ASP.NET 2.0
Everyday Apps
FOR
DUMMIES®

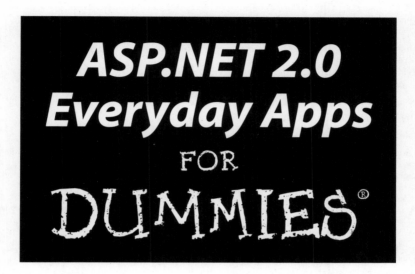

ASP.NET 2.0 Everyday Apps FOR DUMMIES®

by Doug Lowe

WILEY

Wiley Publishing, Inc.

ASP.NET 2.0 Everyday Apps For Dummies®

Published by
Wiley Publishing, Inc.
111 River Street
Hoboken, NJ 07030-5774
www.wiley.com

WILEY

About the Author

Doug Lowe has written a whole bunch of computer books, including more than 35 *For Dummies* books, including the *Java All-in-One Desk Reference For Dummies*, *Networking For Dummies*, 7th Edition, the *Networking All-in-One Desk Reference For Dummies*, *PowerPoint 2003 For Dummies*, and the *Word 2003 All-in-One Desk Reference For Dummies*. He lives in sunny Fresno, California, where the motto is, "We almost beat USC!" with his wife, the youngest of his three daughters, and a couple of outrageously cute puppies. He is the Information Technology Director for Blair, Church & Flynn, an engineering firm in nearby Clovis, CA, and he is also one of those obsessive-compulsive decorating nuts who used to put up tens of thousands of lights at Christmas until his wife saw the electric bill, so now he creates energy-efficient computer-controlled Halloween decorations that rival Disney's Haunted Mansion.

Dedication

To Sarah and Hunter.

Author's Acknowledgments

I'd like to thank everyone involved with making this book a reality, especially project editor Paul Levesque, who did a great job following through on all the little editorial details needed to put a book of this scope together on time, and didn't panic when the "on time" part of that equation was in question. Thanks also to Ken Cox, who gave the manuscript a thorough review and offered many excellent suggestions for improvements, and to copy editor Barry Childs-Helton, who crossed all the i's and dotted all the t's, or something like that, and in the process somehow turned my strange prose into readable English. And, as always, thanks to all the behind-the-scenes people who chipped in with help I'm not even aware of.

Publisher's Acknowledgments

We're proud of this book; please send us your comments through our online registration form located at `www.dummies.com/register/`.

Some of the people who helped bring this book to market include the following:

Acquisitions, Editorial, and Media Development

Senior Project Editor: Paul Levesque

Acquisitions Editor: Katie Feltman

Copy Editor: Barry Childs-Helton

Technical Editor: Ken Cox

Editorial Manager: Leah Cameron

Media Development Manager: Laura VanWinkle

Media Development Supervisor: Richard Graves

Editorial Assistant: Amanda Foxworth

Cartoons: Rich Tennant (`www.the5thwave.com`)

Composition Services

Project Coordinator: Adrienne Martinez

Layout and Graphics: Carl Byers, Andrea Dahl, Lauren Goddard, Denny Hager, Joyce Haughey, Barbara Moore, Lynsey Osborn, Heather Ryan

Proofreaders: Laura Albert, Leeann Harney, Jessica Kramer, TECHBOOKS Production Services

Indexer: TECHBOOKS Production Services

Publishing and Editorial for Technology Dummies

Richard Swadley, Vice President and Executive Group Publisher

Andy Cummings, Vice President and Publisher

Mary Bednarek, Executive Acquisitions Director

Mary C. Corder, Editorial Director

Publishing for Consumer Dummies

Diane Graves Steele, Vice President and Publisher

Joyce Pepple, Acquisitions Director

Composition Services

Gerry Fahey, Vice President of Production Services

Debbie Stailey, Director of Composition Services

Contents at a Glance

Table of Contents

Introduction

• •

Welcome to *ASP.NET 2.0 Everyday Apps For Dummies,* the book that
teaches ASP.NET 2.0 Web programming by example. In this book,
you'll find eight complete ASP.NET applications. We're not talking trivial
Hello-World-type applications here. Instead, they're real-world applications
like shopping carts and discussion forums. You can use any of them as-is, or
modify them as you see fit. So you've got workable stuff already included.
(What a concept.)

About This Book

This book is a practical introduction to ASP.NET 2.0 Web programming. It provides you with actual working code to build the most popular types of applications on the Web. These applications enable you to:

- Restrict access to registered users, for all or part of your Web site
- Sell products online via your Web site
- Provide back-end functions for your public Web site, such as file mainte-
  nance and reporting
- Let users manage specific types of online content
- Create discussion forums and blogs

ASP.NET 2.0 Everyday Apps For Dummies doesn't pretend to be a comprehensive reference for every detail of ASP.NET programming. Instead, it takes a
learn-by-example approach, under the assumption that you are already a
pretty competent programmer who can best learn by seeing real-world examples. Designed using the easy-to-follow *For Dummies* format, this book helps
you get the information you need without laboring to find it.

Conventions Used in This Book

This book has a lot of code in it. You'll find complete listing of every line of
code, both C# and Visual Basic, for each of the eight applications presented
in this book. You'll also find listings for supporting files such as SQL scripts
to generate databases and `web.config` files that provide configuration information for the applications.

Most of these listings include reference numbers that correspond to numbered explanations in the text. In most cases, these explanations apply to both the C# and the Visual Basic versions of the code. (For example, the code explanation identified with reference number 3 applies to the line indicated with reference number 3 in both the C# and the Visual Basic versions of the listing.)

To keep page-flipping to a minimum, I always present the C# version of a listing first, followed by the text that explains it, followed by the Visual Basic listing. Thus, if you're a C# programmer, you can flip forward from your listing to the text that explains it. And if you're a Visual Basic programmer, you can flip *backward* from your listing to the corresponding blow-by-blow description.

On occasion, I'll show a console prompt along with commands you need to enter. In that case, the command is presented as follows:

```
sqlcmd -S localhost\SQLExpress -s createdb.sql
```

How This Book Is Organized

This book is divided into six parts, with two or three chapters in each part. Chapters 4 through 11 present the applications themselves. In these particular chapters, you're going to find the same basic structure, which (hopefully) gets the following information across for each one:

- ✔ A discussion of design issues for the application.

- ✔ An overview of the application's user interface, including a diagram that shows the flow of the application's pages, along with images of each page.

- ✔ A description of the design for the database used by the application, along with listings of the scripts used to create the database and populate it with sample test data.

- ✔ Listings of the .aspx files for each of the application's pages.

- ✔ Where appropriate, listings of the code-behind file in both C# and Visual Basic.

- ✔ Explanations of the key parts of the listings.

If you're up for a quick summary, the following sections offer a bird's-eye view of what you can find in each part of the book.

Part I: Introducing ASP.NET 2.0 Application Development

Chapter 1 in this part is a general introduction to ASP.NET application development. It explains bedrock concepts such as the system-development life cycle, using layered architectures in ASP.NET applications, and designing relational databases. Then Chapter 2 presents a quick introduction to building ASP.NET applications using Visual Studio 2005 or Visual Web Developer 2005 Express Edition.

Part II: Building Secure Applications

This part shows you how to build security into your applications. Chapter 3 is an introduction to ASP.NET 2.0 security. Then, behold: Chapter 4 presents the first application in this book — a user-authentication application that you can incorporate into any application that requires users to register and log in.

Part III: Building E-Commerce Applications

This part provides two complete e-commerce applications. The first is an online product catalog that lets users view your products via a Web site. The second is a shopping-cart application that lets users purchase products. In fact, the shopping-cart application is an extension of the product-catalog application: It lets users purchase products they've had a chance to view via the online catalog.

Part IV: Building Back-End Applications

Just about all public Web applications have a back end that isn't visible to the general public. This part presents two applications you'll often need in the back end. The first is a file-maintenance application that lets you add, update, or delete records in a products database. And the second is a report application that generates reports based on data gathered from Web visitors.

Part V: Building Community Applications

The three applications in this part let users create Web-based communities. Chapter 9 presents a content-management system for users' Web sites; Chapter 10 presents a forum application for posting messages and replies. And Chapter 11 presents a blog application that lets users create blog articles that visitors can then read and comment upon.

Part VI: The Part of Tens

No *For Dummies* book would be complete without a Part of Tens. In Chapter 12, you get an overview of the most important new features of ASP.NET 2.0. If you're an experienced ASP.NET programmer but haven't worked with version 2.0 yet, you may want to read this chapter first to see what new features have been added for this version.

Next Chapter 13 describes ten-or-so rookie mistakes that (with any luck) you can avoid. And finally, Chapter 14 presents ten-or-so tips for designing your databases.

About the CD

The CD that's glued into the back of this book contains all the source code for the applications presented in this book. You'll find two versions of each application: a C# version and a Visual Basic version. The CD lets you choose which versions of the applications to install. If you want, you can install both versions of the applications; C# and VB can easily coexist within the same ASP.NET system. (Although it's uncommon, C# and VB can even coexist within the same ASP.NET application.)

Icons Used in This Book

Like any *For Dummies* book, this book is chock-full of helpful icons that draw your attention to items of particular importance. You find the following icons throughout this book:

Pay special attention to this icon; it lets you know that some particularly useful tidbit is at hand.

Did I tell you about the memory course I took?

Danger, Will Robinson! This icon highlights information that may help you avert disaster.

Watch out! Some technical drivel is just around the corner. Read it only if you have your pocket protector firmly attached.

Where to Go from Here

Yes, you can get there from here. With this book in hand, you're ready to get right to the task of creating ASP.NET 2.0 Web applications. Browse through the table of contents and decide which type of application interests you most. Then, jump in and hang on. Be bold! Be courageous! Be adventurous! And above all, have fun!

Part I
Introducing ASP.NET 2.0 Application Development

The 5th Wave   By Rich Tennant

"Our automated response policy to a large, company-wide data crash is to notify management, back up existing data and sell 90% of my shares in the company."

In this part . . .

This part presents a basic introduction to building applications with ASP.NET version 2.0. First, Chapter 1 provides an overall introduction to building Web applications, providing an overview of the typical development cycle for ASP.NET applications — as well as some ideas for designing them. This chapter also includes a helpful tutorial on database design.

Then Chapter 2 takes you step by step through the process of using Visual Studio to create a very simple ASP.NET application. This walk-through helps you prepare for developing more complex applications like the ones presented later in this book.

Chapter 1

Designing ASP.NET 2.0 Applications

ASP.NET is Microsoft's platform for developing Web applications. With the new release of version 2.0, Microsoft has added powerful new features such as Master Pages and automatic site navigation, which make it one of the most powerful (yet easy-to-use) Web-development tools out there.

And it's inexpensive. Although the professional versions of Visual Studio will set you back some, Visual Web Developer Express Edition will cost you only about $100 and can be used to develop sophisticated ASP.NET applications, using your choice of programming languages — Visual Basic or C#.

One way to learn ASP.NET is to buy a beginning ASP.NET book. There are plenty of good ones out there, including (in all due modesty) my own *ASP.NET 2.0 All-In-One Desk Reference For Dummies* (published by Wiley, of course). But this book takes a different approach. Instead of belaboring the myriad of details that go into ASP.NET programming, this book presents a series of complete popular applications, such as a shopping cart and a forum host, and explains in detail how these applications work. You can study these applications to see how real-world ASP.NET programming is done, and you can even copy them to give your own applications a running start.

You'll need to modify the applications, of course, to make them work for your own situation. Still, the samples presented in this book should provide an excellent starting point. Even so, before you base your app on any of the applications presented in this book, take a step back: Carefully analyze the problem the application is intended to solve — and design an appropriate solution. This chapter presents a brief introduction to this process, known in software development circles as *analysis and design*. Along the way, you get a look at the basics of designing relational databases, as well as designing objects to work with an ASP.NET application.

The Development Treadmill

Over the years, computer gurus have observed that computer projects have a life of their own, which goes through natural stages. The *life cycle* of an application-development project typically goes something like this:

1. **Feasibility study:** This is the conception phase, in which the decision to undertake a new computer system is made based on the answers to questions such as:

   - What business problem will the new system solve?

   - Will the new system actually be an improvement over the current system?

   - If so, can the value of this improvement be quantified?

   - Is the new system possible?

   - What will the new system cost to develop and run?

   - How long will the system take to develop?

   The result of the feasibility study is a charter for the new project that defines the scope of the project, user requirements, budget constraints, and so on.

2. **Analysis:** This is the process of deciding exactly what a computer system is to do. The traditional approach to analysis is to thoroughly document the existing system that the new system is intended to replace, even if the existing system is entirely manual and rife with inefficiency and error. Then, a specification for a new system to replace the old system is created. This specification defines exactly what the new system will do, but not necessarily how it will do it.

3. **Design:** This process creates a plan for implementing the specification for a new system that results from the analysis step. It focuses on how the new system will work.

4. **Implementation:** Here's where the programs that make up the new system are coded and tested, the hardware required to support the system is purchased and installed, and the databases required for the system are defined and loaded.

5. **Acceptance testing:** In this phase, all pieces of the system are checked out to make sure that the system works the way it should.

6. **Production:** This is another word for "put into action." If the system works acceptably, it's put into production: Its users actually begin using it.

7. **Maintenance:** The moment the computer system goes into production, it needs maintenance. In this dreaded phase, errors — hopefully minor — that weren't caught during the implementation and acceptance phases are corrected. As the users work with the system, they invariably realize that what they *really* need isn't what they said they wanted, so they request enhancements — which are gradually incorporated into the system.

The biggest challenge of this phase is making sure that corrections and enhancements don't create more problems than they solve.

8. **Obsolescence:** Eventually, the new system becomes obsolete. Of course, this doesn't mean the system dies; it probably remains in use for years, perhaps even decades, *after* it becomes "obsolete." Many obsolete COBOL systems are still in production today, and Web applications being built today will be in production long after ASP.NET becomes passé.

Only the most obsessive project managers actually lead projects through these phases step by step. In the real world, the phases overlap to some degree. In fact, modern development methods often overlap all phases of a highly *iterative* process where the approach is "try, hit a snag, make changes, try again with a new version."

I omitted two important pieces of the computer-system-development puzzle because they should be integrated throughout the *entire* process: *quality assurance* and *documentation*. Quality needs to be built into each phase of development, and shouldn't be tacked on to the end as an afterthought. Likewise, documentation of the system should be built constantly as the system is developed, to minimize confusion.

Building Models

When it comes right down to it, computer system analysis and design is nothing more than glorified model-building. (Minus the glue fumes.)

Most engineering disciplines involve model-building. In fact, that's what engineers do all day: sit around building fancy models of skyscrapers, bridges, freeway overpasses, culverts, storm drains, whatever.

These models usually aren't the kind made of molded plastic parts and held together with cement (though sometimes they are). Instead, they're conceptual models drawn on paper. Architects draw floor plans, electrical engineers draw schematic circuit diagrams, structural engineers draw blueprints; these are all nothing more than models.

The reason engineers build models is that they're cheaper to build (and break) than the real thing. It's a lot easier to draw a picture of a bridge and examine it to make sure it won't collapse the first time the wind blows too fast or the river is too full than it is to build an actual bridge and *then* find out.

The same holds true for computer-application design. Building a computer system is an expensive proposition. It's far cheaper to build a paper model of the system first, and then test the model to make sure it works before building the actual system.

What Is an Application Design?

Glad you asked. An *application design* is a written model of a system that can be used as a guide when you actually construct a working version of the system. The components of an application design can vary, but the complete design typically includes the following:

- **A statement of the purpose and scope of the system:** This statement of purpose and scope is often written in the form of a *use case*, which describes the actors and actions (users and uses) that make up the system and shows what it's for. Sometimes the use case is a graphic diagram; most often it's plain text.

- **A data model:** Normally this is an outline of the database structure, consisting of a set of *Entity-Relationship Diagrams* (*ERDs*) or other diagrams. These describe the details of how the application's database will be put together. Each application in this book uses a database and includes an ERD, which describes how the database tables relate to each other.

- **Data Flow Diagrams (DFDs):** Some application designs include these diagrams, which show the major processes that make up the application and how data flows among the processes. The data flow is pretty straightforward for most of the applications presented in this book, so I don't include Data Flow Diagrams for them.

- **User Interface Flow Diagrams:** These are sometimes called *storyboards* and are often used to plan the application's user interface. I include a User Interface Flow Diagram for each application in this book so you can see how the application flows from one page to the next.

Using Layered Architectures

One approach to designing Web applications is to focus on clearly defined layers of the application's architecture. This approach is similar to the way an architect designs a building. If you've ever seen detailed construction plans for a skyscraper, you know what I'm talking about. The construction plans include separate blueprints for the foundation, frame, roof, plumbing, electrical, and other floors of the building.

With a layered architecture, specialists can design and develop the "floors" — called *layers* — independently, provided that the connections between the layers (the *interfaces*) are carefully thought out.

The layers should be independent of one another, as much as possible. Among other things, that means heeding a few must-dos and shalt-nots:

- ✓ **Each layer must have a clearly defined focus.** To design the layers properly, you must clearly spell out the tasks and responsibilities of each layer.

- ✓ **Layers should mind their own business.** If one layer is responsible for user interaction, only that layer is allowed to communicate with the user. Other layers that need to get information from the user must do so through the User Interface Layer.

- ✓ **Clearly defined protocols must be set up for the layers to interact with one another.** Interaction between the layers occurs only through these protocols.

Note that the layers are not tied directly to any particular application. For example, an architecture might work equally well for an online ordering system and for an online forum. As a result, layered architecture has nothing to do with the ERDs that define a database or the Data Flow Diagrams that define how the data flows within the application. It's a separate structure.

How many layers?

There are several common approaches to application architecture that vary depending on the number of layers used. One common scheme is to break the application into two layers:

- ✓ **Application Layer:** The design of the user interface and the implementation of business policies are handled in this layer. This layer may also handle *transaction logic* — the code that groups database updates into transactions and ensures that all updates within a transaction are made consistently.

- ✓ **Data Access Layer:** The underlying database engine that supports the application. This layer is responsible for maintaining the integrity of the database. Some or all the transaction logic may be implemented in this layer.

In the two-layer model, the Application Layer is the ASP.NET Web pages that define the pages presented to the user as well as the code-behind files that implement the application's logic. The Data Access Layer is the database server that manages the database, such as Microsoft SQL Server or Oracle.

Note that ASP.NET 2.0 doesn't require that you place the application's logic code in a separate code-behind file. Instead, you can intersperse the logic code with the presentation code in the same file. However, it's almost always a good idea to use separate code-behind files to separate the application's logic from its presentation code. All of the applications presented in this book use separate code-behind files.

Using objects in the Data Access Layer

One of the fundamental architecture decisions you need to make when developing ASP.NET applications is whether to create customized data classes for the Data Access Layer. For example, an application that accesses a Products database might incorporate a class named `ProductDB` that includes methods for retrieving, inserting, updating, and deleting data in the Products database. Then, the other layers of the application can simply call these methods to perform the application's data access.

Creating custom data-access classes like this has several advantages:

✔ The data-access code is isolated in a separate class, so you can assign your best database programmers to work on those classes.

✔ You can fine-tune the database performance by spending extra time on the data-access classes without affecting the rest of the application.

✔ If you need to migrate the application from one database server to another (for example, from SQL Server to Oracle), you can do so by changing just the data-access classes.

✔ You can design the data-access classes so they work with a variety of databases. Then,

you can let the user configure which database to use when the application is installed.

However, this flexibility isn't without cost. ASP.NET is designed to work with the data-source controls embedded in your `.aspx` pages. If you want to create your own data-access classes, you have basically two choices:

✔ Don't use the ASP.NET data sources, which means you can't use data binding. Then, you must write all the code that connects your user interface to your data-access classes. That's a lot of work.

✔ Use the new ASP.NET 2.0 object data sources, which are designed to let you bind ASP.NET controls to custom data-access classes. Unfortunately, this adds a layer of complexity to the application and often isn't worth the trouble.

The applications in this book don't use custom data-access classes. However, you should be able to adapt them to use object data sources if you want.

For more information about designing objects for ASP.NET applications, see the "Designing Objects" section, later in this chapter.

The division between the Application and Data Access layers isn't always as clear-cut as it could be. For performance reasons, transaction logic is often shifted to the database server (in the form of stored procedures), and business rules are often implemented on the database server with constraints and triggers. Thus, the database server often handles some of the application logic.

If this messiness bothers you, you can use a *three-layer architecture*, which adds an additional layer to handle business rules and policies:

- ✔ **Presentation Layer:** This layer handles the user interface.

- ✔ **Business Rules Layer:** This layer handles the application's business rules and policies. For example, if a sales application grants discounts to certain users, the discount policy is implemented in this layer.

- ✔ **Data Access Layer:** The underlying database model that supports the application.

Creating a separate layer for business rules enables you to separate the rules from the database design and the presentation logic. Business rules are subject to change. By placing them in a separate layer, you have an easier task of changing them later than if they're incorporated into the user interface or database design.

Model-View-Controller

Another common model for designing Web applications is called *Model-View-Controller (MVC)*. In this architecture, the application is broken into three parts:

- ✔ **Model:** The *model* is, in effect, the application's business layer. It usually consists of objects that represent the business entities that make up the application, such as customers and products.

- ✔ **View:** The *view* is the application's user interface. In a Web application, this consists of one or more HTML pages that define the look and feel of the application.

- ✔ **Controller:** The *controller* manages the events processed by the application. The events are usually generated by user-interface actions, such as the user clicking a button or selecting an item from a drop-down list.

In a typical ASP.NET application, the `.aspx` file implements the view; the model and controller functions are combined and handled by the code-behind file. Thus, the code-behind file can be thought of as the *model-controller*.

You can, of course, separate the model and controller functions by creating separate classes for the business entities. For simplicity, the applications in this book keep the model and controller functions combined in the code-behind file.

Designing the user interface

Much of the success of any Web application depends on the quality of its user interface. As far as end-users are concerned, the user interface *is* the application: Users aren't interested in the details of the data model or the design of the data-access classes.

In an ASP.NET Web application, the user interface consists of a series of .aspx pages that are rendered to the browser using standard HTML. Designing the user interface is simply a matter of deciding which pages are required (and in what sequence) — and populating those pages with the appropriate controls.

Standard HTML has a surprisingly limited set of user-input controls:

- Buttons
- Text boxes
- Drop-down lists
- Check boxes
- Radio buttons

However, ASP.NET offers many controls that build on these basic controls. For example, you can use a GridView control to present data from a database in a tabular format.

All ASP.NET controls are eventually rendered to the browser, using standard HTML. As a result, even the most complicated ASP.NET controls are simply composites made of standard HTML controls and HTML formatting elements (such as tables).

Designing the user interface can quickly become the most complicated aspect of a Web application. Although user interface design has no hard-and-fast rules, here are a few guidelines you should keep in mind:

- Consider how frequently the user will use each page and how familiar he or she will be with the application. If the user works with the same page over and over again all day long, try to make the data entry as efficient as possible. However, if the user will use the page only once in a while, err on the side of making the page self-explanatory so the user doesn't have to struggle to figure out how to use the page.

- Remember that the user is in control of the application and users are pretty unpredictable. Users might give up in the middle of a data-entry sequence, or unexpectedly hit the browser's Back button.

- Some users like the mouse, others like the keyboard. Don't force your preference on the user: make sure your interface works well for mouse as well as keyboard users.

✔ Review prototypes of the user-interface design with *actual users*. Listen to their suggestions seriously. They probably have a better idea than you do of what the user interface should look like and how it should behave.

✔ Study Web sites that you consider to have good interfaces.

Designing the Business Rules Layer

Business rules are the portion of a program that implements the business policies dictated by the application. Here are some examples of business rules:

✔ Should a customer be granted a credit request?

✔ How much of a discount should be applied to a given order?

✔ How many copies of Form 10432/J need to be printed?

✔ How much shipping and handling should be tacked onto an invoice?

✔ When should an inventory item that is running low on stock be reordered?

✔ How much sick leave should an employee get before managers wonder whether he or she has been skiing rather than staying home sick?

✔ When should an account payable be paid to take advantage of discounts while maximizing float?

The key to designing the business-rules portion of an application is simply to identify the business rules that must be implemented and separate them as much as possible from other parts of the program. That way, if the rules change, only the code that implements the rules needs to be changed.

For example, you might create a class to handle discount policies. Then, you can call methods of this class whenever you need to calculate a customer's discount. If the discount policy changes, the discount class can be updated to reflect the new policy.

Ideally, each business rule should be implemented only once, in a single class that's used by each program that needs it. All too often, business policies are implemented over and over again in multiple programs — and if the policy changes, dozens of programs need to be updated. (That even hurts to think about, doesn't it?)

Designing the Data Access Layer

Much of the job of designing the Data Access Layer involves designing the database itself. Here are some pointers on designing the Data Access Layer:

✔ For starters, you must decide what database server to use (for example, SQL Server or Oracle).

   ✔ You'll need to design the tables that make up the database and determine which columns each table will require. For more information about designing the tables, refer to the section "Designing Relational Databases," later in this chapter.

   ✔ You must also decide what basic techniques you'll use to access the data. For example, will you write custom data-access classes that access the database directly, or will you use ASP.NET's `SqlDataSource` control to access the database? And will you use stored procedures or code the SQL statements used to access the data directly in the application code?

Designing Relational Databases

Most ASP.NET applications revolve around relational databases. As a result, one of the keys to good application design is a good database design.

Database design is the type of process that invites authors to create step-by-step procedures, and I certainly don't want to be left out. So what follows is an ordered list of steps you can use to create a good database design for your ASP.NET application. (Keep in mind, however, that in real life most designers manage to do many, if not all, of these steps at once.)

Step 1: Create a charter for the database

Every database has a reason for being, and you'll be in a much better position to create a good database design if you start by considering why the database needs to exist and what will be expected of it.

Database designers sometimes fall into one of two traps: Assuming that the data exists for its own sake, or assuming that the database exists for the sake of the Information Technology (IT) department. Of course, the database exists for its users. Before designing a database, you'd better find out why the users need the database — and what they expect to accomplish with it.

You can think of this purpose statement as a *mission statement* or a *charter* for the database. Here's an example of a charter for a database for a store that sells supplies for pirates:

> The purpose of the Pirate Supply Store database is to keep track of all the products sold at the Acme Pirate Supply store. The database should include detailed information about each product and should enable us to categorize the products into one of several categories. It should also allow us to add new categories later on if we decide to sell additional types of products. And it should provide a way to display a picture of each product on our Web page. It should also keep track of our customers and keep track of each sale.

For a more complicated application, the charter will probably be more detailed than this. But the key point is that the charter should identify the unique capabilities that the user expects from the database. In this case, the flexibility to add new product categories down the road and the ability to show pictures on the Web site are key features that the user wants.

An important part of this step is examining how the data is currently being stored and to uncover the weaknesses in the status quo. If the data is currently stored in an Excel spreadsheet, carefully examine the spreadsheet. If paper forms are used, study the forms to see what kind of data is included on them. If the data is scribbled on the back of napkins, collect the napkins and scrutinize them.

Step 2: Make a list and check it twice

Once you're sure you understand the purpose of the database, sit down with a yellow pad and a box of freshly sharpened #2 pencils and start writing. (You can use a word processor if you prefer, but I like to have something I can crumple up when I change my mind.) Start by listing the major tables that the database includes.

When creating and fiddling with the lists of tables and data items, it helps to think in terms of *entities*: tangible, real-world objects that the database needs to keep track of, such as people and things. For the `Pirate Supply Store` database mentioned in Step 1, you might list the following entities:

✔ Products

✔ Categories

✔ Customers

✔ Orders

After you identify the major tables in the database, list the data elements that fall under each one. For example:

```
Products
    Name
    Category Name
    Description
    Vendor name
    Vendor address
    Vendor phone number
    Price
    Image file name

Category
```

```
        Name

Customers
        Last Name
        First Name
        Address
        City
        State
        Zip Code
        Phone Number
        E-mail
        Credit Card Number

Order
        Order number
        Date
        Customer
        Product
        Quantity
        Price
        Subtotal
        Shipping
        Tax
        Total
```

Don't be afraid to crumple up the paper and start over a few times. In fact, if you're doing this step right, you'll end up with wads of yellow paper on your floor. You can clean up when you're done.

For example, you may realize that the vendor information stored in the Products table should actually be its own table. So you break the Products table into two tables, Products and Vendors:

```
Products
        Name
        Category Name
        Description
        Price
        Image file name

Vendor
        Name
        Address
        City
        State
        Zip Code
        Phone Number
        E-mail
```

As you design the database, creating additional tables like this will become a regular occurrence. You'll discover tables that need to be split because they have data for two distinct entities, or you'll discover entities that you simply forgot to include. The number of tables in a database rarely goes *down* as you refine the design.

Note that the `Orders` table has several problems in its current form. For example, how do you identify which customer is associated with an order? And, more importantly, what if more than one product is ordered? We'll solve these problems in subsequent steps.

Step 3: Add keys

In an SQL database, every table should have a column or combination of columns that uniquely identifies each row in the table. This column (or combination of columns) is called the *primary key*. In this step, you revisit all the entities in your design and make sure each one has a useful primary key.

Selecting the primary key for a table is sometimes a challenge. For example, what field should you use as the primary key for the `Customers` table? Several choices come to mind:

- **Last Name:** This works fine until you get your *second* customer named Smith. It can also be a problem when you get a customer named Zoldoske. Every time you type this name, you'll probably spell it differently: Zoldosky, Soldoskie, Zaldosky, and so on. (Trust me on this one. My wife's maiden name is Zoldoske; she's seen it spelled each of these ways — and many more.)

- **Last and First Name combined:** This works better than Last Name alone, but you still may have *two* Lucy McGillicuddys who want to buy your stuff.

- **Phone Number:** Everyone has a unique phone number, but some phone numbers are shared by several individuals (say, roommates or family members). And when people move, they often change their phone numbers.

- **E-mail Address:** This isn't too bad a choice; people rarely share e-mail addresses and don't change them nearly as often as phone numbers.

If no field in the table jumps out as an obvious primary key, you may need to create an otherwise meaningless key for the table. For example, you could add a `Customer Number` to the `Customers` table. The `Customer Number` would be a unique number that has no meaning other than as an identifier for a specific customer. You can let the user enter a unique value for the key field, or you can let the database automatically generate a unique value. In the latter case, the key is known as an *identity column*.

In the `Pirate Supply Store` database, I decided to use the `E-mail Address` field for the primary key of the `Customers` table. For the Products table, I added a `Product ID` field that represents a unique product code determined by the users. I did the same for the `Categories` table. For the `Orders` table, I used the `Order Number` column and designated it as an identify column so it will be automatically generated.

As you add primary keys to your tables, you can also add those primary keys columns as *foreign keys* in related tables. For example, a `Vendor ID` column could be added to the `Products` table so each product is related to a particular vendor.

After the key columns have been added, the list looks like this:

```
Products
     Product ID (primary key)
     Name
     Category ID (foreign key)
     Category Name
     Description
     Price
     Image file name
     Vendor ID (foreign key)

Vendor
     Vendor ID (primary key)
     Name
     Address
     City
     State
     Zip Code
     Phone Number
     E-mail

Category
     Category ID (primary key)
     Name

Customers
     Last Name
     First Name
     Address
     City
     State
     Zip Code
     Phone Number
     E-mail (primary key)
     Credit Card Number

Order
     Order number (primary key)
     Date
```

```
Customer ID (foreign key)
Product ID (foreign key)
Quantity
Price
Subtotal
Shipping
Tax
Total
```

Step 4: Normalize the database

Normalization refers to the process of eliminating redundant information and other problems in the database design. To normalize a database, you identify problems in the design and correct them, often by creating additional tables. After normalizing your design, you almost always have more tables than you had when you started.

Five different levels of normalization exist, known as the *five normal forms*. You'll find a list of all five of these normal forms (which actually look sort of monstrous) in the sidebar at the end of this chapter, "The Five Abby-Normal Forms."

To normalize the `Pirate Supply Store` database, I made several changes to the design:

- ✔ I changed all the table names to plural. Before, I had a mixture of singular and plural names. (This is just a consistency issue.)

- ✔ I broke the `Orders` table into two tables: `Orders` and `Line Items`. When a customer places an order, one row is created in the `Orders` table for the entire order, and one row is created in the `Line Items` table for each product ordered. This allows the customer to order more than one product in a single order.

- ✔ I removed the `Category Name` field from the `Products` table because this data is contained in the `Categories` table.

- ✔ I removed the `Subtotal` column from the `Orders` table. The `Line Items` table contains an `Item Total` column, and the subtotal for an order can be calculated by adding up the item totals for each line item that belong to the order.

- ✔ I designated the `Item Total` column in the `Line Items` table as a calculated value. Rather than being stored in the table, this value is calculated by multiplying the quantity times the price for the row being retrieved.

> ✔ While interviewing the users, I discovered that some of the products are available from two or more vendors. Thus, the Products⇨Vendors relationship isn't many-to-one, but many-to-many. As a result, I added a new table named `Product Vendor` to implement this relationship. Each row in this table represents a vendor that supplies a particular product.

The resulting design now looks like this:

```
Products
    Product ID
    Name
    Category ID
    Description
    Price
    Image file name

Vendors
    Vendor ID
    Name
    Address
    City
    State
    Zip Code
    Phone Number
    E-mail

Categories
    Category ID
    Name

Customers
    E-mail
    Last Name
    First Name
    Address
    City
    State
    Zip Code
    Phone Number
    Credit Card Number

Orders
    Order number
    Date
    Customer E-mail
    Shipping
    Tax
    Total

Line Items
    Order number
    Product ID
```

```
        Quantity
        Price
        Item Total

Product Vendor
        Product ID
        Vendor ID
```

Even though I did mention at the beginning of this section that five degrees of normality exist (It's a good thing these apply to databases and not to people, because some of us would be off the chart.), most database designers settle for the first through third normal forms. That's because the requirements of the fourth and fifth normal forms are a bit picky. As a result, I don't go into the fourth and fifth normal forms here. However, the following sections describe the first three normal forms.

First normal form (1NF)

A database is in 1NF when each table row is free of repeating data. For example, you might be tempted to design the `Orders` table like this:

```
Orders
    Order number
    Date
    Customer ID
    Product ID 1
    Quantity 1
    Price 1
    Product ID 2
    Quantity 2
    Price 2
    Product ID 3
    Quantity 3
    Price 3
    Subtotal
    Shipping
    Tax
    Total
```

This design allows the customer to purchase as many as three different products on a single order. But what if the customer wants to purchase four products? The solution is to create a separate table for the line items. The `Line Items` table uses a foreign key to relate each line item to an order.

Second normal form (2NF)

Second normal form applies only to tables that have composite keys — that is, a primary key that's made up of two or more table columns. When a table has a composite key, every column in the table must depend on the entire key, not just on part of the key, for the table to be in second normal form.

For example, consider the following table, in which the primary key is a combination of the Order Number and Product ID columns:

```
Line Items
    Order Number
    Product ID
    Name
    Quantity
    Price
```

This table breaks 2NF because the `Name` column depends solely on the Product ID, not on the combination of Order Number and Product ID. The solution is to remove the Name column from the `Line Items` table, and retrieve the product name from the `Products` table whenever it's required.

You might wonder whether the `Price` column also violates second normal form. The answer depends on the application's requirements. A product's price can change over time, but the price for a given order should be the price that was effective when the order was created. So in a way, the price *does* depend on the order number. Thus, including the `Price` column in the `Line Items` table doesn't violate 2NF.

Third normal form (3NF)

A table is in *third normal form* if every column in the table depends on the entire primary key, and none of the non-key columns depend on each other.

The Five Abby-Normal Forms

No, this stuff didn't come from an abnormal brain in a jar; it only seems that way. In case you're interested (and just to point out how esoteric these things can be), here's a list of the original definitions of the five normal forms, in the original Greek, as formulated by C. J. Date in his classic book, *An Introduction to Database Systems* (Addison-Wesley, 1974):

First Normal Form (1NF): A relation *R* is in *first normal form* (1NF) if and only if all underlying domains contain atomic values only.

Second Normal Form (2NF): A relation *R* is in *second normal form* (2NF) if and only if it is in 1NF and every nonkey attribute is fully dependent on the primary key.

Third Normal Form (3NF): A relation *R* is in *third normal form* (3NF) if and only if it is in 2NF and every nonkey attribute is nontransitively dependent on the primary key.

Fourth Normal Form (4NF): A relation *R* is in *fourth normal form* (4NF) if and only if, whenever there exists an MVD in R, say A⇨⇨B, then all attributes of R are also functionally dependent on A (that is, A⇨X for all attributes X of R).

(An *MVD* is a *multivalued dependence*.)

Fifth Normal Form (5NF): A relation *R* is in *fifth normal form* (5NF) — also called projection-join normal form (PJ/NF) — if and only if every join dependency in R is implied by the candidate keys of R.

Suppose the store gives a different discount percentage for each category of product, and the `Products` and `Categories` tables are designed like this:

```
Product
    Product ID
    Category ID
    Name
    Price
    Image file
    Discount Percent

Categories
    Category ID
    Name
```

Here, the `Discount Percent` column depends not on the `Product ID` column, but on the `Category ID` column. Thus the table is not in 3NF. To make it 3NF, you'd have to move the `Discount Percent` column to the `Categories` table.

Step 5: Denormalize the database

What?! After all that fuss about normalizing the data, now I'm telling you to *de*-normalize it? Yes — sometimes. Many cases occur in which a database will operate more efficiently if you bend the normalization rules a bit. In particular, building a certain amount of redundancy into a database for performance reasons is often wise. Intentionally adding redundancy back into a database is called *denormalization* — and it's perfectly normal. (Groan.)

Here are some examples of denormalization you might consider for the `Pirate Supply Store` database:

- ✔ Restoring the `Subtotal` column to the `Orders` table so the program doesn't have to retrieve all the `Line Items` rows to calculate an order total.

- ✔ Adding a `Name` field to the `Line Items` table so the program doesn't have to retrieve rows from the `Products` table to display or print an order.

- ✔ Adding the customer's name and address to the `Orders` table so that the application doesn't have to access the `Customers` table to print or display an order.

- ✔ Adding the `Category Name` to the `Products` table so the application doesn't have to look it up in the `Categories` table each time.

In each case, deciding whether to denormalize the database should depend on a specific performance tradeoff — updating the redundant data in several places versus improving the access speed.

Step 6: Pick legal SQL names

All through the data-design process, I use names descriptive enough that I can remember exactly what each table and column represents. However, most SQL dialects don't allow tables with names like Line Items or columns with names like Product ID or Discount Percent, because of the embedded spaces. At some point in the design, you'll have to assign the tables and columns actual names that SQL allows. When picking names, stick to these rules:

- ✔ No special characters, other than $, #, and _.
- ✔ No spaces.
- ✔ No more than 128 characters.

Shorter names are better, as long as the meaning is preserved. Although you can create names as long as 128 characters, I suggest you stick to names with 15 or fewer characters.

Step 7: Draw a picture

Computer professionals love to draw pictures, possibly because it's more fun than real work, but mostly because (as they say) a picture is worth 1,024 words. So they often draw a special type of diagram — an *Entity-Relationship Diagram (ERD)* — when creating a data model. Figure 1-1 shows a typical ERD. Visual Studio 2005 includes a handy feature that automatically creates these diagrams for you.

The ERD shows each of the tables that make up a database and the relationships among the tables. Usually you see the tables as rectangles and the relationships as arrows. Sometimes, the columns within each table are listed in the rectangles; sometimes they aren't. Arrowheads are used to indicate one-to-one, one-to-many, many-to-one, and many-to-many relationships. Other notational doodads may be attached to the diagram, depending on which drawing school the database designers attended — and whether they're using UML (more about that shortly).

That's it for the steps needed to design relational databases. In the next section, I describe another important aspect of application design: designing the various objects that will make up the application.

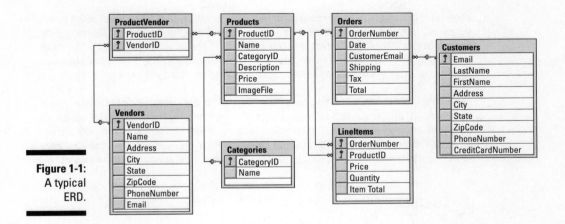

Figure 1-1:
A typical
ERD.

Designing Objects

The Microsoft .NET Framework is inherently object-oriented, so all ASP.NET applications are object-oriented applications. At minimum, each Web page that makes up the application is represented as two classes, as described by the Model-View-Controller (MVC) pattern:

✔ The *view* defines the appearance of the page.

✔ The *model-controller* represents the methods called to handle events, such as when the user clicks a button or selects an item from a drop-down list.

Many ASP.NET applications need additional classes to represent other types of objects. As a result, you might find yourself defining objects that represent business objects, or even some that implement business rules. Then you can write C# or VB code to implement those objects.

The task of designing these objects boils down to deciding what classes the application requires and what the public interface to each of those classes must be. If you plan your classes well, implementing the application is easy; plan your classes poorly, and you'll have a hard time getting your application to work.

Diagramming Classes with UML

Since the beginning of computer programming, programmers have loved to create diagrams of their programs. Originally they drew *flowcharts,* graphic representations of a program's procedural logic (the steps it took to do its job).

Flowcharts were good at diagramming procedures, but they were way too detailed. When the Structured Programming craze hit in the 1970s, programmers started thinking about the overall structure of their programs. Before long, they switched from flowcharts to *structure charts*, which illustrate the organizational relationships among the modules of a program or system.

Now that object-oriented programming is the thing, programmers draw *class diagrams* to illustrate the relationships among the classes that make up an application. For example, the simple class diagram shown in Figure 1-2 shows a class diagram for a simple system that has four classes. The rectangles represent the classes themselves; the arrows represent relationships among classes.

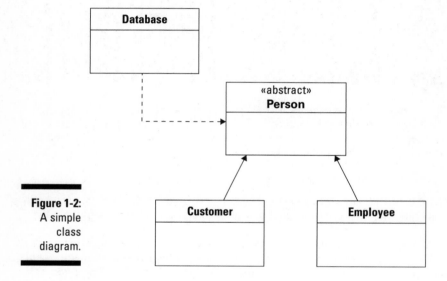

Figure 1-2:
A simple
class
diagram.

You can draw class diagrams in many ways, but most programmers use a standard diagramming approach called *UML* (which stands for *Unified Modeling Language*) to keep theirs consistent. The class diagram in Figure 1-2 is a simple example of a UML diagram; they can get much more complicated.

The following sections describe the details of creating UML class diagrams. Note that these sections don't even come close to explaining all the features of UML. I include just the basics of creating UML class diagrams so that you can make some sense of UML diagrams when you see them, and so that you know how to draw simple class diagrams to help you design the class structure for your applications. If you're interested in digging deeper into UML, check out *UML 2 For Dummies* by Michael Jesse Chonoles and James A. Schardt (Wiley).

Drawing classes

The basic element in a class diagram is a *class* — drawn as a rectangle in UML. At minimum, the rectangle must include the class name. However, you can subdivide the rectangle into two or three compartments that can contain additional information about the class, as shown in Figure 1-3.

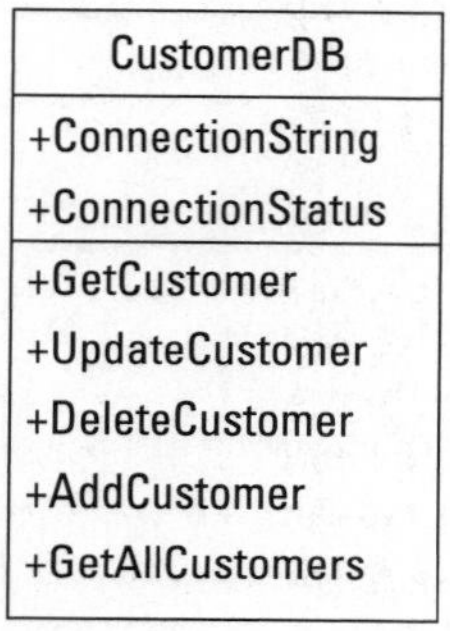

CustomerDB
+ConnectionString
+ConnectionStatus
+GetCustomer
+UpdateCustomer
+DeleteCustomer
+AddCustomer
+GetAllCustomers

Figure 1-3: A class.

The middle compartment of a class lists the class variables; the bottom compartment lists the class methods. You can precede the name of each variable or method with a *visibility indicator* — one of the symbols listed in Table 1-1 — although actual practice commonly omits the visibility indicator and lists only those fields or methods that have public visibility. (*Visibility* refers to whether or not a variable or method can be accessed from outside of the class.)

Table 1-1   Visibility Indicators for Class Variables and Methods

Indicator	Description
+	Public
-	Private
#	Protected

If you want, you can include type information in your class diagrams — not only for variables, but for methods and parameters as well. A variable's type is indicated by adding a colon to the variable name and then adding the type, as follows:

```
connectionString: String
```

A method's return type is indicated in the same way:

```
getCustomer(): Customer
```

Parameters are specified within the parentheses; both the name and type are listed, as in this example:

```
getCustomer(custno: int): Customer
```

Note: The type and parameter information are often omitted from UML diagrams to keep them simple.

Interfaces are drawn pretty much the same way as classes, except the class name is preceded by the word *interface,* like this:

```
«interface»
  ProductDB
```

Note: The word *interface* is enclosed within a set of double-left and double-right arrows. These double arrows are often called *chevrons* and can be accessed in Microsoft Word via the Insert Symbol command.

Drawing arrows

Besides rectangles to represent classes, class diagrams also include arrows that represent relationships among classes. UML uses various types of arrows; this section shows a basic set of them.

A solid line with a hollow, closed arrow at one end represents inheritance:

⟶▷

The arrow points to the base class.

A dashed line with a hollow, closed arrow at one end indicates that a class implements an interface:

- - -▷

The arrow points to the interface.

A solid line with an open arrow indicates an association:

- - -→

An *association* simply indicates that two classes work together. It may be that one of the classes creates objects of the other class, or that one class requires an object of the other class to perform its work. Or perhaps instances of one class contain instances of the other class.

You can add a name to an association arrow to indicate its purpose. For example, if an association arrow indicates that instances of one class create objects of another class, you can place the word `Creates` next to the arrow.

Chapter 2

Using Visual Studio 2005

*T*echnically, everything you need to create ASP.NET 2.0 applications is free. You can download the .NET Framework from Microsoft's Web site for free, most versions of Windows come with the IIS Web server, and the only development environment you need is Notepad.

But building ASP.NET applications with Notepad is kind of like cutting down your own trees and milling your own lumber to build a doghouse. Yes, you can do it, but it's much easier to go to Home Depot and buy the two-by-fours already cut.

Likewise, ASP.NET applications are much easier to develop if you use Visual Studio, Microsoft's development environment for creating .NET applications. The least expensive edition of Visual Studio you need if you're going to create an ASP.NET 2.0 application is Visual Web Developer 2005 Express Edition (also known as *VWDE*). You can purchase it for about a hundred bucks — even less if you're a student. Although you can use one of the more expensive versions of Visual Studio 2005, VWDE is sufficient for the applications presented in this book.

This chapter walks you step-by-step through the process of creating a simple ASP.NET 2.0 application using VWDE. Before you get started, you should first install VWDE according to the instructions that come with it. After you've installed VWDE, you're ready to go.

If you're using one of the professional editions of Visual Studio, the steps for creating Web applications are the same. However, you can't create Web applications using one of the language-specific Express editions of Visual Studio such as Visual Basic 2005 Express Edition or Visual C# 2005 Express Edition. Those editions can only create Windows-based applications.

Creating a Basic Hello World Application

Many classic programming books begin with a simple Hello World application that displays the text `Hello, World!` on the screen. Because I'd like this book to become a classic, we start with a Hello World program and develop it step by step, adding new features as we go.

To get started, fire up Visual Web Developer. The Start Page will appear, as shown in Figure 2-1. As you can see, this page gives you fast access to the projects you've been recently working on. You can click one of the links in the Recent Projects section to open a project.

The Start Page also shows recent information from Microsoft's MSDN site, which contains useful information for developers. If any of these items interests you, click it to read more.

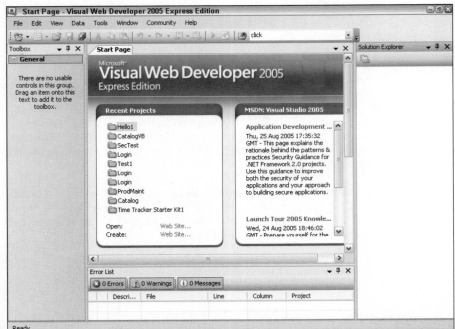

Figure 2-1:
Visual Web
Developer's
Start page.

Creating a new Web site

To create a new Web site, follow these steps:

1. **Choose File⇨New Web Site.**

   This brings up the New Web Site dialog box, as shown in Figure 2-2. This dialog box lists the templates available for creating Web sites. By default, the ASP.NET Web Site template is selected. That's the one you want to use to create a basic Web site.

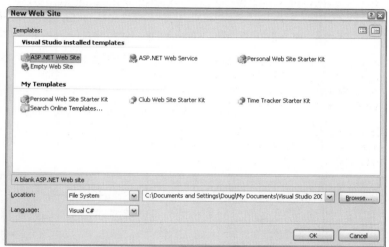

Figure 2-2:
The New
Web Site
dialog box.

2. **Choose File System from the Location drop-down menu.**

   The Location drop-down list enables you to choose one of three types of Web sites you can create:

   • **File System:** This option creates a Web site that's run by Visual Web Developer's built-in Web server, which is called the ASP.NET Development Server. For the applications in this book, file system Web sites are adequate.

   • **HTTP:** This option creates a Web site on an IIS server (*IIS* refers to *Internet Information Services*, Microsoft's Web server). The IIS server can run on your own computer or another server computer you have access to. This is the option used most often for professional Web site development.

- **FTP:** This option creates a Web site on a remote IIS server to which you don't have HTTP access. It uses the File Transfer Protocol (FTP) to upload your Web site files to the server.

  FTP sites are used mostly when you're working with a hosting service to host your site.

3. **Type the name and location for your Web site in the path text box.**

   By default, file system Web sites are created in My Documents\Visual Studio 2005\WebSites. You'll have to scroll to the end of this long path to type the name of your Web site at the end of this path.

   You can use the Browse button to bring up a dialog box that enables you to browse to the location where you want to create the Web site.

4. **Choose the language you want to use from the Language drop-down menu.**

   The choices are Visual Basic, Visual C#, and Visual J#.

5. **Click OK.**

   Visual Web Developer grinds and whirs for a moment as it creates your Web site. When it's finished, a screen similar to the one shown in Figure 2-3 appears. Here, the `Default.aspx` page is opened in Source view.

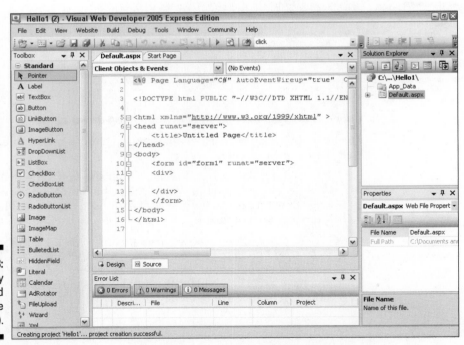

Figure 2-3: A newly created Web site (C#).

Note that if you selected Visual Basic as the language for the Web site, the `Default.aspx` page is opened in Design view rather than in Source view. I guess Microsoft figures that C# programmers like the hard-coding efficiency of Source view, while Visual Basic programmers prefer the drag-and-drop comfort of Design view. Either way, you can switch between Design and Source view by clicking the Design and Source buttons located at the bottom of the Designer window.

Adding a label control

To display the "Hello, World!" greeting, we'll add a label control to the `Default.aspx` page. Follow these steps:

1. **If the page is currently displayed in Source view, click the Design button at the bottom of the Designer window.**

   This switches the Designer to Design view.

2. **Drag a Label control from the Toolbox onto the page.**

   The Toolbox is located to the left of the Designer. If the Label control isn't visible, click the + icon next to the word `Standard` in the Toolbox.

   Figure 2-4 shows how the label should appear.

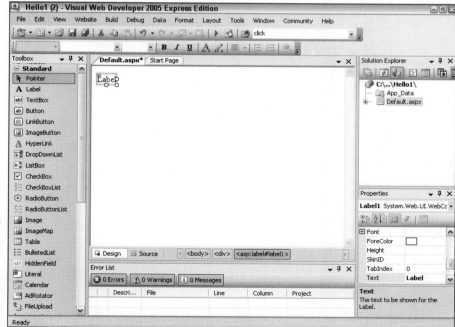

Figure 2-4:
The
`Default.`
`aspx` page
with a Label
control.

3. **In the Properties window, set the Text property of the label to** Hello, World!.

   You can set the Text property by using the Properties window, which is usually located at the bottom-right edge of the Visual Web Designer window. First, select the label. Then, locate the Text property in the Properties window and change its value to "Hello, World!" by clicking the Text property and typing the new value. (If the Properties window isn't visible, press F4 to display it.)

4. **Expand the** Font **property in the Properties window, and then set the** Size **property to** X-Large.

   To expand the Font property, click the + icon next to the word Font.

   Figure 2-5 shows what the page looks like after you've set the properties for the label.

Note that when you add a control in Design view, Visual Web Developer automatically adds code to the Default.aspx file to declare the control. You can switch back to Source view to see this code. Here's the code that's generated for the label in the Hello World application:

```
<asp:Label ID="Label1" runat="server" Font-Size="X-Large"
          Text="Hello, World!"></asp:Label>
```

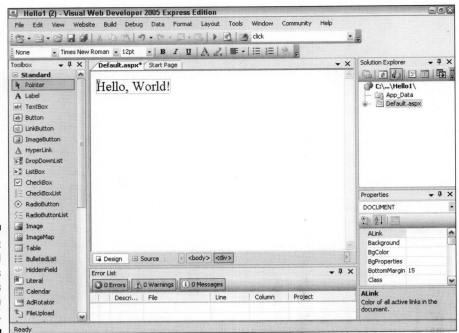

Figure 2-5:
The label after its properties have been set.

Here, the `<asp:Label>` element defines the label control. The `ID` attribute identifies the label's name as `Label1`. The `runat` attribute is required for all ASP.NET controls; it simply indicates that the control runs on the server rather than on the client. Next, the `Font-Size` attribute specifies the size of the font used to display the label's text, and the `Text` attribute provides the text displayed in the label.

Running the application

The Hello World application is now ready to run. There are several ways to run an application from Visual Web Developer; the easiest is simply to click the Start button (pictured in the margin). Here are a few other alternatives:

- ✔ Choose Debug➪Start Debugging
- ✔ Press F5
- ✔ Right-click the `Default.aspx` page in the Solution Explorer window and choose View In Browser.

The first time you run an ASP.NET application, Visual Web Developer displays the dialog box shown in Figure 2-6. This dialog box appears because in order to debug an ASP.NET application, debugging must be enabled in the `web.config` file. Unfortunately, the default template for new ASP.NET applications doesn't include a `web.config` file. So, this dialog box offers to create a `web.config` file for you so that the application can be run in debugging mode.

Figure 2-6:
The dialog box that's displayed the first time you run an ASP.NET application.

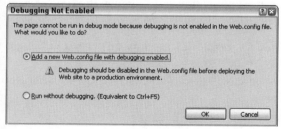

To run the application, click OK. Visual Web Developer then compiles the application. Assuming there are no compiler errors, the built-in development Web server starts and the application runs. After a few moments, a Browser window appears and shows the application's start page (usually `Default.aspx`), as shown in Figure 2-7.

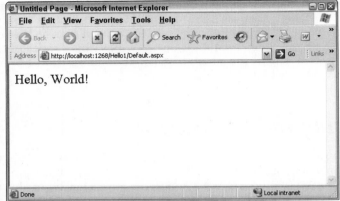

Figure 2-7:
The Hello
World
application
in action.

 When you're satisfied that the application has run correctly, you can stop the application by closing the Browser window. Alternatively, you can return to the Visual Web Developer window and click the Stop Debugging button (shown in the margin).

Adding a Code-Behind File

So far, the Hello World application doesn't do anything other than display a static message on a Web page. To make the application a little more interesting, in this section we add a *code-behind file* — a separate file that contains the program logic for the application — to display the time as well as the "Hello, World!" greeting. Here are the steps:

1. **If the** Default.aspx **page isn't already on-screen in Design view, switch to Design view now.**

   To switch to Design view, click the Design button at the bottom of the Designer window.

2. **Double-click anywhere on the background of the page.**

   This opens the code-behind file for the Default.aspx page and creates a Page_Load method that's executed each time the page is loaded. Figure 2-8 shows how this appears when C# is the selected language. (For VB, the code-behind file is similar, but naturally is coded in Visual Basic rather than C#.)

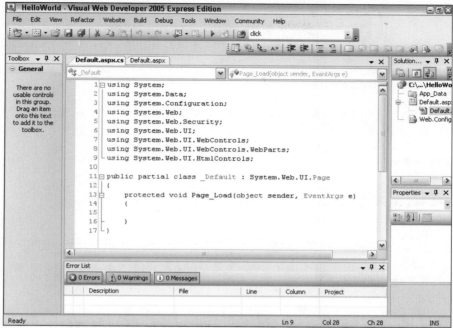

Figure 2-8:
The code-
behind file
for the
Default.
aspx page.

3. Add code to the Page_Load **method.**

If you're working in C#, add this code:

```
Label1.Text = "Hello, World!<br /><br />"
    + DateTime.Now.ToLongDateString() + "<br />"
    + DateTime.Now.ToLongTimeString();
```

If you're working in Visual Basic, add this code instead:

```
Label1.Text = "Hello, World!<br /><br />" _
    + DateTime.Now.ToLongDateString() + "<br />" _
    + DateTime.Now.ToLongTimeString()
```

4. Run the application again.

This time the date and time should appear on the page, as shown in Figure 2-9.

Note that the Page_Load method is executed each time the page is loaded. As a result, you can update the date and time by clicking the browser's Refresh button.

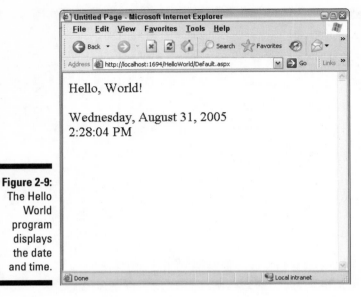

Figure 2-9:
The Hello
World
program
displays
the date
and time.

Adding a Text Box and a Button

To show how you can accept user input in an ASP.NET application, in this section we modify the Hello World application so it includes a text box and a button. The user can enter his or her name in the text box. Then, when the user clicks the button, a personalized greeting is added to the page. Figure 2-10 shows the revised Hello World application in action.

To add the text box and button to the page, switch to Design view and follow these steps:

1. **Place the insertion point right after the existing label, hit the Enter key a couple of times, and type** `Your Name:`.

   Type it as text string, not as your name. (But you knew that.) Doing so creates the descriptive text that will identify the text box.

2. **Double-click the TextBox icon in the toolbox.**

   This adds a text box to the page.

3. **Press the right-arrow key to move the cursor to the end of the line, then press Enter twice.**

   This adds a blank line after the text box.

4. **Double-click the Button icon in the toolbox.**

   This adds a button to the page.

Figure 2-10:
The Hello
World
program
displays a
personalized
greeting.

5. **Click the text box to select it, and then use the Properties window to change the** ID **property from** TextBox1 **to** txtName.

   This gives the text box a more meaningful name than TextBox1.

6. **Click the button to select it, and then use the Properties window to change the** Text **property to** Submit.

   This changes the button text to Submit.

   If you want, you can switch to Source view to see the ASPX code that's generated for the text box and the button.

7. **Double-click the button.**

   The code-behind file appears and a skeleton method is created to handle the Click event for the button. In C#, this skeleton method looks like this:

   ```
   protected void Button1_Click(object sender, EventArgs e)
   {
   }
   ```

   If you're working in Visual Basic, the skeleton method looks more like this:

   ```
   Protected Sub Button1_Click(ByVal sender As Object,
           ByVal e As System.EventArgs) Handles
           Button1.Click

   End Sub
   ```

8. **Add code to the Click Event handler.**

   For C#, you should add the following code:

   ```
   Label1.Text += "<br />Hello, "
       + txtName.Text;
   ```

   For Visual Basic, use this code instead:

   ```
   Label1.Text += "<br />Hello, " _
       + txtName.Text
   ```

9. **Run the application.**

   This time, the text box and button should appear. When you enter a name and click the button, a greeting will be added to text displayed in the label.

For your reference, Listing 2-1 shows the complete `Default.aspx` file, Listing 2-2 shows the C# version of the code-behind file, and Listing 2-3 shows the Visual Basic version of the code-behind file.

To use the Visual Basic code-behind file, you must change the `Language` attribute of the `Page` directive from C# to VB, and you should change the `CodeFile` attribute from `Default.aspx.cs` to `Default.aspx.vb`.

Listing 2-1: The `Default.aspx` page

```
<%@ Page Language="C#" AutoEventWireup="true"
CodeFile="Default.aspx.cs" Inherits="_Default" %>

<!DOCTYPE html PUBLIC "-//W3C//DTD XHTML 1.1//EN"
"http://www.w3.org/TR/xhtml11/DTD/xhtml11.dtd">

<html xmlns="http://www.w3.org/1999/xhtml" >
<head runat="server">
    <title>Untitled Page</title>
</head>
<body>
    <form id="form1" runat="server">
    <div>
        <asp:Label ID="Label1" runat="server"
            Font-Size="X-Large"
            Text="Hello, World!"></asp:Label><br />
        <br />
        Your name:
        <asp:TextBox ID="txtName"
            runat="server"></asp:TextBox><br />
        <br />
        <asp:Button ID="Button1" runat="server"
            Text="Submit" OnClick="Button1_Click" />
    </div>
    </form>
</body>
</html>
```

Listing 2-2:   The C# code-behind file

```
using System;
using System.Data;
using System.Configuration;
using System.Web;
using System.Web.Security;
using System.Web.UI;
using System.Web.UI.WebControls;
using System.Web.UI.WebControls.WebParts;
using System.Web.UI.HtmlControls;

public partial class _Default : System.Web.UI.Page
{
    protected void Page_Load(object sender,
        EventArgs e)
    {
        Label1.Text = "Hello, World!<br /><br />"
            + DateTime.Now.ToLongDateString() + "<br />"
            + DateTime.Now.ToLongTimeString();
    }

    protected void Button1_Click(object sender,
        EventArgs e)
    {
        Label1.Text += "<br />Hello, "
            + txtName.Text;
    }
}
```

Listing 2-3:   The Visual Basic code-behind file

```
Partial Class _Default
    Inherits System.Web.UI.Page

    Protected Sub Page_Load(ByVal sender As Object, _
        ByVal e As System.EventArgs) Handles Me.Load
            Label1.Text = "Hello, World!<br /><br />" _
            + DateTime.Now.ToLongDateString() + "<br />" _
            + DateTime.Now.ToLongTimeString()
    End Sub

    Protected Sub Button1_Click(ByVal sender As Object, _
        ByVal e As System.EventArgs) _
        Handles Button1.Click
            Label1.Text += "<br />Hello, " _
            + txtName.Text
    End Sub

End Class
```

Working with Folders and Other Project Items

By default, a new ASP.NET Web project includes just one subfolder, named App_Data. This folder is designed to hold databases used by the application, but in practice it sees action only if the application uses Access databases or text files. If the application uses a SQL Server database or a database managed by some other database server, the actual database is usually stored in a location that's independent of the Web application.

You can add other folders to a Web project by right-clicking the project node in the Solution Explorer and choosing the Add New Item command. This brings up a dialog box that enables you to add a variety of items to the project — including Web forms, HTML files, text files, Master Pages, and so on.

When you add a Web form to a project, you must supply the name and language to use for the page. In addition, check boxes let you indicate whether you want to use a Master Page and place the code in a separate code-behind file. You should almost always select both of these options. You can also add additional folders to a project by right-clicking the project in the Solution Explorer and selecting the Add Folder command. This brings up a submenu, from which you can choose to add any of the following types of folders:

- ✔ **Regular folder:** Adds a regular Windows folder to the project. Use regular folders to organize the application's Web pages into groups or to store related items such as images.

- ✔ **Bin folder:** Adds a folder to store pre-compiled class libraries.

- ✔ **App_GlobalResources:** Adds a folder that contains *global resources* that can be accessed by any page in the application.

    Consider carefully which resources you want to place in this folder.

- ✔ **App_LocalResources:** Adds a folder that contains *local resources*, which are available only to pages in the same folder as the App_LocalResources folder. App_LocalResources folders are sometimes used along with regular folders that contain logically related pages to hold resources available only to those pages.

- ✔ **App_WebReferences:** Adds a folder that holds references to Web services.

- ✔ **App_Browsers:** Adds a folder that can hold browser-definition files. ASP.NET uses these files to identify the capabilities of individual browsers.

- ✔ **Themes:** Adds a folder that holds files related to *themes* — a new ASP.NET feature that helps ensure a consistent appearance throughout a Web site and makes it easier to change the Web site's appearance when necessary.

Note that none of the applications in this book use the App_
GlobalResources, App_LocalResources, App_WebReferences,
App_Browsers, or Themes folders. As a result, you can safely ignore
these folders until you're ready to dig deeper.

Debugging Web Applications

Visual Web Developer includes a variety of built-in debugging features that
can help you track down the nasty bugs that are sure to creep into your
application. With the application we've presented so far, it's hard for
anything to go wrong because the application doesn't really do any signifi-
cant work. So, this section starts by presenting a simple calculator application that we can use to explore Visual Web Developer's debugging features.

Creating a calculator page

Figure 2-11 shows a simple Web page that accepts two numbers as input
and displays the sum of the numbers when the user clicks the button. The
.aspx file for this page is shown in Listing 2-4. Listing 2-5 shows the C# version of the code-behind file for this page, and Listing 2-6 shows the Visual
Basic version.

Note that for the Visual Basic version of the code-behind file to work, you
must change the language reference in the .aspx file, the CodeFile attribute
to Default.aspx.vb, and the AutoEventWireup attribute to "false". Thus,
the Page directive for the VB version should look like this:

```
<%@ Page Language="VB"
    AutoEventWireup="false"
    CodeFile="Default.aspx.vb"
    Inherits="_Default" %>
```

In addition, you should remove the OnClick attribute for the Button control.

You can see right away the problem waiting to happen with this application.
It parses whatever the user enters into the two text boxes to decimal types,
and then adds the numbers and displays the result. The application will work
fine as long as the user enters valid numbers in both text boxes. But if the
user leaves one or both boxes blank, or enters something other than a valid
number, the program will fail.

In this case, the problem is easy enough to find. However, this simple program is adequate to demonstrate most of Visual Web Developer's debugging
features.

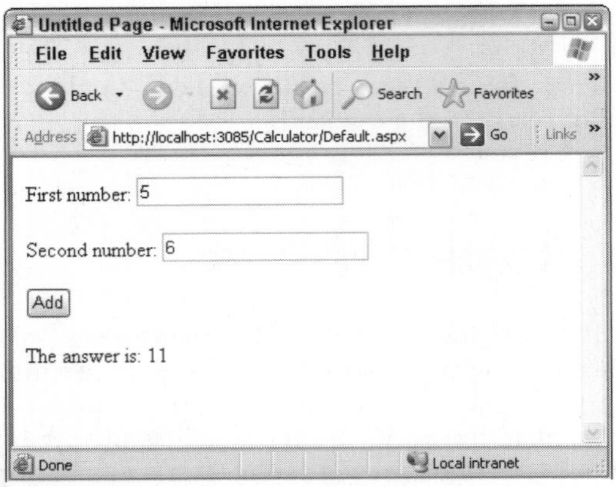

Figure 2-11:
A simple
calculator
program in
action.

Listing 2-4:   The Default.aspx page for the Calculator application

```
<%@ Page Language="C#" AutoEventWireup="true"
    CodeFile="Default.aspx.cs" Inherits="_Default" %>

<!DOCTYPE html PUBLIC "-//W3C//DTD XHTML 1.1//EN"
"http://www.w3.org/TR/xhtml11/DTD/xhtml11.dtd">

<html xmlns="http://www.w3.org/1999/xhtml" >
<head runat="server">
    <title>Untitled Page</title>
</head>
<body>
    <form id="form1" runat="server">
    <div>
        First number:
        <asp:TextBox ID="txtFirst" runat="server">
        </asp:TextBox>
        <br /><br />
        Second number:
        <asp:TextBox ID="txtSecond" runat="server">
        </asp:TextBox>
        <br /><br />
        <asp:Button ID="btnAdd" runat="server"
            OnClick="btnAdd_Click" Text="Add" />
        <br /><br />
        The answer is:
        <asp:Label ID="lblAnswer" runat="server">
        </asp:Label>
    </div>
    </form>
</body>
</html>
```

Listing 2-5: **The C# code-behind file for the Calculator application (Default.aspx.cs)**

```
using System;
using System.Data;
using System.Configuration;
using System.Web;
using System.Web.Security;
using System.Web.UI;
using System.Web.UI.WebControls;
using System.Web.UI.WebControls.WebParts;
using System.Web.UI.HtmlControls;

public partial class _Default : System.Web.UI.Page
{
    protected void btnAdd_Click(object sender, EventArgs
          e)
    {
        decimal a = decimal.Parse(txtFirst.Text);
        decimal b = decimal.Parse(txtSecond.Text);
        decimal c = a + b;
        lblAnswer.Text = c.ToString();
    }
}
```

Listing 2-6: **The Visual Basic code-behind file for the Calculator application (Default.aspx.vb)**

```
Partial Class _Default
    Inherits System.Web.UI.Page

    Protected Sub btnAdd_Click(ByVal sender As Object, _
      ByVal e As System.EventArgs) _
      Handles btnAdd.Click
        Dim a, b, c As Decimal
        a = Decimal.Parse(txtFirst.Text)
        b = Decimal.Parse(txtSecond.Text)
        c = a + b
        lblAnswer.Text = c.ToString()
    End Sub

End Class
```

Working in Break mode

Run the Calculator application by pressing F5, which starts the application in debugging mode. Just to make sure it works, enter a number in each of the text boxes and click Add. The program should add the numbers together and display the result. Now enter 5 for the first number and abc for the second and click Add again. This causes the program to throw an uncaught exception, which in turn throws Visual Web Developer into Break mode, as shown in Figure 2-12.

As you can see, Visual Web Developer highlights the statement that threw the exception and displays the details of the exception. In this case, the message FormatException was unhandled by user code indicates that a FormatException was thrown and wasn't handled.

Displaying data values

One of the most useful debugging features in Visual Web Developer is the *DataTips* feature, which displays the value of a variable when you point at it while the system is in Break mode. For example, if you point at the Text property for the txtSecond text box, a tip balloon will appear showing the current value of this property, as shown in Figure 2-13.

You can even use a data tip to change the actual value of a variable while the program is running. Just click the value in the data tip, and then type a new value.

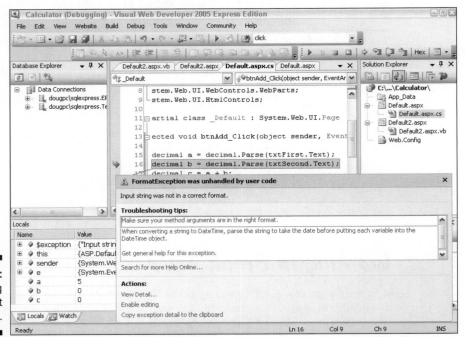

Figure 2-12:
Debugging an uncaught exception.

Figure 2-13:
Displaying a
data tip.

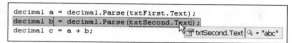

```
decimal a = decimal.Parse(txtFirst.Text);
decimal b = decimal.Parse(txtSecond.Text);
decimal c = a + b;                          txtSecond.Text  - "abc"
```

Another way to determine the values of variables is to use the Locals
window. Looking back at, Figure 2-12, you'll find the Locals window in the
lower-left corner of the screen. As you can see, the value of the a variable has
been properly parsed to the value 5, but the b and c variables remain at their
default values: 0 (zero).

To find the value of the Text property in the Locals window, first expand the
this node. (If you're working in Visual Basic, use the Me node instead.) This
lists all the controls on the current page. Locate and expand the txtSecond
node, and then locate the Text property.

Controlling execution and setting breakpoints

You can control the execution of the application by stepping through the
application one or more lines at a time. In addition, you can set *breakpoints,*
which cause the debugger to interrupt the program when they are encoun-
tered. The following buttons appear on the Debug toolbar to help you control
the program's execution:

 ✔ **Continue:** Continues execution with the next statement.

✔ **Break:** Interrupts the application and places Visual Web Developer into
Break mode.

 ✔ **Stop Debugging:** Stops the application.

 ✔ **Restart:** Restarts the application.

 ✔ **Show Next Statement:** Highlights the next statement to be executed.

 ✔ **Step Into:** Executes the next statement and then breaks. If the statement
calls a method, execution stops with the first statement in the method.

 ✔ **Step Over:** Executes the next statement, and then breaks. If the statement calls a method, the entire method is executed without breaking.

 ✔ **Step Out:** Finishes the current method and then breaks.

You can set a *breakpoint* at any statement in your program by clicking in the gray border on the left edge of the Designer window, next to the statement where you want the program to break. A large dot appears in the gray border to mark the breakpoint.

Deploying ASP.NET Applications

Eventually, the Big Day comes: You've finished the application, tracked down and removed all the bugs, and you're ready for the application to go live. That's when Visual Web Developer's *deployment features* come in handy.

In general, there are three ways to deploy an ASP.NET application:

- ✔ **Xcopy deployment:** This is the simplest type of deployment. You simply copy the files from your development server to the production server. You can use this deployment method by choosing the Web Site⇨Copy Web Site command.

    One problem with Xcopy deployment is that the application isn't compiled on the production server until the first time the application is accessed. To solve that problem, you can use precompiled deployment instead.

- ✔ **Precompiled deployment:** In this type of deployment, the entire application is compiled. Then the compiled assemblies are copied to the production server. To use precompiled deployment, choose the Build⇨ Publish Web Site command. Or use the aspnet_compiler command from a command prompt. (Note that the Publish Web Site command isn't available in Visual Web Developer 2005 Express Edition.)

- ✔ **Setup project:** A third way to deploy a Web application is to create a Setup project for the Web site. Then you can deploy the application by running the Setup program on the target server. This is the most complicated (and least used) form of deployment for ASP.NET applications. (Setup projects are only available if you use Visual Studio 2005; VWDE doesn't provide Setup projects.)

Before you deploy an ASP.NET application, be sure to nail down a few final changes to make the application ready for production — in particular, these:

- ✔ Turn off debugging in the web.config file:

    ```
    <compilation defaultLanguage="C#" debug="false" />
    ```

- ✔ Check the Page directive for all pages; make sure tracing is not turned on by removing any trace="True" attributes.

- ✔ Make sure the web.config file contains this line:

    ```
    <customErrors mode="RemoteOnly" />
    ```

    That way detailed error pages won't be displayed for production users.

Part II
Building Secure Applications

In this part . . .

This part covers one of the most important aspects of building ASP.NET applications: security. Chapter 3 begins with an overview of security issues for ASP.NET application developers. Then Chapter 4 shows you how to develop a complete user-registration-and-authentication application.

Many of the other applications in this book can be integrated with the application presented in Chapter 4. For example, you may want to require users to register before they can use the Shopping Cart application (presented in Chapter 6). And for the back-end applications shown in Part IV, you may want to limit access to users who have been registered as administrative personnel.

Chapter 3

Designing Secure ASP.NET Applications

In This Chapter

▶ Understanding user authentication and authorization

▶ Looking at membership providers

▶ Using ASP.NET 2.0 login controls

▶ Examining other security issues

*I*n the 1960s television series *Get Smart*, they had a top-secret security device known as the Cone of Silence. Whenever Max (Agent 86) and The Chief were about to discuss matters of importance, Max would insist that they use the Cone of Silence. The Chief would protest, but Max would eventually win out and they'd lower the Cone over themselves.

Of course, the gag was that the Cone of Silence was so effective they couldn't even hear themselves talk. Computer security is sometimes like that. The key is designing an application secure enough that sensitive data is protected, but not so secure that the application becomes unusable.

This chapter describes some of the most important techniques for creating secure Web applications using ASP.NET 2.0. Most of this chapter explores ASP.NET's built-in features for user authentication, including the new login controls. You'll also find tips for creating applications that are safe from various types of security threats such as cross-site scripting and SQL injections (more about those shortly).

Understanding ASP.NET User Authentication

Many Web applications require that the user register with the system and log in before using the application. For example, a shopping-cart application requires that the user log in before completing a purchase. That way, the application knows who is purchasing the items, who to ship the items to, and who to send the bill to. Similarly, community applications such as forums and blogs require users to log in before posting content to the application.

Some applications require the user to log in before he or she can view any page in the application. Other applications have some pages that can be viewed anonymously and others that require a log in. For example, an online store might allow users to view a catalog and add items to a shopping cart without logging in, but require a login to complete a purchase. And a forum or blog might allow anyone to view other users' posts without logging in, but the user must log in to make a post of his or her own.

In addition, some applications have more than one kind of user. For example, most of the users of a shopping-cart application can view the company's products, add items to a shopping cart, and make purchases, but can't make changes to the items in the Products database. To do that, the user must be an administrator. Similarly, forums typically distinguish between normal users (who are allowed to post information) and moderators (who can delete questionable posts or ban abusive users).

There are two aspects of user registration and login security in ASP.NET:

- ✔ **Authentication,** which refers to the process of determining who a user is, and whether the user really is who he or she claims to be.

- ✔ **Authorization,** which refers to the process of determining whether a particular user, once authenticated, can access a particular Web site page.

The following sections describe the authentication and authorization features available in ASP.NET.

Examining three types of authentication

ASP.NET provides three basic methods for authenticating users:

- ✔ **Forms-based authentication:** Uses a membership database to store the names and passwords of valid users. Whenever a user attempts to access a restricted page, ASP.NET automatically redirects the user to a login page (normally named Login.aspx), which prompts the user for a name and password and attempts to authenticate the user. The originally requested page is then displayed if the user is valid. This is the most common type of authentication for Web sites that allow public access but require that users create login accounts to access the application.

- ✔ **Windows-based authentication:** Uses existing Windows accounts to authenticate users. This type of authentication is used mostly for intranet applications, where the users already have valid Windows accounts.

✔ **Passport authentication:** Uses Microsoft's Passport service to authenticate users. When you use Passport authentication, a user must have a valid Passport account to access the application. Of the three authentication modes, this one is the least used.

The rest of this chapter (and the rest of this book) assumes you will use forms-based authentication when you need to restrict access to your Web applications.

Configuring forms-based authentication

To configure an ASP.NET application to use forms-based authentication, add an `<authentication>` element to the `<system.web>` section of the application's root `web.config` file. In its simplest form, this element looks like this:

```
<system.web>
    <authentication mode="Forms" />
</system.web>
```

That's all you need do to enable the authentication of forms, if you're okay with using the default settings. If you want, you can customize the settings by adding a `<forms>` subelement beneath the `<authentication>` element. Here's an example:

```
<system.web>
    <authentication mode="Forms" >
        <forms loginUrl="Login.aspx" />
    </authentication>
</system.web>
```

Here, forms-based authentication is configured so that the login page is named `Signin.aspx` rather than the default `Login.aspx`.

You can also add a `<Credentials>` element that lists the names and passwords of the users. However, it's considered bad form (groan) to list the passwords directly in the `web.config` file because of security risks. So a separate database is usually used instead.

Configuring authorization

Authorization — that is, the process of determining which users are allowed to access what resources in a Web application — is another capability you configure via the `web.config` file. The key to configuring authorization is realizing two vital aspects of how it works:

✔ Each folder within a Web application can have its own `web.config` file.

✔ The authorization settings in a given `web.config` file apply only to the files in the folder where a `web.config` file appears, plus any subfolders. (Note, however, that a subfolder can have its own `web.config` file, which overrides the settings it gets from the parent folder's `web.config` file.)

To configure access restrictions for the files in a folder, add a `web.config` file to the folder, then add an `<authorization>` element to the `web.config` file's `<system.web>` element. Then, add one or more `<allow>` or `<deny>` elements. Here's an example:

```
<system.web>
    <authorization>
        <deny users="?" />
    </authorization>
</system.web>
```

In this example, the `?` wildcard prohibits anonymous users. As a result, only authenticated users will be allowed to access the pages in the folder where this `web.config` file appears.

You can also allow or deny access to specific users. Here's an example:

```
<system.web>
    <authorization>
        <allow users="Tom, Dick, Harry" />
        <deny users="*" />
    </authorization>
</system.web>
```

Here, the `<allow>` element grants access to users named `Tom`, `Dick`, and `Harry`, and the `<deny>` element uses a wildcard to deny access to all other users.

Here are a few additional points regarding these elements:

✔ The `?` wildcard refers only to users who haven't logged in. The `*` wildcard refers to all users, whether they've logged in or not.

✔ If you list more than one user name in an `<allow>` or `<deny>` element, separate the names with commas.

✔ The order in which you list the `<allow>` and `<deny>` elements is important. As soon as ASP.NET finds an `<allow>` or `<deny>` rule that applies to the current user, the rule is applied and any remaining elements are ignored. Thus, you should list rules that list specific users first, followed by rules that use the `?` wildcard, followed by rules that use the `*` wildcard.

If you don't want to mess with coding the authorization elements yourself, you can use the new browser-based configuration tool instead. From Visual Studio, choose Web Site⇨ASP.NET Configuration to access this tool.

Understanding membership providers

Prior to ASP.NET 2.0, you had to develop custom programming to store and retrieve user data from a database. Now, ASP.NET 2.0 uses a *provider model* that provides a standardized interface to the objects that maintain the user-account information. In addition, ASP.NET 2.0 comes with a *standard membership provider,* an application that stores basic user-account information in a SQL Server database. The Login controls are designed to work with this membership provider.

If the standard provider isn't adequate to your needs, you can write your own membership provider to use instead. As long as your custom provider conforms to the ASP.NET membership provider interface, the Login controls can work with it.

To create a custom provider, you simply create a class that inherits the abstract class System.Web.Security.MembershipProvider. This class requires that you implement about two dozen properties and methods. (For example, you must implement a CreateUser method that creates a user account and a ValidateUser method that validates a user based on a name and password. For openers.) For more information about creating your own membership provider, refer to the Help.

After you've created a custom membership provider, you can use settings in the web.config file to indicate that you want to use it instead of the standard membership provider. Here's an example:

```
<system.web>
    <membership defaultProvider="MyMemberProvider" >
        <providers>
            <add name="MyMemberProvider"
                type="MyNameSpace.MyMemberProvider"
                connectionStringName="MyProviderConn"
                enablePasswordRetrieval="false"
                enablePasswordReset="true"
                requiresQuestionAndAnswer="true"
            />
        </providers>
    </membership>
</system.web>
```

Here, a custom membership provider named MyMemberProvider is created using the class MyNameSpace.MyMemberProvider. This provider is designated as the *default provider*, used throughout the application unless you specify otherwise.

Fortunately, the standard membership provider is suitable for most applications. So you don't have to create your own membership provider unless your application has unusual requirements.

Using ASP.NET Login Controls

One of the most useful new features in ASP.NET 2.0 is a suite of seven controls designed to simplify applications that authenticate users. In Visual Studio 2005, these controls are located in the toolbox under the Login tab. The seven controls are as follows:

- ✔ Login: Lets the user log in by entering a user name and password.
- ✔ CreateUserWizard: Lets the user create a new user account.
- ✔ PasswordRecovery: Lets the user retrieve a forgotten password.
- ✔ ChangePassword: Lets the user change his or her password.
- ✔ LoginView: Displays the contents of a template based on the user's login status.
- ✔ LoginStatus: If the user is logged in, displays a link that logs the user out. If the user isn't logged in, displays a link that leads to the application's login page.
- ✔ LoginName: Displays the user's login name if the user is logged in.

The following sections describe the basics of using each of these controls.

Using the Login control

The Login control provides a convenient way to let users log in to an application. You should use the Login control on a page named Login.aspx. That way, the Login control will be displayed automatically whenever a user tries to access a page that requires the user to be logged in.

In its simplest form, the Login control looks like this:

```
<asp:Login id="Login1" runat="Server" />
```

The Login control displays text boxes that let the user enter a user name and password. When those are filled in, the Login control uses the membership provider to look up the user name and password in the membership database. If the user name and password are valid, the user is logged in and the page that was originally requested is displayed. If not, an error message is displayed and the user is not logged in.

You can customize the Login control by using any of the optional attributes listed in Table 3-1. For example, here's a Login control that uses custom titles and displays links to a new user-registration page and a password-recovery page:

```
<asp:Login id="Login1" runat="Server"
    TitleText="Please enter your user name and password:"
    UserNameLabelText="Your user name:"
    PasswordLabelText="Your password:"
    CreateUserText="Register as a new user"
    CreateUserUrl="~/Login/Register.aspx"
    PasswordRecoveryText="Forgot your password?"
    PasswordRecoveryUrl="~/Login/Recover.aspx" />
```

Table 3-1	Attributes for the Login control
Attribute	*Explanation*
id	The ID associated with the Login control.
runat	Runat="Server" is required for all ASP.NET server controls.
CreateUserIconUrl	The URL of an image used as a link to a page that registers a new user.
CreateUserText	Text that's displayed as a link to a page that registers a new user.
CreateUserUrl	The URL of a page that registers a new user.
DestinationPageUrl	Sets the URL of the page that's displayed when the user successfully logs in. If this attribute is omitted, the page that was originally requested is displayed.
DisplayRememberMe	A Boolean that indicates whether the Login control should display a check box that lets the user choose to leave a cookie so the user can automatically be logged in in the future.
FailureText	The text message that's displayed if the user name or password is incorrect. The default reads: Your login attempt has failed. Please try again.
InstructionText	A text value displayed immediately beneath the title text, intended to provide login instructions for the user. The default is an empty string.
LoginButtonText	The text that's displayed on the Login button.

(continued)

Table 3-1 *(continued)*

Attribute	*Explanation*
LoginButtonType	The button type for the Login button. You can specify Button, Link, or Image. (If you specify Image, then you should also specify the LoginButtonImageUrl attribute.)
Orientation	Specifies the layout of the login controls. You can specify Horizontal or Vertical. The default is Vertical.
PasswordLabelText	The text that's displayed in the label that identifies the Password field.
PasswordRecoveryIconUrl	The URL of an image used as a link to a page that recovers a lost password.
PasswordRecoveryText	Text that's displayed as a link to a page that recovers a lost password.
PasswordRecoveryUrl	The URL of a page that recovers a lost password.
RememberMeText	The text displayed for the Remember Me check box.
TextLayout	Specifies the position of the labels relative to the user name and password text boxes. If you specify TextOnLeft, the labels appear to the left of the text boxes. If you specify TextOnTop, the labels appear above the text boxes.
TitleText	The text that's displayed at the top of the Login control.
UserNameLabelText	The text that's displayed in the label that identifies the User Name field.

Using the CreateUserWizard control

The CreateUserWizard control automates the task of entering the information for a new user and creating a record for the user in the membership database. It displays text boxes that let the user enter a user name, a password, an e-mail address, a security question, and the answer to the security question. Note that there are actually two text boxes for the password; the user must enter the same password in both text boxes.

When the user clicks the New User button, the `CreateUserWizard` control attempts to create a new user account, basing it on the information entered by the user. If the account is successfully created, the user is logged in to the new account. If the account can't be created (for example, because an account with the same user name already exists), an error message is displayed.

In its simplest form, the `CreateUserWizard` control looks like this:

```
<asp:CreateUserWizard id="CreateUserWizard1"
    runat="Server" />
```

You can customize the `CreateUserWizard` control with the attributes listed in Table 3-2. Here's an example:

```
<asp:CreateUserWizard id="CreateUserWizard1"
        runat="Server"
    HeaderText="New User Registration"
    InstructionText="Please enter your user information:"
    UserNameLabelText="Your user name:"
    PasswordLabelText="Your password:"
    ConfirmPasswordLabelText="Confirm password:"
    EmailLabelText="Your e-mail address:"
    QuestionLabelText="Your secret question:"
    AnswerLabelText="The answer:" />
```

In this example, attributes are used to set the text values displayed by the labels that identify the data-entry text boxes.

Table 3-2	Attributes for the CreateUserWizard control
Attribute	**Explanation**
`id`	The ID associated with the `CreateUserWizard` control.
`runat`	`Runat="Server"` is required for all ASP.NET server controls.
`AnswerLabelText`	The text that's displayed in the label for the `Answer` field.
`CancelButtonImageUrl`	The URL of an image used on the Cancel button.
`CancelButtonText`	The text displayed on the Cancel button.
`CancelButtonType`	The button type for the Cancel button. You can specify `Button`, `Link`, or `Image`.
`CancelDestinationPageUrl`	The URL of the page that's displayed if the user clicks the Cancel button.

(continued)

Table 3-2 *(continued)*

Attribute	Explanation
CompleteStepText	The text displayed when the user successfully creates an account. (Note that the Complete step isn't shown unless LoginCreatedUser is set to False.)
ContinueButtonImageUrl	The URL of an image used on the Continue button on the Success page.
ContinueButtonText	The text displayed on the Continue button on the Success page.
ContinueButtonType	The button type for the Continue button on the Success page. You can specify Button, Link, or Image.
ContinueDestinationPageUrl	The URL of the page that's displayed if the user clicks the Continue button on the Success page.
ConfirmPasswordLabelText	The text that's displayed in the label that identifies the Password Confirmation field.
CreateUserButtonImageUrl	The URL of an image used on the Create User button.
CreateUserButtonText	The text displayed on the Create User button.
CreateUserButtonType	The button type for the Create User button. You can specify Button, Link, or Image.
DisableCreatedUser	A Boolean that indicates whether the new user should be allowed to log in. The default is False. You can set this to True if you require an administrator to approve a new account before allowing the user to log in.
DisplayCancelButton	A Boolean that indicates whether to display the Cancel button. The default is False.
EmailLabelText	The text that's displayed in the label for the Email field.
HeaderText	The text that's displayed in the header area of the control.
InstructionText	The text that's displayed in the instruction area, immediately below the header text.

Attribute	Explanation
LoginCreatedUser	A Boolean that indicates whether the new user should automatically be logged in. The default is True.
PasswordLabelText	The text that's displayed in the label for the Password field.
QuestionLabelText	The text that's displayed in the label for the Security Question field.
UserNameLabelText	The text that's displayed in the label for the User Name field.

Here are a few other things you should know about the CreateUserWizard control:

✔ You can apply an AutoFormat to the CreateUserWizard control. Or you can use style attributes (not listed in Table 3-2) to customize the appearance of the wizard. For more information, refer to the Help.

✔ By default, the user is logged in the moment an account is created. You can prevent this by specifying LoginCreatedUser="False".

✔ You can disable a new user account by specifying DisableCreatedUser="True". This capability is especially handy when you want to require an administrator's approval before you allow new users to access the site.

✔ The CreateUserWizard control inherits the new Wizard control. As a result (you guessed it), many of the CreateUserWizard control's basic features are derived from the Wizard control. For more information about the Wizard control, refer to Chapter 6.

✔ By default, the wizard has two steps, named CreateUserWizardStep and CompleteWizardStep. You can add additional steps if you want. You can also add a sidebar that displays a link to each of the wizard's steps. Each wizard step is represented by a template in a <WizardSteps> child element. For example, when you create a CreateUserWizard control in Visual Studio, the default steps are defined with code similar to this:

```
<asp:CreateUserWizard runat="server"
    ID="CreateUserWizard1" >
    <WizardSteps>
        <asp:CreateUserWizardStep runat="server"
            ID="CreateUserWizardStep1">
        </asp:CreateUserWizardStep>
        <asp:CompleteWizardStep runat="server"
            ID="CompleteWizardStep1">
        </asp:CompleteWizardStep>
    </WizardSteps>
</asp:CreateUserWizard>
```

For more information about defining your own wizard steps, see the Help.

✔ The `CreateUserWizard` control can send a confirmation e-mail to the new user. For that to work, you can add a `<MailDefinition>` child element, like this:

```
<MailDefinition
    From="name@domain.com"
    Subject="Subject Line"
    BodyFileName="BodyFile.txt" />
```

If you prefer, you can use `MailDefinition` attributes directly in the `<CreateUserWizard>` element, like this:

```
<asp:CreateUserWizard runat="server"
    ID="CreateUserWizard1" >
    MailDefinition-From="name@domain.com"
    MailDefintion-Subject="Subject Line"
    MailDefinition-BodyFileName="BodyFile.txt" >
```

Either method is an acceptable way to specify mail-definition settings.

The body of the e-mail message will be taken from the file indicated by the `BodyFileName` attribute. Note that this text file can include the special variables `<%UserName%>` and `<%Password%>` to include the user's account name and password in the message.

✔ Besides the `<MailDefinition>` child element, you must also provide a `<MailSettings>` element in the application's `web.config` file. Here's a simple example:

```
<system.net>
  <mailSettings>
    <smtp>
      <network host="smtp.somewhere.com"
      from="Admin@MyDomain.com" />
    </smtp>
  </mailSettings>
</system.net>
```

Here the network host is `smtp.somewhere.com` and the `from` address for the e-mail is `Admin@MyDomain.com`. Naturally, you'll need to change these settings to reflect the host name of the SMTP server that delivers the mail, as well as the `from` address you want to use.

Using the PasswordRecovery control

The `PasswordRecovery` control lets a user retrieve a forgotten password. The user must correctly answer the secret question on file for the user. Then the password is reset to a random value, and the new password is e-mailed to the e-mail address on file with the user.

E-mail is inherently insecure, and the password sent to the user is not encrypted. As a result, you should carefully evaluate your application's security requirements before you use this control.

In its simplest form, the `PasswordRecovery` control looks like this:

```
<asp:PasswordRecovery id="PasswordRecovery1"
    runat="Server" >
    <MailDefinition
        From="name@domain.com"
        Subject="Subject Line"
        BodyFileName="BodyFile.txt" />
</asp:PasswordRecovery>
```

If you prefer, you can code the mail-definition settings directly into the `<PasswordRecovery>` element, like this:

```
<asp:PasswordRecovery id="PasswordRecovery1"
    runat="Server"
    MailDefinition-From="name@domain.com"
    MailDefinition-Subject="Subject Line"
    MailDefinition-BodyFileName="BodyFile.txt" />
</asp:PasswordRecovery>
```

As you can see, the `<MailDefinition>` child element is required to provide the information necessary to send an e-mail message with the user's name and password. As with the `CreateUserWizard` control, the body of the e-mail message is supplied by a text file that can include the variables `<%UserName%>` and `<%Password%>`, which are replaced by the user's name and password when the mail is sent.

The attributes listed in Table 3-3 let you customize the appearance of the `PasswordRecovery` control. Here's an example that changes the text labels displayed by the control:

```
<asp:PasswordRecovery id="PasswordRecovery1" runat="Server"
    UserNameTitleText=
        "Forgot Your Password Again, Eh?<br /><br />"
    UserNameInstructionText=
        "Enter your user name.<br /><br />"
    UserNameLabelText="User name:"
    QuestionTitleText=
        "Forgot Your Password Again, Eh?<br /><br />"
    QuestionInstructionText=
        "Answer the secret question.<br /><br />"
    QuestionLabelText="<br />Secret question:"
    AnswerLabelText="<br />Your answer:"
    SuccessText="Your new password has been e-mailed to
        you."
    />
```

Table 3-3   **Attributes for the PasswordRecovery control**

Attribute	Explanation
id	The ID associated with the PasswordRecovery control.
runat	Runat=Server is required for all ASP.NET server controls.
AnswerLabelText	The text that's displayed in the label for the Answer field.
GeneralFailureText	The text that's displayed if the password can't be recovered.
QuestionFailureText	The text that's displayed if the user provides the wrong answer for the secret question.
QuestionInstructionText	The text that's displayed in the label that instructs the user to answer the secret question.
QuestionLabelText	The text that's displayed in the label that identifies the secret question.
QuestionTitleText	The text that's displayed in the title area when the secret question is asked.
SubmitButtonImageUrl	The URL of an image used on the Submit button.
SubmitButtonText	The text displayed on the Submit button.
SubmitButtonType	The button type for the Submit button. You can specify Button, Link, or Image.
SuccessPageUrl	The URL of the page to be displayed when the password has been successfully recovered.
SuccessText	The text to display when the password has been successfully recovered. Note that this text is not displayed if the SuccessPageUrl is provided.
TextLayout	Specifies the position of the labels relative to the user name and password text boxes. If you specify TextOnLeft, the labels appear to the left of the text boxes. If you specify TextOnTop, the labels appear above the text boxes.

Attribute	Explanation
UserNameFailureText	The text that's displayed if the user provides an incorrect user name.
UserNameInstructionText	The text that's displayed in the instruction area when the user name is requested.
UserNameLabelText	The text that's displayed in the label that identifies the User Name field.
UserNameTitleText	The text that's displayed in the title area when the user name is requested.

Using the ChangePassword control

The ChangePassword control lets a user change his or her password. The ChangePassword control can be configured to accept the user name of the account whose password you want to change. If the control isn't configured to accept the user name, then the actual user must be logged in to change the password.

The ChangePassword control can also be configured to e-mail the new password to the user. Note that because e-mail is inherently insecure, you should carefully evaluate your application's security requirements before you use this feature.

In its simplest form, the ChangePassword control looks like this:

```
<asp:ChangePassword id="ChangePassword1"
    runat="Server" />
```

If you want to e-mail the changed password to the user, you should add a <MailDefinition> child element, like this:

```
<asp:ChangePassword id="ChangePassword1"
    runat="Server" >
    <MailDefinition
        From="name@domain.com"
        Subject="Subject Line"
        BodyFileName="BodyFile.txt" />
</asp:ChangePassword>
```

Here, the body of the e-mail message is supplied by a text file that can include the variables <%UserName%> and <%Password%>. When the message is sent, these variables are replaced by the user's name and password. (You can see an example of how this works in Chapter 4.)

You can customize the appearance and behavior of the ChangePassword using the attributes listed in Table 3-4. Here's an example:

```
<asp:ChangePassword id="ChangePassword1" runat="Server"
    ChangePasswordTitleText=
        "Change Your Password<br /><br />"
    PasswordLabelText="Enter your current password:"
    NewPasswordLabelText="Enter the new password:"
    ConfirmNewPasswordLabelText="Confirm the new
        password:"
/>
```

Table 3-4   Attributes for the ChangePassword control

Attribute	Explanation
id	The ID associated with the ChangePassword control.
runat	Runat="Server" is required for all ASP.NET server controls.
CancelButtonImageUrl	The URL of an image used on the Cancel button.
CancelButtonText	The text displayed on the Cancel button.
CancelButtonType	The button type for the Cancel button. You can specify Button, Link, or Image.
CancelDestinationPageUrl	The URL of the page that's displayed if the user clicks the Cancel button.
ChangePasswordButtonImageUrl	The URL of an image used on the Change Password button.
ChangePasswordButtonText	The text displayed on the Change Password button.
ChangePasswordButtonType	The button type for the Change Password button. You can specify Button, Link, or Image.
ChangePasswordFailureText	The text that's displayed if the password can't be changed.
ChangePasswordTitleText	The text that's displayed as the title for the Change Password control.

Attribute	Explanation
ConfirmNewPasswordLabelText	The text that's displayed in the label that identifies the Confirm Password field.
ContinueButtonImageUrl	The URL of an image used on the Continue button.
ContinueButtonText	The text displayed on the Continue button.
ContinueButtonType	The button type for the Continue button. You can specify Button, Link, or Image.
ContinueDestinationPageUrl	The URL of the page that's displayed if the user clicks the Continue button.
CreateUserText	The text displayed as a link to the application's Create User page.
CreateUserUrl	The URL of the application's Create User page.
DisplayUserName	A Boolean that indicates whether the user will be asked to enter a user name. If True, the ChangePassword control can be used to change the password of an account other than the one to which the user is currently logged in.
InstructionText	The text that's displayed in the instruction area of the ChangePassword control.
NewPasswordLabelText	The text that's displayed in the label that identifies the New Password field.
NewPasswordRegularExpression	A regular expression used to validate the new password.
PasswordHintText	The text that's displayed to inform the user of any password requirements, such as minimum length or required use of special characters.
PasswordLabelText	The text that's displayed by the label that identifies the Current Password field.

(continued)

Table 3-4 *(continued)*

Attribute	Explanation
PasswordRecoveryText	The text displayed as a link to the application's Password Recovery page.
PasswordRecoveryUrl	The URL of the application's Password Recovery page.
SuccessPageUrl	The URL of the page to be displayed when the password has been successfully changed.
SuccessText	The text to display when the password has been successfully changed. Note that this text is not displayed if the SuccessPageUrl is provided.
UserNameLabelText	The text that's displayed in the label that identifies the User Name field.

Here are a couple of additional details you need to know about the ChangePassword control:

✔ By default, the ChangePassword control requires that the user be logged in already. However, that changes if you specify DisplayUserName="True". Then, the ChangePassword control displays a user name text box. The ChangePassword control then lets the user change the password for any user, provided the user enters a valid user name and password.

✔ The ChangePassword control has two views. The initial view — the Change Password view — includes the text boxes that let the user enter a new password. The Success view is displayed only if the password is successfully changed. It displays a confirmation message. Note that if you specify the SuccessPageUrl attribute, Success view is never displayed. Instead, the page at the specified URL is displayed.

Using the LoginView control

The LoginView control is a templated control that displays the contents of one of its templates, depending on the login status of the user. This enables you to customize the content of your Web site for different types of users. For example, the User Authentication application presented later in this chapter uses a LoginView control to display a link to the administration page that's visible only to members of the Admin role.

Unlike the other login controls presented so far in this chapter, the LoginView control doesn't rely much on the use of attributes to customize its appearance or behavior. Instead, you customize the LoginView control by using three types of templates, each of which is coded as a child element:

✔ Anonymous template: Displayed if the user isn't logged in.

✔ LoggedIn template: Displayed if the user is logged in.

✔ RoleGroup template: Displayed if the user is logged in and is a member of a particular role group.

The first two template types are simply specified as child elements of the LoginView control. Consider this example:

```
<asp:LoginView runat="Server" id="LoginView1">
    <AnonymousTemplate>
        This template is displayed for anonymous users.
    </AnonymousTemplate>
    <LoggedInTemplate>
        This template is displayed for logged in users.
    </LoggedInTemplate>
</asp:LoginView>
```

The role group templates are a little more complicated. They're coded like this:

```
<asp:LoginView runat="Server" id="LoginView1">
    <RoleGroups>
        <asp:RoleGroup Roles="Admin">
            <ContentTemplate>
            This template is displayed for
        administrators.
            </ContentTemplate>
        </asp:RoleGroup>
    </RoleGroups>
</asp:LoginView>
```

Note that the <RoleGroups> element can contain more than one <RoleGroup> element. In addition, <RoleGroup> elements can be used along with Anonymous and LoggedIn templates.

Using the LoginName control

The LoginName control is straightforward: It simply displays the user's name, assuming the user is logged in. If the user is not logged in, the LoginName control displays nothing.

In its simplest form, the LoginName control looks like this:

```
<asp:LoginName runat="server" id="LoginName1" />
```

You might be tempted to precede the `LoginName` control with text, like this:

```
Hello, <asp:LoginName runat="server" id="LoginName1" />
```

Unfortunately, this technique won't work right if the user isn't logged in — the text literal (`Hello,`) will be displayed but the name won't be. Instead, you can specify a format string, like this:

```
<asp:LoginName runat="server" ID="LoginName1"
    FormatString="Hello, {0}" />
```

That way, `Hello,` will be added as a prefix to the name if the user is logged in. If the user isn't logged in, nothing is displayed.

Using the LoginStatus control

The `LoginStatus` control displays a link that lets the user log in to — or log out of — a Web site. If the user is already logged in, the link lets the user log out. If the user isn't logged in, the link lets the user log in.

The simple form of the `LoginStatus` control looks like this:

```
<asp:LoginStatus runat="server" id="LoginStatus1" />
```

You can customize the control by using the attributes listed in Table 3-5.

Table 3-5	Attributes for the LoginStatus control
Attribute	**Explanation**
`id`	The ID associated with the `LoginStatus` control.
`runat`	`Runat="Server"` is required for all ASP.NET server controls.
`LoginImageUrl`	The URL of an image used for the `Login` link.
`LoginText`	The text displayed by the <u>Login</u> link.
`LogoutAction`	Specifies what happens when the user logs out. You can specify `Redirect` to redirect the user to the page specified in the `LogoutPageUrl` attribute, `RedirectToLoginPage` to redirect the user to the application's login page, or `Refresh` to refresh the current page.

Attribute	Explanation
LogoutImageUrl	The URL of an image used for the <u>Logout</u> link.
LogoutPageUrl	The URL of the page to redirect to when the user logs out if the LogoutAction attribute specifies Redirect.
LogoutText	The text displayed by the <u>Logout</u> link.

Protecting Against Other Threats

Although the main security technique for ASP.NET applications is user authentication and authorization, not all security threats are related to unauthorized users accessing Web pages. The following sections describe some of the more common types of threats besides unauthorized access — and offer pointers to protect your ASP.NET applications against those threats.

Avoid malicious scripts

Cross-site scripting (also known as *XSS*) is a hacking technique in which a malicious user enters a short snippet of JavaScript into a text box, hoping that the application will save the JavaScript in the database and redisplay it later. Then, when the script gets displayed, the browser will execute the script.

For example, suppose your application asks the user to enter his or her name into a text box — and instead of entering a legitimate name, the user enters the following:

```
<script>alert("Gotcha!");</script>
```

Then this string gets saved in the user's Name column in the application's database. Later on, when the application retrieves the name to display it on a Web page, the browser sees the <script> element and executes the script. In this case, the script simply displays an alert dialog box with the message Gotcha! But the script could easily be up to more malicious business — for example, stealing values from cookies stored on the user's computer.

Fortunately, ASP.NET includes built-in protection against this type of script attack. By default, every input value is checked; if the value is potentially dangerous input, the server refuses to accept it. ASP.NET throws an exception and displays an unattractive error page, as shown in Figure 3-1.

Figure 3-1:
The error
page
displayed
when a user
enters
potentially
dangerous
input.

You can manually disable this process that checks for dangerous input — page by page — if you add `ValidateRequest="False"` to the `Page` directive for each page. Or you can disable the check for an entire site by adding the following code to the `web.config` file:

```
<system.web>
    <pages validateRequest="False" />
</system.web>
```

If you do this, however, you must be careful to *manually validate any input* to make sure it doesn't contain suspicious content. The easiest way to do that is to call the `HtmlEncode` method of the `Server` class before you save any text-input data to a database. Here's an example:

```
string Name = Server.HtmlEncode(txtName.Text);
```

This method replaces any HTML special characters (such as < and >) with codes such as `&lt` and `&gt`, which a browser will display *but not execute*.

By default, *bound controls* (that is, controls that automatically display data derived from a database) automatically encode data before they display it. As a result, XSS protection is automatic for data displayed by the `GridView` and other bound controls. Sure, you *can* disable this protection (by specifying `HtmlEncode="False"` for any bound fields you don't want encoded) — but I wouldn't recommend it. Doing so leaves your application vulnerable to script attacks.

Preventing SQL-injection attacks

The typical *SQL-injection attack* happens when a hacker enters data that includes a SQL command into a data-entry text box. To understand how this can pose a threat, suppose your application uses the data entered into a text box to construct a command in SQL, like this:

```
string cmd = "SELECT * FROM Cust WHERE CustID ='"
    + txtCustID.Text + "'";
```

Then, the program proceeds to execute the command contained in the cmd string variable. For example, if the user enters 12345 in the CustID text box, the following SQL command will be entered:

```
SELECT * FROM Cust WHERE CustID ='12345'
```

The SQL-injection attack isn't all that hard to do: The hacker enters text that tricks the program into executing a batch of statements. This requires knowledge of both the database structure and the statement that's supposed to be executed, but the hacker can often gain that knowledge by trial and error.

For example, suppose that instead of entering 12345, the hacker enters this:

```
12345'; Delete * From Customers; Select * from Cust where
          CustID='.
```

Then the cmd string variable will contain the following text:

```
SELECT * FROM Cust WHERE CustID ='12345'; Delete * From
          Cust; Select * from Cust where CustID=''
```

Here, three SQL commands will be executed. The first retrieves a customer, the second deletes all customers from the Cust table, and the third (again) tries to retrieve a customer. In effect, the hacker has discovered how to delete all of your customers!

Note that the only purpose of the third SQL command is to provide a matching quotation mark for the final quotation mark that's appended by the assignment statement in the program. Without a matching quotation mark, the SQL statement would contain a syntax error — and wouldn't execute.

The moral of the story is this: *never* build SQL statements using literals obtained from data-entry fields. Instead, put any data entered by the user into parameters, and write your SQL statements so they use those parameter values instead of the literals. For example, the program's SQL statement could be written like this:

```
string cmd = "SELECT * FROM Cust WHERE CustID = @CustID;
```

Then, the program could create a SQL parameter named `@CustID` to hold the value entered by the user.

Hiding error messages

ASP.NET provides a wealth of information that's useful while you're testing and debugging an application. For example, when an unhandled exception is thrown, a detailed error page appears, showing the exact cause of the error — as well as several source statements immediately before and after the statement that threw the exception.

This information is useful during testing and debugging, but can lead to serious security breaches once the program is in production. For example, consider a hacker attempting to break into your application using the type of SQL-injection attack described in the previous section. His or her nefarious efforts will be *much* easier if the application displays error pages that include the text of the actual SQL statements being submitted to the server!

To prevent these detailed error pages from being displayed, you'll need to provide custom error pages and configure the application's `web.config` file to use them. To do that, add a `<customErrors>` element to the `web.config` file, like this:

```
<customErrors mode="RemoteOnly"
    defaultRedirect="ErrorDefault.aspx">
    <error statusCode="404"
        redirect="Error404.aspx" />
</customErrors>
```

Here, any `404` errors (`Page Not Found`) will be redirected to `Error404.aspx`, and all other errors will be redirected to `ErrorDefault.aspx`. You can include whatever error information you want your users to see on these pages.

The `mode` attribute of the `<customErrors>` element can have one of three settings:

  ✔ **Off:** No custom error pages are displayed. Use this setting while you're testing and debugging your application.

  ✔ **On:** Custom error pages are displayed whenever an unhandled exception is thrown. This setting is useful while you're testing and debugging the error pages themselves.

  ✔ **RemoteOnly:** Custom error pages are shown for remote users, but not for local users. This is the ideal setting to use after the application is in production; it lets you see the default error pages so you can diagnose any problems the application encounters, but it still shows the custom error pages to the end-users.

Chapter 4

Building a User Authentication Application

I'm a big fan of the TV series *M*A*S*H*. In one of its best episodes ("Officer of the Day"), Hawkeye reluctantly assumes the role of Officer of the Day and must deal with local residents who come in to request medical assistance. To prove they are friendly, the residents must present identification. The first person to come in shows an identification card with the name Kim Luck. A few minutes later, a second person comes in and also presents an identification card with the name Kim Luck. Hawkeye asks, "Can you identify yourself?" and the man points to himself and says emphatically "This is me!"

Many Web applications require a similar type of identification before the user is allowed to access the Web site — *user authentication:* The user must provide a name as well as a password, and the name and password combination must be on file before the user is allowed to enter the application. No surprise, however, that most Web applications have more stringent security requirements than the 4077. In particular, user names must be unique (they can't all be "Kim Luck"), and the password must be more complicated than "This is me!"

Because logging in is such a common requirement for Web applications, ASP.NET 2.0 provides a sophisticated set of login controls that can handle almost all aspects of user-account management with little, if any, programming. This chapter presents an application that uses these controls to implement basic user authentication. In particular, the application requires users to log in to gain access to the application's content pages (which don't actually contain any content). If the user hasn't registered, the application allows the user to create an account. And if the user forgets his or her password, a password recovery feature can send the user's password via e-mail. The application also includes a page that lists the name of each user that's currently logged in. And finally, the application distinguishes between ordinary users and administrators, who can access a special administrator's page.

The Application's User Interface

Figure 4-1 shows the user interface flow for the User Authentication Application. As you can see, the user interface consists of seven distinct pages. The diagram indicates how the user's interaction with the interface flows from page to page.

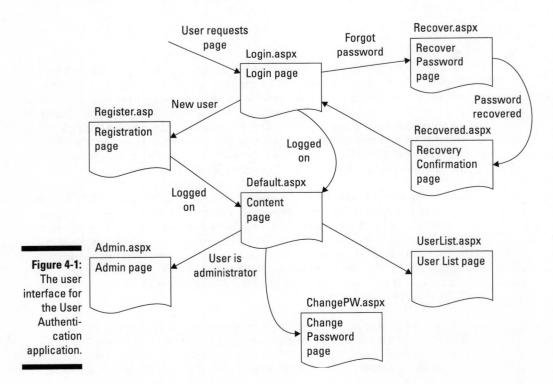

Figure 4-1: The user interface for the User Authentication application.

✔ **The Login page:** The Login page, shown in Figure 4-2, is the first page a user sees when he or she tries to access the Content page. The Login page requires the user to enter his or her user name and password. Then, assuming the user name and password are valid, the application displays the Content page. If the user name and password *aren't* valid, the Login page is redisplayed so the user has another chance to enter a correct user name and password.

This page also has links to the Register page and the Recover Password page.

✔ **The Content page:** This page, shown in Figure 4-3, is the page that the user is trying to gain access to. This page is displayed only if the user enters a valid user name and password in the Login page. For this application, the content page will be named `Default.aspx` and won't actually contain any useful information. Instead, it just displays a message that says (in effect), "Congratulations, you have reached the content page." Of course, in an actual application, this page would have to be more interesting. Otherwise why would users go to the trouble to register and log in just to see an essentially blank page?

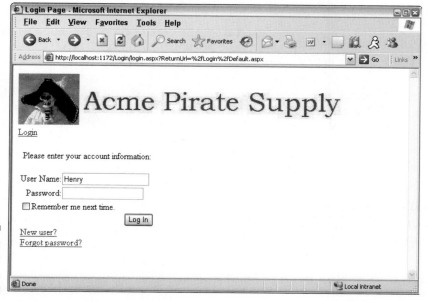

Figure 4-2:
The Login
page.

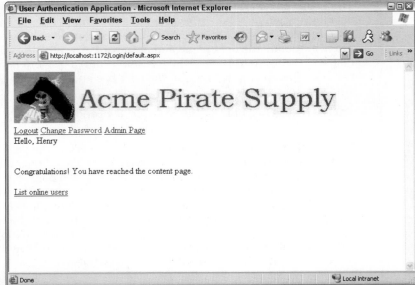

Figure 4-3:
The Content
page.

If the user has logged in with an administrator account, this page will
also contain a link to the Administration page. Then the user can click
this link to perform administrative functions. Note that this link doesn't
appear if the user is not an administrator.

✓ **The Admin page:** The Admin page, shown in Figure 4-4, can only be
reached by those users who have logged in with an administrator
account. For this application, the Admin page doesn't do anything
other than display a message indicating that the Admin page has been
reached. In a real application, this page would contain links to administrative functions, such as updating databases or managing Web site
content. (The Admin page also includes a button that leads back to the
Main Content page.)

✓ **The Registration page:** Figure 4-5 shows the Registration page, which
lets the user create a new user account. More specifically, it lets the
user enter the required account information — which includes a user
name, a password (the password must be entered twice), an e-mail
address, a secret question, and the answer to the secret question.
Assuming the user enters correct information, the account is created,
the user is automatically logged in using the new account, and the
Content page is displayed.

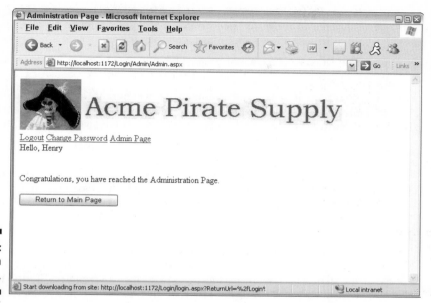

Figure 4-4:
The Admin
page.

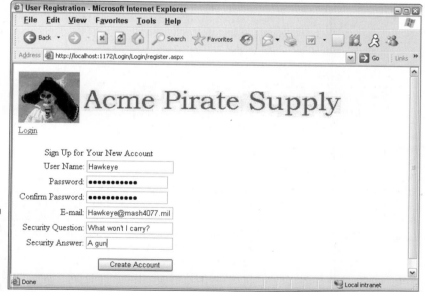

Figure 4-5:
The
Registration
page.

If the registration is successful, the Registration page sends an e-mail message to the address entered by the user. (Figure 4-6 gives you an idea what this kind of e-mail message looks like.)

✔ **The Recover Password page:** The user can use the Recover Password page, shown in Figure 4-7, to retrieve a forgotten password.

This page first asks for the user name. Then, if the user name is valid, it displays the secret question and allows the user to enter the answer. Finally, if the answer is correct, the user's password is changed to a random value and the new password is e-mailed to the e-mail address on file for the user.

✔ **The Recovery Confirmation page:** The page shown in Figure 4-8 is displayed when the Recover Password page successfully e-mails the user's password. It displays a confirmation message indicating that the password has been e-mailed and a button the user can click to return to the Login page.

Figure 4-9 shows the e-mail message that's sent when the password has been recovered. Note that the Recover Password page actually changes the user's password, assigning a random combination of alphanumeric characters and symbols. The resulting password is not likely to be very friendly.

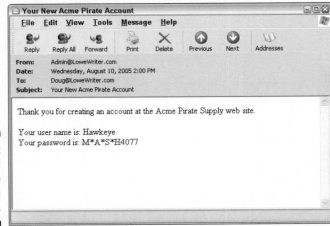

Figure 4-6:
The e-mail
sent to
confirm a
registration.

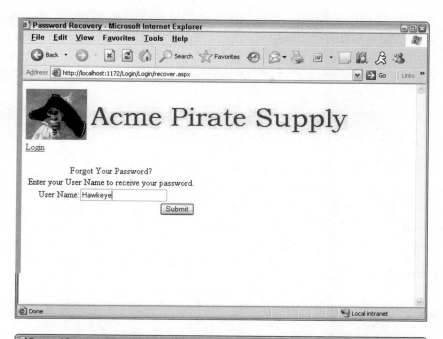

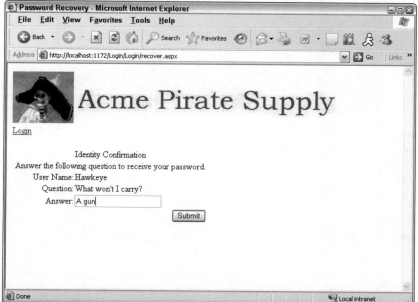

Figure 4-7:
The
Recover
Password
pages.

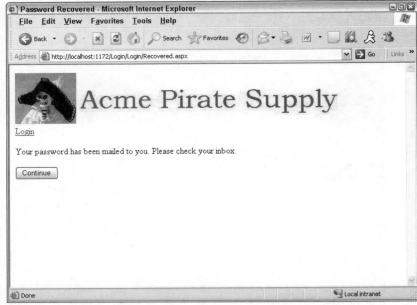

Figure 4-8:
The
Recovery
Confirmation
page.

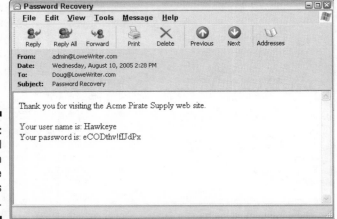

Figure 4-9:
The e-mail
sent when
the
password is
recovered.

✔ **The Change Password page:** The Change Password page, shown in Figure 4-10, lets the user change his or her password. The user can access this page from any content page once the user has logged in.

✔ **The User List page:** The User List page, shown in Figure 4-11, displays the name of each user currently logged in to the system. Any registered user can access this page from the Content page. As a result, the user must be logged in to the application to view the User List page.

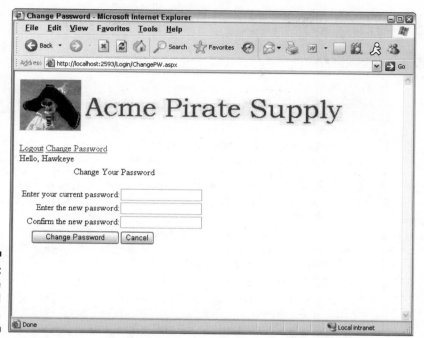

Figure 4-10:
The Change
Password
page.

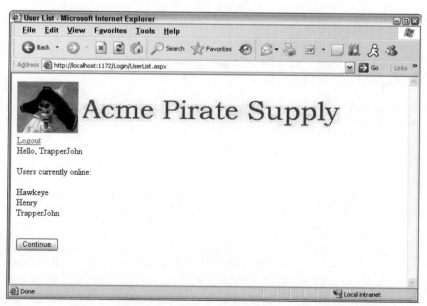

Figure 4-11:
The User
List page.

Designing the User Authorization Application

To keep the User Authorization application simple to use, it takes advantage of built-in ASP.NET authorization features — as many as possible, especially these:

✔ It uses the supplied **SQL membership provider** to manage the user database. If you want to extend the application so that it tracks additional data besides the user name, password, and the secret question and answer, or if you want to use your own database to store the member information, you can code your own provider. For most applications, however, the supplied provider should be adequate.

✔ It relies on the **new login controls** as much as possible and uses as little C# or Visual Basic code as possible. In fact, the only page that requires a code-behind file is the User List page. The other pages rely entirely on the declarative features of the new login controls.

✔ The application uses a **Master Page** (`MasterPage.master`) to provide a consistent layout for each page of the application. Even so, I refrained from using fancy formatting features; the resulting pages may be plainlooking, but they're easier to modify and adapt to your application's unique needs. You can easily add formatting to the pages by applying AutoFormats or themes.

The Application's Folders

As with most ASP.NET applications, the User Authorization application includes several folders. These folders are used to determine which pages can be viewed by users who haven't yet logged in, which ones are visible to normal users who have logged in, and which ones can only be seen by administrators who have logged in. The application uses the following folders:

✔ **Root:** The application's root folder (though the Solution Explorer doesn't call it that) contains the pages that can be viewed by a user once he or she has logged in. These include the application's main content page (`Default.aspx`), the user list page (`UserList.aspx`), the Change Password page (`ChangePW.aspx`), and the Master Page (`MasterPage.master`). In addition, this folder contains the Login page itself (`Login.aspx`).

✔ **App_Data:** This folder contains the membership database (`ASPNETDB.MDF`). The membership database is generated automatically, so you don't have to create it yourself.

✔ **Images:** This folder contains the banner graphic that's displayed by the Master Page. This folder also contains a `web.config` file that allows anonymous users to access its files. That's required so the banner can be displayed by the `Login.aspx`, `Register.aspx`, and `Recover.aspx` pages that appear on-screen before a user has logged in.

✔ **Login:** This folder contains the files necessary to display the Register and Recover Password pages. In addition, this folder contains a `web.config` file that allows anonymous users to access the files it contains. That way, users who haven't logged in can display the Register and Recover Password pages.

✔ **Admin:** This folder contains the Administration page (`Admin.aspx`) and a `web.config` file that restricts access to administrative users (that is, users who are assigned to the Admin role).

The root and `App_Data` folders are created automatically when you create a new Web site in Visual Studio. You'll have to create the Images, Login, and Admin folders manually, using the Solution Explorer. (To create a folder in the Solution Explorer, right-click the root folder and choose the New➪Folder command.)

The web.config Files

The User Authentication application relies on `web.config` files to configure its authentication features. Listing 4-1 shows the `web.config` file that appears in the application's root folder. The following paragraphs point out the highlights of this `web.config` file:

→ **1**   The `<authorization>` section contains a `<deny>` element that denies access to anonymous users, as indicated by the question mark in the users attribute.

→ **2**   The `<roleManager>` element is required to enable roles. The roles themselves are defined in the membership database.

→ **3**   The `<authentication>` element specifies that the application will use forms-based authentication. As a result, the application will automatically redirect to the Login.aspx page whenever necessary.

→ **4**   The `<mailSettings>` section provides the information necessary to access a mail server to send e-mail when the user registers or requests a password recovery. The host attribute specifies the name of the mail host, and the `from` attribute specifies the address listed in the from field for any e-mail messages sent. Depending on how your mail server is configured, you may also need to supply a user name and password via the user and password attributes.

Listing 4-1:   The main web.config file

```
<?xml version="1.0"?>
<configuration xmlns=
    "http://schemas.microsoft.com/.NetConfiguration/v2.0">
  <appSettings />
  <connectionStrings/>

  <system.web>
    <compilation debug="true"/>
    <authorization>                                        →1
      <deny users="?" />
    </authorization>
    <roleManager enabled="true" />                         →2
    <authentication mode="Forms" />                        →3
  </system.web>

  <system.net>
    <mailSettings>                                         →4
      <smtp>
         <network host="my.mail.server" />
      </smtp>
    </mailSettings>
  </system.net>

</configuration>
```

In addition to the main web.config file, the User Authentication application has three other web.config files that specify access to the Login, Admin, and Images folders. The web.config files for the Login and Images folders are the same:

```
<?xml version="1.0" encoding="utf-8"?>
<configuration xmlns=
  "http://schemas.microsoft.com/.NetConfiguration/v2.0">
   <system.web>
      <authorization>
          <allow users="?" />
      </authorization>
   </system.web>
</configuration>
```

As you can see, this web.config file specifically allows access for anonymous users (the ? wildcard refers to anonymous users).

The `web.config` file for the Admin folder is a little different:

```
<?xml version="1.0" encoding="utf-8"?>
<configuration xmlns=
  "http://schemas.microsoft.com/.NetConfiguration/v2.0">
    <system.web>
        <authorization>
            <allow roles="Admin" />
            <deny users="*" />
        </authorization>
    </system.web>
</configuration>
```

Here, the `<allow>` element allows users who are assigned to the Admin role to access files in the folder. Then the `<deny>` element denies access to all other users.

The order is important here. If you listed the `<deny>` element before the `<allow>` element, no one would be able to access pages in the Admin folder.

Building Pages for the User Authentication Application

The following sections present the `.aspx` file for each of the User Authentication application's pages and, where appropriate, both C# and Visual Basic versions of the code-behind files. Note that `.aspx` files assume that C# is for the code-behind files.

To make these pages work with the Visual Basic code-behind files, you must change the `Language` attribute in the Page directive from C# to VB, and the `CodeFile` attribute will need to specify the Visual Basic version of the code-behind file, using `.vb` as the extension instead of `.cs`.

Building the Master Page

Before we look at the individual Content pages that make up the User Authentication application, Listing 4-2 presents the Master Page that's used by the Content pages. This Master Page displays four elements on every page of the application:

🖮 A banner.

🖮 A link that lets the user log in or out.

✔ If the user is logged in, a greeting such as `Hello, Hawkeye`.

✔ If the user is a member of the Admin role, a link to the `Admin.aspx` page. (To assign a member to the Admin role, use the Web-based administration tool.)

Listing 4-2:   The Master Page (MasterPage.master)

```
<%@ Master Language="C#" AutoEventWireup="true"          →1
    CodeFile="MasterPage.master.cs"
    Inherits="MasterPage" %>

<!DOCTYPE html PUBLIC "-//W3C//DTD XHTML 1.1//EN"
           "http://www.w3.org/TR/xhtml11/DTD/xhtml11.dtd">

<html xmlns="http://www.w3.org/1999/xhtml" >

<head runat="server">
    <title>User Authentication Application</title>
</head>

<body>
  <form id="form1" runat="server">
  <div>

    <asp:Image ID="Image1" runat="server"              →2
        ImageUrl="~/Images/Banner.jpg"/>
    <br />

    <asp:LoginStatus ID="LoginStatus1"                 →3
        runat="server" />

    <asp:LoginView ID="LoginView1" runat="server">     →4
      <RoleGroups>
        <asp:RoleGroup Roles="Admin">
          <ContentTemplate>
            <a href="Admin/Admin.aspx">Admin Page</a>
          </ContentTemplate>
        </asp:RoleGroup>
      </RoleGroups>
    </asp:LoginView><br />

    <asp:LoginName ID="LoginName1" runat="server"       →5
        FormatString="Hello, {0}" /><br />

    <asp:contentplaceholder runat="server"             →6
        id="ContentPlaceHolder1" >
    </asp:contentplaceholder>

  </div>
  </form>
</body>
</html>
```

The following paragraphs describe the key lines of the Master Page:

→ **1**   The `Master` directive identifies the file as a Master Page.

→ **2**   The Image control displays a banner image at the top of each page. The `Banner.jpg` file is stored in the Images folder.

Notice the tilde used in the `ImageUrl` attribute ("`~/Images/Banner.jpg`"). The tilde signifies the application's root folder and can be used in URLs in any ASP.NET control.

→ **3**   The `LoginStatus` control is a new ASP.NET 2.0 control that displays one of two links, depending on whether the user is logged in or not. If the user is not logged in, a <u>Login</u> link is displayed to allow the user to log in. If the user is logged in, a <u>Logout</u> link is displayed to allow the user to log out. The <u>Login</u> or <u>Logout</u> link appears immediately beneath the banner image.

→ **4**   The `LoginView` control is another new ASP.NET 2.0 control. It displays the contents of a template depending on the user's login status. As this `LoginView` control shows, you can use the `<RoleGroups>` element to create content that's rendered if the user is logged in and is assigned to the specified role. In this case, the `LoginView` control renders a link to the `Admin.aspx` page if the user is logged in and belongs to the Admin role. Although this example doesn't show it, you can also use an `<AnonymousTemplate>` or a `<LoggedInTemplate>` element to create content that's rendered if the user is anonymous or logged in.

→ **5**   The `LoginName` control displays the user's name if the user is logged in. If the user isn't logged in, the `LoginName` control doesn't display anything. Notice that the `LoginName` control in this listing uses a format string to format the name by adding "Hello, " before the name. You might be tempted to just specify "Hello, " as a text literal immediately before the `LoginName` control. But if you do that, the text will be displayed even if the user isn't logged in. By using a format string, the text won't be displayed if the user isn't logged in.

→ **6**   The `ContentPlaceHolder` control provides an area in which the content from the individual pages can be displayed. Each content page includes a `Content` control that refers to the ID of this `ContentPlaceHolder` control.

Building the Content page

The content page (`Default.aspx`) is pretty simple, as it merely displays a label indicating that the user has reached the page along with a link to the UserList page. The code is shown in Listing 4-3. (Refer back to Figure 4-3 to catch a glimpse of this page displayed in a browser window.)

Listing 4-3:   The Content Page (Default.aspx)

```
<%@ Page Language="C#" AutoEventWireup="true"              →1
    MasterPageFile="~/MasterPage.master"
    CodeFile="Default.aspx.cs"
    Inherits="_Default" %>
<asp:Content ID="Content1" Runat="Server"                 →2
    ContentPlaceHolderID="ContentPlaceHolder1" >
    <br /><br />
    Congratulations! You have reached the content page.
    <br /><br />
    <a href="UserList.aspx">List online users</a>
</asp:Content>
```

The following paragraphs describe the high points of this listing:

→ **1**   The Page directive for a content page uses the MasterPageFile attribute to specify the name of the Master Page, ~/MasterPage. master.

If you haven't worked with Master Pages before, you might be wondering where the HTML <Head>, <Body>, and <Form> elements are. Those elements aren't required here because this is a content page that references a Master Page. As a result, those elements appear in the Master Page.

→ **2**   The <Content> element holds the content that's displayed when the page is rendered. The ContentPlaceHolderID attribute provides the name of the content placeholder defined in the Master Page. In this case, the content is displayed in the placeholder named ContentPlaceHolder1.

Building the Admin page

Like the Content page, the Admin page (Admin.aspx) is simpler. It displays a label indicating that the user has reached the page and a button that returns the user to the main content page. In an actual application, this page would contain links to administrative functions such as database maintenance pages. The code for the Admin page is shown in Listing 4-4. You can refer back to Figure 4-4 to see this page displayed in a browser window.

This page is stored in the Admin folder, which contains a web.config file that restricts access to users who are logged in and are assigned to the Admin role. As a result, the page can be viewed only by administrative users.

Listing 4-4: The Admin Page (Admin.aspx)

```
<%@ Page Language="C#" AutoEventWireup="true"          →1
    MasterPageFile="~/MasterPage.master"
    CodeFile="Admin.aspx.cs"
    Inherits="Admin_Admin"
    Title="Administration Page" %>
<asp:Content ID="Content1" Runat="Server"              →2
    ContentPlaceHolderID="ContentPlaceHolder1" >
    <br /><br />
    Congratulations, you have reached the
    Administration Page.
    <br /><br />
    <asp:Button ID="Button1" runat="server"            →3
        PostBackUrl="~/Default.aspx"
        Text="Return to Main Page" />
</asp:Content>
```

The following paragraphs describe the key lines in this listing:

→ **1**   The Page directive uses the `MasterPageFile` attribute to specify the name of the Master Page, `~/MasterPage.master`.

→ **2**   The `<Content>` element displays a message that lets the user know the Admin page has been reached.

→ **3**   The `Button` control that defines the "Return to Main Page" button includes a new ASP.NET 2.0 feature: the `PostBackUrl` attribute. `PostBackUrl` specifies the URL of the page that is posted when the user clicks the button. This effectively allows the button to act as a link to another page. With previous versions of ASP.NET, you'd have to write an event handler for the button and use `Server.Transfer` or `Response.Redirect` to return to the Admin page — or use a hyperlink rather than a button.

Building the Login page

ASP.NET displays the Login page (`Login.aspx`) automatically whenever an anonymous user tries to access a protected page. Other than designating which pages are denied access via the `web.config` file, you don't have to do anything special to make the Login page appear. All you have to do is create a page named `Login.aspx` in the application's root folder and provide a login control on the page. ASP.NET will then take care of the details for you.

Listing 4-5 shows the Login page for the User Authentication application. To see how this page looks in a browser window, you can refer back to Figure 4-2.

Listing 4-5: The Login Page (Login.aspx)

```
<%@ Page Language="C#" AutoEventWireup="true"        →1
    MasterPageFile="~/MasterPage.master"
    CodeFile="Login.aspx.cs"
    Inherits="Login_Login"
    Title="Untitled Page" %>
<asp:Content ID="Content1" Runat="Server"            →2
    ContentPlaceHolderID="ContentPlaceHolder1" >
    <asp:Login ID="Login1" runat="Server"            →3
    DestinationPageUrl="~/Default.aspx"              →4
    TitleText=
    "Please enter your account information:<br /><br />"
    CreateUserText="New user?"                        →5
    CreateUserUrl="~/Login/Register.aspx"
    PasswordRecoveryText="Forgot password?"           →6
    PasswordRecoveryUrl="~/Login/Recover.aspx" />
</asp:Content>
```

The following paragraphs describe the high points of this listing:

→ **1** The `Page` directive specifies that `~/MasterPage.master` is the Master Page for this content page.

→ **2** The `<Content>` element provides the content that's displayed for the Login page.

→ **3** The `Login` control allows the user to log in. It displays text boxes that let the user enter his or her user name and password and a Log In button the user can click to log in.

→ **4** The `DestinationPageUrl` attribute specifies the page that should be displayed when the user successfully logs in. In this case, the `Default.aspx` page is displayed.

→ **5** The `CreateUserText` attribute specifies the text that's displayed in a link the user can click to create a new user account. Then the `CreateUserUrl` attribute provides the URL of the page that handles the user registration. In this case, the text is `New user?` and the registration page is `~/Login/Register.aspx`.

→ **6** The `PasswordRecoveryText` attribute specifies the text that's displayed in a link the user can click if he or she forgets his or her password. Then the `PasswordRecoveryUrl` attribute supplies the URL of the page that handles password recovery. In this case, the text is `Forgot password?` and the password-recovery page is `~/Login/Recover.aspx`.

Building the Register page

The Register page (`Register.aspx`) is displayed when the user clicks the <u>Not Registered?</u> link on the Login page. This page should be created in the Login directory.

Listing 4-6 shows the listing for the Register page. To see how this page looks in a browser window, you can refer back to Figure 4-5. Note that this page doesn't require a code-behind file. That's because the `CreateUserWizard` control handles all functions required to register a user — automatically — including the updating of the user-account database and reporting errors if someone enters a duplicate user name or other invalid data.

Listing 4-6:   The Register Page (Register.aspx)

```
<%@ Page Language="C#" AutoEventWireup="true"            →1
    MasterPageFile="~/MasterPage.master"
    CodeFile="Register.aspx.cs"
    Inherits="Login_Register"
Title="User Registration" %>
<asp:Content ID="Content1" Runat="Server"               →2
    ContentPlaceHolderID="ContentPlaceHolder1" >
  <asp:CreateUserWizard ID="CreateUserWizard1"           →3
      runat="server"
      ContinueDestinationPageUrl="~/Default.aspx"
      CreateUserButtonText="Create Account">
    <WizardSteps>                                        →4
      <asp:CreateUserWizardStep
          ID="CreateUserWizardStep1" runat="server">
      </asp:CreateUserWizardStep>
      <asp:CompleteWizardStep
          ID="CompleteWizardStep1" runat="server">
      </asp:CompleteWizardStep>
    </WizardSteps>
    <MailDefinition                                      →5
        From="Admin@AcmePirate.com"
        Subject="Your New Acme Pirate Account"
        BodyFileName="~/Login/NewUser.txt" />
  </asp:CreateUserWizard>
</asp:Content>
```

The following paragraphs elucidate the salient aspects of this listing:

→ **1**   The `Page` directive specifies that `~/MasterPage.master` is the Master Page for this content page.

→ **2**   The `<Content>` element provides the content that's displayed for the Register page.

→ 3 The `CreateUserWizard` control lets the user create a new user account. It displays labels and text boxes that allow the user to enter the user's account name, password (the password must be entered twice), e-mail address, a secret question, and the answer to the question.

The `ContinueDestinationPageUrl` attribute provides the name of the page displayed when the user successfully creates an account. In this case, the default page (`~/Default.aspx`) is specified. Note that the user is automatically logged in after the account is created, so the user is not redirected to the Login page.

The `CreateUserButtonText` attribute changes the text displayed on the Create User button from the default (`Create User`) to `Create Account`.

→ 4 The `<WizardSteps>` element defines the two steps for the `CreateUserWizard` control. This `<WizardSteps>` element indicates that the default settings for the two steps of the Wizard (`<CreateUserWizardStep>` and `<CompleteWizardStep>`) will be used.

→ 5 The `<MailDefinition>` element provides the information needed to e-mail a confirmation message when the user creates an account. As you can see, this element specifies that the From address for the message will be `Admin@AcmePirate.com`, the subject will be `Your New Acme Pirate Account`, and the body of the message will be taken from the text file named `NewUser.txt`.

The `NewUser.txt` file is a simple text file that contains the following:

```
Thank you for creating an account at the Acme Pirate
        Supply Web site.

Your user name is: <%UserName%>
Your password is: <%Password%>
```

Here, the user's name is substituted for the `<%UserName%>` variable and the password is substituted for the `<%Password%>` variable.

Building the Recover Password page

The Recover Password page (`Recover.aspx`) is displayed when the user clicks the <u>Forgot Password?</u> link on the Login page. This page lets the user recover a forgotten account password. For security's sake, the user must first answer a question that was provided when the account was created. Then the password is e-mailed to the account on file for the user.

Note that the password is automatically changed when it is recovered. So the previous password on file for the account will no longer work once the password has been recovered.

This Recover Password page is stored in the Login folder so it can be accessed by users who have not successfully logged in.

Listing 4-7 shows the Recover Password page. To see how this page looks in a browser window, you can refer back to Figure 4-7.

Listing 4-7:   The Recover Password Page (Recover.aspx)

```
<%@ Page Language="C#" AutoEventWireup="true"              →1
    MasterPageFile="~/MasterPage.master"
    CodeFile="Recover.aspx.cs"
    Inherits="Login_Recover"
    Title="Password Recovery" %>
<asp:Content ID="Content1" Runat="Server"                 →2
    ContentPlaceHolderID="ContentPlaceHolder1" >
    <asp:PasswordRecovery ID="PasswordRecovery1"           →3
        runat="server"
        SuccessPageUrl="~/Login/Recovered.aspx" >          →4
        <MailDefinition                                    →5
            From="admin@LoweWriter.com"
            Subject="Password Recovery"
            BodyFileName="~/Login/PasswordMessage.txt">
        </MailDefinition>
    </asp:PasswordRecovery>
</asp:Content>
```

The following paragraphs elucidate the salient aspects of this listing:

→ **1**   The `Page` directive specifies that `~/MasterPage.master` is the Master Page for this content page.

→ **2**   The `<Content>` element provides the content that's displayed for the Recover Password page.

→ **3**   The `PasswordRecover` control lets the user recover a lost password. This control uses a wizard to walk the user through the steps necessary to recover the password. First, the user is prompted for the user name. If the user name is valid, the user is prompted with the secret question. Then, if the user answers the question correctly, the user's password is changed to a random value, an e-mail revealing the new password is sent to the address on file for the user, and a success message is displayed. (Note, however, that this application overrides the success message as described in the next paragraph.)

→ 4   The success message displayed by default when the user recovers a forgotten password doesn't include a link or button that lets the user return to the login page. As a result, the user must use the browser's Back button to return to the Login page. To avoid that inconvenience, the User Authentication application uses a separate page to confirm that the password e-mail has been sent. This page is identified by the SuccessPageUrl attribute. As a result, the PasswordRecovery control's default success message is never displayed in this application.

→ 5   The <MailDefinition> element for the PasswordRecover control works just like it does for the CreateUserWizard control. As you can see, the From address is set to Admin@AcmePirate.com, the subject is Password Recovery, and the body of the message is provided by the text file named PasswordMessage.txt.

The PasswordMessage.txt file contains the following:

```
Thank you for visiting the Acme Pirate Supply Web
    site.

Your user name is: <%UserName%>
Your password is: <%Password%>
```

Once again, the user's name is substituted for the <%UserName%> variable and the password is substituted for the <%Password%> variable.

Building the Password Confirmation page

The Password Confirmation page displays a message that indicates that the user's password has been e-mailed along with a button that lets the user return to the Login page. The only reason I included this page in the application is to get around a default behavior of the PasswordRecovery control: it displays a message indicating success but leaves the user stranded on the page, with no easy way to get back to the Login page. As a result, rather than display the default success message, the PasswordRecovery control displays the Password Confirmation page, which includes a link back to the Login page.

The code for the Password Confirmation page (`Recovered.aspx`) is shown in Listing 4-8. Refer back to Figure 4-8 to see this page displayed in a browser window.

Listing 4-8:   The Password Confirmation Page (Recovered.aspx)

```
<%@ Page Language="C#" AutoEventWireup="true"                     →1
    MasterPageFile="~/MasterPage.master"
    CodeFile="Recovered.aspx.cs"
    Inherits="Login_Recovered"
    Title="Password Recovered" %>
<asp:Content ID="Content1" Runat="Server"                         →2
    ContentPlaceHolderID="ContentPlaceHolder1" >
    Your password has been e-mailed to you.
    Please check your inbox.<br /><br />
    <asp:Button ID="Button1" runat="server"                       →3
        PostBackUrl="~/Default.aspx"
        Text="Continue" />
</asp:Content>
```

The following paragraphs describe the key lines in this listing:

→ **1**   The `Page` directive uses the `MasterPageFile` attribute to specify the name of the Master Page, `~/MasterPage.master`.

→ **2**   The `<Content>` element displays a message that lets the user
know that the password has been sent via e-mail.

→ **3**   The `Button` control that defines the "Continue" button uses the
new `PostBackUrl` attribute to return to the main content page.
Of course, the user hasn't logged in; the user will automatically
be redirected to the Login page instead.

Building the Change Password page

The Change Password page (`ChangePW.aspx`) is displayed when the user clicks the <u>Change Password</u> link that appears beneath the banner image on any of the application's content pages. This link is displayed by a `LoginView` control in the Master Page, so it only appears when the user is logged in.

Listing 4-9 shows the Change Password page. To see how this page appears when it's displayed in a browser window, you can refer back to Figure 4-10.

Listing 4-9:   The Change Password Page (ChangePW.aspx)

```
<%@ Page Language="C#" AutoEventWireup="true"          →1
    MasterPageFile="~/MasterPage.master"
    CodeFile="ChangePW.aspx.cs"
    Inherits="ChangePW"
    Title="Change Password" %>
<asp:Content ID="Content1"                             →2
    ContentPlaceHolderID="ContentPlaceHolder1"
    Runat="Server">
    <asp:ChangePassword ID="ChangePassword1"           →3
        runat="server"
        ChangePasswordTitleText=
            "Change Your Password<br /><br />"
        PasswordLabelText="Enter your current password:"
        NewPasswordLabelText="Enter the new password:"
        ConfirmNewPasswordLabelText=
            "Confirm the new password:"
    />
</asp:Content>
```

The following paragraphs (ahem) elucidate the salient aspects of this listing:

→ **1**   The `Page` directive specifies that `~/MasterPage.master` is the Master Page for this content page.

→ **2**   The `<Content>` element provides the content that's displayed for the Recover Password page.

→ **3**   The `ChangePassword` control lets the user change his or her password. The attributes on this control simply customize the labels displayed for the password, new password, and confirm new password fields.

Building the User List page

The User List page is the only page of the User Authentication application that uses a code-behind file. It displays a list of all the users who are currently logged in to the application. The list itself is created by retrieving the user names from the .NET Membership class. The list is assigned to a single label, with break tags (`<br />`) used to separate the names. As a result, all the users are displayed on a single page.

If you expect the application to have more than a few dozen users logged in at once, you may want to provide a way to page the list. I suggest using a `DataGridView` control to do that.

Listing 4-10 shows the `.aspx` file for the User List page.

Listing 4-10:   The User List Page (UserList.aspx)

```
<%@ Page Language="C#" AutoEventWireup="true"              →1
    MasterPageFile="~/MasterPage.master"
    CodeFile="UserList.aspx.cs"
    Inherits="UserList" Title="User List" %>
<asp:Content ID="Content1" Runat="Server"                 →2
    ContentPlaceHolderID="ContentPlaceHolder1" >
    <br />
    Users currently online:
    <br /><br />
    <asp:Label ID="lblUsers" runat="server" />             →3
    <br /><br />
    <asp:Button ID="Button1" runat="server"               →4
        Text="Continue"
        PostBackUrl="~/Default.aspx"/>
</asp:Content>
```

The following paragraphs describe the key lines in this listing:

→ **1**   The `Page` directive specifies `~/MasterPage.master` as the Master Page.

→ **2**   The `<Content>` element displays the user list and a button that links back to the main content page.

→ **3**   The `Label` control is used by the code-behind file to display the list of logged in users. The `ID` attribute specifies `lblUsers` as the ID for this label.

→ **4**   The Continue button uses the `PostBackUrl` attribute to return to the main content page.

Listing 4-11 shows the C# version of the code-behind file for the User List page. As you can see, the user list is generated during the Page Load event for the page. The static `GetAllUsers` method of the `Membership` class returns a collection of all the members in the membership database. This collection is defined by the `MembershipUserCollection` class. Then a `foreach` statement serves to examine each item in the collection of users. If a user is currently online (as indicated by the `IsOnline` property), that user's name is added to the `Text` value of the label, along with a `<br />` tag so that each user is listed on a separate line.

Listing 4-11: The code-behind file for the User List Page (C# version)

```csharp
using System;
using System.Data;
using System.Configuration;
using System.Collections;
using System.Web;
using System.Web.Security;
using System.Web.UI;
using System.Web.UI.WebControls;
using System.Web.UI.WebControls.WebParts;
using System.Web.UI.HtmlControls;

public partial class UserList : System.Web.UI.Page
{
    protected void Page_Load(object sender, EventArgs e)
    {
        MembershipUserCollection users;
        users = Membership.GetAllUsers();
        foreach (MembershipUser user in users)
        {
            if (user.IsOnline)
                lblUsers.Text += user.UserName + "<br />";
        }
    }
}
```

Listing 4-12 shows the Visual Basic version of the code-behind file. It works the same as the C# version.

Listing 4-12: The code-behind file for the User List page (VB version)

```vbnet
Partial Class UserListVB
    Inherits System.Web.UI.Page

    Protected Sub Page_Load(ByVal sender As Object, _
        ByVal e As System.EventArgs) Handles Me.Load
        Dim users As MembershipUserCollection
        users = Membership.GetAllUsers()
        For Each user As MembershipUser In users
            If user.IsOnline Then
                lblUsers.Text += user.UserName + "<br />"
            End If
        Next

    End Sub
End Class
```

Part III

Building E-Commerce Applications

"Okay, I think I forgot to mention this, but we now have a Web management function that automatically alerts us when there's a broken link on The Aquarium's Web site."

In this part . . .

*I*n this part, I show you two ASP.NET 2.0 applications that help you sell products in an online store. The first is a product catalog that lets Web users see what products you have for sale; the second is a shopping-cart application that lets users purchase items from your catalog. It's a fairly standard practice to combine these applications so users can both browse through the product catalog and (ideally) buy your products.

Chapter 5

Building a Product Catalog Application

*P*roduct catalogs used to be phone-book-size tomes; now they're applications — among the most common found on the Web. That's because most companies want to show off their products. Small companies sometimes create Web sites that have just a few products. Other companies, such as Amazon.com, have online catalogs with hundreds of thousands of products. Still, the idea is the same: online product catalogs exist because they drive sales.

Many Web sites not only let users browse the product catalog, but also let users purchase products directly from the Web site. You'll see an example of an online purchasing application in the next chapter. The application presented in this chapter focuses on presenting product information that's stored in a database in an interesting and useful way.

The Application's User Interface

Figure 5-1 shows the user-interface flow for the Product Catalog application that's built in this chapter. This application's user interface has just three pages:

- ✔ `default.aspx` displays a list of products for a category selected by the user.
- ✔ `product.aspx` displays details about a specific product selected by the user.
- ✔ `cart.aspx` is displayed when the user chooses to purchase a product.

For this application, the `cart.aspx` page simply displays a message indicating that the shopping cart isn't implemented. (You'll find an implementation of the Shopping Cart page in the next chapter.)

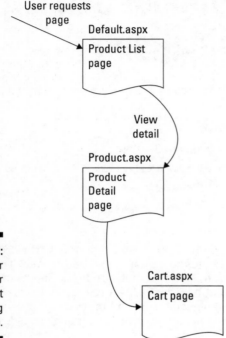

User requests page

Default.aspx

Product List page

View detail

Product.aspx

Product Detail page

Cart.aspx

Cart page

Figure 5-1:
The user interface for the Product Catalog application.

The Product List page

Figure 5-2 shows the Product List page (`default.aspx`) displayed in a browser window. This page displays a list of products for a category selected by the user. This is the default start page for the application.

The following paragraphs describe the more interesting aspects of the Product List page:

✔ The page uses a Master Page named `default.master`. The Master Page simply displays the banner image that appears at the top of the page.

✔ The application's database includes a separate table for featured products that includes a sale price and space for a promotional message.

Any products in this table are listed at the top of the Product List page. Then the user can click the <u>Details</u> link to go to the Product page for the featured product.

🗸 A drop-down list is used to select a product category. When the user selects a category from this list, the page is updated to list the products for the selected category. Note that the category values aren't hard-coded into the program. Instead, they're retrieved from the application's database.

🗸 The product list shows the products for the selected category. The user can click the <u>View</u> link to go to the Product page for a particular product. Note that if the product is currently on sale, the sale price is shown in the Product List.

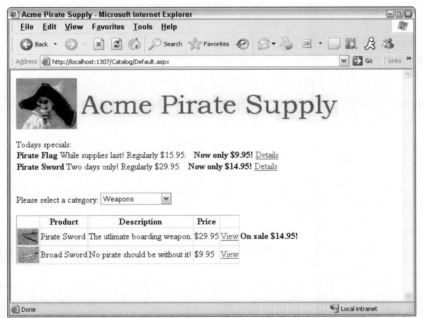

Figure 5-2:
The Product
List page.

The Product Detail page

Figure 5-3 shows the Product Detail page (`product.aspx`) displayed in a browser window. As you can see, this page displays the details for a particular product. The user can reach this page by clicking the <u>View</u> or <u>Details</u> link for a product on the Product List page.

Figure 5-3:
The Product
Detail page.

The following paragraphs describe some of the more interesting details about this page:

✔ Like the Product List page, this page also uses the default.Master Page as its Master Page. However, I scrolled down a bit to show the entire contents of the page. As a result, the banner that appears at the top of the page isn't visible in the figure.

✔ Because this product is listed as one of the featured products, its sale price is shown.

✔ The buttons at the bottom of the page let the user add the current product to the shopping cart or return to the Product List page.

✔ Notice that the URL that appears in the browser's address bar includes two query string fields: `prod=sword01` and `cat=weap`. The first field indicates which product the user selected in the Product List page. The Product Detail page uses this field to retrieve the correct product from the database. The second field saves the category selected by the user on the Product List page (the Product Detail page doesn't use this field). However, if the user clicks the Back to List button to return to the Product List page, the `cat` field is passed back to the Product List page. Then the Product List page uses it to select the category that the user had previously selected.

The Cart page

This application provides a dummy Cart page, as shown in Figure 5-4. As you can see, this page simply indicates that the shopping cart function hasn't yet been implemented. For an implementation of the shopping-cart page, refer to the next chapter.

Notice that the URL in this figure includes a query string that indicates which product the user wants to add to the cart. The dummy Cart page used in this application doesn't do anything with this query string — but the actual Shopping Cart application (presented in Chapter 6) has plenty of use for it.

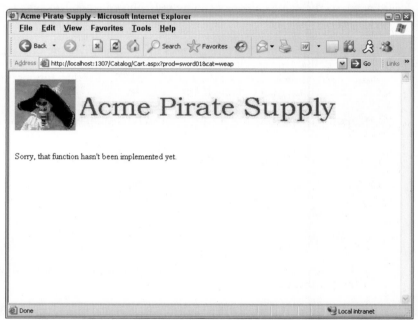

Figure 5-4:
The Cart
page.

Designing the Product Catalog Application

The Product Catalog Application is designed to be simple enough to present in this book, yet complicated enough to realistically address some of the design considerations that go into this type of application. There are several important decisions that need to be made for any application of this sort.

For example, how will the database be designed to store the product information? In particular, how will the database represent products and categories, and how will the products featured on sale be represented? In addition, the database design must address how images of the product will be accessed. For more details on the database design for this application, refer to the section "Designing the Product Database" later in this chapter.

Another important aspect of the design is how the application keeps track of the state information, such as which product the user is viewing. For example, when the user chooses to see more detail for a specific product, how will the application pass the selected product from the Product List page to the Product Detail page so the Product Detail page knows which product to display? And how will the application remember which product category was being viewed, so the same category can be redisplayed when the user returns to the Product List page?

Although there are several alternatives for storing this type of state information in ASP.NET, this application saves the product and category information in query strings appended to the end of the URLs used to request the application's pages. Two query-string fields are used:

✔ `prod`: Passes the ID of the product to be displayed by the Product Detail page.

✔ `cat`: Passes the ID of the category that's selected on the Product List page.

For example, suppose the user selects the Weapons category and clicks the <u>View</u> link for the first sword. Then the URL used to display the `Product.aspx` page will look like this:

```
~\Product.aspx?prod=sword01&cat=weap
```

Here, the ID of the product to be displayed is `sword01` and the ID of the selected category is `weap`.

If the user clicks the Back to List button, the application returns to the `Default.aspx` page via the following URL:

```
~\Default.aspx?cat=weap
```

That way, the `Default.aspx` page will know to set the category drop-down list to `Weapons`.

If, on the other hand, the user clicks the Add to Cart button to order the product, this URL will be used to display the `Cart.aspx` page:

```
~\Product.aspx?prod=sword01&cat=weap
```

Thus, the product and category ID values are passed from the `Product.aspx` page to the `Cart.aspx` page. (For more information about what the actual Cart page does with these values, refer to Chapter 6.)

Note that when the application is first started, the URL used to display the `Default.aspx` page doesn't include any query strings. As a result, the `Default.aspx` page is designed so that if it isn't passed a `cat` query-string field, it defaults to the first category.

Designing the Product Database

The Product Catalog application requires a database to store the information about the products to be displayed. Figure 5-5 shows a diagram of the database. As you can see, it consists of three tables:

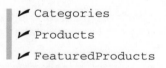

- Categories
- Products
- FeaturedProducts

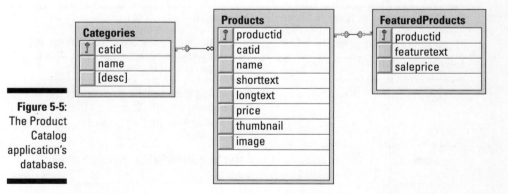

Figure 5-5: The Product Catalog application's database.

The following sections describe the details of each of these tables.

The Categories table

The `Categories` table contains one row for each category of product represented in the database. Table 5-1 lists the columns defined for this table.

Table 5-1		The Categories Table
Column name	**Type**	**Description**
catid	VARCHAR(10)	An alphanumeric code (up to 10 characters) that uniquely identifies each category. This is the primary key for the Categories table.
name	VARCHAR(50)	A text field that provides the name of the category.
desc	VARCHAR(MAX)	A text field that provides a description of the category.

The Products table

The Products table contains one row for each product represented in the database. Table 5-2 lists the columns used by the Products table.

Table 5-2		The Products Table
Column name	**Type**	**Description**
productid	VARCHAR(10)	An alphanumeric code (up to 10 characters) that uniquely identifies each product. This is the primary key for the Products table.
catid	VARCHAR(10)	A code that identifies the product's category. A foreign-key constraint ensures that only values present in the Categories table can be used for this column.
name	VARCHAR(50)	A text field that provides the name of the product.
shorttext	VARCHAR(MAX)	A text field that provides a short description of the product.
longtext	VARCHAR(MAX)	A text field that provides a longer description of the product.
price	MONEY	The price for a single unit of the product.
thumbnail	VARCHAR(40)	The name of the thumbnail image file.
image	VARCHAR(40)	The name of the main image file.

Note that the `thumbnail` and `image` fields contain just the filename of the image files, not the complete path to the images. The application adds `~\Images\` to the filenames to locate the files. (For example, `sword01.jpg` will become `~\Images\sword01.jpg`.)

The FeaturedProducts table

The `FeaturedProducts` table contains one row for each product that's currently on sale or being featured. Note that each row in this table corresponds to a row in the `Products` table. Table 5-3 lists the columns used by the `FeaturedProducts` table.

Table 5-3	The FeaturedProducts Table	
Column name	*Type*	*Description*
productid	VARCHAR(10)	An alphanumeric code (up to 10 characters) that uniquely identifies the product featured. This is the primary key for the `FeaturedProducts` table, and a foreign-key constraint ensures that the value must match a value present in the `Products` table.
featuretext	VARCHAR(MAX)	Promotional text that describes the item being featured.
saleprice	MONEY	The sale price for the item.

Note that each row in the `FeaturedProducts` table corresponds to a row in the `Products` table, and the relationship is one-to-one. Each row in the `Products` table can have only one corresponding row in the `FeaturedProducts` table. However, not every row in the `Products` table has a corresponding row in the `FeaturedProducts` table, which is (by definition) only for those products currently being featured.

I could just as easily combined these tables by including the saleprice and featuretext columns in the `Products` table. I chose to implement `FeaturedProducts` as a separate table to simplify the query that retrieves the list of featured products.

However, most design decisions involve trade-offs, and this one is no exception. Although using a separate table for the featured products list simplifies the query that retrieves the featured products, it complicates the queries that retrieve product rows. That's because whenever you retrieve a product row, you must also check to see if that product is on sale. Otherwise the user won't know the actual price of the product. As a result, the query that retrieves products for the `Default.aspx` and `Product.aspx` pages must use an outer join to retrieve data from both tables.

For more information about the queries used to access this database, see the section "Querying the database," later in this chapter.

Creating the database

You can create the `Products` database manually from within Visual Studio by using the Database Explorer. Alternatively, you can run the `CreateProducts.sql` script that's shown in Listing 5-1. To run this script, open a command-prompt window and change to the directory that contains the script. Then enter this command:

```
sqlcmd -S localhost\SQLExpress -i CreateProducts.sql
```

Note that this command assumes you're running SQL Server Express on your own computer. If you're using SQL Server on a different server, you'll need to change `localhost\SQLExpress` to the correct name. If you're not sure what name to use, ask your database administrator.

Listing 5-1: The CreateProducts.sql script

```
USE master                                          →1
GO

IF EXISTS(SELECT * FROM sysdatabases                →2
    WHERE name='Products')
  DROP DATABASE Products
GO

CREATE DATABASE Products                            →3
ON (NAME=Product,
    FILENAME = 'C:\APPS\Products.mdf',
    SIZE=10 )
GO
```

```
USE Products                                            →4
GO

CREATE TABLE Categories (                               →5
   catid VARCHAR(10)   NOT NULL,
   name  VARCHAR(50)   NOT NULL,
   [desc]  VARCHAR(MAX) NOT NULL,                        →6
   PRIMARY KEY(catid) )
GO

CREATE TABLE Products (                                 →7
   productid VARCHAR(10)   NOT NULL,
   catid      VARCHAR(10)   NOT NULL,
   name       VARCHAR(50)   NOT NULL,
   shorttext VARCHAR(MAX)  NOT NULL,
   longtext   VARCHAR(MAX)  NOT NULL,
   price      MONEY          NOT NULL,
   thumbnail VARCHAR(40)   NOT NULL,
   image      VARCHAR(40)   NOT NULL,
   PRIMARY KEY(productid),
   FOREIGN KEY(catid) REFERENCES Categories(catid) )
GO

CREATE TABLE FeaturedProducts (                         →7
   productid    VARCHAR(10)   NOT NULL,
   featuretext VARCHAR(MAX)  NOT NULL,
   saleprice   MONEY          NOT NULL,
   PRIMARY KEY(productid),
   FOREIGN KEY(productid) REFERENCES Products(productid) )
GO
```

The following paragraphs describe the highlights of this script:

→ **1**   Sets the database context to master. This is usually the default context, but it's a good idea to set it just in case.

→ **2**   Deletes the existing Products database if it exists.

→ **3**   Creates a database named Products. The database file will be created in the C:\Apps directory. You should change this location if you want to place the database file in a different folder.

→ **4**   Creates the Categories table.

→ **5**   Note that the column name desc is a SQL keyword, so it must be enclosed in brackets.

→ **6**   Creates the Products table.

→ **7**   Creates the FeaturedProducts table.

Adding some test data

When you run the `CreateProduct` script, the database will be created, but it will be empty. Your online store will look pretty bare! To add some test data, run the `InsertProducts.sql` script that's included on this book's CD along with the `CreateProduct.sql` script. It creates the sample data shown in Tables 5-4, 5-5, and 5-6. (Note that to keep Table 5-5 presentable, I omitted the `shorttext` and `longtext` columns. Don't worry — the script does create data for these columns.)

To run the script, open a command window, change to the directory that contains the script, and then run this command:

```
sqlcmd -S localhost\SQLExpress -i InsertProducts.sql
```

Once again, you'll need to change the server name if you're not running SQL Server Express on your own computer.

You'll know the script works if you see a series of messages like this one:

```
(1 rows affected)
```

Table 5-4	Test data for the Categories Table	
catid	name	desc
booty	Booty	Treasure for the Scallywags.
equip	Equipment	Equipment and gear for yer ship.
weap	Weapons	Proper weapons for a scurvy pirate.

Table 5-5		Test data for the Products			
Productid	catid	name	price	thumbnail	image
chain01	equip	Anchor Chain	6.95	chainT.jpg	chain.jpg
crown1	booty	Royal Crown	14.95	crown1T.jpg	crown1.jpg
flag01	equip	Pirate Flag	15.95	flag01T.jpg	flag01.jpg
flag02	equip	Pirate Flag	12.95	flag02T.jpg	flag02.jpg
gold01	booty	Gold Coins	8.95	gold01T.jpg	gold01.jpg

Productid	*catid*	*name*	*price*	*thumbnail*	*image*
polly	equip	Polly the Parrot	15.95	pollyT.jpg	polly.jpg
rat01	equip	Bilge Rat	9.95	rat01T.jpg	rat01.jpg
scope1	equip	Pirate Telescope	15.95	scope1T.jpg	scope1.jpg
sign01	equip	Pirate Sign	25.95	sign01T.jpg	sign01.jpg
sword01	weap	Pirate Sword	29.95	sword01T.jpg	sword01.jpg
sword02	weap	Broad Sword	9.95	sword02T.jpg	sword02.jpg

Table 5-6	Test data for the Table	
productid	*featuretext*	*saleprice*
flag01	While supplies last!	9.95
sword01	Two days only!	14.95

Querying the database

The Product Catalog application uses several queries to retrieve data from the Products database. In particular, the application must perform the following queries:

✔ Retrieve all rows from the Categories table to fill the drop-down list on the Default.aspx page so the user can select a product.

✔ Retrieve all rows from the FeaturedProducts table to display at the top of the Default.aspx page. Note that some data is also required from the Products table, so this query requires a join.

✔ Retrieve all products for a given category, including the sale price indicated in the FeaturedProducts table.

✔ Retrieve all data for a specified product to display on the Product.aspx page. Note that this query must also retrieve the sale price from the FeaturedProducts table.

These queries will appear in the SqlDataSource controls defined in the application's .aspx files.

The query to retrieve all rows from the Categories table uses this SQL statement:

```
SELECT catid,
    name,
    [desc]
FROM Categories
ORDER BY name
```

Note that because desc is a SQL keyword, it must be enclosed in brackets. (Some SQL programmers like to enclose all column names in brackets just to be safe.)

The query to retrieve the featured product rows requires a join to retrieve data from the FeaturedProducts table as well as the Products table:

```
SELECT FeaturedProducts.productid,
    FeaturedProducts.featuretext,
    FeaturedProducts.saleprice,
    Products.name,
    Products.price
FROM FeaturedProducts
    INNER JOIN Products
        ON FeaturedProducts.productid = Products.productid
```

This query retrieves all rows from the FeaturedProducts table, and joins the corresponding rows from the Products table to get the name and price columns.

The query to retrieve the products for a given category also requires a join:

```
SELECT Products.productid,
    Products.catid,
    Products.name,
    Products.shorttext,
    Products.longtext,
    Products.price,
    Products.image,
    Products.thumbnail,
    FeaturedProducts.saleprice
FROM Products
    LEFT OUTER JOIN FeaturedProducts
        ON Products.productid = FeaturedProducts.productid
WHERE (Products.catid = @catid)
```

Here, the outer join retrieves data from the `FeaturedProducts` table and provides nulls for the `saleprice` column of any product that doesn't have a row in the `FeaturedProducts` table. Notice also that the `WHERE` clause specifies a parameter. As you'll see later in this chapter, the `@catid` parameter will be set to the category ID value selected by the user via the drop-down list.

The last query used by the program retrieves the data for a specific product:

```
SELECT Products.productid,
    Products.catid,
    Products.name,
    Products.shorttext,
    Products.longtext,
    Products.price,
    Products.image,
    FeaturedProducts.saleprice,
    FeaturedProducts.featuretext
FROM Products
    LEFT OUTER JOIN FeaturedProducts
        ON Products.productid = FeaturedProducts.productid
WHERE (Products.productid = @productid)"
```

Here, a parameter named `@productid` indicates which product to retrieve. This parameter's value will be obtained from the `prod` query string field that's passed to the `Product.aspx` page.

Notice also that an outer join is used to retrieve the `saleprice` and `featuretext` columns from the `FeaturedProducts` table. If there is no corresponding product in the `FeaturedProducts` table, these columns will be set to null.

Connecting to the database

The connection string used to access the `Products` database is stored in the application's `web.config` file, like this:

```
<connectionStrings>
    <add name="ConnectionString"
        connectionString="Data
        Source=localhost\SQLExpress;
Initial Catalog=Products;Integrated Security=True"/>
</connectionStrings>
```

These lines should go right after the opening `<system.web>` tag in the `web.config` file. Note that the connection string is the only place in the application that references the database name and the server information. As a result, you can move the database to a different server or use a different database simply by changing the connection string specified in the `web.config` file.

The Application's Folders

Like most ASP.NET applications, the Product Catalog application includes several folders. The following folders are particularly important:

- ✔ (Root): The application's root folder contains the application's three pages (`Default.aspx`, `Product.aspx`, and `Cart.aspx`) as well as the Master Page (`Default.master`).

- ✔ App_Data: This folder is created by default by Visual Studio when the application is created. However, because the database may be used by other applications, it's stored in a folder that isn't part of the application's folder hierarchy.

- ✔ Images: This folder contains the banner graphic that's displayed by the Master Page as well as image files that picture the various products. For each product, the Images folder contains two image files: one is a larger image that's approximately 200 pixels square; the other is a thumbnail image that's about 30 pixels square. Note that not all the images are perfectly square. For the rectangular images, the height is held at 200 pixels (or less) for the large image and 30 pixels for the thumbnail images.

Building the Master Page

Listing 5-2 shows the code for the master page (`MasterPage.master`), which is used by both the `Default.aspx` and the `Product.aspx` pages. It simply displays a banner at the top of each page. In an actual application, you'd probably want to provide a more developed Master Page. But for this application, the simple Master Page shown here will do.

Listing 5-2: The Master Page (MasterPage.master)

```
<%@ Master Language="C#"
    AutoEventWireup="true"
    CodeFile="MasterPage.master.cs"          →1
    Inherits="MasterPage" %>
```

```
<!DOCTYPE html PUBLIC "-//W3C//DTD XHTML 1.1//EN"
    "http://www.w3.org/TR/xhtml11/DTD/xhtml11.dtd">

<html xmlns="http://www.w3.org/1999/xhtml" >
<head runat="server">
    <title>Acme Pirate Supply</title>
</head>
<body>
    <form id="form1" runat="server">
    <div>
        <img src="Images/Banner.jpg" />                    →2
        <br /><br />
        <asp:contentplaceholder                            →3
            id="ContentPlaceHolder1" runat="server">
        </asp:contentplaceholder>
    </div>
    </form>
</body>
</html>
```

The following paragraphs describe the key lines of the Master Page:

→ **1**   The `Master` directive identifies the file as a Master Page.

→ **2**   The `Image` control displays a banner image at the top of each page. The `Banner.jpg` file is stored in the Images folder.

→ **3**   The `ContentPlaceHolder` control provides the area where the content for the application's content pages will be displayed.

Building the Product List Page

The Product List page (`Default.aspx`) is the default page for the Product Catalog application. It displays a drop-down list that lets the user select a product category as well as a list of all products for the category selected by the user. In addition, this page displays a list of all featured products.

The Product List page includes the following controls:

✔ `DataList1`: A `DataList` control that lists the products in the FeaturedProducts table. The `DataList` control is a templated control that renders an instance of its `ItemTempate` for each row in the data source. The controls in the `ItemTemplate` can use special binding expressions to bind to data in the data source. The `ItemTemplate` for this `DataList` control contains the following bound controls:

- • `NameLabel`: Displays the `name` column from the data source.

- • `FeatureTextLabel`: Displays the `featuretext` column from the data source.

- • `PriceLabel`: Displays the `price` column from the data source.

- • `SalePriceLabel`: Displays the `saleprice` column from the data source.

- • `btnFeature`: Displays a link button that lets the user display more information about one of the featured products.

✔ `SqlDataSource1`: A `SqlDataSource` control that's used as the data source used by the `DataList1` control. This data source queries the FeaturedProducts and Products tables to return the `name`, `featuretext`, `price`, and `saleprice` for each featured product. Note that `SqlDataSource` controls aren't visible to the user when the page is rendered.

✔ `ddlCategory`: A drop-down list that displays each row of the `Categories` table. This drop-down list is bound to the `SqlDataSource` control named `SqlDataSource2`.

✔ `SqlDataSource2`: A `SqlDataSource` control that's used as the data source for the `ddlCategories` drop-down list. This data source simply retrieves all the rows from the Categories table.

✔ `GridView1`: A `GridView` control that lists all the products for the category selected by the `ddlCategory` drop-down list. The `GridView` control is a new control for ASP.NET 2.0. It serves the same purpose as the old `DataGrid` control, but provides many more options. This `GridView` control is bound to a data source named `SqlDataSource3` and defines following columns to display the thumbnail image, name, short text, price, and sale price fields from the data source. In addition, a command field column displays a Select button.

✔ `SqlDataSource3`: A `SqlDataSource` control that's used as the data source for the `GridView` control. This data source retrieves rows from the Products and FeaturedProducts tables. A parameter limits the rows to those whose `catid` column matches the `catid` of the category selected in the drop-down list.

The Default.aspx file

Listing 5-3 shows the `Default.aspx` file, which defines the Product List page. You can refer back to Figure 5-2 to see how this page appears in a browser window.

The SqlDataSource Control

The SqlDataSource control is one of the new data controls provided with ASP.NET 2.0. It lets controls such as DataList, GridView, and DetailsView bind to SQL data retrieved from SQL databases such as Microsoft's own SQL Server and Access. The SqlDataSource control doesn't render on the page, so it's not visible to the user.

The following list describes the most important attributes used with the SqlDataSource control:

✔ ID: Provides a name used to identify the SqlDataSource control.

✔ Runat: As with all ASP.NET controls, you must specify runat=server.

✔ ConnectionString: Provides the connection string used to connect to the database. You can store the connection string in the web.config file, then use an expression such as <%$ Connection Strings:ConnectionString %> to retrieve the connection string from the web.config file.

✔ SelectStatement: Provides the SELECT statement used to retrieve the data.

✔ DataSourceMode: DataReader or DataSet to specify whether the data should be retrieved via a data reader or a dataset. If you specify DataSourceMode= DataSet, you can also specify Enable

Caching=True to place the dataset in cache memory.

✔ InsertCommand: An INSERT command that inserts rows into the database.

✔ UpdateCommand: An UPDATE command that updates rows in the database.

✔ DeleteCommand: A DELETE command that deletes rows.

If the SQL commands used by the data source require parameters, you must use a <Select Parameters>, <InsertParameters>, <UpdateParameters>, or <Delete Parameters> element to define the parameters. You can define the parameters using any of the following elements:

✔ <ControlParameter>: A parameter whose value is taken from another ASP.NET control.

✔ <CookieParameter>: A parameter whose value is taken from a cookie.

✔ <FormParameter>: A parameter whose value is taken from a form field.

✔ <QueryStringParameter>: A parameter whose value is taken from a query string.

✔ <SessionParameter>: A parameter whose value is taken from a session variable.

Listing 5-3: The Product List Page (Default.aspx)

```
<%@ Page Language="C#"
    MasterPageFile="~/MasterPage.master"          →1
    AutoEventWireup="true"
    CodeFile="Default.aspx.cs"
    Inherits="_Default"
    Title="Acme Pirate Supply" %>
```

(continued)

Listing 5-3 *(continued)*

```
<asp:Content ID="Content1" Runat="Server"                    →2
    ContentPlaceHolderID="ContentPlaceHolder1" >
    Todays specials:<br />
  <asp:DataList ID="DataList1" runat="server"                →3
      DataKeyField="ProductID"
      DataSourceID="SqlDataSource1"
      OnSelectedIndexChanged=
      "DataList1_SelectedIndexChanged">
    <ItemTemplate>                                           →4
      <b>
        <asp:Label ID="NameLabel" runat="server"             →5
            Text='<%# Eval("name") %>'>
        </asp:Label>
      </b>
      <asp:Label ID="FeatureTextLabel"                       →6
          runat="server"
          Text='<%# Eval("FeatureText") %>'>
      </asp:Label>
      <asp:Label ID="PriceLabel" runat="server"              →7
          Text=
          '<%# Eval("price", " Regularly {0:c}. ") %>'>
      </asp:Label> 
      <b>
      <asp:Label ID="SalePriceLabel" runat="server"          →8
          Text=
          '<%# Eval("SalePrice", "Now only {0:c}! ") %>'>
      </asp:Label>
      </b>
      <asp:LinkButton ID="btnFeature" runat="server"         →9
          CommandName="Select" Text="Details" >
      </asp:LinkButton>
      <br />
    </ItemTemplate>
  </asp:DataList>
  <asp:SqlDataSource ID="SqlDataSource1"                     →10
    runat="server"
    ConnectionString=
      "<%$ ConnectionStrings:ConnectionString %>"
    SelectCommand="SELECT FeaturedProducts.productid,
        FeaturedProducts.featuretext,
        FeaturedProducts.saleprice,
        Products.name,
        Products.price
      FROM FeaturedProducts
        INNER JOIN Products
          ON FeaturedProducts.productid =
        Products.productid">
```

```
</asp:SqlDataSource>
<br /><br />
Please select a category:
<asp:DropDownList ID="ddlCategory" runat="server"          →11
    AutoPostBack="True"
    DataSourceID="SqlDataSource2"
    DataTextField="name"
    DataValueField="catid"
    Width="127px">
</asp:DropDownList><br />
<asp:SqlDataSource ID="SqlDataSource2"                     →12
    runat="server"
    ConnectionString=
        "<%$ ConnectionStrings:ConnectionString %>"
    SelectCommand="SELECT catid,
        name,
        [desc]
        FROM Categories ORDER BY name">
</asp:SqlDataSource>
<br />
<asp:GridView ID="GridView1" runat="server"               →13
    AutoGenerateColumns="False"
    BorderStyle="None"
    DataKeyNames="productid"
    DataSourceID="SqlDataSource3"
    OnSelectedIndexChanged=
        "GridView1_SelectedIndexChanged"
    AllowPaging="True">
    <Columns>
      <asp:ImageField                                      →14
          DataImageUrlField="thumbnail"
          DataImageUrlFormatString="~\Images\{0}">
      </asp:ImageField>
      <asp:BoundField DataField="name"                     →15
          HeaderText="Product" />
      <asp:BoundField DataField="shorttext"                →16
          HeaderText="Description" />
      <asp:BoundField DataField="price"                    →17
          DataFormatString="{0:c}"
          HeaderText="Price" />
      <asp:CommandField SelectText="View"                  →18
          ShowSelectButton="True" />
      <asp:BoundField DataField="SalePrice"                →19
          DataFormatString="On sale {0:c}!"
          SortExpression="SalePrice">
          <HeaderStyle BorderStyle="None" />
          <ItemStyle BorderStyle="None"
              Font-Bold="True" />
      </asp:BoundField>
```

(continued)

Listing 5-3 *(continued)*

```
        </Columns>
        <PagerSettings Mode="NextPrevious" />                  →20
    </asp:GridView>
    <asp:SqlDataSource ID="SqlDataSource3"                     →21
        runat="server"
        ConnectionString=
          "<%$ ConnectionStrings:ConnectionString %>"
        SelectCommand="SELECT Products.productid,
                Products.catid,
                Products.name,
                Products.shorttext,
                Products.longtext,
                Products.price,
                Products.image,
                Products.thumbnail,
                FeaturedProducts.saleprice
            FROM Products
                LEFT OUTER JOIN FeaturedProducts
                  ON Products.productid =
                      FeaturedProducts.productid
            WHERE (Products.catid = @catid)">
        <SelectParameters>                                     →22
          <asp:ControlParameter Name="catid"
              ControlID="ddlCategory"
              PropertyName="SelectedValue"
              Type="String" />
        </SelectParameters>
      </asp:SqlDataSource>
    </asp:Content>
```

The following paragraphs describe the key parts of the Product List page:

→ **1**   The Page directive uses the MasterPageFile attribute to specify the name of the Master Page, ~/MasterPage.master.

→ **2**   The <Content> element identifies the content for the Product
List page.

→ **3**   The DataList control displays the featured products. As you can
see, its data source is SqlDataSource1. In addition, a method
named DataList1_SelectedIndexChanged is called if the user
selects one of the items in this DataList.

→ **4**   The DataList control renders one instance of the ItemTemplate
for each row in the data source.

→ **5**   The NameLabel label displays the name from the data source. It
uses ASP.NET 2.0's simplified binding syntax, which uses the Eval
method to specify the data source column you want to display.

→ **6**   The FeatureTextLabel label uses the simplified binding syntax
to display the featuretext column from the data source.

→ **7**   The `PriceLabel` label uses the simplified binding syntax to display the price column from the data source. Note that in this case, I used a version of the `Eval` method that accepts a format string as a second parameter. Here the format string formats the price as `currency` and adds the word `Regularly` before the price value.

→ **8**   Similarly, the `SalePriceLabel` uses a format string to format the sale price as `currency` and adds some peppy text to highlight the sale price. Note also that this label is bracketed by `<b>` and `</b>` tags to display the sale price in boldface.

→ **9**   The `LinkButton` control provides a link button the user can click to display additional information about a featured product. Here, the `CommandName` attribute specifies `Select` as the button's command name. As a result, the row will be selected when the user clicks this button. Selecting the row causes the `SelectedIndexChanged` event to fire, which then causes the `DataList1_SelectedIndexChanged` method to be called.

→ **10**   The first `SqlDataSource` control provides the data source for the `DataList`. Notice how the connection string is specified:

```
<%$ ConnectionStrings:ConnectionString %>
```

This refers to the connection string identified by the name `ConnectionString` in the `ConnectionStrings` section of the `web.config` file. As a result, the actual connection string is determined at run time by reading the `web.config` file.

The `SelectCommand` attribute specifies the `SELECT` statement used to retrieve data for this data source. In this case, the `SELECT` statement uses an inner join to retrieve information from both the `FeaturedProducts` and `Products` tables.

→ **11**   The `drop-down list` control lets the user choose which category of products to display. `AutoPostBack` is set to true so that the page will be posted when the user selects a product. The data source is set to `SqlDataSource2`. The `DataTextField` attribute specifies that the `name` field should be displayed in the drop-down list, and the `DataValueField` specifies that the `catid` field should be used as the value for the selected item.

→ **12**   The second `SqlDataSource` control provides the data for the drop-down list. It uses a simple `SELECT` statement to retrieve all rows from the Categories table.

→ **13**   The `GridView` control displays the product rows that match the category selected by the user via the drop-down list. As you can see, it specifies `SqlDataSource3` as its data source. In addition, the `GridView1_SelectedIndexChanged` method is called when the user selects a row. Finally, the `AllowPaging` attribute enables the `GridView` control's built-in paging features, which by default display only ten rows at a time.

→ 14   The first column defined for the `GridView` control is an `ImageField` that displays the thumbnail image for each product. The `DataImageUrlField` attribute identifies the name of the data source field that contains the URL of the images to be displayed, and the `DataImageUrlFormatString` attribute provides a format string that's applied to the URL. In this case, the data source field contains just the filename of the image file. Then the format string completes the path by adding `~\Images\` to the filename. For example, if the `thumbnail` field contains the value `sword01T.jpg`, the complete URL will be `~\Images\sword01T.jpg`.

→ 15   This `BoundField` column displays the `name` column from the data source. The header text for the column is set to `Product`.

→ 16   This `BoundField` column displays the `shorttext` column from the data source. The header text for the column is set to `Description`.

→ 17   This `BoundField` column displays the `price` column from the data source. A format string displays the price in `currency` format, and the header text is set to `Price`.

→ 18   A `CommandField` column displays a Select button with the text `View`. When the user clicks this button, the row is selected and the `SelectedIndexChanged` event is raised for the `GridView` control. As a result, the `GridView1_SelectedIndexChanged` method in the code-behind file is executed.

→ 19   The last column in the `GridView` control is a `BoundField` column that displays the `saleprice` column from the data source. A format string is used to add the text `On sale` and to apply the `currency` format. Note that nothing is displayed if the `saleprice` column is null. Notice also that `<HeaderStyle>` and `<ItemStyle>` elements are used to display this column without a border.

→ 20   The `<PagerSettings>` element indicates what type of paging controls you want to appear on the `GridView` control. In this example, the `Mode` attribute specifies `NextPrevious`, so Next and Previous buttons are displayed. Other options for this attribute are `NextPreviousFirstLast`, `Numeric`, and `NumericFirstLast`. Besides the `Mode` attribute, the `<PagerSettings>` element enables you to use other attributes that affect various aspects of the paging controls — such as the text or image displayed for each pager button.

→ 21   The third `SqlDataSource` control provides the data that's displayed by the `GridView` control. Notice that the `SELECT` statement refers to a parameter named `catid` to indicate which products to select.

→ **22**   The `<SelectParameters>` element defines the parameters used by a data source. In this example, only one parameter, named `catid`, is required. To define the `catid` parameter, a `<ControlParameter>` element is used. The `<ControlParameter>` element defines a parameter whose value is taken from another control on the page. In this case, the control is the drop-down list (`ddlCategory`), and the parameter value will be taken from the `SelectedValue` property of the control.

The GridView Control

The `GridView` control, new with ASP.NET 2.0, is designed to replace the old `DataGrid` control. Like the `DataGrid` control, the `GridView` control is designed to present data from a data source in a tabular format. However, the `GridView` control has several features that weren't available in the `DataGrid` control, such as automatic paging and sorting. And it's designed to work with the new ASP.NET 2.0 data sources.

Here are the attributes you'll use most often on the `<GridView>` element to define a `GridView` control:

✔ `ID`: Provides a name used to identify the `GridView` control.

✔ `Runat`: As with all ASP.NET controls, you must specify `runat=server`.

✔ `DataSourceID`: The ID of the data source.

✔ `DataKeyNames`: The names of the key fields. If the data source has more than one key field, the names should be separated by commas.

✔ `AutoGenerateColumns`: You'll usually specify `False` for this attribute to prevent the `GridView` control from automatically generating columns for each field in the data source. Then you can use a `<Columns>` child element to manually define the columns.

✔ `AllowPaging`: Specify `True` to enable paging for the `GridView` control.

✔ `AllowSorting`: Specify `True` to enable sorting for the `GridView` control.

The columns are defined by creating a `<Columns>` child element, and then adding one of the following child elements for each column you want to create:

✔ `BoundField`: Creates a column that's bound to a field in the data source.

✔ `ButtonField`: Creates a column that contains a button.

✔ `CheckBoxField`: Creates a column with a check box that's bound to a Boolean value.

✔ `CommandField`: Creates a column with one or more command buttons (command buttons include Select, Edit, and Delete).

✔ `HyperLinkField`: Creates a column that displays a field from the data source as a hyperlink.

✔ `ImageField`: Creates a column that displays an image. The URL for the image is obtained from a field in the data source.

✔ `TemplateField`: Creates a field that uses a template to specify the field's contents.

The code-behind file for the Default.aspx page (C# version)

The `Default.aspx` page requires a code-behind file to handle the `PageLoad` event and the `SelectedIndexChanged` event for the `DataList` and the `GridView` controls. The C# version of this code-behind file is shown in Listing 5-4. If you're working in Visual Basic, you can skip this section and use the VB version of the code-behind file presented in the next section instead.

Listing 5-4:   The code-behind file for the Default.aspx page (C#)

```
using System;
using System.Data;
using System.Configuration;
using System.Collections;
using System.Web;
using System.Web.Security;
using System.Web.UI;
using System.Web.UI.WebControls;
using System.Web.UI.WebControls.WebParts;
using System.Web.UI.HtmlControls;

public partial class _Default : System.Web.UI.Page
{
    protected void Page_Load(object sender,              →1
        EventArgs e)
    {
        if (!IsPostBack)
        {
            string CatID = Request.QueryString["cat"];
            if (CatID != null)
            {
                ddlCategory.SelectedValue = CatID;
            }
        }
    }

    protected void DataList1_ SelectedIndexChanged       →2
        (object sender, EventArgs e)
    {
        string ProductID =
            DataList1.SelectedValue.ToString().Trim();
        string CatID = ddlCategory.SelectedValue;
        Response.Redirect("Product.aspx?prod="
            + ProductID
            + "&cat="
            + CatID);
    }
```

```
protected void GridView1_ SelectedIndexChanged        →3
    (object sender, EventArgs e)
{
    string ProductID =
        GridView1.SelectedValue.ToString().Trim();
    string CatID = ddlCategory.SelectedValue;
    Response.Redirect("Product.aspx?prod="
        + ProductID
        + "&cat="
        + CatID);
}
}
```

Here's a closer look at each of the methods in this code-behind file:

→ **1**   Page_Load: This method is called each time the page is loaded. Its purpose is to set the drop-down list's selection to the category indicated by the cat query string field. Note that the query string field is used only when IsPostBack is false. That's because the query string field should be used only when the Default.aspx page is posted from another page, such as the Product.aspx page. If the query string field were used when the Default.aspx page posts back from itself, then any selection made by the user would be replaced by the query string field's value — which isn't what you want. Note also that the code checks to make sure that the cat field exists before using its value.

→ **2**   DataList1_SelectedIndexChanged: This method is called whenever the user selects an item in the DataList control, which lists the currently featured products. It uses the SelectedValue property of the DataList control to extract the ID of the selected product and the SelectedValue property of the drop-down list to extract the ID of the selected category. Then it calls the Response.Redirect method to redirect to the Product.aspx page, with the prod and cat query strings set to the appropriate values.

→ **3**   GridView1_SelectedIndexChanged: This method is called whenever the user selects an item in the GridView control, which lists the products for the currently selected category. It works pretty much the same as the DataList1_SelectedIndexChanged method, but the product ID is extracted from the GridView control instead of the DataList control.

The code-behind file for the Default.aspx page (Visual Basic version)

The Visual Basic version of this code-behind file is shown in Listing 5-5. If you're working in C#, you can skip this section and use the C# version (presented in the previous section) instead.

To use the Visual Basic version, you must change the Language specification in the Page directive of the Default.aspx file from C# to VB — *and* change the name of the code-behind file from Default.aspx.cs to Default.aspx.vb.

Listing 5-5:   The code-behind file for the Default.aspx page (VB)

```
Partial Class _Default
    Inherits System.Web.UI.Page

    Protected Sub Page_Load( _                              →1
       ByVal sender As Object, _
       ByVal e As System.EventArgs) _
       Handles Me.Load
         If Not IsPostBack Then
            Dim CatID As String
            CatID = Request.QueryString("cat")
            If Not CatID = Nothing Then
                ddlCategory.SelectedValue = CatID
            End If
         End If
    End Sub

    Protected Sub DataList1_SelectedIndexChanged( _         →2
       ByVal sender As Object, _
       ByVal e As System.EventArgs) _
       Handles DataList1.SelectedIndexChanged
         Dim ProductID As String
         Dim CatID As String
         ProductID =
             DataList1.SelectedValue.ToString().Trim()
         CatID = ddlCategory.SelectedValue
         Response.Redirect("Product.aspx?prod=" _
             + ProductID + "&cat=" + CatID)
    End Sub
```

```
Protected Sub GridView1_SelectedIndexChanged( _          →3
   ByVal sender As Object, _
   ByVal e As System.EventArgs) _
   Handles GridView1.SelectedIndexChanged
      Dim ProductID As String
      Dim CatID As String
      ProductID =
         GridView1.SelectedValue.ToString().Trim()
      CatID = ddlCategory.SelectedValue
      Response.Redirect("Product.aspx?prod=" _
         + ProductID + "&cat=" + CatID)
   End Sub

End Class
```

The following paragraphs describe each of the methods in this code-behind file:

→ **1**   Page_Load: This method is called each time the page is loaded.
Its purpose is to set the drop-down list's selection to the category
indicated by the cat query string field. Note that the query string
field is used only when IsPostBack is false. That's because the
query string field should be used only when the Default.aspx
page is posted from another page, such as the Product.aspx
page. If the query-string field were used when the Default.aspx
page posts back from itself, then any selection made by the user
would be replaced by the query-string field's value — which isn't
what you want. Also, the code checks to make sure the cat field
exists before using it.

→ **2**   DataList1_SelectedIndexChanged: This method is called whenever the user selects an item in the DataList control, which lists
the currently featured products. It uses the SelectedValue property of the DataList control to extract the ID of the selected
product and the SelectedValue property of the drop-down list to
extract the ID of the selected category. Then it calls the Response.
Redirect method to redirect to the Product.aspx page, with
the prod and cat query strings set to the appropriate values.

→ **3**   GridView1_SelectedIndexChanged: This method is called whenever the user selects an item in the GridView control, which lists
the products for the currently selected category. It works pretty
much the same as the DataList1_SelectedIndexChanged
method, but the product ID is extracted from the GridView control instead of the DataList control.

Building the Product Detail page

The Product Detail page (`Product.aspx`) displays the data for a specific product selected by the user. This page is displayed when the user selects a product from either the `DataList` or the `GridView` control in the `Default.aspx` page. It uses a `DetailsView` control (one of the new data controls provided by ASP.NET 2.0) to display the product details.

The Product.aspx file

The Product Details page is defined by the `Product.aspx` file, which is shown in Listing 5-6.

Listing 5-6:   The Product Details Page (Product.aspx)

```
<%@ Page Language="C#"                                              →1
    MasterPageFile="~/MasterPage.master"
    AutoEventWireup="true"
    CodeFile="Product.aspx.cs"
    Inherits="Product"
    Title="Acme Pirate Supply" %>
<asp:Content ID="Content1" Runat="Server"
    ContentPlaceHolderID="ContentPlaceHolder1" >
    <asp:DetailsView ID="DetailsView1"                              →2
        runat="server"
        AutoGenerateRows="False"
        BorderStyle="None"
        BorderWidth="0px"
        DataKeyNames="productid"
        DataSourceID="SqlDataSource1"
        Height="50px"
        Width="125px">
        <Fields>
            <asp:BoundField DataField="name"                        →3
                ShowHeader="False" >
                <ItemStyle Font-Size="Large" />
            </asp:BoundField>
            <asp:ImageField                                         →4
                DataImageUrlField="image"
                DataImageUrlFormatString="~\Images\{0}"
                ShowHeader="False">
            </asp:ImageField>
            <asp:BoundField DataField="shorttext"                   →5
                ShowHeader="False" >
                <ItemStyle Font-Size="Medium" />
            </asp:BoundField>
            <asp:BoundField DataField="longtext"                    →6
                DataFormatString="<br />{0}"
```

```
                    ShowHeader="False" >
                    <ItemStyle Font-Size="Small" />
                </asp:BoundField>
                <asp:BoundField DataField="price"              →7
                    DataFormatString="<br />{0:c}"
                    ShowHeader="False" >
                    <ItemStyle Font-Size="Large" />
                </asp:BoundField>
                <asp:BoundField DataField="SalePrice"          →8
                    DataFormatString="<br />Sale Price {0:c}!"
                    ShowHeader="False" >
                    <ItemStyle Font-Size="Large" />
                </asp:BoundField>
                <asp:BoundField DataField="productid"          →9
                    DataFormatString=
                      "<br />Product code: {0}"
                    ReadOnly="True"
                    ShowHeader="False" />
            </Fields>
        </asp:DetailsView>
        <asp:SqlDataSource ID="SqlDataSource1"                 →10
            runat="server"
            ConnectionString=
                "<%$ ConnectionStrings:ConnectionString %>"
            SelectCommand="SELECT Products.productid,
                Products.catid,
                Products.name,
                Products.shorttext,
                Products.longtext,
                Products.price,
                Products.image,
                FeaturedProducts.saleprice,
                FeaturedProducts.featuretext
                FROM Products
                LEFT OUTER JOIN FeaturedProducts
                  ON Products.productid =
                        FeaturedProducts.productid
                WHERE (Products.productid = @productid)">
            <SelectParameters>                                 →11
                <asp:QueryStringParameter
                    Name="productid"
                    QueryStringField="prod"
                    Type="String" />
            </SelectParameters>
        </asp:SqlDataSource>
        <br />
        <asp:Button ID="btnAdd" runat="server"                 →12
            OnClick="btnAdd_Click"
            Text="Add to Cart" /> 
        <asp:Button ID="btnBack" runat="server"                →13
            OnClick="btnBack_Click"
            Text="Back to List" />
</asp:Content>
```

The DetailsView Control

The DetailsView control is a new data control introduced with ASP.NET 2.0. It's designed to display one row from a data source at a time. The DetailsView control is rendered as an HTML table, with one table row for each field in the data source.

Here are the attributes you'll use most often on the DetailsView control:

- ID: Provides a name used to identify the DetailsView control.

- Runat: As with all ASP.NET controls, you must specify runat=server.

- DataSourceID: The ID of the data source.

- DataKeyNames: The names of the key fields. If the data source has more than one key field, the names should be separated by commas.

- AutoGenerateRows: You'll usually specify False for this attribute to prevent the DetailsView control from automatically generating a row for each field in the data source. Then you can use a <Fields> child element to manually define the fields displayed by the DetailsView control.

- AllowPaging: Specify True to enable paging for the DetailsView control.

Next, to define the fields displayed by a DetailsView control, you add a <Fields> child element. Add one following child element for each field you want to create:

- BoundField: Creates a field that's bound to a field in the data source.

- ButtonField: Creates a field that contains a button.

- CheckBoxField: Creates a field with a check box that's bound to a Boolean value.

- CommandField: Creates a field with one or more command buttons (command buttons include Select, Edit, and Delete).

- HyperLinkField: Creates a field that displays a field from the data source as a hyperlink.

- ImageField: Creates a field that displays an image. The URL for the image is obtained from a field in the data source.

- TemplateField: Creates a field that uses a template to specify the field's contents.

The following paragraphs describe the key points of this listing:

→ 1 The Page directive specifies that the page will use MasterPage.master as its Master Page.

→ 2 The DetailsView control displays the details for a single row in its data source, identified by the DataSourceID field as SqlDataSource1. The AutoGenerateRows attribute is set to False so the control won't automatically generate a row for each field in the data source. Instead, this DetailsView control uses a <Fields> element to define the data to be displayed.

→ **3**   The first field displayed by the `DetailsView` control displays the `name` field from the data source.

→ **4**   The second field displays the full-size image, identified by the `image` field. Note that the `DataImageUrlFormatString` attribute adds `~\Images\` to the URL. Thus, if the `image` field specifies that the image file is named `sword01.jpg`, the complete URL for the image will be `~\Images\sword01.jpg`.

→ **5**   This field displays the `shorttext` field. The `<ItemStyle>` element specifies that the font size should be `medium`.

→ **6**   This field displays the `longtext` field. The `DataFormatString` attribute adds a line break (`<br />`) before the text. The `<ItemStyle>` element specifies that the font size should be `small`.

→ **7**   This field displays the `price` field. The `DataFormatString` attribute formats the price as `currency`, and the `<ItemStyle>` element specifies that the font size should be `Large`.

→ **8**   The sales price is displayed with a format string that display the words `Sale Price` and formats the sales price as `currency`.

→ **9**   The last field in the `DetailsView` control displays the product ID. A format string adds the text `Product code:` before the product ID.

→ **10**   This `SqlDataSource` control defines the data source used by the `DetailsView` control. The connection string is retrieved from the `web.config` file, and the `SELECT` statement retrieves the product data for the product selected by the user. A join is used because data must be retrieved from both the Products and the FeaturedProducts tables, and the `WHERE` clause uses a parameter named `productid`.

→ **11**   The `<SelectParameters>` element defines the parameter used by the `SELECT` statement in the data source. The parameter is defined by the `<QueryStringParameter>` element, which retrieves the parameter value from a query string. In this case, the parameter is named `productid` and the value is retrieved from a query string named `prod`.

→ **12**   The Add button lets the user add the current product to the shopping cart.

→ **13**   The Back button lets the user return to the Product List page to continue shopping.

The code-behind file for the Product.aspx page (C# version)

Listing 5-7 shows the C# version of the code-behind file for the Product.aspx page. If you're working in Visual Basic, you may want to skip this section and go instead to the VB version of the code-behind file (presented in the next section).

Listing 5-7: **The code-behind file for the Product.aspx page (C#)**

```csharp
using System;
using System.Data;
using System.Configuration;
using System.Collections;
using System.Web;
using System.Web.Security;
using System.Web.UI;
using System.Web.UI.WebControls;
using System.Web.UI.WebControls.WebParts;
using System.Web.UI.HtmlControls;

public partial class Product : System.Web.UI.Page
{
    protected void btnAdd_Click(object sender,          →1
        EventArgs e)
    {
        string ProductID = Request.QueryString["prod"];
        string CatID = Request.QueryString["cat"];
        Response.Redirect("Cart.aspx?prod="
            + ProductID + "&cat=" + CatID);
    }
    protected void btnBack_Click(object sender,         →2
        EventArgs e)
    {
        string CatID = Request.QueryString["cat"];
        Response.Redirect("Default.aspx?cat=" + CatID);
    }
}
```

The following paragraphs describe the two methods in this code-behind file:

→ 1   btnAdd_Click: This method is called when the user clicks the Add to Cart button. It simply redirects to the Cart.aspx page, passing the product and category information via query-string fields.

→ 2   btnBack_Click: This method is called when the user clicks the Back to List button. It redirects to the Default.aspx page. The category ID is passed via a query string.

The code-behind file for the Product.aspx page (Visual Basic version)

The Visual Basic version of the Product.aspx code-behind file is shown in Listing 5-8. To use this code-behind file, you must change the Language specification in the Page directive of the Product.aspx file from C# to VB.

If you're working in C#, you should use the C# version of the code-behind file (presented in the previous section) instead of the version in Listing 5-8.

Listing 5-8:   The code-behind file for the Default.aspx page (VB)

```
Partial Class Product
    Inherits System.Web.UI.Page

    Protected Sub btnAdd_Click( _                            →1
      ByVal sender As Object, _
      ByVal e As System.EventArgs) _
      Handles btnAdd.Click
        Dim ProductID As String
        Dim CatID As String
        ProductID = Request.QueryString("prod")
        CatID = Request.QueryString("cat")
        Response.Redirect("Cart.aspx?prod=" _
            + ProductID + "&cat=" + CatID)
    End Sub

    Protected Sub btnBack_Click( _                           →2
      ByVal sender As Object, _
      ByVal e As System.EventArgs) _
      Handles btnBack.Click
        Dim CatID As String
        CatID = Request.QueryString("cat")
        Response.Redirect("Default.aspx?cat=" + CatID)
    End Sub

End Class
```

The following paragraphs describe the two methods in this code-behind file:

→ **1**   btnAdd_Click: This method is called when the user clicks the Add to Cart button. It simply redirects to the Cart.aspx page, passing the product and category information via query-string fields.

→ **2**   btnBack_Click: This method is called when the user clicks the Back to List button. It redirects to the Default.aspx page. The category ID is passed via a query string.

Building the Cart Page

This application doesn't support a shopping cart. However, to make this application compatible with the Shopping Cart application presented in the next chapter, the `Product.aspx` page includes an Add to Cart button that redirects to a page named `Cart.aspx`. Listing 5-9 shows a dummy version of the Cart page that simply displays a message indicating that the shopping cart function isn't implemented. For a working version of this page, refer to Chapter 6.

Listing 5-9:   The Cart page (Cart.aspx)

```
<%@ Page Language="C#"
    MasterPageFile="~/MasterPage.master"
    AutoEventWireup="true"
    CodeFile="Cart.aspx.cs"
    Inherits="Cart"
    Title="Acme Pirate Supply" %>
<asp:Content ID="Content1" Runat="Server"
    ContentPlaceHolderID="ContentPlaceHolder1" >
    <br />
    Sorry, that function hasn't been implemented yet.
</asp:Content>
```

Chapter 6

Building a Shopping Cart Application

*T*his chapter presents a simple online Shopping Cart application that lets your customer purchase products directly from your Web site by adding products to a list for purchase. It's integrated with the Product Catalog application shown in Chapter 5. When the user is ready to purchase the items, a Check Out page gathers the user's shipping and payment information so the order can be processed.

Of all the applications in this book, this one is the most code-intensive. That's because it doesn't use ASP.NET data binding or data sources for the Shopping Cart and Check Out pages. Instead, they use code to directly manage the data displayed for the shopping cart and to write the order data to the database. It's common for large applications to use separate classes to handle database access so that the database access code can be separated from the presentation and business logic code. As with the other applications in this book, you'll find both C# and Visual Basic versions of this code in this chapter.

Because the application is an extension of the Product Catalog application shown in Chapter 5, you may want to refer to that chapter to remind yourself how the Product List and Product Detail pages work.

Considering Some Basic Decisions

Before we get into the specifics of the Shopping Cart application's design, consider some basic decisions that will affect both the application and its design:

✔ **Will customers be required to log in?** One of the first decisions you'll need to make is whether you want to require users to log in before they can purchase items. Requiring users to log in has several advantages. For example, you can store the customer information in a database and retrieve it when the user logs in, eliminating the need for the user to re-enter his or her name and address. On the other hand, some users avoid sites where they have to register precisely for that reason: They don't like the idea that you're keeping their information on file.

ASP.NET makes it easy to require customers to log in to a Web site before they can access certain pages, and Chapter 4 presents a basic user registration and login application that uses those features. The Shopping Cart application in this chapter doesn't require the user to log in, but you can easily incorporate the features from the User Authentication application (see Chapter 4) with this Shopping Cart application.

✔ **How will you handle international shipments?** For simplicity, the application in this figure accepts orders only within the 50 states of the United States. You'll have to modify it somewhat to accept orders from outside of the U.S.

✔ **How will you store the shopping cart data?** There are two common options for how you will store the contents of the user's shopping cart. One is to keep the shopping cart in a database table. Then the shopping cart data will continue to exist apart from the application. The other is to use one of ASP.NET's temporary state features — most likely *session state* — to hold the shopping cart.

The advantage of putting the shopping cart in a database is that the user can leave the application and come back later and find the items still in his or her shopping cart. But there are several disadvantages. One is that you'll have to devise a way to associate the data for a particular user's shopping cart with that user. The easiest way to do that is to require the user to register and log in. Another disadvantage is that the Shopping Cart table can quickly become filled with abandoned data. You'll need to clean up the table periodically, removing the data from old shopping carts that users have abandoned.

The main advantage of using a feature such as session state to store shopping cart data is the ease of programming. ASP.NET takes care of associating the data with the user and deleting the cart when the user ends the session.

An alternative to session state is the new ASP.NET 2.0 Profile feature. Profile is similar to session state but automatically saves data to a database when the session ends. Then, if the user visits the Web site again later, that user's profile data is automatically retrieved.

The application shown in this chapter uses session state to store the shopping cart.

✔ **How will you handle credit cards?** Most Web sites allow the user to pay for the purchase with a credit card. Then the application must be careful to provide adequate security to protect the customer's credit card information. At the least, the application should use SSL (Secure Socket Layers) to secure the connection so the user's credit card information is transmitted securely (although you must also take precautions to *store* it securely if you save it in your database).

The application in this chapter accepts the user's credit card information, but doesn't save it in the database. In addition, the credit card information isn't properly validated and the credit card account isn't charged for the purchase. The exact procedures for doing that vary depending on the credit card processing company you use. As a result, the application presented in this chapter doesn't actually charge the customer's credit card for the order. You'll have to develop the code to do that yourself.

As an alternative to credit cards, you may want to let your customers pay for their orders using PayPal. See www.paypal.com for information about how to incorporate PayPal into your Web site.

✔ **How will you calculate shipping charges?** The easiest way to charge customers for shipping is to charge a simple flat rate for each item sold. Alternatively, you can calculate the order's exact shipping costs by using a combination of the order's total weight and the destination Zip code. The application presented in this chapter simply charges $2.00 for each item ordered. You may want to develop a routine that calculates the shipping charges more accurately.

The User Interface

Figure 6-1 shows the user interface flow for the Shopping Cart application. This application's user interface has just five pages. The first two, default.aspx and product.aspx, are almost identical to the pages of the Product Catalog application presented in Chapter 5. The cart.aspx page displays the user's shopping cart, and the CheckOut.aspx page lets the user enter the information required to complete the order, including the shipping and credit card information. Finally, when the user submits the order, the completed.aspx page is displayed to confirm that the order has been submitted.

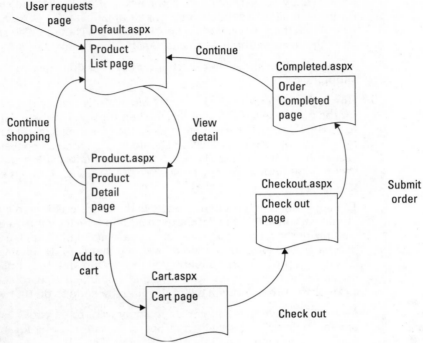

Figure 6-1:
The user interface for the Shopping Cart application.

The Product List page

Figure 6-2 shows the Product List page (`default.aspx`). It's almost identical to the `default.aspx` page from Chapter 5, with one subtle difference: there's a line just beneath the banner that displays information about the user's shopping cart as well as a link that goes to the cart page. This line is part of the Master Page, so it's displayed on every page of the application.

The Product Detail page

Figure 6-3 shows the Product Detail page (`product.aspx`), which displays the details for the product selected by the user. The Add to Cart button at the bottom of the page adds the item to the user's shopping cart, and then takes the user to the Shopping Cart page.

The Cart page

Figure 6-4 shows the Shopping Cart page, which displays the contents of the user's shopping cart.

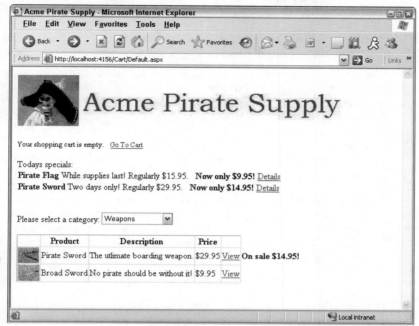

Figure 6-2:
The Product
List page.

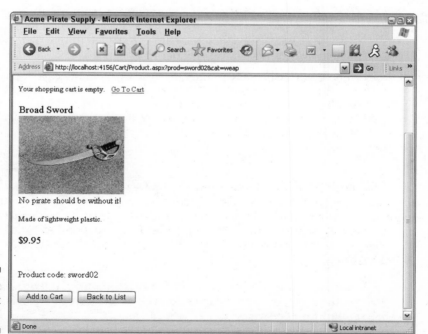

Figure 6-3:
The Product
Detail page.

Following are some of the salient points to notice about this page:

- ✔ The shopping cart shown here contains two items. Notice that the message in the Master Page indicates the number of items in the cart.

- ✔ When the user clicks the Add to Cart button in the Product Detail page, the item is added to the cart and the quantity field is set to 1. If the user has previously added the same item to the cart, the quantity for that item is increased by one. (In other words, if the user were to click the Continue Shopping button to return to the Product Detail page for the Pirate Flag, then click the Add to Cart button again, the quantity field for the Pirate Flag line in the shopping cart would be changed to 2.)

- ✔ The user can click the Delete link to remove an item from the cart.

- ✔ The user can click the Change link to change the quantity for an item in the cart. Then the Quantity field for that item changes from a label to a text box, and the Change and Delete links are replaced by Update and Cancel links. The user can then change the quantity and click Update, or click Cancel to keep the existing quantity unchanged.

- ✔ If the shopping cart is empty, the following message is displayed in place of the cart:

```
Your shopping cart is empty.
```

    In addition, the Check Out button is disabled.

- ✔ The user can click the Continue Shopping button to return to the product pages. If the user came to the Cart page by clicking Add to Cart from the page for a specific product, the user is returned to that page. Otherwise, the user is returned to the Product List page.

- ✔ When the user is ready to purchase the items in the cart, he or she can click the Check Out button. This redirects the user to the Check Out page, which is described in the next section.

The Check Out page

The Check Out page uses the new ASP.NET 2.0 `Wizard` control to walk the user through the process of completing an order. The `Wizard` control does this by displaying separate steps that the user can navigate through using Next and Previous buttons that appear at the bottom of the wizard. The user can also go directly to one of the steps by using navigation links to the left of the wizard.

The three steps for the Check Out process are: Shipping, Billing, and Confirmation. The pages displayed for each of these steps are described in the following sections.

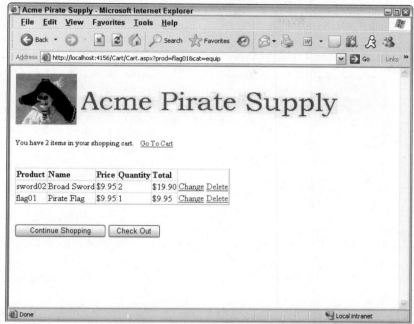

Figure 6-4:
The Cart
page.

The Shipping step

Figure 6-5 shows the page displayed for the first step of the check-out wizard, which gathers the customer's contact information.

The following paragraphs describe the operation of this page:

- ✔ The links at the left side of the page let the user go directly to any of the three steps of the Wizard.

- ✔ The text boxes let the user enter his or her name, address, zip code, phone number, and email address.

- ✔ The drop-down list is filled with the names of all 50 states in the United States. If you want to accept orders from outside of the U.S., you'll need to modify this step, perhaps by adding a drop-down list or text box for the country.

- ✔ All of the text boxes have validators that require the user to enter data. However, any data is accepted. You may want to modify this step to provide more comprehensive validation. For example, you may want to use a Regular Expression validator to validate the phone number and e-mail address. (I'll leave it to you to figure out how to do that.)

- ✔ When the user clicks the Next button, the Payment step of the wizard is displayed, as described in the next section.

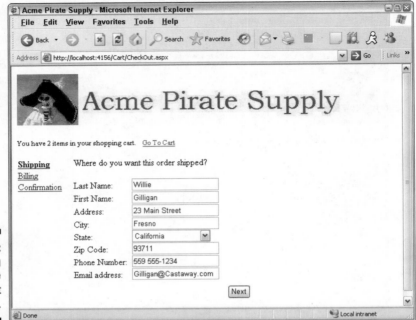

Figure 6-5:
The Shipping
Step of the
Check Out
page.

The Payment step

Figure 6-6 shows the Payment step of the check-out wizard, which lets the user enter credit card information to pay for the order.

Here are the important details:

- ✔ Again, the links at the left side of the page let the user go directly to any of the three wizard steps.

- ✔ The first drop-down list lets the user select which type of credit card to use. The options are Visa, MasterCard, and American Express. You can easily modify the application to accept other types of cards.

- ✔ The first text box accepts the credit card number. A required-field validator forces the user to enter a value, but other than requiring an entry, no further validation is done. The validation requirements for credit card numbers are different for each type of card, and the validation checks can get pretty complicated. I'll leave it to you to add validation checking for this field once you determine what credit cards you want to accept.

- ✔ The second drop-down list lets the user indicate the credit card's expiration month. This drop-down list is filled with the names of the months of the year.

✔ The second text box lets the user enter the expiration year for the credit card. Validators are used to ensure the user enters an integer that's between 2005 and 2099.

✔ The user can click the Next button to go to the Confirmation step or the Previous button to return to the Shipping step.

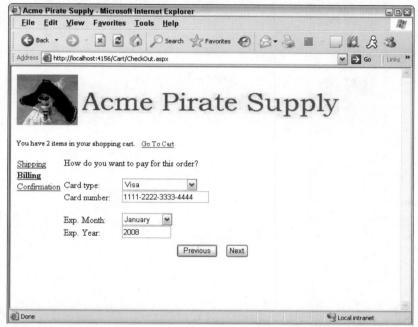

Figure 6-6:
The
Payment
step of the
Check Out
page.

The Confirmation step

Figure 6-7 shows the Confirmation step of the check-out wizard, which displays the final total for the order (including sales tax and shipping) and allows the user to submit the order for processing.

Here are the details of how this page works:

✔ As with the other two steps, the links to the left of the wizard let the user go directly to either of the other two steps.

✔ The labels display the subtotal calculated by adding up prices of the items ordered, the sales tax, the shipping charges, and the order total.

✔ Sales tax is calculated at 7.75 percent for California orders only.

✔ Shipping charges are $2.00 per item.

✔ The user can click the Submit Order button to submit the order or the Previous button to return to the Payment step. If the user submits the order, the Completed page is displayed, as described in the next section.

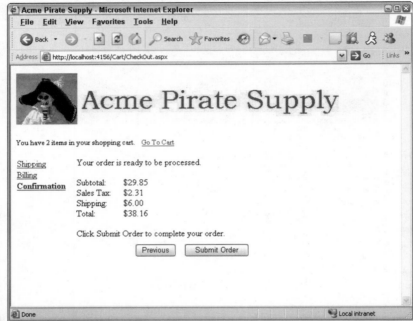

Figure 6-7:
The
Confirmation
step of the
Check Out
page.

The Completed page

Figure 6-8 shows the Completed page, which is displayed when the user submits the order. As you can see, this page simply displays a message indicating that the order has been processed. The user can then click the Continue button to return to the `Default.aspx` page.

Note that if an error occurs while processing the order, the following message is displayed instead of the one shown in Figure 6-8:

```
There was a problem with your order. Please try again
       later.
```

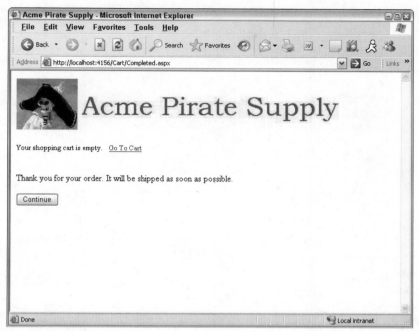

Figure 6-8:
The
Completion
page.

Designing the Cart Database

The Shopping Cart application uses a SQL Server database to store information about the products, customers, and orders. Figure 6-9 shows an Entity-Relationship Diagram of the database. As you can see, it consists of six tables:

- ✔ Categories
- ✔ Products
- ✔ FeaturedProducts
- ✔ Customers
- ✔ Orders
- ✔ OrderItems

The first three of these tables are the same as in the Products database used for the application that was presented in Chapter 5. So I refer you to that chapter for more information about those tables. The following sections describe the three new tables.

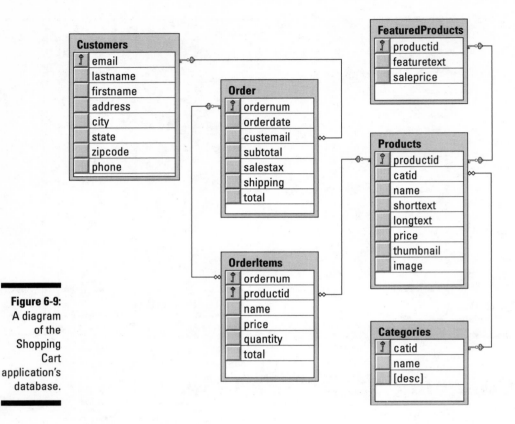

Figure 6-9:
A diagram
of the
Shopping
Cart
application's
database.

The Customers table

The Customers table contains one row for each customer who has purchased a product. Table 6-1 lists the columns defined for this table.

Column name	Type	Description
Table 6-1		The Customers Table
email	VARCHAR(50)	The customer's e-mail address. This column also serves as the table's primary key.
lastname	VARCHAR(50)	The customer's last name.
firstname	VARCHAR(50)	The customer's first name.

Column name	Type	Description
address	VARCHAR(50)	The customer's street address.
city	VARCHAR(50)	The customer's city.
state	VARCHAR(2)	The customer's two-character state code.
zipcode	VARCHAR(9)	The customer's Zip code, up to nine characters.
phone	VARCHAR(20)	The customer's phone number.

The Orders table

The Orders table contains one row for each order that has been submitted. Table 6-2 lists the columns used by the Orders table.

Table 6-2		The Orders Table
Column name	**Type**	**Description**
ordernum	INT	An identity column that uniquely identifies each order. This column is the primary key for the table.
orderdate	SMALLDATETIME	The date the order was placed.
custemail	VARCHAR(50)	The customer's e-mail address. This serves as a foreign key that relates the order to a particular row in the Customers table.
subtotal	MONEY	The sum of the totals for each item associated with the order.
salestax	MONEY	The sales tax for the order.
shipping	MONEY	The shipping charges for the order.
total	n/a	The order total. This field is calculated by adding the subtotal, salestax, and shipping fields.

Note that the total column doesn't actually store the order total. Instead, it's a calculated field that adds the subtotal, sales tax, and shipping charges to determine the total for the order.

The OrderItems table

The OrderItems table contains one row for each line item associated with an order. Table 6-3 lists the columns used by the OrderItems table.

Table 6-3		The OrderItems Table
Column name	*Type*	*Description*
ordernum	INT	The order number for the order this item is associated with.
productid	VARCHAR(10)	The ID for the product represented by this item. Note that this column and the ordernum column comprise the primary key for this table.
name	VARCHAR(50)	The product's name.
price	MONEY	The product's price.
quantity	SMALLINT	The quantity ordered.
total	n/a	The total for the item, calculated by multiplying the price by the quantity.

Note that this table uses a primary key composed of the ordernum and productid columns. As a result, although there can be duplicate order numbers and product IDs in the table, each combination of order number and product ID must be unique. That makes sense when you think about it: Each order can have more than one order item, and each product can appear on many different orders, but a particular order can have only one line item for each product.

Note also that the name column is included in the OrderItems table as a convenience so the application doesn't have to retrieve it from the Products table. You could omit the name from the OrderItems table, but that would complicate the database access required to display the line items for an order. This is an example of *denormalization* (as described in Chapter 1).

You might suspect that the price could also be omitted, but the price is a bit different than the name. Product prices are likely to change. Suppose a customer places an order for a product that's priced at $9.95 at the time the order is submitted, but within moments of when the user submits the order, the price is increased to $11.95. If you then charge the customer $11.95 for the product, the customer will be justifiably upset. To prevent that from happening, the price at the time of the order should be stored in the OrderItems table when the order is submitted.

Creating the database

You can create the `Cart` database manually from within Visual Studio by using the Server Explorer. Or you can run the `CreateCartDB.sql` script that's shown in Listing 6-1. The easiest way to run this script is to open a command-prompt window, change to the directory that contains the script, and enter this command:

```
sqlcmd -S localhost\SQLExpress -i CreateCartDB.sql
```

This command assumes you're running SQL Server Express on your own computer. If you're using SQL Server on a different server, you'll need to change `localhost\SQLExpress` to the correct name. If you're not sure what name to use, ask your database administrator.

Listing 6-1: The CreateCartDB.sql script

```
USE master                                              →1
GO

IF EXISTS(SELECT * FROM sysdatabases                    →2
    WHERE name='Cart')
DROP DATABASE Cart
GO

CREATE DATABASE Cart                                    →3
ON (NAME=Product,
    FILENAME = 'C:\APPS\Cart.mdf',
    SIZE=10 )
GO

USE Cart

CREATE TABLE Categories (                               →4
  catid VARCHAR(10)   NOT NULL,
  name  VARCHAR(50)   NOT NULL,
  [desc]  VARCHAR(MAX) NOT NULL,
  PRIMARY KEY(catid) )
  GO

CREATE TABLE Products (                                 →5
  productid VARCHAR(10)   NOT NULL,
  catid     VARCHAR(10)   NOT NULL,
  name      VARCHAR(50)   NOT NULL,
  shorttext VARCHAR(MAX)  NOT NULL,
  longtext  VARCHAR(MAX)  NOT NULL,
  price     MONEY         NOT NULL,
  thumbnail VARCHAR(40)   NOT NULL,
```

(continued)

Listing 6-1 *(continued)*

```
    image      VARCHAR(40)  NOT NULL,
    PRIMARY KEY(productid),
    FOREIGN KEY(catid) REFERENCES Categories(catid) )
    GO

CREATE TABLE FeaturedProducts (                              →6
    productid   VARCHAR(10)  NOT NULL,
    featuretext VARCHAR(MAX) NOT NULL,
    saleprice   MONEY        NOT NULL,
    PRIMARY KEY(productid),
    FOREIGN KEY(productid) REFERENCES Products(productid) )
    GO

    CREATE TABLE Customers (                                 →7
    email      VARCHAR(50)  NOT NULL,
    lastname   VARCHAR(50)  NOT NULL,
    firstname  VARCHAR(50)  NOT NULL,
    address    VARCHAR(50)  NOT NULL,
    city       VARCHAR(50)  NOT NULL,
    state      VARCHAR(2)   NOT NULL,
    zipcode    VARCHAR(9)   NOT NULL,
    phone      VARCHAR(20)  NOT NULL,
    PRIMARY KEY(email) )
    GO

    CREATE TABLE Orders (                                    →8
    ordernum   INT              IDENTITY,
    orderdate  SMALLDATETIME NOT NULL,
    custemail  VARCHAR(50)   NOT NULL,
    subtotal   MONEY         NOT NULL,
    salestax   MONEY         NOT NULL,
    shipping   MONEY         NOT NULL,
    total      AS (subtotal + salestax + shipping),
    PRIMARY KEY(ordernum),
    FOREIGN KEY(custemail) REFERENCES Customers(email) )
    GO

    CREATE TABLE OrderItems (                                →9
    ordernum   INT           NOT NULL,
    productid  VARCHAR(10)   NOT NULL,
    name       VARCHAR(50)   NOT NULL,
    price      MONEY         NOT NULL,
    quantity   SMALLINT      NOT NULL,
    total      AS (price * quantity),
    PRIMARY KEY(ordernum, productid),
    FOREIGN KEY(ordernum) REFERENCES Orders(ordernum),
    FOREIGN KEY(productid) REFERENCES Products(productid) )
    GO
```

Here are some of the more interesting details about this script:

→ **1**   This line sets the database context to `master`. Although that's usually the default, it's a good idea to set it just in case.

→ **2**   Deletes the existing `Cart` database if it exists.

→ **3**   Creates a database named `Cart`, placing the database file in the `C:\Apps` directory. You can change this location if you want to store the database in a different location.

→ **4**   Creates the `Categories` table.

→ **5**   Creates the `Products` table.

→ **6**   Creates the `FeaturedProducts` table.

→ **7**   Creates the `Customers` table.

→ **8**   Creates the `Orders` table.

→ **9**   Creates the `OrderItems` table.

Adding some test data

The CD that comes with this book includes a script named `InsertData.sql` that inserts test data into the `Cart` database. You can run this script from a command prompt like this:

```
sqlcmd -S localhost\SQLExpress -i InsertData.sql
```

(You may need to change the server name if you're not using a local instance of SQL Server Express.)

Querying the database

The Shopping Cart application uses the same queries as the Product Catalog application to retrieve product information from the database. For more information about those queries, refer to Chapter 5.

Inserting order data into the database

To insert the data for an order into the database, several SQL statements must be used. Here's a brief outline of what must be done to successfully process an order:

```
start a transaction
if the customer already exists in the Customers table
    update the Customers row with the new data
else
    insert a new row in the Customers table
insert a new row in the Orders table
get the order number generated for the inserted row
for each item in the shopping cart
    insert a new row in the OrderItems table
if any SQL errors occur
    roll back the transaction
else
    commit the transaction
```

Note that the entire process is contained within a transaction. That way, if any SQL errors occur during the processing of the order, any updates made prior to the error will be rolled back. The updates to the Customers, Orders, and OrderItems tables aren't committed until all of the updates are successfully completed.

There are several ways to handle the logic necessary to insert or update the customer data. One way is to run a query to determine whether the customer exists, then execute an INSERT or UPDATE statement depending on the results of the query. This application uses a simpler technique: It assumes that the customer doesn't already exist, so it executes an INSERT statement to insert the customer data. If this statement fails because of a duplicate primary key, the program executes an UPDATE statement to update the existing customer row with the new data.

The only other challenging bit of SQL code is determining what order number is generated when a row is inserted into the Orders table. This is necessary because the order number must be included in the OrderItems rows for the order. Fortunately, you can determine the order number by issuing this statement:

```
SELECT @@IDENTITY
```

The @@IDENTITY function returns the value of the last identity column generated for the database.

In some cases, the @@IDENTITY function doesn't return the value you might expect. For example, if you insert a row into a table that contains an identity column, you'd expect @@IDENTITY to return the value generated for that identity column. But that's not what happens if the table has a trigger associated with it, and that trigger executes another INSERT statement that inserts data into another table that also has an identity column. In that case, the `@@IDENTITY` function returns the identity value for the second table. Fortunately, the `Cart` database doesn't use triggers, so the `@@IDENTITY` function will correctly return the identity value generated by the `Orders` table.

Connecting to the database

The connection string used to access the `Cart` database is stored in the application's `web.config` file, like this:

```
<connectionStrings>
    <add name="ConnectionString"
        connectionString="Data
            Source=localhost\SQLExpress;
Initial Catalog=Cart;Integrated Security=True"/>
</connectionStrings>
```

The only place in the application that references this connection string is here in the `web.config` file. This makes it easy to relocate the database when you put the application into production.

The Application's Folders

The Shopping Cart application includes the following folders:

- ✔ **(Root):** The application's root folder contains the application's six pages (`Default.aspx`, `Product.aspx`, `Cart.aspx`, `CheckOut.aspx`, and `Completed.aspx`) as well as the Master Page (`Default.master`).

- ✔ **App_Data:** This folder is designed to store databases used by the application. However, this particular application uses a database that's stored in a location that's determined by SQL Server. So the database for our Cart isn't actually stored in this folder. (If you use the script presented in Listing 6-1 to create the database, the database file is stored in `C:\Apps`.)

- ✔ **App_Code:** This folder contains the C# or Visual Basic code files that define the classes used by the application. For more information about these classes, see the section "Designing the Classes" later in this chapter.

- ✔ **Images:** Here, you'll find the banner image displayed by the Master Page and the image files that show pictures of the store's products.

Designing the Classes

Unlike most of the other applications presented in this book, the Shopping Cart application depends on several classes that both define the business objects used by the program as well as provide the database access. In particular, the application uses the following classes:

- *Customer*: Represents a single customer.
- *ShoppingCart*: Represents the user's shopping cart.
- *CartItem*: Represents an item in the user's shopping cart.
- *Order*: Represents an order.
- *OrderDB*: Handles the details of writing an order to the database.

The following sections describe each of these classes in detail.

The Customer class

The *Customer* class represents a single customer. Its constructors and properties are spelled out in Table 6-4.

Table 6-4	The Customer Class
Constructor	*Description*
Customer()	Creates an instance of the Customer class with default property values.
Customer(string lastName, string firstName, string address, string city, string state, string zipCode, string phoneNumber, string email)	Creates an instance of the Customer class with the specified property values.
Property	*Description*
string LastName	The customer's last name.
string FirstName	The customer's first name.

Property	Description
string Address	The customer's street address.
string City	The customer's city.
string State	The customer's state.
string zipCode	The customer's Zip code.
string phoneNumber	The customer's phone number.
string email	The customer's e-mail address.

The ShoppingCart class

The ShoppingCart class represents a user's shopping cart. Its constructors, properties, and methods are listed in Table 6-5.

Table 6-5	The ShoppingCart class
Constructor	**Description**
ShoppingCart()	Creates a new shopping cart with no items.
Property	**Description**
int Count	The number of items in the shopping cart.
Method	**Description**
List<CartItem> GetItems()	Returns a List object that contains one CartItem object for each item in the shopping cart.
void AddItem(string id, string name, decimal price)	Adds a new item with the specified product ID, name, and price.
void UpdateQuantity (int index, int quantity)	Updates the quantity at the specified index.
void DeleteItem(int index)	Deletes the item at the specified index.
string PhoneNumber	The customer's phone number.

The CartItem class

The CartItem class represents an item in the user's shopping cart. Its constructors and properties are listed in Table 6-6.

Table 6-6	The CartItem class
Constructor	**Description**
CartItem()	Creates a new CartItem object with default property values.
CartItem(string ID, string name, decimal price, int quantity)	Creates a new CartItem object with the specified ID, name, price, and quantity.
Property	**Description**
string ID	The Product ID for the product represented by the item.
string Name	The product name.
decimal Price	The price per unit.
int Quantity	The quantity.
decimal Total	The total for the item (read-only).

The Order class

The Order class represents an order submitted by the user. Its constructors and properties are listed in Table 6-7.

Table 6-7	The Order class
Constructor	**Description**
Order ()	Creates a new Order object with default property values.
Order (date OrderDate, Customer cust, ShoppingCart cart)	Creates a new CartItem object with the specified order date, customer, and shopping cart.
Property	**Description**
DateTime OrderDate	The date the order was submitted.
Customer Cust	The customer who submitted the order.

Property	Description
`ShoppingCart Cart`	The shopping cart that specifies the items being ordered.
`decimal SubTotal`	The subtotal, calculated by adding up the total for each item in the order's shopping cart.
`decimal SalesTax`	The sales tax for the order (read-only). The sales tax is calculated as 7.75% of the subtotal if the Customer resides in California. Otherwise, the sales tax is zero.
`decimal Shipping`	The shipping charges for the order (read-only). The shipping charge is calculated as $2.00 per item.
`decimal Total`	The total for the order (read-only). The total is calculated by adding up the subtotal, sales tax, and shipping charges.

The OrderDB class

The `OrderDB` class handles the task of writing an order to the database. It consists of just a single `static` method (`Shared` for all you Visual Basic programmers out there), as described in Table 6-8.

Table 6-8	The OrderDB class
Method	*Description*
`static bool WriteOrder(Order o)`	Writes the order to the `Cart` database. Returns `true` if the order is successfully written; otherwise, returns `false`. The connection string for the database is obtained from the application's `web.config` file.

Building the Master page

The Master Page (`MasterPage.master`) for the Shopping Cart application is shown in Listing 6-2. It's similar to the Master Page that was used in the Product Listing application shown in Chapter 5. However, it includes an additional label that displays information about the user's shopping cart and a link that leads to the Cart page.

Listing 6-2:   The Master Page (MasterPage.master)

```
<%@ Master Language="C#"                                            →1
    AutoEventWireup="true"
    CodeFile="MasterPage.master.cs"
    Inherits="MasterPage" %>

<!DOCTYPE html PUBLIC "-//W3C//DTD XHTML 1.1//EN"
    "http://www.w3.org/TR/xhtml11/DTD/xhtml11.dtd">

<html xmlns="http://www.w3.org/1999/xhtml" >
<head runat="server">
    <title>Acme Pirate Supply</title>
</head>
<body>
    <form id="form1" runat="server">
    <div>
        <img src="Images/Banner.jpg" />                             →2
        <br />
        <asp:Label ID="lblCart" runat="server"                      →3
            Font-Size="Small"/>
         
        <a href="Cart.aspx"                                         →4
            style="font-size: small">
            Go To Cart</a>
        <br /><br />
        <asp:contentplaceholder                                     →5
            id="ContentPlaceHolder1" runat="server">
        </asp:contentplaceholder>
    </div>
    </form>
</body>
</html>
```

The following paragraphs describe the key lines of the Master Page:

→ **1**   The `Master` directive identifies the file as a Master Page.

→ **2**   The `Image` control displays a banner image at the top of each page. The `Banner.jpg` file is stored in the Images folder.

→ **3**   The label that displays the number of items currently in the shopping cart. The text for this label is set in the `Page_Load` method.

→ **4**   The link that leads to the Cart page.

→ **5**   The `ContentPlaceHolder` control provides the area where the content for the application's content pages will be displayed.

The Master Page requires a code-behind file to set the `Text` property of the label. The C# version of this code-behind file is shown in Listing 6-3, and the Visual Basic version is shown in Listing 6-4.

Listing 6-3: The code-behind file for the Master Page (C#)

```csharp
using System;
using System.Data;
using System.Configuration;
using System.Collections;
using System.Web;
using System.Web.Security;
using System.Web.UI;
using System.Web.UI.WebControls;
using System.Web.UI.WebControls.WebParts;
using System.Web.UI.HtmlControls;

public partial class MasterPage : System.Web.UI.MasterPage
{
    protected void Page_Load(object sender, EventArgs e)
    {
        ShoppingCart cart = (ShoppingCart)Session["cart"];
        if (cart == null)
            lblCart.Text = "Your shopping cart is empty.";
        else if (cart.Count == 0)
            lblCart.Text = "Your shopping cart is empty.";
        else if (cart.Count == 1)
            lblCart.Text =
                "You have 1 item in your shopping cart.";
        else
            lblCart.Text = "You have "
                + cart.Count.ToString()
                + " items in your shopping cart.";
    }
}
```

Listing 6-4: The code-behind file for the Master Page (VB)

```vb
Partial Class MasterPage
    Inherits System.Web.UI.MasterPage

    Protected Sub Page_Load( _
            ByVal sender As Object, _
            ByVal e As System.EventArgs) _
            Handles Me.Load
        Dim cart As ShoppingCart
        cart = Session("cart")
        If cart Is Nothing Then
            lblCart.Text = "Your shopping cart is empty."
        ElseIf cart.Count = 0 Then
            lblCart.Text = "Your shopping cart is empty."
        ElseIf cart.Count = 1 Then
            lblCart.Text =
                "You have 1 item in your shopping cart."
        Else
```

(continued)

Listing 6-4 *(continued)*

```
                lblCart.Text = "You have " _
                    + cart.Count.ToString() _
                    + " items in your shopping cart."
            End If
        End Sub

End Class
```

As you can see, the code-behind file has just one method, named `Page_Load`, which is executed when the page is loaded. It retrieves the shopping cart from session state, casts it as a `ShoppingCart` object, then sets the label accordingly. If the cart doesn't exist or is empty, the label is set to "Your shopping cart is empty." If the cart contains exactly one item, the label is set to "You have 1 item in your shopping cart." And if the cart has more than one item, the label is set to "You have *n* items in your shopping cart."

Modifying the Product Detail Page

The Product Detail page (`Product.aspx`) is almost identical to the Product Detail page for the Product Catalog application shown in Chapter 5. However, there's one crucial difference. In the Chapter 5 application, clicking the Add to Cart button simply led the user to a page that indicates that the shopping cart feature hasn't yet been implemented. But in this application, clicking the Add to Cart button must actually add the product to the shopping cart, then redirect the user to the `Cart.aspx` page to see the contents of the shopping cart.

To add this feature to the Product Detail page, you must modify the method that's called when the user clicks the Add to Cart button, `btnAdd_Click`. The rest of the page is unchanged from the Chapter 5 application.

Listing 6-5 shows the C# version of the `btnAdd_Click` method, the method that's called when the user clicks the Add to Cart button. Listing 6-6 shows the Visual Basic version of this method. (To see the `.aspx` file for the Product Detail page, please refer back to Chapter 5.)

Listing 6-5:   The btnAdd_Click method (C#)

```
protected void btnAdd_Click(object sender, EventArgs e)
{
    // get values from data source                          →1
    DataView dv = (DataView)SqlDataSource1.Select(
        DataSourceSelectArguments.Empty);
    DataRowView dr = dv[0];
    string ID = (String)dr["ProductID"];
    string Name = (string)dr["Name"];
```

```
decimal Price;
if (dr["SalePrice"] is DBNull)
    Price = (decimal)dr["Price"];
else
    Price = (decimal)dr["SalePrice"];

// get or create shopping cart                          →2
ShoppingCart cart;
if (Session["cart"] == null)
{
    cart = new ShoppingCart();
    Session["cart"] = cart;
}
else
{
    cart = (ShoppingCart)Session["cart"];
}

// add item to cart                                     →3
cart.AddItem(ID, Name, Price);

// redirect to cart page                                →4
string ProductID = Request.QueryString["prod"];
string CatID = Request.QueryString["cat"];
Response.Redirect("Cart.aspx?prod=" + ProductID
    + "&cat=" + CatID);
}
```

The following paragraphs describe the key points of this method:

→ **1**   The btnAdd_Click method begins by retrieving the ID, name, and price information for the current product from the data source. You'd think that it would be pretty easy to retrieve the product data displayed by the form, but it turns out to be a little tricky. The easiest technique is to use the Select method of the data source to retrieve a *data view* object that contains the data retrieved by the data source's SELECT statement. Because the SELECT statement for this data source retrieves the data for a single product, the resulting data view will have just one row. The indexer for the DataView object lets you retrieve the individual rows of the data view. Thus, index 0 is used to retrieve a DataRowView object for the data view's only row. Then the individual columns are retrieved from the DataRowView object using the column names as indexes.

Note that if a SalePrice column is present, it is used instead of the Price column for the product's price.

→ **2**   Once the product information has been retrieved from the data source, session state is checked to see if a shopping cart already exists. If so, the shopping cart is retrieved from session state. If not, the application creates a new shopping cart by calling the

ShoppingCart class constructor. Then the new shopping cart is added to session state under the name "cart."

→ **3**   The AddItem method of the shopping cart is called to add the product to the shopping cart.

→ **4**   The user is redirected to the Cart.aspx page, with the product and category IDs passed on as query string fields.

Listing 6-6:   The btnAdd_Click method (VB)

```vb
Protected Sub btnAdd_Click( _
  ByVal sender As Object, _
  ByVal e As System.EventArgs) _
  Handles btnAdd.Click

    ' get values from data source                        →1
    Dim dv As DataView
    dv = SqlDataSource1.Select( _
        DataSourceSelectArguments.Empty)
    Dim dr As DataRowView = dv(0)
    Dim ID As String = dr("ProductID")
    Dim name As String = dr("Name")
    Dim Price As Decimal
    If TypeOf (dr("SalePrice")) Is DBNull Then
        Price = dr("Price")
    Else
        Price = dr("SalePrice")
    End If

    ' get or create shopping cart                        →2
    Dim cart As ShoppingCart
    If Session("cart") Is Nothing Then
        cart = New ShoppingCart()
        Session("cart") = cart
    Else
        cart = Session("cart")
    End If

    ' add item to cart                                   →3
    cart.AddItem(ID, name, Price)

    ' redirect to cart page                              →4
    Dim ProductID As String
    ProductID = Request.QueryString("prod")
    Dim CatID As String
    CatID = Request.QueryString("cat")
    Response.Redirect( _
        "Cart.aspx?prod=" + ProductID _
        + "&cat=" + CatID)
End Sub
```

Building the Cart Page

The Cart page (`Cart.aspx`) displays the user's shopping cart and lets the user modify the shopping cart by changing the quantity ordered or by deleting items. There are two ways the user can display this page. One is to click the Add to Cart button on the Product Detail page. The other is to click the <u>Go To Cart</u> link that appears beneath the banner at the top of each page of the application. To see what this page looks like, refer to Figure 6-4.

The following sections present the `.aspx` code for the cart page and the C# and Visual Basic versions of the code-behind file.

The Cart.aspx file

The Cart page is defined by the `Cart.aspx` file, which is shown in Listing 6-7.

Listing 6-7:   The Cart Page (Cart.aspx)

```
<%@ Page Language="C#"                                   →1
    MasterPageFile="~/MasterPage.master"
    AutoEventWireup="true"
    CodeFile="Cart.aspx.cs"
    Inherits="Cart"
    Title="Acme Pirate Supply" %>
<asp:Content ID="Content1" Runat="Server"
    ContentPlaceHolderID="ContentPlaceHolder1" >
    <br />
    <asp:GridView ID="GridView1" runat="server"          →2
        AutoGenerateColumns="False"
        EmptyDataText="Your shopping cart is empty."
        OnRowDeleting="GridView1_RowDeleting"
        OnRowEditing="GridView1_RowEditing"
        OnRowUpdating="GridView1_RowUpdating"
        OnRowCancelingEdit="GridView1_RowCancelingEdit">
        <Columns>
            <asp:BoundField DataField="ID"               →3
                HeaderText="Product" ReadOnly="True" >
                <HeaderStyle HorizontalAlign="Left" />
            </asp:BoundField>
            <asp:BoundField DataField="Name"             →4
                HeaderText="Name" ReadOnly="True" >
                <HeaderStyle HorizontalAlign="Left" />
            </asp:BoundField>
            <asp:BoundField DataField="Price"            →5
                HeaderText="Price" ReadOnly="True"
                DataFormatString="{0:c}" >
                <HeaderStyle HorizontalAlign="Left" />
```

(continued)

Listing 6-7 *(continued)*

```
            </asp:BoundField>
            <asp:BoundField DataField="Quantity"              →6
                HeaderText="Quantity" >
                <HeaderStyle HorizontalAlign="Left" />
            </asp:BoundField>
            <asp:BoundField DataField="Total"                 →7
                HeaderText="Total" ReadOnly="True"
                DataFormatString="{0:c}" >
                <HeaderStyle HorizontalAlign="Left" />
            </asp:BoundField>
            <asp:CommandField EditText="Change"               →8
                ShowDeleteButton="True"
                ShowEditButton="True" >
                <ItemStyle BorderStyle="None" />
                <HeaderStyle BorderStyle="None" />
            </asp:CommandField>
        </Columns>
    </asp:GridView>
    <br /><br />
    <asp:Button ID="btnContinue" runat="server"              →9
        OnClick="btnContinue_Click"
        Text="Continue Shopping" /> 
    <asp:Button ID="btnCheckOut" runat="server"              →10
        PostBackUrl="~/CheckOut.aspx"
        Text="Check Out" />
</asp:Content>
```

The following paragraphs describe the important elements of this listing:

→ **1**   The `Page` directive specifies that the page will use `MasterPage.master` as its Master Page.

For the Visual Basic version of this application, be sure to change the `AutoEventWireup` attribute of the `Page` directive to `false`. That enables the Handles clause of the Sub procedures. (If you don't change this setting, the events for the `GridView` control included on this page won't be processed correctly.)

→ **2**   The `GridView` control displays the user's shopping cart. Notice that unlike the `GridView` controls used on the `Default.aspx` page, this `GridView` control doesn't specify a data source. Instead, the data source will be specified at run time, when the `Page_Load` method is executed.

For the Visual Basic version of this application, you need to remove the four attributes that specify the event handling for this control. Specifically, you need to remove the following four attributes:

- `OnRowDeleting`
- `OnRowEditing`

- OnRowUpdating

- OnRowCancelingEdit

If you don't remove these attributes, the corresponding events in the Visual Basic code-behind file will be executed *twice* each time the event is raised.

Notice that AutoGenerateColumns is set to false. Then the GridView control doesn't automatically create a column for each field in the data source. Instead, you must manually configure the columns by using the <Columns> element.

→ **3**   The first column in the GridView control is bound to the data source field named ID. The heading for this column is set to "Product," and the column is defined as read-only to prevent the user from modifying it.

→ **4**   The second column in the GridView control is bound to the Name field. This column is also defined as read-only to prevent the user from modifying it.

→ **5**   The next column is bound to the Price field. It uses a format string to display the price in currency format. It too is read-only.

→ **6**   Unlike the other columns in the GridView control, the Quantity column isn't read-only. As a result, the user can modify its contents when the row is placed into Edit mode.

→ **7**   The Total column displays the item total (the price times the quantity) in currency format. It is read-only.

→ **8**   The last column in the shopping cart GridView control is a command column that lets the user edit or delete a shopping cart row. The ShowEditButton and ShowDeleteButton attributes are required to display the Edit and Delete buttons, and the EditButtonText attribute changes the text displayed in the edit button from the default ("Edit") to "Change."

→ **9**   The Continue button lets the user continue shopping by returning to the product pages.

→**10**   The Check Out button lets the user proceed to the checkout page.

For the Visual Basic version of this application, you should remove the OnClick attribute for this control.

The code-behind file for the Cart page

Listing 6-8 shows the C# version of the code-behind file for the Cart page, and Listing 6-9 shows the Visual Basic version.

Listing 6-8:   The code-behind file for the Cart page (C# version)

```csharp
using System;
using System.Data;
using System.Configuration;
using System.Collections;
using System.Web;
using System.Web.Security;
using System.Web.UI;
using System.Web.UI.WebControls;
using System.Web.UI.WebControls.WebParts;
using System.Web.UI.HtmlControls;
using System.Collections.Generic;

public partial class Cart : System.Web.UI.Page
{
    ShoppingCart cart;

    protected void Page_Load(object sender,                     →1
        EventArgs e)
    {
        CheckTimeStamps();

        if (Session["cart"] == null)
        {
            cart = new ShoppingCart();
            Session["cart"] = cart;
        }
        else
        {
            cart = (ShoppingCart)Session["cart"];
        }

        GridView1.DataSource = cart.GetItems();
        if (!IsPostBack)
            GridView1.DataBind();

        btnCheckOut.Enabled = (cart.Count > 0);
    }

    protected void GridView1_RowDeleting(                       →2
        object sender, GridViewDeleteEventArgs e)
    {
        cart.DeleteItem(e.RowIndex);
        GridView1.DataBind();
    }

    protected void GridView1_RowEditing(                        →3
        object sender, GridViewEditEventArgs e)
    {
        GridView1.EditIndex = e.NewEditIndex;
        GridView1.DataBind();
```

```
    }

    protected void GridView1_RowUpdating(              →4
        object sender, GridViewUpdateEventArgs e)
    {
        DataControlFieldCell cell =
            (DataControlFieldCell)GridView1
                .Rows[e.RowIndex].Controls[3];
        TextBox t = (TextBox)cell.Controls[0];
        try
        {
            int q = int.Parse(t.Text);
            cart.UpdateQuantity(e.RowIndex, q);
        }
        catch (FormatException)
        {
            e.Cancel = true;
        }
        GridView1.EditIndex = -1;
        GridView1.DataBind();
    }

    protected void GridView1_RowCancelingEdit(         →5
        object sender, GridViewCancelEditEventArgs e)
    {
        e.Cancel = true;
        GridView1.EditIndex = -1;
        GridView1.DataBind();
    }

    protected void btnContinue_Click(                  →6
        object sender, EventArgs e)
    {
        string ProductID = Request.QueryString["prod"];
        string CatID = Request.QueryString["cat"];
        if (ProductID == null)
            if (CatID == null)
                Response.Redirect("Default.aspx");
            else
                Response.Redirect("Default.aspx?cat="
                    + CatID);
        else
            Response.Redirect("Product.aspx?prod="
                + ProductID
                + "&cat=" + CatID);
    }

    private void CheckTimeStamps()                     →7
    {
        if (IsExpired())
            Response.Redirect(Request.Url.OriginalString);
```

(continued)

Listing 6-8 *(continued)*

```
        else
        {
            DateTime t = DateTime.Now;
            ViewState.Add("$$TimeStamp", t);
            String page = Request.Url.AbsoluteUri;
            Session.Add(page + "_TimeStamp", t);
        }
    }

    private bool IsExpired()                                    →8
    {
        String page = Request.Url.AbsoluteUri;
        if (Session[page + "_TimeStamp"] == null)
            return false;
        else if (ViewState["$$TimeStamp"] == null)
            return false;
        else if (Session[page + "_TimeStamp"].ToString()
                == ViewState["$$TimeStamp"].ToString())
            return false;
        else
            return true;
    }
}
```

The following paragraphs describe the methods in this code-behind file. Note that these comments apply to both the C# and the VB versions.

→ **1** Page_Load: This method is called when the page loads. It begins by calling a method named CheckTimeStamps. I'll explain how this method works later in this section. For now, just realize that this method forces the page to refresh if the user has come to the page by using the browser's back button. This approach prevents problems that can occur when the user backs up to a version of the page that shows a shopping cart with contents that differ from the shopping cart that's stored in session state.

Assuming that the CheckTimeStamps method didn't force the page to refresh, the Page_Load method next checks to see if session state contains an item named cart. If not, a new shopping cart is created and saved in session state. But if an item named cart does exist, the cart item is retrieved, cast to a ShoppingCart object, and assigned to the cart variable.

Next, the shopping cart's GetItems method is called. This returns a List object that holds a CartItem object for each item in the shopping cart. This List object is used as the data source for the GridView control. And if this is the first time the page has been posted, the DataBind method of the GridView control is called so it displays the contents of the shopping cart.

The last line of this method checks to see if the number of items in the cart is greater than zero. If so, the Check Out button is enabled. But if the cart is empty, the Check Out button is disabled. That prevents the user from checking out with an empty shopping cart.

→ **2** `GridView1_RowDeleting`: This method is called whenever the user clicks the Delete button for a shopping cart row. The e argument has a property named `RowIndex` which indicates the row to be deleted. This property is passed to the shopping cart's `DeleteItem` method, which removes the item from the cart. Then the `GridView` control's `DataBind` method is called to update the `GridView` control so the deleted row isn't displayed.

→ **3** `GridView1_RowEditing`: This method is called when the user clicks the Edit button to edit a row. Its e argument includes a property named `NewEditIndex`, which indicates the index of the row to be edited. What this method actually does is to set the `EditIndex` property of the `GridView` control to this index value. Then it calls the `DataBind` method to update the `GridView` control. This, in turn, causes the Quantity column (the only column in the `GridView` control that isn't read-only) to display as a text box instead of a label. That way, the user can enter a new value for the quantity.

→ **4** Here the `GridView1_RowUpdating` method is executed when the user clicks the Update button after modifying the quantity field for the row being edited. The code in this method is a little tricky because, surprisingly, there's no easy way to get the value entered by the user into the text box. So the first statement uses the `Rows` and `Controls` collections of the `GridView` control to get to the fourth cell (index 3) in the row being edited. This returns an object of type `DataControlFieldCell`, which has its own `Controls` collection. The text box that contains the quantity is the first control in this collection. As a result, the second statement in this method retrieves this text box and assigns it to the variable t.

Next, the `int.Parse` method attempts to parse the text entered by the user as an integer. If the text can be parsed to an integer, the result is passed to the shopping cart's `UpdateQuantity` method to update the quantity. If not, a `FormatException` exception is thrown. When this exception is caught, the `Cancel` property of the e argument is set to `true`, which tells the `GridView` control to cancel the update.

Finally, the `EditIndex` property of the `GridView` control is set to −1 to indicate that no row is being edited, and the `DataBind` method is called to update the `GridView` control with the updated contents of the shopping cart.

→ **5** `GridView1_RowCancelingEdit`: This method is called if the user clicks the Edit button to edit a row, then clicks the Cancel button to cancel the edit. It sets the `Cancel` property of the e argument to `true` to cancel the edit. Then it sets the `EditIndex` property of the `GridView` control to -1 to indicate that no row is being edited and calls `DataBind` to refresh the `GridView` control from the data source.

→ **6** `btnContinue_Click`: This method is called if the user clicks the Continue Shopping button. It examines the `prod` and `cat` query strings to determine which page the user should be redirected to. If there is no `prod` or `cat` query string, the user is redirected to the `Default.aspx` page. If there is a `cat` string but no `prod` string, the user is redirected to the `Default.aspx` page and the `cat` string is passed on so that the drop-down list will show the category that was previously selected by the user. And if both a `prod` and a `cat` query string are present, the user is redirected to the `Product.aspx` page. In that case, both query strings are passed on so the product that was previously displayed will be shown.

→ **7** `CheckTimeStamps`: This method is called at the start of the `Page_Load` method to determine if the user has reached this page by clicking the browser's Back button. To determine this, a timestamp is generated and saved in two places: in the page's view state and in the application's session state. If the user posts a page that was reached by using the browser's Back button, the timestamp saved in view state for that page won't match the time-stamp stored in session state. In that case, the application forces the page to refresh so it will display the shopping cart accurately.

The `CheckTimeStamps` method begins with an `if` statement that calls the `IsExpired` method. This method compares the time-stamps to determine if the page is outdated. If so, the user is redirected to `Request.Url.OriginalString`, which contains the URL of the page that was posted. This forces the page to be refreshed.

If the `IsExpired` method indicates that the page is not outdated, a new timestamp is generated by calling `DateTime.Now`. Then this timestamp is stored in the page's view state under the name `$$TimeStamp` and in session state using the absolute URL of the page.

→ **8** `IsExpired`: This method is called to determine if a page should be refreshed because it has expired. Here are the rules it uses to determine whether the page has expired:

- If there is no timestamp item in session state for the page, the page is not expired.
- If there is no timestamp item in view state for the page, the page is not expired.
- If there is a timestamp in both view state and session state and the timestamps are the same, the page is not expired.
- If there is a timestamp in both view state and session state and the timestamps are different, the page is expired.

Listing 6-9:   The code-behind file for the Cart page (VB version)

```
Partial Class Cart
    Inherits System.Web.UI.Page

    Private cart As ShoppingCart

    Protected Sub Page_Load( _                              →1
            ByVal sender As Object, _
            ByVal e As System.EventArgs) _
            Handles Me.Load
        CheckTimeStamps()
        If Session("cart") Is Nothing Then
            cart = New ShoppingCart()
            Session("cart") = cart
        Else
            cart = Session("cart")
        End If
        GridView1.DataSource = cart.GetItems()
        If Not IsPostBack Then
            GridView1.DataBind()
        End If
        btnCheckOut.Enabled = (cart.Count > 0)
    End Sub

    Protected Sub GridView1_RowDeleting( _                  →2
            ByVal sender As Object, _
            ByVal e As
        System.Web.UI.WebControls.GridViewDeleteEventAr
        gs) _
            Handles GridView1.RowDeleting
        cart.DeleteItem(e.RowIndex)
        GridView1.DataBind()
    End Sub

    Protected Sub GridView1_RowEditing( _                   →3
            ByVal sender As Object, _
            ByVal e As
        System.Web.UI.WebControls.GridViewEditEventArgs
        ) _
            Handles GridView1.RowEditing
        GridView1.EditIndex = e.NewEditIndex
        GridView1.DataBind()
    End Sub

    Protected Sub GridView1_RowUpdating( _                  →4
            ByVal sender As Object, _
            ByVal e As
        System.Web.UI.WebControls.GridViewUpdateEventAr
        gs) _
        Handles GridView1.RowUpdating
        Dim cell As DataControlFieldCell
```

(continued)

Listing 6-9 *(continued)*

```vb
        cell = GridView1.Rows(e.RowIndex) _
            .Controls(3)
        Dim t As TextBox = cell.Controls(0)
        Try
            Dim q As Integer
            q = Integer.Parse(t.Text)
            cart.UpdateQuantity(e.RowIndex, q)
        Catch ex As FormatException
            e.Cancel = True
        End Try
        GridView1.EditIndex = -1
        GridView1.DataBind()
    End Sub

    Protected Sub GridView1_RowCancelingEdit( _          →5
            ByVal sender As Object, _
            ByVal e As
        System.Web.UI.WebControls.GridViewCancelEditEve
        ntArgs) _
            Handles GridView1.RowCancelingEdit
        e.Cancel = True
        GridView1.EditIndex = -1
        GridView1.DataBind()
    End Sub

    Protected Sub btnContinue_Click( _                   →6
            ByVal sender As Object, _
            ByVal e As System.EventArgs) _
            Handles btnContinue.Click
        Dim ProductID As String
        ProductID = Request.QueryString("prod")
        Dim CatID As String
        CatID = Request.QueryString("cat")
        If ProductID Is Nothing Then
            If CatID Is Nothing Then
                Response.Redirect("Default.aspx")
            Else
                Response.Redirect( _
                "Default.aspx?cat=" + CatID)
            End If
        Else
            Response.Redirect( _
                "Product.aspx?prod=" + ProductID _
                + "&cat=" + CatID)
        End If
    End Sub

    Private Sub CheckTimeStamps()                        →7
        If IsExpired() Then
            Response.Redirect(Request.Url.OriginalString)
```

```
        Else
            Dim t As DateTime
            t = DateTime.Now
            ViewState.Add("$$TimeStamp", t)
            Dim page As String
            page = Request.Url.AbsoluteUri
            Session.Add(page + "_TimeStamp", t)
        End If
    End Sub

    Private Function IsExpired() As Boolean               →8
        Dim page As String
        page = Request.Url.AbsoluteUri
        If Session(page + "_TimeStamp") Is Nothing Then
            Return False
        ElseIf ViewState("$$TimeStamp") Is Nothing Then
            Return False
        ElseIf Session(page + "_TimeStamp").ToString() _
            = ViewState("$$TimeStamp").ToString() Then
            Return False
        Else
            Return True
        End If
    End Function

End Class
```

Building the Check Out Page

The Check Out page uses a `Wizard` control to walk the user through the three-step process of completing an order. In the first step, the user enters his or her name, address, e-mail address, and phone number. In the second step, the user enters credit card payment information. And in the third step, the user confirms the order. Once the order is confirmed, the Check Out page calls the `InsertOrder` method of the `OrderDB` class to actually write the order to the database.

The following sections present the `.aspx` code for the Check Out page and the C# and VB code-behind files.

The CheckOut.aspx file

Listing 6-10 shows the `.aspx` code for the Check Out page.

Listing 6-10: The Check Out Page (CheckOut.aspx)

```
<%@ Page Language="C#"                                            →1
    MasterPageFile="~/MasterPage.master"
    AutoEventWireup="true"
    CodeFile="CheckOut.aspx.cs"
    Inherits="CheckOut"
    Title="Acme Pirate Supply" %>
<asp:Content ID="Content1" Runat="Server"
    ContentPlaceHolderID="ContentPlaceHolder1">
  <asp:Wizard ID="Wizard1" runat="server"                        →2
    Width="425px"
    ActiveStepIndex="0"
    FinishCompleteButtonText="Submit Order"
    OnFinishButtonClick="Wizard1_FinishButtonClick">
    <WizardSteps>
      <asp:WizardStep runat="server"                             →3
          Title="Shipping">
        Where do you want this order shipped?<br />
        <br />

        <asp:Label ID="Label1" runat="server"                    →4
            BorderStyle="None" Text="Last Name:"
            Width="100px" />
        <asp:TextBox ID="txtLastName" runat="server" />
        <asp:RequiredFieldValidator
            ID="RequiredFieldValidator1" runat="server"
            ControlToValidate="txtLastName"
            ErrorMessage="Required."
            Display="Dynamic" />
        <br />

        <asp:Label ID="Label2" runat="server"                    →5
            BorderStyle="None" Text="First Name:"
            Width="100px" />
        <asp:TextBox ID="txtFirstName" runat="server" />
        <asp:RequiredFieldValidator
            ID="RequiredFieldValidator2" runat="server"
            ControlToValidate="txtFirstName"
            ErrorMessage="Required."
            Display="Dynamic" />
        <br />

        <asp:Label ID="Label3" runat="server"                    →6
            BorderStyle="None" Text="Address:"
            Width="100px" />
        <asp:TextBox ID="txtAddress" runat="server" />
        <asp:RequiredFieldValidator
            ID="RequiredFieldValidator3" runat="server"
            ControlToValidate="txtAddress"
            ErrorMessage="Required."
            Display="Dynamic" />
```

```
<br />

<asp:Label ID="Label4" runat="server"                      →7
    BorderStyle="None" Text="City:"
    Width="100px" />
<asp:TextBox ID="txtCity" runat="server" />
<asp:RequiredFieldValidator
    ID="RequiredFieldValidator4" runat="server"
    ControlToValidate="txtCity"
    ErrorMessage="Required."
    Display="Dynamic" />
<br />

<asp:Label ID="Label5" runat="server"                      →8
    BorderStyle="None" Text="State:"
    Width="100px" />
<asp:DropDownList ID="ddlState" runat="server">
  <asp:ListItem Value="AL">Alabama</asp:ListItem>
  <asp:ListItem Value="AK">Alaska</asp:ListItem>
  <asp:ListItem Value="AZ">Arizona</asp:ListItem>
  <asp:ListItem Value="AR">Arkansas</asp:ListItem>
  <asp:ListItem Value="CA">California
      </asp:ListItem>
  <asp:ListItem Value="CO">Colorado</asp:ListItem>
  <asp:ListItem Value="CT">Connecticut
      </asp:ListItem>
  <asp:ListItem Value="DE">Deleware</asp:ListItem>
  <asp:ListItem Value="DC">District of Columbia
      </asp:ListItem>
  <asp:ListItem Value="FL">Florida</asp:ListItem>
  <asp:ListItem Value="GA">Georgia</asp:ListItem>
  <asp:ListItem Value="HI">Hawaii</asp:ListItem>
  <asp:ListItem Value="ID">Idaho</asp:ListItem>
  <asp:ListItem Value="IL">Illinois</asp:ListItem>
  <asp:ListItem Value="IN">Indiana</asp:ListItem>
  <asp:ListItem Value="IA">Iowa</asp:ListItem>
  <asp:ListItem Value="KS">Kansas</asp:ListItem>
  <asp:ListItem Value="KY">Kentucky</asp:ListItem>
  <asp:ListItem Value="LA">Louisianna
      </asp:ListItem>
  <asp:ListItem Value="ME">Maine</asp:ListItem>
  <asp:ListItem Value="MD">Maryland</asp:ListItem>
  <asp:ListItem Value="MA">Massachusetts
      </asp:ListItem>
  <asp:ListItem Value="MI">Michigan</asp:ListItem>
  <asp:ListItem
   Value="MN">Minnesota</asp:ListItem>
  <asp:ListItem Value="MS">Mississippi
      </asp:ListItem>
  <asp:ListItem Value="MO">Missouri</asp:ListItem>
  <asp:ListItem Value="MT">Montana</asp:ListItem>
```

(continued)

Listing 6-10 *(continued)*

```
      <asp:ListItem Value="NE">Nebraska</asp:ListItem>
      <asp:ListItem Value="NV">Nevada</asp:ListItem>
      <asp:ListItem Value="NH">New Hampshire
          </asp:ListItem>
      <asp:ListItem Value="NJ">New Jersey
          </asp:ListItem>
      <asp:ListItem Value="NM">New Mexico
          </asp:ListItem>
      <asp:ListItem Value="NY">New York</asp:ListItem>
      <asp:ListItem Value="NC">North Carolina
          </asp:ListItem>
      <asp:ListItem Value="ND">North Dakota
          </asp:ListItem>
      <asp:ListItem Value="OH">Ohio</asp:ListItem>
      <asp:ListItem Value="OK">Oklahoma</asp:ListItem>
      <asp:ListItem Value="OR">Oregon</asp:ListItem>
      <asp:ListItem Value="PA">Pennsylvania
          </asp:ListItem>
      <asp:ListItem Value="RI">Rhode Island
          </asp:ListItem>
      <asp:ListItem Value="SC">South Carolina
          </asp:ListItem>
      <asp:ListItem Value="SD">South Dakota
          </asp:ListItem>
      <asp:ListItem
       Value="TN">Tennessee</asp:ListItem>
      <asp:ListItem Value="TX">Texas</asp:ListItem>
      <asp:ListItem Value="UT">Utah</asp:ListItem>
      <asp:ListItem Value="VT">Vermont</asp:ListItem>
      <asp:ListItem Value="VA">Virginia</asp:ListItem>
      <asp:ListItem Value="WA">Washington
          </asp:ListItem>
      <asp:ListItem Value="WV">West Virginia
          </asp:ListItem>
      <asp:ListItem
       Value="WI">Wisconsin</asp:ListItem>
      <asp:ListItem Value="WY">Wyoming</asp:ListItem>
</asp:DropDownList>
<br />

<asp:Label ID="Label6" runat="server"                →9
    BorderStyle="None" Text="Zip Code:"
    Width="100px" />
<asp:TextBox ID="txtZipCode" runat="server" />
<asp:RequiredFieldValidator
    ID="RequiredFieldValidator5" runat="server"
    ControlToValidate="txtZipCode"
    ErrorMessage="Required."
    Display="Dynamic" />
<br />

<asp:Label ID="Label7" runat="server"                →10
```

```
             BorderStyle="None" Text="Phone Number:"
             Width="100px" />
      <asp:TextBox ID="txtPhoneNumber" runat="server" />
      <asp:RequiredFieldValidator
          ID="RequiredFieldValidator6" runat="server"
          ControlToValidate="txtPhoneNumber"
          ErrorMessage="Required."
          Display="Dynamic" />
      <br />

      <asp:Label ID="Label8" runat="server"                →11
          BorderStyle="None" Text="Email address:"
          Width="100px" />
      <asp:TextBox ID="txtEmail" runat="server" />
      <asp:RequiredFieldValidator
          ID="RequiredFieldValidator7" runat="server"
          ControlToValidate="txtEmail"
          ErrorMessage="Required."
          Display="Dynamic" />
      <br />
</asp:WizardStep>

<asp:WizardStep runat="server"                           →12
      Title="Billing">
   How do you want to pay for this order?<br />
   <br />

   <asp:Label ID="Label11" runat="server"                →13
       BorderStyle="None" Text="Card type:"
       Width="100px" />
   <asp:DropDownList ID="ddlCardType"
       runat="server">
     <asp:ListItem Value="VISA">Visa</asp:ListItem>
     <asp:ListItem Value="MC">MasterCard
        </asp:ListItem>
     <asp:ListItem Value="AMEX">American Express
        </asp:ListItem>
   </asp:DropDownList>
   <br />

   <asp:Label ID="Label13" runat="server"                →14
       BorderStyle="None" Text="Card number:"
       Width="100px" />
   <asp:TextBox ID="txtCardNumber" runat="server" />
   <asp:RequiredFieldValidator
       ID="RequiredFieldValidator8" runat="server"
       ControlToValidate="txtCardNumber"
       ErrorMessage="Required." Display="Dynamic" />
   <br /><br />

   <asp:Label ID="Label15" runat="server"                →15
       BorderStyle="None" Text="Exp. Month:"
```

(continued)

Listing 6-10 *(continued)*

```
            Width="100px" />
    <asp:DropDownList ID="ddlExpirationMonth"
        runat="server">
      <asp:ListItem Value="1">January</asp:ListItem>
      <asp:ListItem Value="2">February</asp:ListItem>
      <asp:ListItem Value="3">March</asp:ListItem>
      <asp:ListItem Value="4">April</asp:ListItem>
      <asp:ListItem Value="5">May</asp:ListItem>
      <asp:ListItem Value="6">June</asp:ListItem>
      <asp:ListItem Value="7">July</asp:ListItem>
      <asp:ListItem Value="8">August</asp:ListItem>
      <asp:ListItem Value="9">September</asp:ListItem>
      <asp:ListItem Value="10">October</asp:ListItem>
      <asp:ListItem Value="11">November</asp:ListItem>
      <asp:ListItem Value="12">December</asp:ListItem>
    </asp:DropDownList>
    <br />

    <asp:Label ID="Label16" runat="server"                 →16
        BorderStyle="None" Text="Exp. Year:"
        Width="100px" />
    <asp:TextBox ID="txtExpirationYear" runat="server"
        Width="82px" />
    <asp:RequiredFieldValidator
        ID="RequiredFieldValidator9" runat="server"
        ControlToValidate="txtExpirationYear"
        ErrorMessage="Required." Display="Dynamic" />
    <asp:RangeValidator ID="RangeValidator1"
        runat="server"
        ControlToValidate="txtExpirationYear"
        Display="Dynamic"
        ErrorMessage="Incorrect date."
        MaximumValue="2099"
        MinimumValue="2005"
        Type="Integer" />
</asp:WizardStep>

<asp:WizardStep runat="server"                             →17
    Title="Confirmation">
  Your order is ready to be processed.<br />
  <br />
  <asp:Label ID="Label9" runat="server"
      BorderStyle="None" Text="Subtotal:"
      Width="80px" />
  <asp:Label ID="lblSubtotal"                              →18
      runat="server" />
  <br />
  <asp:Label ID="Label10" runat="server"
      BorderStyle="None" Text="Sales Tax:"
      Width="80px" />
  <asp:Label ID="lblSalesTax"                              →19
      runat="server" />
```

```
        <br />
        <asp:Label ID="Label12" runat="server"
            BorderStyle="None" Text="Shipping:"
            Width="80px" />
        <asp:Label ID="lblShipping"                          →20
            runat="server" />
        <br />
        <asp:Label ID="Label14" runat="server"
            BorderStyle="None" Text="Total:"
            Width="80px" />
        <asp:Label ID="lblTotal"                             →21
            runat="server" />
        <br /><br />
        Click Submit Order to complete your order.<br />
    </asp:WizardStep>

  </WizardSteps>
  <SideBarStyle VerticalAlign="Top" />                       →22
  </asp:Wizard>
</asp:Content>
```

This is a long listing because the `Wizard` control has three steps, each of which is like an entire Web page unto itself. The following list describes each of the controls defined for this page:

→ **1**   In the `Page` directive, remember to change the `Language` attribute to `VB` and the `AutoEventWireup` attribute to `false` if you're working with Visual Basic.

→ **2**   The `Wizard` control defines the wizard displayed by the Check Out page. The `ActiveStepIndex` attribute specifies the index of the step the wizard should start with when the page is first displayed, and the `FinishCompleteButtonText` attribute specifies the text displayed on the Finish button in the final step of the wizard.

Whenever you run the application from Visual Studio, this attribute is changed to match the step that is currently displayed in the design window. As a result, you should always switch to the first Wizard step before running the application from Visual Studio.

If you're working in Visual Basic instead of C#, you should remove the `OnFinishButtonClick` attribute.

→ **3**   The `<WizardSteps>` element defines the steps used by the wizard. Each of these steps is then defined by an `<asp:WizardStep>` element. This one defines the first step in the Wizard, titled "Shipping." The content for this step begins with the text "Where do you want this order shipped?" Then items →4 through →11 define the controls that allow the user to enter the shipping information.

→ **4**   A label, text box, and required-field validator let the user enter his or her last name.

→ 5 A label, text box, and required-field validator let the user enter his or her first name.

→ 6 A label, text box, and required-field validator let the user enter his or her address.

→ 7 A label, text box, and required-field validator let the user enter the city.

→ 8 A label and a drop-down list let the user select the state. As you can see, 51 <ListItem> elements are used to populate the drop-down list with the names and abbreviations of the 50 states plus the District of Columbia.

→ 9 A label, text box, and required-field validator let the user enter his or her Zip code.

→ 10 A label, text box, and required-field validator let the user enter his or her phone number.

→ 11 A label, text box, and required-field validator let the user enter his or her e-mail address. This is the last set of controls for the first wizard step.

→ 12 The second wizard step defines the controls that let the user enter his or her credit card information. This step is titled "Billing."

→ 13 A label and a drop-down list let the user choose the credit card type. <ListItem> elements are used to fill the drop-down list with three popular credit card types: Visa, MasterCard, and American Express. If you want to accept additional credit card types, you can add additional <ListItem> elements.

→ 14 A label, text box, and required-field validator let the user enter the credit card number. For an actual application, you'll want to do more validation than a simple required-field validator provides. In particular, you'll want to make sure that the number entered conforms to the requirements for each credit card type. (The requirements vary depending on card type; I'll leave it to you to provide this validation.)

→ 15 A label and drop-down list let the user select the credit card's expiration month. Twelve <ListItem> elements fill the list with the months of the year.

→ 16 A label, text box, and two validators let the user enter the year the credit card expires. The required-field validator ensures that the user enters a value, and the range validator requires that the entry be an integer between 2005 and 2099.

Note that this validation logic doesn't prevent the user from entering data based on a card that's already expired. You may want to provide more extensive validation here to ensure that the year is greater than or equal to the current year — *and* (if the year is equal to the current year) that the month is greater than or equal to the current month.

→ **17** The third wizard step defines the final step of the check-out process, which simply displays a summary of the order and allows the user to submit the order for final processing. The title of this step is "Confirmation."

→ **18** This label displays the order subtotal, obtained by adding the total for each item in the shopping cart.

→ **19** This label displays the sales tax for the order.

→ **20** This label displays the shipping charges for the order.

→ **21** This label displays the order total. This is the last control in the third wizard step.

→ **22** The `Wizard` control ends with a `<SideBarStyle>` element that defines how the sidebar navigation links will be aligned. In this case, `VerticalAlign="Top"` indicates that the links will appear at the top of the sidebar area. By default, they are centered vertically.

The code-behind file for the Check Out page

Mercifully, the code-behind file for the Check Out page is not nearly as long as the `.aspx` file (or as long as the code-behind for the Cart page, for that matter). Listing 6-11 shows the C# version, and the Visual Basic version is shown in Listing 6-12.

Listing 6-11:   The code-behind file for the Check Out page (C#)

```
using System;
using System.Data;
using System.Configuration;
using System.Collections;
using System.Web;
using System.Web.Security;
using System.Web.UI;
using System.Web.UI.WebControls;
using System.Web.UI.WebControls.WebParts;
using System.Web.UI.HtmlControls;

public partial class CheckOut : System.Web.UI.Page
{
    private Order order;                                    →1
    private Customer cust;
    private ShoppingCart cart;

    protected void Page_Load(object sender,                 →2
        EventArgs e)
    {
```

(continued)

Listing 6-11 *(continued)*

```
        cart = (ShoppingCart)Session["cart"];

        if (Session["order"] == null)                          →3
        {
            order = new Order(DateTime.Now,
                null, (ShoppingCart)Session["cart"]);
            Session["order"] = order;
        }
        else
        {
            order = (Order)Session["order"];
            cart = order.Cart;
        }

        cust = new Customer(txtLastName.Text,                  →4
            txtFirstName.Text,
            txtAddress.Text,
            txtCity.Text,
            ddlState.SelectedValue,
            txtZipCode.Text,
            txtPhoneNumber.Text,
            txtEmail.Text);
        order.Cust = cust;

        lblSubtotal.Text                                       →5
            = order.SubTotal.ToString("c");
        lblSalesTax.Text
            = order.SalesTax.ToString("c");
        lblShipping.Text
            = order.Shipping.ToString("c");
        lblTotal.Text
            = order.Total.ToString("c");
    }

    protected void Wizard1_FinishButtonClick(                  →6
        object sender, WizardNavigationEventArgs e)
    {
        // process credit card information here

        bool success = OrderDB.WriteOrder(order);
        Session["cart"] = null;
        Session["order"] = null;
        if (success)
            Response.Redirect("Completed.aspx");
        else
            Response.Redirect("Completed.aspx?Error=1");
    }

}
```

The Wizard Control

The `Wizard` control is a new feature in ASP.NET 2.0 that makes it easy to create wizards that walk the user through a series of steps. A wizard consists of one or more steps and navigation buttons that let the user move from step to step. Only the content defined for the current step is displayed when the page containing a Wizard control is rendered.

The steps for the Wizard control are defined by the `<WizardSteps>` element, which can contain one or more `<WizardStep>` child elements. There are five different types of steps you can create:

✔ **Start:** The first step. This step includes a Next button but not a Previous button.

✔ **Step:** An intermediate step. This step includes both a Next and a Previous button.

✔ **Finish:** The final step that collects data from the user. Instead of a Next button, this step includes a Finish button.

✔ **Complete:** The last step displayed by the wizard, after the user clicks the Finish button. No navigation buttons are included on this step.

✔ **Auto:** A step whose type is determined by its position in the `<WizardSteps>` element. (For example, the first step declared is the start step.)

Here's a basic skeleton of a simple Wizard control with three steps:

```
<asp:Wizard id="Wizard1" runat="server">
    <WizardSteps>
        <asp:WizardStep steptype="Start" title="Step One">
            Content for step one goes here.
        </asp:WizardStep>
        <asp:WizardStep steptype="Step" title="Step Two">
            Content for step two goes here.
        </asp:WizardStep>
        <asp:WizardStep steptype="Finish" title="Step
Three">
            Content for step three goes here.
        </asp:WizardStep>
    </WizardSteps>
</asp:Wizard>
```

Note that you can edit the steps individually in Visual Studio using the Smart Tag menu, which you can summon by clicking the small arrow that appears in the upper-right corner of the Wizard when you're working in Design view. You can select the step you want to edit from a drop-down list that appears in the Smart Tag menu. And you can add or remove steps by choosing Add/Remove WizardSteps from the Smart Tag menu.

The following paragraphs explain the key points of this code-behind file:

→ **1** Three variables are defined so they can be accessed throughout the class. The first, `order`, references the `Order` object for the order to be processed. The second, `cust`, references the `Customer` object. And the third, `cart`, references the user's shopping cart.

→ **2** The `Page_Load` method is executed each time the page loads. It begins by retrieving the shopping cart from session state and assigning it to the `cart` variable.

→ **3** This `if` statement retrieves the `order` item from session state if it exists. If there is no `order` item already in session state, a new `Order` object is created using the current time for the order date, `null` (C#) or `Nothing` (VB) for the customer, and the `cart` item from session state for the shopping cart. Then the new `Order` object is added to session state.

→ **4** Next, a new `Customer` object is created, using values entered by the user in the first wizard step. Note that if the user hasn't yet completed this step, these values will be blank. The new `Customer` object is then assigned to the `Cust` property of the `order` object.

→ **5** These four assignment statements assign formatted values to the labels in the Confirmation step of the wizard, using properties of the `Order` object.

→ **6** The `Wizard1_FinishButtonClick` method is called when the user clicks the Submit Order button in the third wizard step. It begins with a comment that indicates where you should place the code that processes the customer's credit card. Then it calls the `WriteOrder` method of the `OrderDB` class to write the order to the database. The result of this call is saved in the Boolean variable `success`. Next, the `cart` and `order` items in session state are cleared. Finally, the user is redirected to the `Completed.aspx` page. A query string field named `Error` is passed if the `WriteOrder` method returned `false`.

Listing 6-12:   The code-behind file for the Check Out page (VB)

```
Partial Class CheckOut
    Inherits System.Web.UI.Page

    Private order As Order                                    →1
    Private cust As Customer
    Private cart As ShoppingCart

    Protected Sub Page_Load( _                                →2
        ByVal sender As Object, _
        ByVal e As System.EventArgs) _
        Handles Me.Load
```

```
        cart = Session("cart")

        If Session("order") Is Nothing Then              →3
            order = New Order(DateTime.Now, _
                Nothing, Session("cart"))
            Session("order") = order
        Else
            order = Session("order")
            cart = order.Cart
        End If

        cust = New Customer(txtLastName.Text, _          →4
            txtFirstName.Text, _
            txtAddress.Text, _
            txtCity.Text, _
            ddlState.SelectedValue, _
            txtZipCode.Text, _
            txtPhoneNumber.Text, _
            txtEmail.Text)
        order.Cust = cust

        lblSubtotal.Text _                               →5
            = order.SubTotal.ToString("c")
        lblSalesTax.Text _
            = order.SalesTax.ToString("c")
        lblShipping.Text _
            = order.Shipping.ToString("c")
        lblTotal.Text _
            = order.Total.ToString("c")
    End Sub

    Protected Sub Wizard1_FinishButtonClick( _           →6
        ByVal sender As Object, _
        ByVal e As
          System.Web.UI.WebControls.WizardNavigationEvent
          Args) _
        Handles Wizard1.FinishButtonClick

        ' process credit card information here

        Dim success As Boolean
        success = OrderDB.WriteOrder(order)
        Session("cart") = Nothing
        Session("order") = Nothing
        If success Then
            Response.Redirect("Completed.aspx")
        Else
            Response.Redirect("Completed.aspx?Error=1")
        End If
    End Sub
End Class
```

Creating the Customer Class

The Customer class provides the customer information required to process an order. Its constructors and properties are spelled out earlier in this chapter (refer to Table 6-4). Listing 6-13 shows the C# version of this class. The Visual Basic version is shown in Listing 6-14.

Listing 6-13:   The Customer class (C# version)

```csharp
using System;
using System.Data;
using System.Configuration;
using System.Web;
using System.Web.Security;
using System.Web.UI;
using System.Web.UI.WebControls;
using System.Web.UI.WebControls.WebParts;
using System.Web.UI.HtmlControls;

public class Customer
{
    private string _lastName;                          →1
    private string _firstName;
    private string _address;
    private string _city;
    private string _state;
    private string _zipCode;
    private string _phoneNumber;
    private string _email;

    public Customer()                                  →2
    {
    }

    public Customer(string lastName,                   →3
        string firstName, string address,
        string city, string state,
        string zipCode, string phoneNumber,
        string email)
    {
        this.LastName = lastName;
        this.FirstName = firstName;
        this.Address = address;
        this.City = city;
        this.State = state;
        this.ZipCode = zipCode;
        this.PhoneNumber = phoneNumber;
        this.Email = email;
    }

    public string LastName                             →4
```

```
{
    get
    {
        return _lastName;
    }
    set
    {
        _lastName = value;
    }
}

public string FirstName                                    →5
{
    get
    {
        return _firstName;
    }
    set
    {
        _firstName = value;
    }
}

public string Address                                      →6
{
    get
    {
        return _address;
    }
    set
    {
        _address = value;
    }
}

public string City                                         →7
{
    get
    {
        return _city;
    }
    set
    {
        _city= value;
    }
}

public string State                                        →8
{
    get
    {
```

(continued)

Listing 6-13 *(continued)*

```
            return _state;
        }
        set
        {
            _state = value;
        }
    }

    public string ZipCode                                    →9
    {
        get
        {
            return _zipCode;
        }
        set
        {
            _zipCode = value;
        }
    }

    public string Email                                      →10
    {
        get
        {
            return _email;
        }
        set
        {
            _email = value;
        }
    }

    public string PhoneNumber                                →11
    {
        get
        {
            return _phoneNumber;
        }
        set
        {
            _phoneNumber = value;
        }
    }
}
```

The following paragraphs define each component of this class:

→ **1**   The class begins by defining private instance variables that are
         used to hold the values associated with the class properties.
         By convention, each of these variable names begins with an

underscore to indicate that it corresponds to a property with the same name.

→ **2**   The default constructor creates a `Customer` object with default values for each of its properties.

→ **3**   This constructor accepts arguments that initialize the customer data. Notice that the assignment statements don't directly assign values to the instance variables of the class. Instead, they use the properties to assign these values. That way, any validation routines written in the property setters will be used. (In this example, none of the property setters have validation routines. Still, it's a good practice to follow just in case.)

→ **4**   The `LastName` property represents the customer's last name. Its get routine simply returns the value of the `_lastName` instance variable, and its set routine simply sets the `_lastName` variable to the value passed via the `value` argument.

→ **5**   The `FirstName` property represents the customer's first name, which is stored in the `_firstName` instance variable.

→ **6**   The `Address` property represents the customer's address, stored in the `_address` instance variable.

→ **7**   The `City` property represents the customer's city, stored in the `_city` instance variable.

→ **8**   The `State` property represents the customer's state, stored in the `_state` instance variable.

→ **9**   The `ZipCode` property represents the customer's Zip code, stored in the `_zipCode` instance variable.

→ **10** The `Email` property represents the customer's e-mail address, stored in the `_email` instance variable.

→ **11** The `PhoneNumber` property represents the customer's phone number, stored in the `_phoneNumber` instance variable.

Listing 6-14:   The Customer class (VB version)

```
Imports Microsoft.VisualBasic

Public Class Customer
    Private _lastName As String                                    →1
    Private _firstName As String
    Private _address As String
    Private _city As String
    Private _state As String
    Private _zipCode As String
    Private _phoneNumber As String
```

(continued)

Listing 6-14 *(continued)*

```
Private _email As String

Public Sub New()                                            →2
End Sub

Public Sub New(ByVal lastName As String, _                  →3
        ByVal firstName As String, _
        ByVal address As String, _
        ByVal city As String, _
        ByVal state As String, _
        ByVal zipCode As String, _
        ByVal phoneNumber As String, _
        ByVal email As String)
    Me.LastName = lastName
    Me.FirstName = firstName
    Me.Address = address
    Me.City = city
    Me.State = state
    Me.ZipCode = zipCode
    Me.PhoneNumber = phoneNumber
    Me.Email = email
End Sub

Public Property LastName() As String                        →4
    Get
        Return _lastName
    End Get
    Set(ByVal value As String)
        _lastName = value
    End Set
End Property

Public Property FirstName() As String                       →5
    Get
        Return _firstName
    End Get
    Set(ByVal value As String)
        _firstName = value
    End Set
End Property

Public Property Address() As String                         →6
    Get
        Return _address
    End Get
    Set(ByVal value As String)
        _address = value
    End Set
End Property

Public Property City() As String                            →7
    Get
```

```
            Return _city
        End Get
        Set(ByVal value As String)
            _city = value
        End Set
    End Property

    Public Property State() As String              →8
        Get
            Return _state
        End Get
        Set(ByVal value As String)
            _state = value
        End Set
    End Property

    Public Property ZipCode() As String            →9
        Get
            Return _zipCode
        End Get
        Set(ByVal value As String)
            _zipCode = value
        End Set
    End Property

    Public Property Email() As String              →10
        Get
            Return _email
        End Get
        Set(ByVal value As String)
            _email = value
        End Set
    End Property

    Public Property PhoneNumber() As String        →11
        Get
            Return _phoneNumber
        End Get
        Set(ByVal value As String)
            _phoneNumber = value
        End Set
    End Property
End Class
```

Creating the ShoppingCart Class

The ShoppingCart class represents the user's virtual shopping cart, as
described in detail earlier in this chapter (see Table 6-5). Now, Listing 6-15
presents the C# version of the ShoppingCart class, and the Visual Basic version is shown in Listing 6-16.

Listing 6-15:   The ShoppingCart class (C# version)

```csharp
using System;
using System.Data;
using System.Configuration;
using System.Web;
using System.Web.Security;
using System.Web.UI;
using System.Web.UI.WebControls;
using System.Web.UI.WebControls.WebParts;
using System.Web.UI.HtmlControls;
using System.Collections.Generic;

public class ShoppingCart
{
    private List<CartItem> _cart;                               →1

    public ShoppingCart()                                       →2
    {
        _cart = new List<CartItem>();
    }

    public List<CartItem> GetItems()                            →3
    {
        return _cart;
    }

    public void AddItem(string id, string name,                 →4
        decimal price)
    {
        bool itemFound = false;
        foreach (CartItem item in _cart)
        {
            if (item.ID == id)
            {
                item.Quantity += 1;
                itemFound = true;
            }
        }
        if (!itemFound)
        {
            CartItem item =
                new CartItem(id, name, price, 1);
            _cart.Add(item);
        }
    }

    public void UpdateQuantity(int index,                       →5
        int quantity)
    {
        CartItem item = _cart[index];
        item.Quantity = quantity;
```

```
    }

    public void DeleteItem(int index)                     →6
    {
        _cart.RemoveAt(index);
    }

    public int Count                                      →7
    {
        get
        {
            return _cart.Count;
        }
    }
}
```

The following paragraphs describe the important details of this class:

→ **1**   A private instance variable named _cart holds the contents of the shopping cart. This variable uses the new Generics feature to create a list object that can only hold objects of type CartItem. (For more information about generics, see the sidebar "Using Generics" later in this section.)

To use the List class, you must provide an imports (C#) or Using (VB) statement that specifies the namespace System. Collections.Generic.

→ **2**   The constructor for this class creates an instance of the List class and assigns it to the _cart variable.

→ **3**   The GetItems method returns a List that contains CartItem objects. It simply returns the _cart variable.

→ **4**   The AddItem method adds an item to the shopping cart, using the product ID, name, and price values passed as parameters. It uses a for each loop to search the items in the cart. If one of the items already in the cart has a product ID that matches the ID passed as a parameter, that item's quantity is incremented and a local variable named itemFound is set to true. If a matching item is not found by the for each loop, a new CartItem object is created with a quantity of 1. Then the new cart item is added to the list.

→ **5**   The UpdateQuantity method changes the quantity for a specified product. It uses the index value passed as a parameter to access the cart item, then sets the item's Quantity property to the value passed via the quantity parameter.

→ **6**   The DeleteItem method uses the RemoveAt method of the List class to remove the item at the index passed via the parameter.

→ **7**   The Count property simply returns the Count property of the _cart list. Notice that since this is a read-only property, no set routine is provided.

Listing 6-16: The ShoppingCart class (VB version)

```vb
Imports Microsoft.VisualBasic
Imports System.Collections.Generic

Public Class ShoppingCart

    Private _cart As List(Of CartItem)                          →1

    Public Sub New()                                            →2
        _cart = New List(Of CartItem)()
    End Sub

    Public Function GetItems() As List(Of CartItem)            →3
        Return _cart
    End Function

    Public Sub AddItem(ByVal id As String, _                    →4
            ByVal name As String, _
            ByVal price As Decimal)
        Dim itemFound As Boolean = False
        For Each item As CartItem In _cart
            If item.ID = id Then
                item.Quantity += 1
                itemFound = True
            End If
        Next
        If Not itemFound Then
            Dim item As CartItem
            item = New CartItem(id, name, price, 1)
            cart.Add(item)
        End If
    End Sub

    Public Sub UpdateQuantity( _                                →5
            ByVal index As Integer,
            ByVal quantity As Integer)
        Dim item As CartItem
        item = _cart(index)
        item.Quantity = quantity
    End Sub

    Public Sub DeleteItem(ByVal index As Integer)               →6
        _cart.RemoveAt(index)
    End Sub

    Public ReadOnly Property Count() As Integer                 →7
        Get
            Return _cart.Count
        End Get
    End Property

End Class
```

Using Generics

Generics is a new feature of both the C# and the Visual Basic programming languages. The purpose of the Generics feature is to prevent a common problem when dealing with .NET collection classes. Suppose you want to store a collection of `Customer` objects. You can do that by declaring an `ArrayList` object, then adding `Customer` objects to the array list. However, nothing prevents you from adding other types of objects to the array list. If you were careless, you could also add a `ShoppingCart` object to the array list.

With the new Generics feature, you can create collections that are designed to hold only objects of a specified type. For example, you can create a list that can hold only `Customer` objects. Then, if you try to add a `ShoppingCart` object to the list by accident, an exception will be thrown.

Along with the Generics feature comes a new namespace (`System.Collections.Generic`) with a set of collection classes that are designed to work with the Generics feature. Here are the classes you'll probably use most:

- **List**: A generic array list.

- **SortedList**: A generic list that's kept in sorted order.

- **LinkedList**: A generic linked list.

- **Stack**: A generic last-in, first-out stack.

- **Queue**: A generic first-in, first-out queue.

- **Dictionary**: A generic collection of key/value pairs.

- **SortedDictionary**: A generic collection of key/value pairs kept in sorted order.

The syntax for using the Generics feature takes a little getting used to. Here's a C# example that defines a variable of type `List` whose objects are `Customer` types, then creates an instance of the list and assigns it to the variable:

```
List<Customer> custlist;
    custlist = new
    List<Customer>();
```

Notice how the generic type is enclosed in greater-than and less-than symbols.

Here's the same example in Visual Basic:

```
Dim custlist As List(Of
    Customer)
    custlist = New List(Of
    Customer)()
```

As you can see, Visual Basic uses the `Of` keyword to indicate the generic type.

Creating the CartItem Class

The `CartItem` class defines an item in the user's shopping cart. The `ShoppingCart` class itself (presented in the previous section) is basically a list of `CartItem` objects. For a list of properties provided by the `CartItem` class, refer to Table 6-6. Listings 6-17 and 6-18 present the C# and Visual Basic versions of this class.

Listing 6-17: **The CartItem class (C# version)**

```csharp
using System;
using System.Data;
using System.Configuration;
using System.Web;
using System.Web.Security;
using System.Web.UI;
using System.Web.UI.WebControls;
using System.Web.UI.WebControls.WebParts;
using System.Web.UI.HtmlControls;

public class CartItem
{
    private string _id;                                          →1
    private string _name;
    private decimal _price;
    private int _quantity;

    public CartItem()                                            →2
    {
        this.ID = "";
        this.Name = "";
        this.Price = 0.0m;
        this.Quantity = 0;
    }

    public CartItem(string id, string name,                      →3
        decimal price, int quantity)
    {
        this.ID = id;
        this.Name = name;
        this.Price = price;
        this.Quantity = quantity;
    }


    public string ID                                             →4
    {
        get
        {
            return _id;
        }
        set
        {
            _id = value;
        }
    }

    public string Name                                           →5
    {
        get
        {
            return _name;
```

```
        }
        set
        {
            _name = value;
        }
    }

    public decimal Price                                    →6
    {
        get
        {
            return _price;
        }
        set
        {
            _price = value;
        }
    }

    public int Quantity                                     →7
    {
        get
        {
            return _quantity;
        }
        set
        {
            _quantity = value;
        }
    }

    public decimal Total                                    →8
    {
        get
        {
            return _price * _quantity;
        }
    }
}
```

Here are the key points to take note of in these listings:

→ **1**　　The private instance variables _id, _name, _price, and _quantity hold the values for the cart item's properties.

→ **2**　　The first constructor, which has no parameters, simply initializes the class properties to default values.

→ **3**　　The second constructor lets you create a CartItem object and set the ID, Name, Price, and Quantity properties at the same time.

→ **4**　　The ID property provides the ID of the product referred to by the cart item. It uses the private instance variable id to store its value.

→ **5**   The Name property represents the name of the product referred to by the cart item. It uses the private instance variable name.

→ **6**   The Price property represents the price of the product. It uses the _price variable to store its value.

→ **7**   The Quantity property records the quantity for the cart item. It stores its value in the _quantity variable.

→ **8**   The Total property returns the value Price property multiplied by the Quantity property. Notice that this property's value isn't stored in an instance variable. Instead, the value is recalculated each time it is accessed.

Listing 6-18:   The CartItem class (VB version)

```
Imports Microsoft.VisualBasic

Public Class CartItem
    Private _id As String                                →1
    Private _name As String
    Private _price As Decimal
    Private _quantity As Integer

    Public Sub New()                                     →2
        Me.ID = ""
        Me.Name = ""
        Me.Price = 0.0
        Me.Quantity = 0
    End Sub

    Public Sub New(ByVal id As String, _                 →3
            ByVal name As String, _
            ByVal price As Decimal, _
            ByVal quantity As Integer)
        Me.ID = id
        Me.Name = name
        Me.Price = price
        Me.Quantity = quantity
    End Sub

    Public Property ID() As String                       →4
        Get
            Return _id
        End Get
        Set(ByVal value As String)
            _id = value
        End Set
    End Property

    Public Property Name() As String                     →5
        Get
            Return _name
```

```
            End Get
            Set(ByVal value As String)
                _name = value
            End Set
        End Property

        Public Property Price() As Decimal          →6
            Get
                Return _price
            End Get
            Set(ByVal value As Decimal)
                _price = value
            End Set
        End Property

        Public Property Quantity() As Integer        →7
            Get
                Return _quantity
            End Get
            Set(ByVal value As Integer)
                _quantity = value
            End Set
        End Property

        Public ReadOnly Property Total() As Decimal   →8
            Get
                Return _price * _quantity
            End Get
        End Property
End Class
```

Creating the Order Class

The Order class represents the order placed by the user. Its main purpose in life is to serve as the parameter passed to the WriteOrder method of the OrderDB class. The constructors and properties of this class appear back in Table 6-7; Listings 6-19 and 6-20 provide the C# and Visual Basic versions of this class.

Listing 6-19:   The Order class (C# version)

```
using System;
using System.Data;
using System.Configuration;
using System.Web;
using System.Web.Security;
```

(continued)

Listing 6-19 *(continued)*

```csharp
using System.Web.UI;
using System.Web.UI.WebControls;
using System.Web.UI.WebControls.WebParts;
using System.Web.UI.HtmlControls;

public class Order
{
    private DateTime _orderDate;                              →1
    private Customer _cust;
    private ShoppingCart _cart;

    public Order()                                           →2
    {
        _cust = new Customer();
        _cart = new ShoppingCart();
    }

    public Order(DateTime orderDate,                         →3
        Customer Cust, ShoppingCart Cart)
    {
        this.OrderDate = orderDate;
        this.Cust = Cust;
        this.Cart = Cart;
    }

    public DateTime OrderDate                                →4
    {
        get
        {
            return _orderDate;
        }
        set
        {
            _orderDate = value;
        }
    }

    public Customer Cust                                     →5
    {
        get
        {
            return _cust;
        }
        set
        {
            _cust = value;
        }
    }

    public ShoppingCart Cart                                 →6
    {
        get
```

```
            {
                return _cart;
            }
        set
            {
                _cart = value;
            }
    }

    public decimal SubTotal                              →7
    {
        get
        {
            decimal subTotal = 0;
            foreach (CartItem item in _cart.GetItems())
                subTotal += item.Total;
            return subTotal;
        }
    }

    public decimal SalesTax                              →8
    {
        get
        {
            if (this.Cust.State.Equals("CA"))
                return this.SubTotal * 0.0775m;
            else
                return 0.0m;

        }
    }

    public decimal Shipping                              →9
    {
        get
        {
            int count = 0;
            foreach (CartItem item in _cart.GetItems())
                count += item.Quantity;
            return count * 2.00m;
        }
    }

    public decimal Total                                 →10
    {
        get
        {
            return this.SubTotal + this.Shipping
                + this.SalesTax;
        }
    }
}
```

The following paragraphs draw your attention to the highlights of this class:

→ **1**   Private instance variables hold the data for the order. The _orderDate variable holds the order's date, while the _cust and _cart variables hold the Customer and ShoppingCart objects associated with the order.

→ **2**   The parameterless constructor creates new Customer and ShoppingCart objects for the order.

→ **3**   The second constructor lets you create an Order object by passing the order date, customer, and shopping cart data as parameters.

→ **4**   The OrderDate property lets you set or retrieve the order date.

→ **5**   The Cust property lets you set or retrieve the order's Customer object.

→ **6**   The Cart property lets you set or retrieve the order's shopping cart.

→ **7**   The SubTotal property is a read-only property that returns the total for the items in the order's shopping cart. It uses a for each loop to calculate this value by adding up the Total property for each item in the shopping cart. Notice that the cart's GetItems method is called to retrieve the items.

→ **8**   The SalesTax property is a read-only property that calculates the sales tax. If the customer lives in California, the tax is calculated at 7.75 percent. Otherwise no tax is charged.

In a real application, you wouldn't hard-code the tax rate into the program. Instead, you'd store the tax rate in a file, a database, or perhaps in the application's web.config file. That way you wouldn't have to recompile the application when the governor reneges on that campaign promise about not raising taxes.

→ **9**   The Shipping property calculates the shipping charges by adding up the quantities for each item in the shopping cart, then multiplying the total number of items ordered by $2.00.

Of course, hard-coding the shipping charges into the program is an even worse idea than hard-coding the tax rate. In an actual application, you'll almost certainly want to choose a more flexible way to store the shipping charges, such as in a file, a database, or in the web.config file.

→ **10**   The Total property is calculated by adding the values of the SubTotal, Shipping, and SalesTax properties.

Listing 6-20:   The Order class (VB version)

```
Imports Microsoft.VisualBasic
Imports System.Data

Public Class Order
    Private _orderDate As DateTime                              →1
    Private _cust As Customer
    Private _cart As ShoppingCart

    Public Sub New()                                           →2
        _cust = New Customer()
        _cart = New ShoppingCart()
    End Sub

    Public Sub New(ByVal orderDate As DateTime, _              →3
            ByVal Cust As Customer, _
            ByVal Cart As ShoppingCart)
        Me.OrderDate = orderDate
        Me.Cust = Cust
        Me.Cart = Cart
    End Sub

    Public Property OrderDate() As DateTime                    →4
        Get
            Return _orderDate
        End Get
        Set(ByVal value As DateTime)
            _orderDate = value
        End Set
    End Property

    Public Property Cust() As Customer                         →5
        Get
            Return _cust
        End Get
        Set(ByVal value As Customer)
            _cust = value
        End Set
    End Property

    Public Property Cart() As ShoppingCart                     →6
        Get
            Return _cart
        End Get
        Set(ByVal value As ShoppingCart)
            _cart = value
        End Set
    End Property

    Public ReadOnly Property SubTotal() As Decimal             →7
        Get
```

(continued)

Listing 6-20 *(continued)*

```
                Dim d As Decimal = 0D
                For Each item As CartItem In _cart.GetItems()
                    d += item.Total
                Next
                Return d
            End Get
        End Property

        Public ReadOnly Property SalesTax() As Decimal        →8
            Get
                If Me.Cust.State = ("CA") Then
                    Return Me.SubTotal * 0.0775D
                Else
                    Return 0D
                End If
            End Get
        End Property

        Public ReadOnly Property Shipping() As Decimal        →9
            Get
                Dim count As Integer = 0
                For Each item As CartItem In _cart.GetItems()
                    count += item.Quantity
                Next
                Return count * 2D
            End Get
        End Property

        Public ReadOnly Property Total() As Decimal           →10
            Get
                Return Me.SubTotal + Me.Shipping _
                    + Me.SalesTax
            End Get
        End Property
    End Class
```

Creating the OrderDB Class

The last class for this application, OrderDB, contains just a single public
method to write an order to the database. However, several private methods
are required to support this method. The C# version of this class is shown in
Listing 6-21, and Listing 6-22 shows the Visual Basic version.

Listing 6-21: **The OrderDB class (C# version)**

```csharp
using System;
using System.Data;
using System.Configuration;
using System.Web;
using System.Web.Security;
using System.Web.UI;
using System.Web.UI.WebControls;
using System.Web.UI.WebControls.WebParts;
using System.Web.UI.HtmlControls;
using System.Web.Configuration;
using System.Data.SqlClient;

public static class OrderDB                                        →1
{
    static SqlTransaction tran;                                    →2
    static SqlConnection con;

    public static bool WriteOrder(Order o)                        →3
    {
        string cs = WebConfigurationManager
            .ConnectionStrings["ConnectionString"]
                .ConnectionString;
        con = new SqlConnection(cs);
        con.Open();
        tran = con.BeginTransaction();
        try
        {
            InsertCustomer(o.Cust);
            int oNum = InsertOrder(o);
            foreach (CartItem item in o.Cart.GetItems())
                InsertItem(item, oNum);
            tran.Commit();
            con.Close();
            return true;
        }
        catch (Exception ex)
        {
            tran.Rollback();
            return false;
        }
    }

    private static void InsertCustomer(Customer cust)            →4
    {
        SqlCommand cmd = new SqlCommand();
        cmd.Connection = con;
        cmd.Transaction = tran;
        try
        {
            cmd.CommandText = "INSERT INTO Customers "
```

(continued)

Listing 6-21 *(continued)*

```
                + "(lastname, firstname, "
                + "address, city, state, zipcode,"
                + "phone, email) "
                + "VALUES (@LastName, @FirstName, "
                + "@Address, @City, @State, @ZipCode,"
                + "@PhoneNumber, @Email)";
        cmd.Parameters.AddWithValue(
            "@LastName", cust.LastName);
        cmd.Parameters.AddWithValue(
            "@FirstName", cust.FirstName);
        cmd.Parameters.AddWithValue(
            "@Address", cust.Address);
        cmd.Parameters.AddWithValue(
            "@City", cust.City);
        cmd.Parameters.AddWithValue(
            "@State", cust.State);
        cmd.Parameters.AddWithValue(
            "@ZipCode", cust.ZipCode);
        cmd.Parameters.AddWithValue(
            "@PhoneNumber", cust.PhoneNumber);
        cmd.Parameters.AddWithValue(
            "@Email", cust.Email);
        cmd.ExecuteNonQuery();
    }
    catch (SqlException ex)
    {
        if (ex.Number == 2627) // Duplicate key
        {
            cmd.CommandText = "UPDATE Customers "
                + "SET lastname = @LastName, "
                + "firstname = @FirstName, "
                + "address = @Address, "
                + "city = @City, "
                + "state = @State, "
                + "zipcode = @ZipCode, "
                + "phone = @PhoneNumber "
                + "WHERE email = @Email ";
            cmd.ExecuteNonQuery();
        }
        else
            throw ex;
    }
}

private static int InsertOrder(Order o)          →5
{
    SqlCommand cmd = new SqlCommand();
    cmd.Connection = con;
    cmd.Transaction = tran;
    cmd.CommandText = "INSERT INTO Orders "
        + "(orderdate, custemail, "
        + "subtotal, salestax, "
```

```
            + "shipping) "
            + "VALUES (@OrderDate, @Custemail, "
            + "@subtotal, @salestax, "
            + "@shipping)";
        cmd.Parameters.AddWithValue(
            "@OrderDate", DateTime.Now);
        cmd.Parameters.AddWithValue(
            "@Custemail", o.Cust.Email);
        cmd.Parameters.AddWithValue(
            "@subtotal", o.SubTotal);
        cmd.Parameters.AddWithValue(
            "@salestax", o.SalesTax);
        cmd.Parameters.AddWithValue(
            "@shipping", o.Shipping);
        cmd.ExecuteNonQuery();
        cmd.CommandText = "SELECT @@IDENTITY";
        return Convert.ToInt32(cmd.ExecuteScalar());
    }

    private static void InsertItem(CartItem item,          →6
        int oNum)
    {
        SqlCommand cmd = new SqlCommand();
        cmd.Connection = con;
        cmd.Transaction = tran;
        cmd.CommandText = "INSERT INTO OrderItems "
            + "(ordernum, productid, "
            + "name, price, quantity) "
            + "VALUES (@OrderNum, @ProductID, "
            + "@Name, @Price, @Quantity)";
        cmd.Parameters.AddWithValue(
            "@OrderNum", oNum);
        cmd.Parameters.AddWithValue(
            "@ProductID", item.ID);
        cmd.Parameters.AddWithValue(
            "@Name", item.Name);
        cmd.Parameters.AddWithValue(
            "@Price", item.Price);
        cmd.Parameters.AddWithValue(
            "@Quantity", item.Quantity);
        cmd.ExecuteNonQuery();
    }
}
```

The following list spells out the most important details of this class:

→ **1** The C# version of the OrderDB class is defined with the static keyword. That simply means that the class can't contain any instance properties or members. Instead, all methods and properties must be declared as static. That's a new feature of C# for ASP.NET 2.0. Visual Basic doesn't have this feature, which is why the Shared keyword doesn't appear on the class declaration for

→ **2**

the VB version of the `OrderDB` class. (This class uses static methods so that the application doesn't have to create an instance of the class to use its methods for database access.)

A pair of `static` (`Shared` in VB) variables are used to store the `SqlTransaction` and `SqlConnection` objects used by the `WriteOrder` method. The `SqlTransaction` object is used to place all of the updates performed by the `WriteOrder` method in a safety net so that if any of the updates fail, any updates performed up to that point are reversed. And the `SqlConnection` object provides a connection to the database.

→ **3**

The `WriteOrder` method is the only public method provided by the `OrderDB` class. It begins by using the `WebConfigurationManager` class to retrieve the database connection string from `web.config`. Then it creates and opens a connection and obtains a transaction that can be used to coordinate the updates.

Next, it calls the `InsertCustomer` method to insert the customer data into the Customers table, calls the `InsertOrder` method to insert a row into the Orders table, and uses a `for each` loop to call the `InsertItem` method once for each item in the order's shopping cart. Notice that the `InsertOrder` method returns the order number generated for the order. This value is then passed to the `InsertItem` method so the order items will be associated with the correct order.

After all of the data has been inserted, the `Commit` method is called on the transaction object to commit the updates, the connection is closed, and the method returns with a return value of `true` to indicate that the data was written successfully.

If an exception occurs during any of the database updates, however, the exception will be caught by the `Catch` statement. Then the `Rollback` method of the transaction is called to reverse any updates that were previously made. Then the `WriteOrder` method returns `false` so the caller knows the order was not successfully written.

→ **4**

The `InsertCustomer` method inserts or updates the customer data in the `Customers` table. It begins by issuing the following SQL statement to attempt to insert the customer data:

```
INSERT INTO Customers
        (lastname, firstname,
         address, city, state, zipcode,
         phone, email)
VALUES(@LastName, @FirstName,
         @Address, @City, @State, @ZipCode,
         @PhoneNumber, @Email)
```

After defining the INSERT statement, the InsertCustomer method uses the cmd.Parameters collection to set the parameters required by the INSERT statement. Then, it calls the ExecuteNonQuery method to execute the INSERT statement. If a customer with the specified e-mail address already exists in the Customers table, this statement will fail, throwing a specific SqlException whose Number property is 2627. In that case, the InsertCustomer method issues the following SQL statement to update the customer with the new data:

```
UPDATE Customers
    SET lastname = @LastName,
        firstname = @FirstName,
        address = @Address,
        city = @City,
        state = @State,
        zipcode = @ZipCode,
        phone = @PhoneNumber
    WHERE email = @Email
```

→ **5**   The InsertOrder method inserts data into the Orders table by executing this SQL statement:

```
INSERT INTO Orders
            (orderdate, custemail,
             subtotal, salestax,
             shipping)
    VALUES (@OrderDate, @Custemail,
            @subtotal, @salestax,
            @shipping)
```

After the order has been inserted, the ExecuteScalar method is called to execute this SQL statement:

```
SELECT @@IDENTITY
```

This statement returns the identity value generated by the INSERT statement. The ExecuteScalar method returns this value as an object, so it must be converted to an integer by using Convert.ToInt32.

→ **6**   The InsertItem method inserts a single item into the OrderItems table. It does so by calling ExecuteNonQuery to execute the following SQL command:

```
INSERT INTO OrderItems
            (ordernum, productid,
             name, price, quantity)
    VALUES (@OrderNum, @ProductID,
            @Name, @Price, @Quantity)
```

Listing 6-22:   The OrderDB class (VB version)

```
Imports Microsoft.VisualBasic
Imports System.Data.SqlClient
Imports System.Web.Configuration

Public Class OrderDB                                    →1

    Shared tran As SqlTransaction                       →2
    Shared con As SqlConnection

    Public Shared Function WriteOrder( _                →3
            ByVal o As Order) As Boolean
        Dim cs As String
        cs = WebConfigurationManager _
            .ConnectionStrings("ConnectionString") _
                .ConnectionString
        con = New SqlConnection(cs)
        con.Open()
        tran = con.BeginTransaction()
        Try
            InsertCustomer(o.Cust)
            Dim oNum As Integer
            oNum = InsertOrder(o)
            For Each item As CartItem _
                    In o.Cart.GetItems()
                InsertItem(item, oNum)
            Next
            tran.Commit()
            con.Close()
            Return True
        Catch ex As Exception
            tran.Rollback()
            Return False
        End Try
    End Function

    Private Shared Sub InsertCustomer( _                →4
            ByVal cust As Customer)
        Dim cmd As New SqlCommand()
        cmd.Connection = con
        cmd.Transaction = tran
        Try
            cmd.CommandText = "INSERT INTO Customers " _
                + "(lastname, firstname, " _
                + "address, city, state, zipcode," _
                + "phone, email) " _
                + "VALUES (@LastName, @FirstName, " _
                + "@Address, @City, @State, @ZipCode," _
                + "@PhoneNumber, @Email)"
            cmd.Parameters.AddWithValue( _
                "@LastName", cust.LastName)
            cmd.Parameters.AddWithValue( _
                "@FirstName", cust.FirstName)
```

```vb
            cmd.Parameters.AddWithValue( _
                "@Address", cust.Address)
            cmd.Parameters.AddWithValue( _
                "@City", cust.City)
            cmd.Parameters.AddWithValue( _
                "@State", cust.State)
            cmd.Parameters.AddWithValue( _
                "@ZipCode", cust.ZipCode)
            cmd.Parameters.AddWithValue( _
                "@PhoneNumber", cust.PhoneNumber)
            cmd.Parameters.AddWithValue( _
                "@Email", cust.Email)
            cmd.ExecuteNonQuery()
        Catch ex As SqlException
            If ex.Number = 2627 Then 'Duplicate Key
                cmd.CommandText = "UPDATE Customers " _
                    + "SET lastname = @LastName, " _
                    + "firstname = @FirstName, " _
                    + "address = @Address, " _
                    + "city = @City, " _
                    + "state = @State, " _
                    + "zipcode = @ZipCode, " _
                    + "phone = @PhoneNumber " _
                    + "WHERE email = @Email "
                cmd.ExecuteNonQuery()
            Else
                Throw ex
            End If
        End Try
End Sub

Private Shared Function InsertOrder( _                    →5
        ByVal o As Order) As Integer
    Dim cmd As New SqlCommand()
    cmd.Connection = con
    cmd.Transaction = tran
    cmd.CommandText = "INSERT INTO Orders " _
        + "(orderdate, custemail, " _
        + "subtotal, salestax, " _
        + "shipping) " _
        + "VALUES (@OrderDate, @Custemail, " _
        + "@subtotal, @salestax, " _
        + "@shipping)"
    cmd.Parameters.AddWithValue( _
        "@OrderDate", DateTime.Now)
    cmd.Parameters.AddWithValue( _
        "@Custemail", o.Cust.Email)
    cmd.Parameters.AddWithValue( _
        "@subtotal", o.SubTotal)
    cmd.Parameters.AddWithValue( _
        "@salestax", o.SalesTax)
```

(continued)

Listing 6-22 *(continued)*

```
        cmd.Parameters.AddWithValue( _
            "@shipping", o.Shipping)
        cmd.ExecuteNonQuery()
        cmd.CommandText = "SELECT @@IDENTITY"
        Return Convert.ToInt32(cmd.ExecuteScalar())
    End Function

    Private Shared Sub InsertItem( _                        →6
            ByVal item As CartItem, _
            ByVal oNum As Integer)
        Dim cmd As New SqlCommand()
        cmd.Connection = con
        cmd.Transaction = tran
        cmd.CommandText = "INSERT INTO OrderItems " _
            + "(ordernum, productid, " _
            + "name, price, quantity) " _
            + "VALUES (@OrderNum, @ProductID, " _
            + "@Name, @Price, @Quantity)"
        cmd.Parameters.AddWithValue( _
            "@OrderNum", oNum)
        cmd.Parameters.AddWithValue( _
            "@ProductID", item.ID)
        cmd.Parameters.AddWithValue( _
            "@Name", item.Name)
        cmd.Parameters.AddWithValue( _
            "@Price", item.Price)
        cmd.Parameters.AddWithValue( _
            "@Quantity", item.Quantity)
        cmd.ExecuteNonQuery()
    End Sub

End Class
```

Part IV
Building Back-End Applications

In this part . . .

Many Web applications have two faces: a public face that's available to anyone who wanders by, and a back-end interface that only certain users — those responsible for maintaining the application — can access. In this part, I present two typical back-end applications. The first, a database-maintenance application, lets qualified users add, modify, and delete information in a database. The second is a reporting application that generates a report from a database (strictly to those who need to see it, of course).

Chapter 7

Building a Product Maintenance Application

Not all Web applications are intended for use by a company's customers. Just as important are those "behind the scenes" applications that the company's employees use to keep the Web site and its related databases up to date. Some of the most important behind-the-scenes applications are those that do database maintenance — in particular, those that let users update the contents of individual database tables.

In this chapter, I present a simple Product Maintenance application that lets the user update, delete, or insert data into the `Product` and `Category` tables of the database used by the Product Catalog and Shopping Cart applications (Chapters 5 and 6).

To keep this application simple, the database it uses doesn't include the `FeaturedProducts` table used by the applications in Chapters 5 and 6.

The Application's User Interface

Figure 7-1 shows how the pages of the Product Maintenance application work together. This application's user interface has just three pages. `Default.aspx` is simply a menu page with links to the other two pages. `CatMaint.aspx` lets the user add, delete, or modify existing category records. And `ProdMaint.aspx` lets the user maintain product records.

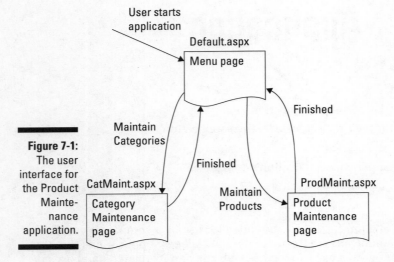

Figure 7-1:
The user interface for the Product Maintenance application.

The Menu page

Figure 7-2 shows the Menu page (`default.aspx`), which displays links to the Category Maintenance and Product Maintenance pages. This is the default start page for the application.

The Category Maintenance page

The Category Maintenance page (`CatMaint.aspx`) is shown in Figure 7-3. As you can see, this page lets the user maintain the data in the `Categories` database table. The user can reach this page by clicking the <u>Maintain Categories</u> link on the Menu page.

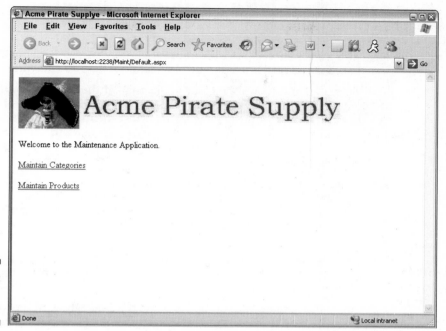

Figure 7-2:
The Menu
page.

Figure 7-3:
The
Category
Mainte-
nance page.

Here are some interesting things to note about the Category Maintenance page:

- ✔ A `GridView` control is used to list all categories in the `Categories` table. Although it isn't apparent from this figure, the `GridView` control's built-in paging feature is used to display no more than 10 categories at a time.

- ✔ The `GridView` control includes links that let the user edit or delete a category. If the user clicks the <u>Edit</u> link, the `GridView` control is placed in Edit mode, as shown in Figure 7-4. Then the user can change the information for the category and click <u>Update</u> to update the database. Or, the user can click <u>Cancel</u> to skip the update. (Note that the `CategoryID` column can't be updated.)

- ✔ The text boxes at the bottom of the page let the user enter the data for a new category. Then the user can click the Add Category button to add the new category to the database. This separate data-entry area is required because although the `GridView` control supports edits and deletions, it doesn't allow insertions.

- ✔ Each of the text boxes at the bottom of the page is followed by a `RequiredFieldValidator` to ensure that the user enters data for all three fields.

- ✔ The link at the bottom of the page lets the user return to the Menu page.

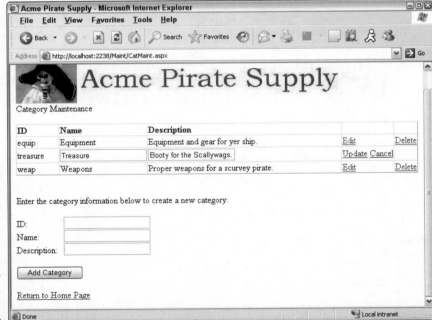

Figure 7-4:
The Category Maintenance page with the `GridView` control in Edit mode.

The Product Maintenance page

The Product Maintenance page (`ProdMaint.aspx`), which lets the user add, change, or delete data from the Products table, is shown in Figure 7-5. The user can reach this page by clicking the <u>Maintain Products</u> link on the Menu page.

Here are some key points to notice about this page:

- A `GridView` control on the left side of the page displays the products in the `Products` table. This `GridView` control uses paging to display ten products on each page. Also, a <u>Select</u> link is shown for each product.

- To the right of the `GridView` control is a `FormsView` control that displays the data for the selected product. The `FormsView` control — a new control introduced with ASP.NET 2.0 — makes it easy to display and update data for a single row of a data source.

- When the Product Maintenance page is first displayed — and no product has yet been selected — the FormsView control simply displays the text Please select a product. The product data isn't displayed until the user clicks the Select link for one of the products displayed by the GridView control.

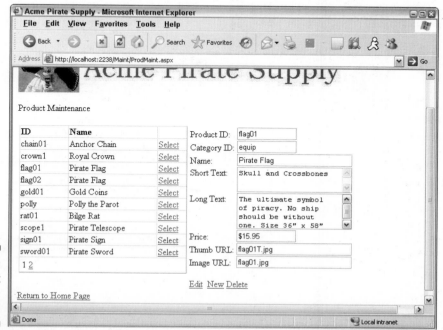

Figure 7-5: The Product Maintenance page.

- The user can edit the data for the selected product by clicking the <u>Edit</u> link at the bottom of the `FormView` control. This places the `FormView` control into Edit mode, as shown in Figure 7-6. Then the user can change the data for the product and click <u>Update</u>. Or, the user can click <u>Cancel</u> to leave Edit mode without updating the data.

- Notice that in Edit mode, the `Category ID` field is displayed by a drop-down list rather than a text box. This drop-down list shows all categories from the `Categories` table.

- Although you can't tell from the figure, each of the text boxes in the `FormView` control is followed by a `RequiredFieldValidator`. That way, the user must enter data for each field.

- Unlike the GridView control, the FormView control does allow for insertions. If the user clicks New, the FormView control enters Insert mode, as shown in Figure 7-7. Then the user can enter the data for a new product and click Insert to insert the row.

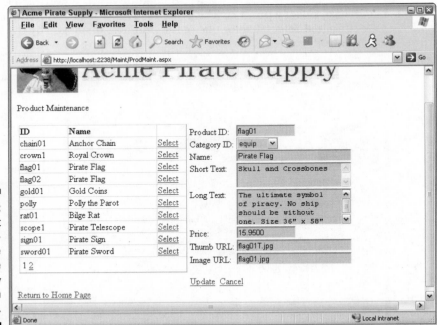

Figure 7-6:
The Product Maintenance page with the `FormView` control in Edit mode.

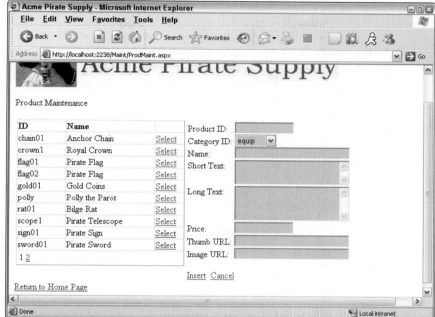

Figure 7-7:
The Product
Mainte-
nance page
with the
`FormView`
control in
Insert mode.

Designing the Application

The Product Maintenance application uses a very simple design. The Menu page uses simple links that post back to the Category Maintenance or Product Maintenance pages. Then these pages use ASP.NET data binding and data sources to connect to and update the databases. This simple design avoids the need for query strings, session states, or other similar features.

There are a few additional considerations to think about whenever you create a maintenance application such as this one. For example, try these on for size:

✔ **How will the user look up the data to be updated?** In this application, a `GridView` control is used to display the Categories and Products tables. That's feasible for this application because there are only a few categories and products. However, what if the database has thousands, or tens of thousands, of products? In that case, you'll want to let the user enter the product ID of the product into a text box to call up a specific product. (Better yet, you can add a search feature to the application.)

✔ **Will you let the user change the primary key fields?** If you do, you must ensure that foreign key constraints are properly handled. For example, if you allow a user to change the category ID for a category, how will you handle products assigned to that category? You have three possible approaches:

   • Cascade the update, so the category IDs change automatically for any related products.

   • Don't allow the category ID to be changed if it appears in any product rows.

   • Don't allow the user to change the category ID. That's the approach taken for this application.

✔ **How will you handle concurrency conflicts that result when two users attempt to update the same data at the same time?** For example, suppose two users simultaneously display the Category Maintenance page and the first user changes the description of the treasure category, while the second user deletes it. If the second user's deletion is posted *before* the first user's update, the update fails because the row no longer exists in the database.

The most common way to handle this situation is to use *optimistic concurrency checking*, a technique in which the original values of each column are saved when the data is initially retrieved. Then the WHEN clauses of the UPDATE or DELETE statements use these values to make sure some other user hasn't changed the data before applying an update or deleting a row. This is the technique used for the Categories table in this application.

The alternative to optimistic concurrency checking is to not do any concurrency checking at all. In that case, the last update posted is the one that's applied. This is the technique used for the Products table in this application.

✔ **How will you handle security?** You don't want to let just anyone modify the data in your database. So you'll certainly want to provide security to authenticate users of your maintenance application. Although the application presented in this chapter doesn't provide for user authentication, you can easily integrate this application with the Login application that was presented in Chapter 4 by simply moving this application's pages to the Admin folder of the Login application. (In addition, you may want to change the name of menu page from Default.aspx to Admin.aspx.)

Designing the Database

The Product Maintenance application obviously uses a database to store the products and categories that the application maintains. Figure 7-8 shows a diagram of this database, named `Maint`. The `Maint` database uses just two tables:

- Categories
- Products

These tables are described in detail in the following sections.

In a real-world application, this maintenance application would maintain the same database used by the front-end applications, such as the Shopping Cart application presented in Chapters 5 and 6. In fact, you can use the Maintenance application presented here with the `Cart` database you created in Chapter 6. If you want to do that, you can skip the sections in this chapter that show you how to create the `Maint` database and insert data into it. Then, in the `web.config` file, you simply connect to the `Cart` database rather than the `Maint` database. I'll show you how to do that in the section "Connecting to the database" later in this chapter.

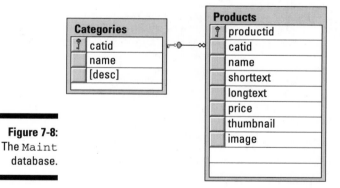

Figure 7-8:
The `Maint`
database.

The Categories table

The `Categories` table stores the information about the categories of products offered by the store. Table 7-1 lists the columns defined for the `Categories` table.

Table 7-1		The Categories Table
Column name	*Type*	*Description*
catid	VARCHAR(10)	An alphanumeric code (up to 10 characters) that uniquely identifies each category. This is the primary key for the Categories table.
name	VARCHAR(50)	A text field that provides the name of the category.
desc	VARCHAR(MAX)	A text field that provides a description of the category.

The Products table

The Products table holds one row for each product. The columns required for this table are listed in Table 7-2.

Table 7-2		The Products Table
Column name	*Type*	*Description*
productid	VARCHAR(10)	An alphanumeric code (up to 10 characters) that uniquely identifies each product. This is the primary key for the Products table.
catid	VARCHAR(10)	A code that identifies the product's category. A foreign key constraint ensures that only values present in the Categories table can be used for this column.
name	VARCHAR(50)	A text field that provides the name of the product.
shorttext	VARCHAR(MAX)	A text field that provides a short description of the product.
longtext	VARCHAR(MAX)	A text field that provides a longer description of the product.
price	MONEY	The price for a single unit of the product.
thumbnail	VARCHAR(40)	The name of the thumbnail image file.
image	VARCHAR(40)	The name of the main image file.

Creating the database

Although you can use Visual Studio to create the `Maint` database, it's better to create it from a script. Then, as you test the application, you can run the script to recreate the database, restoring it to its original state. The SQL script that does these tasks appears in Listing 7-1.

To run this script, open a command-prompt window and change to the directory that contains the script. Then enter this command:

```
sqlcmd -S localhost\SQLExpress -i CreateDB.sql
```

Note that this command assumes you're running SQL Server Express on your own computer. If you're using SQL Server on a different server, you'll need to change `localhost\SQLExpress` to the correct name. If you're not sure what name to use, ask your database administrator.

Listing 7-1: The CreateDB.sql script

```
USE master                                              →1
GO

IF EXISTS(SELECT * FROM sysdatabases                    →2
    WHERE name='Cart')
DROP DATABASE Maint
GO

CREATE DATABASE Maint                                   →3
ON (NAME=Product,
    FILENAME = 'C:\APPS\Maint.mdf',
    SIZE=10 )
GO

USE Maint                                               →4

CREATE TABLE Categories (                               →5
  catid VARCHAR(10)  NOT NULL,
  name  VARCHAR(50)  NOT NULL,
  [desc]  VARCHAR(MAX) NOT NULL,
  PRIMARY KEY(catid) )
  GO

CREATE TABLE Products (                                 →6
  productid VARCHAR(10)  NOT NULL,
  catid     VARCHAR(10)  NOT NULL,
  name      VARCHAR(50)  NOT NULL,
  shorttext VARCHAR(MAX) NOT NULL,
```

(continued)

Listing 7-1 *(continued)*

```
longtext   VARCHAR(MAX) NOT NULL,
price      MONEY        NOT NULL,
thumbnail  VARCHAR(40)  NOT NULL,
image      VARCHAR(40)  NOT NULL,
PRIMARY KEY(productid),
FOREIGN KEY(catid) REFERENCES Categories(catid) )
GO
```

Here's an explanation of the key lines of this script:

→ **1**   Sets the database context to `master`.

→ **2**   Deletes the existing `Maint` database if it exists.

→ **3**   Creates a database named `Maint`, placing the database file in `C:\Apps`.

→ **4**   Sets the database context to `Maint`.

→ **5**   Creates the `Categories` table.

→ **6**   Creates the `Products` table.

Adding some test data

The `CreateDB` script creates the `Maint` database, but doesn't add any data to it. To add data, you can run the `InsertData.sql` script that's included on the CD that comes with this book. This script creates the sample data shown in Table 7-3 and Table 7-4. (Note that the `shorttext` and `longtext` columns aren't listed in Table 7-4.)

You can run the `InsertData.sql` script by opening a command window, changing to the directory that contains the script, and running this command:

```
sqlcmd -S localhost\SQLExpress -i InsertData.sql
```

Be sure to change the server name if you're not running SQL Server Express on your own computer.

Table 7-3	Test Data for the Categories Table	
catid	*name*	*desc*
booty	Booty	Treasure for the Scallywags.
equip	Equipment	Equipment and gear for yer ship.
weap	Weapons	Proper weapons for a scurvy pirate.

Table 7-4		Test Data for the Products Table			
productid	catid	name	price	thumbnail	Image
chain01	equip	Anchor Chain	6.95	chainT.jpg	chain.jpg
crown1	booty	Royal Crown	14.95	crown1T.jpg	crown1.jpg
flag01	equip	Pirate Flag	15.95	flag01T.jpg	flag01.jpg
flag02	equip	Pirate Flag	12.95	flag02T.jpg	flag02.jpg
gold01	booty	Gold Coins	8.95	gold01T.jpg	gold01.jpg
polly	equip	Polly the Parrot	15.95	pollyT.jpg	polly.jpg
rat01	equip	Bilge Rat	9.95	rat01T.jpg	rat01.jpg
scope1	equip	Pirate Telescope	15.95	scope1T.jpg	scope1.jpg
sign01	equip	Pirate Sign	25.95	sign01T.jpg	sign01.jpg
sword01	weap	Pirate Sword	29.95	sword01T.jpg	sword01.jpg
sword02	weap	Broad Sword	9.95	sword02T.jpg	sword02.jpg

SQL statements for the Categories table

The Product Maintenance application uses several SQL statements to retrieve, update, delete, and insert data from the Categories table. These SQL statements have distinct purposes, described in the following paragraphs:

✔ To retrieve all rows from the Categories table, the following SELECT statement is used:

```
SELECT [catid], [name], [desc]
   FROM [Categories] ORDER BY [catid]
```

✔ To delete a row, the following DELETE statement is used:

```
DELETE FROM [Categories]
      WHERE [catid] = @original_catid
        AND [name] = @original_name
        AND [desc] = @original_desc
```

As you can see, this statement — as well as the UPDATE statement presented next — lists all three of the Categories columns in the WHERE clause. That way, if any other user has changed any of the columns in the database row since the row was originally retrieved, the delete (or update) will fail. This technique is called *optimistic concurrency checking*.

✔ To update a row, the following UPDATE statement is used:

```
UPDATE [Categories]
    SET [name] = @name,
        [desc] = @desc
    WHERE [catid] = @original_catid
      AND [name] = @original_name
      AND [desc] = @original_desc
```

Again, the original values for all three columns of the table are listed in the WHERE clause to provide optimistic concurrency checking. Notice also that the catid column is not listed in the SET clause. That's because the application doesn't let the user change the category ID.

✔ To insert a row, the following INSERT statement is used:

```
INSERT INTO [Categories]
            ([catid], [name], [desc])
    VALUES (@catid, @name, @desc)
```

SQL statements for the Products table

The Product Maintenance application also uses several SQL statements to retrieve, update, delete, and insert data from the Products table. Note that the UPDATE and DELETE statements for the Products table — unlike those for the Categories table — don't use optimistic concurrency. (I'll leave it to you to modify the application to provide optimistic concurrency checking for the Products table.)

The following paragraphs describe the SQL statements used for the Products table:

✔ This SELECT statement selects the products to display in the GridView control:

```
SELECT [productid], [name]
    FROM [Products] ORDER BY [productid]
```

✔ This SELECT statement retrieves the product selected by the user in the GridView control so it can be displayed in the FormView control:

```
SELECT [productid], [catid],
       [name], [shorttext], [longtext],
       [price], [thumbnail], [image]
    FROM [Products]
    WHERE ([productid] = @productid)
```

✔ This INSERT statement inserts a new product:

```
INSERT INTO [Products]
            ([productid], [catid], [name], [shorttext],
             [longtext], [price], [thumbnail], [image])
     VALUES (@productid, @catid, @name, @shorttext,
             @longtext, @price, @thumbnail, @image)
```

✔ This UPDATE statement updates a product row:

```
UPDATE [Products]
   SET [catid] = @catid,
       [name] = @name,
       [shorttext] = @shorttext,
       [longtext] = @longtext,
       [price] = @price,
       [thumbnail] = @thumbnail,
       [image] = @image
     WHERE [productid] = @original_productid
```

✔ This DELETE statement deletes a row from the Products table:

```
DELETE FROM [Products]
     WHERE [productid] = @original_productid
```

Connecting to the database

The Maint database uses a connection string that's stored in the application's Web.config file, like this:

```
<connectionStrings>
    <add name="ConnectionString"
         connectionString="Data
           Source=localhost\SQLExpress;
Initial Catalog=Maint;Integrated Security=True"/>
</connectionStrings>
```

Because the connection string is the only place that specifies the database and server name, you can move the database to a different server — or use a different database — by changing the connection string specified in the Web.config file.

If you want to use the database for the Chapter 6 Shopping Cart application rather than the separate Maint database, just change the Initial Catalog setting from Maint to Cart.

The Application's Folders

Like most ASP.NET applications, the Product Catalog application includes several folders. In particular:

- ✔ **(Root):** The application's root folder contains the application's three pages (`Default.aspx`, `Product.aspx`, and `Cart.aspx`) as well as the Master Page (`Default.master`).
- ✔ **App_Data:** This folder is created by default by Visual Studio when the application is created. However, the actual database (managed by SQL Server) is stored in a folder that's not part of the application's folder hierarchy.
- ✔ **Images:** This folder contains the banner graphic that's displayed by the Master Page. The images referred to in the `Thumbnail` and `Image` columns of the `Products` table aren't used by this application, so they aren't included in the Images folder.

Building the Master Page

Listing 7-2 shows the Master Page (`MasterPage.master`). As with the Master Pages shown in previous chapters, this one simply displays a banner at the top of each page.

Listing 7-2:   The Master page (MasterPage.master)

```
<%@ Master Language="C#" %>                                    →1

<!DOCTYPE html PUBLIC "-//W3C//DTD XHTML 1.1//EN"
"http://www.w3.org/TR/xhtml11/DTD/xhtml11.dtd">

<script runat="server">

</script>

<html xmlns="http://www.w3.org/1999/xhtml" >
<head runat="server">
    <title>Acme Pirate Supply</title>
</head>
<body>
    <form id="form1" runat="server">
    <div>
        <asp:Image ID="Image1" runat="server"            →2
            ImageUrl="~/Images/Banner.jpg"/>
        <br />
```

```
        <asp:contentplaceholder runat="server"              →3
            id="ContentPlaceHolder1" >
        </asp:contentplaceholder>
     </div>
     </form>
  </body>
  </html>
```

Here are the key points of this listing:

→ **1**   The `Master` directive indicates that the file is a Master Page.

→ **2**   The `Image` control displays the banner image that appears at the top of each page.

→ **3**   The `ContentPlaceHolder` control indicates where the content for each page that uses this master will appear.

Building the Menu Page

The Menu page (`Default.aspx`) is the default page for the Product Catalog application. It simply displays a pair of links that let the user go to the Category Maintenance page or the Product Maintenance page. Listing 7-3 shows the code for this page.

Listing 7-3:   The Menu page (`Default.aspx`)

```
<%@ Page Language="C#"                                       →1
    MasterPageFile="~/MasterPage.master"
    AutoEventWireup="true"
    CodeFile="Default.aspx.cs"
    Inherits="_Default"
    Title="Acme Pirate Supply" %>
<asp:Content ID="Content1" Runat="Server"                    →2
    ContentPlaceHolderID="ContentPlaceHolder1" >
    <br />
    Welcome to the Maintenance Application.<br />
    <br />
    <asp:LinkButton ID="LinkButton1" runat="server"          →3
        PostBackUrl="CatMaint.aspx">
        Maintain Categories
    </asp:LinkButton>
    <br /><br />
    <asp:LinkButton ID="LinkButton2" runat="server"          →4
        PostBackUrl="ProdMaint.aspx">
        Maintain Products
    </asp:LinkButton>
</asp:Content>
```

Here are some of the key points to note about the code for this page:

→ 1   The `Page` directive uses the `MasterPageFile` attribute to specify the name of the Master Page.

→ 2   The `<Content>` element provides the content that's displayed for the page.

→ 3   The first `<LinkButton>` element provides a link to the `CatMaint.aspx` page. The `PostBackUrl` attribute is used to post to that page when the user clicks the link.

→ 4   The second `<LinkButton>` element provides a link that posts back to the `ProdMaint.aspx` page.

Building the Category Maintenance Page

The Category Maintenance page (`CatMaint.aspx`) lets the user update or delete existing categories or create new categories. It uses a `GridView` control to let the user modify or delete existing categories. In addition, it uses three text boxes that let the user enter data to define a new category. The text boxes are required because the `GridView` control doesn't provide a way for users to insert rows.

The CatMaint.aspx file

Listing 7-4 shows the `.aspx` code for the Category Maintenance page. You may want to refer back to Figure 7-3 to see how this page looks on-screen.

Listing 7-4: **The Category Maintenance page** (`CatMaint.aspx`)

```
<%@ Page Language="C#"                                          →1
    MasterPageFile="~/MasterPage.master"
    AutoEventWireup="true"
    CodeFile="CatMaint.aspx.cs"
    Inherits="CatMaint"
    Title="Acme Pirate Supply" %>
<asp:Content ID="Content1" Runat="Server"                       →2
    ContentPlaceHolderID="ContentPlaceHolder1" >
    Category Maintenance<br />
    <br />
    <asp:GridView ID="GridView1" runat="server"                 →3
        AutoGenerateColumns="False"
        DataKeyNames="catid"
        DataSourceID="SqlDataSource1"
        OnRowDeleted="GridView1_RowDeleted"
        OnRowUpdated="GridView1_RowUpdated">
```

```
        <Columns>
            <asp:BoundField DataField="catid"              →4
                HeaderText="ID" ReadOnly="True">
                <HeaderStyle HorizontalAlign="Left" />
                <ItemStyle Width="80px" />
            </asp:BoundField>
            <asp:BoundField DataField="name"               →5
                HeaderText="Name">
                <HeaderStyle HorizontalAlign="Left" />
                <ItemStyle Width="100px" />
            </asp:BoundField>
            <asp:BoundField DataField="desc"               →6
                HeaderText="Description">
                <HeaderStyle HorizontalAlign="Left" />
                <ItemStyle Width="400px" />
            </asp:BoundField>
            <asp:CommandField                              →7
                CausesValidation="False"
                ShowEditButton="True" />
            <asp:CommandField                              →8
                CausesValidation="False"
                ShowDeleteButton="True" />
        </Columns>
</asp:GridView>
<asp:SqlDataSource ID="SqlDataSource1"                     →9
    runat="server"
    ConflictDetection="CompareAllValues"
    ConnectionString=
    "<%$ ConnectionStrings:ConnectionString %>"
    OldValuesParameterFormatString="original_{0}"
    DeleteCommand="DELETE FROM [Categories]               →10
            WHERE [catid] = @original_catid
            AND [name] = @original_name
            AND [desc] = @original_desc"
    InsertCommand="INSERT INTO [Categories]               →11
                ([catid], [name], [desc])
            VALUES (@catid, @name, @desc)"
    SelectCommand="SELECT [catid],                        →12
                [name], [desc]
            FROM [Categories] ORDER BY [catid]"
    UpdateCommand="UPDATE [Categories]                    →13
            SET [name] = @name, [desc] = @desc
            WHERE [catid] = @original_catid
            AND [name] = @original_name
            AND [desc] = @original_desc">
    <DeleteParameters>                                    →14
        <asp:Parameter Name="original_catid"
            Type="String" />
        <asp:Parameter Name="original_name"
            Type="String" />
        <asp:Parameter Name="original_desc"
            Type="String" />
```

(continued)

Listing 7-4 *(continued)*

```
        </DeleteParameters>
        <UpdateParameters>                          →15
            <asp:Parameter Name="name"
                Type="String" />
            <asp:Parameter Name="desc"
                Type="String" />
            <asp:Parameter Name="original_catid"
                Type="String" />
            <asp:Parameter Name="original_name"
                Type="String" />
            <asp:Parameter Name="original_desc"
                Type="String" />
        </UpdateParameters>
        <InsertParameters>                          →16
            <asp:Parameter Name="catid"
                Type="String" />
            <asp:Parameter Name="name"
                Type="String" />
            <asp:Parameter Name="desc"
                Type="String" />
        </InsertParameters>
    </asp:SqlDataSource>
    <br />
    <asp:Label ID="lblMessage" runat="server"       →17
        EnableViewState="False"
        ForeColor="Red" /><br />
    Enter the category information below
    to create a new category:<br /><br />
    <asp:Label ID="Label1" runat="server"
        BorderStyle="None" Width="80px"
        Text="ID:" />
    <asp:TextBox ID="txtID" runat="server" />        →18
     
    <asp:RequiredFieldValidator
        ID="RequiredFieldValidator1" runat="server"
        ControlToValidate="txtID"
        ErrorMessage="Required." />
    <br />
    <asp:Label ID="Label2" runat="server"
        BorderStyle="None" Width="80px"
        Text="Name:" />
    <asp:TextBox ID="txtName" runat="server" />      →19
     
    <asp:RequiredFieldValidator
        ID="RequiredFieldValidator2" runat="server"
        ControlToValidate="txtName"
        ErrorMessage="Required." />
    <br />
```

```
        <asp:Label ID="Label3" runat="server"
            BorderStyle="None" Width="80px"
            Text="Description:" />
        <asp:TextBox ID="txtDesc" runat="server" />              →20
         
        <asp:RequiredFieldValidator
            ID="RequiredFieldValidator3" runat="server"
            ControlToValidate="txtDesc"
            ErrorMessage="Required." /><br />
        <br />
        <asp:Button ID="btnAdd" runat="server"                   →21
            OnClick="btnAdd_Click"
            Text="Add Category" /><br /><br />
        <asp:LinkButton ID="LinkButton1"                         →22
            runat="server"
            PostBackUrl="~/Default.aspx"
            CausesValidation="false" >
            Return to Home Page
        </asp:LinkButton>
    </asp:Content>
```

Here's a detailed look at each of the numbered lines in this listing:

→ 1   The Page directive specifies the Master Page and other information for the page.

To use the Visual Basic version of the code-behind file — shown in
Listing 7-6 — you must change the AutoEventWireup attribute
to false.

→ 2   The <Content> element provides the content that's displayed
in the <ContentPlaceHolder> element of the Master Page.

→ 3   The GridView control displays the rows from the Categories
table. It's bound to the data source named SqlDataSource1,
which is defined in line 9. Notice also that it specifies methods to
handle the RowDeleted and RowUpdated events.

To use the Visual Basic version of the code-behind file for this
page, you should remove the OnRowDeleted and OnRowUpdated
attributes.

→ 4   The elements under the <Columns> element define the columns
displayed by the GridView control. This one defines the first
column in the grid, which displays the category ID. Notice that
this column is read-only. That prevents the user from changing the
category ID for a category.

→ 5   The column defined by this <BoundField> element displays the
category name.

→ **6**   This column displays the category description.

→ **7**   This line defines a command field that displays an <u>Edit</u> link, which the user can click to edit the row. When the user clicks the <u>Edit</u> link, the labels in the `name` and `desc` columns for the row are replaced by text boxes, and the <u>Edit</u> link is replaced by <u>Update</u> and <u>Cancel</u> links.

→ **8**   This line defines a command field that displays a <u>Delete</u> link, which lets the user delete a row.

→ **9**   This `<SqlDataSource>` element defines the data source used for the `GridView` control. The `ConflictDetection` attribute specifies `CompareAllValues`, which enables optimistic concurrency checking for the data source. Then the `ConnectionString` attribute specifies that the connection string for the data source should be retrieved from the `Web.config` file. Finally, the `OldParameterValuesFormatString` attribute specifies the format string that's used to create the parameter names used to supply the original parameter values. In this case, the word `original_` is simply added to the beginning of each parameter name.

→ **10**   The `<DeleteCommand>` element provides the `DELETE` statement used to delete rows from the table. Notice that the original values of the `catid`, `name`, and `desc` columns are listed in the `WHERE` clause. The values `@original_catid`, `@original_name`, and `@original_desc` parameters are automatically provided by the `GridView` control when the user deletes a row.

→ **11**   The `InsertCommand` attribute provides the `INSERT` statement used to insert a row in the Categories table. Note that the `GridView` control doesn't use this `INSERT` statement, as the `GridView` control doesn't provide a way for the user to insert rows. Instead, the code that's executed when the user clicks the Add Category button (defined in line 21) calls this statement.

→ **12**   This `SELECT` statement is used to retrieve the categories from the Categories table.

→ **13**   The `UPDATE` statement updates a row in the Categories table. Notice that the original values are used in the `WHERE` clause to provide optimistic concurrency checking.

→ **14**   The `<DeleteParameters>` element defines the parameters used by the `DELETE` statement.

→ **15**   The `<UpdateParameters>` element defines the parameters used by the `UPDATE` statement.

→ **16**   The `<InsertParameters>` element defines the parameters used by the `INSERT` statement.

→ **17**   This label is used by the code-behind file to display messages. For example, if an error occurs while trying to update or delete a category, a suitable error message is displayed in this label.

→ **18**   This text box lets the user enter the category ID for a new category. Note that a `RequiredFieldValidator` ensures that the user enters a value into this field.

→ **19**   This text box lets the user enter the name for a new category. A `RequiredFieldValidator` is used to force the user to enter a name.

→ **20**   This text box is where the user enters the description for a new category. Once again, a `RequiredFieldValidator` is present to require an entry for this text box.

→ **21**   The Add Category button lets the user add a new category using the ID, name, and description entered into the text boxes.

            If you're using the Visual Basic version of the code-behind file, you should remove the `OnClick` attribute.

→ **22**   This link button provides a link back to the menu page. Note that `CausesValidation` is set to `false` for this button. That way the `RequiredFieldValidator` isn't enforced for any of the three text boxes when the user clicks the link.

The code-behind file for the Catalog Maintenance page

The `CatMaint.aspx` page requires a code-behind file to handle the button-click event for the Add Category button, as well as the `RowUpdated` and `RowDeleted` events for the `GridView` control. Listing 7-5 shows the C# version of this code-behind file, and Listing 7-6 shows the Visual Basic version.

Listing 7-5:   The code-behind file for the Catalog Maintenance page (C#)

```
using System;
using System.Data;
using System.Configuration;
using System.Collections;
using System.Web;
using System.Web.Security;
using System.Web.UI;
using System.Web.UI.WebControls;
using System.Web.UI.WebControls.WebParts;
using System.Web.UI.HtmlControls;
```

(continued)

Listing 7-5 *(continued)*

```
public partial class CatMaint : System.Web.UI.Page
{

    protected void btnAdd_Click(                         →1
        object sender, EventArgs e)
    {
        setParameter("catid", txtID.Text);
        setParameter("name", txtName.Text);
        setParameter("desc", txtDesc.Text);
        try
        {
            SqlDataSource1.Insert();
            txtID.Text = "";
            txtName.Text = "";
            txtDesc.Text = "";
        }
        catch (Exception)
        {
            lblMessage.Text =
                "There is already a category "
            + "with that ID. Please try another.";
        }
    }

    private void setParameter(string name,              →2
        string value)
    {
        SqlDataSource1.InsertParameters[name]
            .DefaultValue = value;
    }

    protected void GridView1_RowUpdated(                →3
        object sender,
        GridViewUpdatedEventArgs e)
    {
        if (e.Exception != null)
        {
            lblMessage.Text = "Incorrect data. "
                + "Please try again.";
            e.ExceptionHandled = true;
            e.KeepInEditMode = true;
        }
        else if (e.AffectedRows == 0)
        {
            lblMessage.Text = "That category could not "
                + "be updated. Please try again.";
        }
    }

    protected void GridView1_RowDeleted(               →4
        object sender,
        GridViewDeletedEventArgs e)
```

```
        {
            if (e.Exception != null)
            {
                lblMessage.Text = "That category could not "
                    + "be deleted.";
                e.ExceptionHandled = true;
            }
            else if (e.AffectedRows == 0)
            {
                lblMessage.Text = "That category could not "
                    + "be deleted. Please try again.";
            }
        }
    }
}
```

Here's a list that offers a description for every method in this code-behind file:

→ **1**   The btnAdd_Click method is called when the user clicks the Add
      Category button to add a new row to the Categories table. The
      method begins by calling a helper method (named setParameter,
      shown in line 2) to set the value of the catid, name, and desc para-
      meters, and then calls the Insert method of the data source to
      execute the INSERT statement. Assuming the INSERT statement
      is successful, it then clears the three text input fields. However, if
      the INSERT statement fails, an exception will be thrown. Then the
      assignment in the catch statement displays an appropriate error
      message.

→ **2**   The setParameter method provides a simple shorthand for
      setting the value of one of the data source's Insert parameters.
      To set a parameter value, you use the parameter name as an index
      for the InsertParameters property of the data source, then use
      the DefaultValue property to set the value. Because this is a bit
      cumbersome, I created this helper method to make it easier to set
      a parameter value.

→ **3**   The GridView1_RowUpdated method is called whenever a row of
      the GridView control has been updated — regardless of whether
      the update was successful. You can use two properties of the e
      argument to determine whether the update was successful. If the
      update results in an exception (as when the database is unavail-
      able), the Exception property refers to an Exception object;
      otherwise the Exception property is null. And if the UPDATE
      statement did not actually update any data, the AffectedRows
      property will be zero. As you can see, this method tests both prop-
      erties, displaying an appropriate message in the lblMessage label
      if an error has occurred.

→ **4**   The GridView1_RowDeleted method is similar to the
      GridView1_RowUpdated method. It also tests the Exception
      and AffectedRows properties of the e parameter to see whether
      an error has occurred.

Listing 7-6:   **The code-behind file for the Catalog Maintenance page (VB)**

```vb
Partial Class CatMaint
    Inherits System.Web.UI.Page

    Protected Sub btnAdd_Click( _                                →1
            ByVal sender As Object, _
            ByVal e As System.EventArgs) _
            Handles btnAdd.Click
        setParameter("catid", txtID.Text)
        setParameter("name", txtName.Text)
        setParameter("desc", txtDesc.Text)
        Try
            SqlDataSource1.Insert()
            txtID.Text = ""
            txtName.Text = ""
            txtDesc.Text = ""
        Catch ex As Exception
            lblMessage.Text = "There is already a " _
                + "category with that ID. " _
                + "Please try another."
        End Try
    End Sub

    Private Sub setParameter( _                                 →2
            ByVal name As String, _
            ByVal value As String)
        SqlDataSource1.InsertParameters(name) _
            .DefaultValue = value
    End Sub

    Protected Sub GridView1_RowUpdated( _                       →3
            ByVal sender As Object, _
            ByVal e As System.Web.UI.WebControls. _
                GridViewUpdatedEventArgs) _
            Handles GridView1.RowUpdated
        If Not e.Exception Is Nothing Then
            lblMessage.Text = "Incorrect data. " _
                + "Please try again."
            e.ExceptionHandled = True
            e.KeepInEditMode = True
        ElseIf e.AffectedRows = 0 Then
            lblMessage.Text = "That category could not " _
                + "be updated. Please try again."
        End If
    End Sub

    Protected Sub GridView1_RowDeleted( _                       →4
            ByVal sender As Object, _
            ByVal e As System.Web.UI. _
                WebControls.GridViewDeletedEventArgs) _
            Handles GridView1.RowDeleted
```

```
        If Not e.Exception Is Nothing Then
            lblMessage.Text = "That category could not " _
                + "be deleted."
            e.ExceptionHandled = True
        ElseIf e.AffectedRows = 0 Then
            lblMessage.Text = "That category could not " _
                + "be deleted. Please try again."
        End If
    End Sub
End Class
```

Building the Product Maintenance Page

The Product Maintenance page (`ProdMaint.aspx`) lets the user insert, update, and delete rows in the `Products` table. It provides a `GridView` control so the user can select a product, and a `FormView` control to display the information for the selected product. The `FormView` control also lets the user edit, delete, or insert product data.

The following sections present the `.aspx` code that defines this page as well as the code-behind file that handles events raised by the page.

The ProdMaint.aspx file

Listing 7-7 (drum roll, please) shows the complete `.aspx` code for the Product Maintenance page. Refer to Figure 7-5 to see how this page appears when the application is run.

Listing 7-7:   The Product Maintenance page (`ProdMaint.aspx`)

```
<%@ Page Language="C#"                                    →1
    MasterPageFile="~/MasterPage.master"
    AutoEventWireup="true"
    CodeFile="ProdMaint.aspx.cs"
    Inherits="ProdMaint"
    Title="Acme Pirate Supply" %>
<asp:Content ID="Content1" Runat="Server"                 →2
    ContentPlaceHolderID="ContentPlaceHolder1" >
  <br />
  Product Maintenance<br />
  <br />
```

(continued)

Listing 7-7 *(continued)*

```
<table border="0" width="750">                              →3
  <tr>
    <td valign="top" width="300">
        <asp:GridView ID="GridView1"                        →4
            runat="server"
            AllowPaging="True"
            AutoGenerateColumns="False"
            DataKeyNames="productid"
            DataSourceID="SqlDataSource1" Width="300px">
            <Columns>
              <asp:BoundField                                →5
                DataField="productid"
                HeaderText="ID" >
                <HeaderStyle HorizontalAlign="Left" >
              </asp:BoundField>
              <asp:BoundField                                →6
                DataField="name"
                HeaderText="Name"
                SortExpression="name" >
                <HeaderStyle HorizontalAlign="Left" />
              </asp:BoundField>
              <asp:CommandField                              →7
                  ShowSelectButton="True" >
                  <ItemStyle Width="50px" />
              </asp:CommandField>
            </Columns>
        </asp:GridView>
        <asp:SqlDataSource ID="SqlDataSource1"               →8
            runat="server"
            ConnectionString=
              "<%$ ConnectionStrings:ConnectionString
          %>"
            SelectCommand="SELECT [productid], [name]
                FROM [Products] ORDER BY [productid]">
        </asp:SqlDataSource>
    </td>
    <td valign="top" width="450">
        <asp:FormView ID="FormView1"                         →9
            runat="server"
            DataSourceID="SqlDataSource2"
            DataKeyNames="productid"
            Width="400px" >
            <EmptyDataTemplate>                              →10
                Please select a product.
                <br /><br />
                <asp:LinkButton ID="LinkButton2"
                    runat="server"
                    CommandName="New"
                    Text="New Product" />
            </EmptyDataTemplate>
```

```
<ItemTemplate>                              →11
    <asp:Label ID="Label1" runat="server"
        BorderStyle="None" Width="80px"
        Text="Product ID:" />
    <asp:TextBox ID="txtProductID"          →12
        runat="server"
        ReadOnly="True" Width="100px"
        Text='<%# Eval("productid") %>'/>
    <br />
    <asp:Label ID="Label2" runat="server"
        BorderStyle="None" Width="80px"
        Text="Category ID:" />
    <asp:TextBox ID="txtCatID"              →13
        runat="server"
        ReadOnly="True" Width="100px"
        Text='<%# Bind("catid") %>'/><br />
    <asp:Label ID="Label3" runat="server"
        BorderStyle="None" Width="80px"
        Text="Name:" />
    <asp:TextBox ID="txtName"               →14
        runat="server"
        ReadOnly="True" Width="200px"
        Text='<%# Bind("name") %>'/><br />
    <asp:Label ID="Label4" runat="server"
        BorderStyle="None"
        Width="80px" Height="45px"
        Text="Short Text:" />
    <asp:TextBox ID="txtShortText"          →15
        runat="server"
        ReadOnly="True" TextMode="MultiLine"
        Height="40px" Width="200px"
        Text='<%# Bind("shorttext") %>'/>
    <br />
    <asp:Label ID="Label5" runat="server"
        BorderStyle="None"
        Width="80px" Height="65px"
        Text="Long Text:" />
    <asp:TextBox ID="txtLongText"           →16
        runat="server"
        ReadOnly="True" TextMode="MultiLine"
        Height="60px" Width="200px"
        Text='<%# Bind("longtext") %>'/>
    <br />
    <asp:Label ID="Label6" runat="server"
        BorderStyle="None" Width="80px"
        Text="Price:" />
    <asp:TextBox ID="txtPrice"              →17
      runat="server"
      ReadOnly="True" Width="100px"
      Text='<%# Bind("price", "{0:c}") %>'/>
    <br />
```

(continued)

Listing 7-7 *(continued)*

```
                    <asp:Label ID="Label7" runat="server"
                        BorderStyle="None" Width="80px"
                        Text="Thumb URL:" />
                    <asp:TextBox                              →18
                        ID="txtThumbnail" runat="server"
                        ReadOnly="True" Width="200px"
                        Text='<%# Bind("thumbnail") %>'/>
                    <br />
                    <asp:Label ID="Label8" runat="server"
                        BorderStyle="None" Width="80px"
                        Text="Image URL:" />
                    <asp:TextBox                              →19
                        ID="txtImage" runat="server"
                        ReadOnly="True" Width="200px"
                        Text='<%# Bind("image") %>'/><br />
                    <br />
                    <asp:LinkButton ID="LinkButton1"        →20
                        runat="server"
                        CommandName="Edit" Text="Edit" />
                     
                    <asp:LinkButton ID="LinkButton2"        →21
                        runat="server"
                        CommandName="New" Text="New" />
                    <asp:LinkButton ID="LinkButton3"        →22
                        runat="server"
                        CommandName="Delete" Text="Delete"
        />
                </ItemTemplate>
                <EditItemTemplate>                          →23
                    <asp:Label ID="Label1" runat="server"
                        BorderStyle="None" Width="80px"
                        Text="Product ID:" />
                    <asp:TextBox ID="txtProductID"          →24
                        runat="server"
                        ReadOnly="True" Width="100px"
                        BackColor="LightBlue"
                        Text='<%# Eval("productid") %>'/>
                    <br />
                    <asp:Label ID="Label2" runat="server"
                        BorderStyle="None" Width="80px"
                        Text="Category ID:" />
                    <asp:DropDownList                        →25
                        ID="DropDownList1"
                        runat="server"
                        BackColor="LightBlue"
                        DataSourceID="SqlDataSource3"
                        DataTextField="catid"
                        DataValueField="catid"
                        SelectedValue='<%# Bind("catid")
        %>'>
```

```
    </asp:DropDownList><br />
    <asp:Label ID="Label3" runat="server"
        BorderStyle="None" Width="80px"
        Text="Name:" />
    <asp:TextBox ID="txtName"                    →26
        runat="server"
        ReadOnly="False" Width="200px"
        BackColor="LightBlue"
        Text='<%# Bind("name") %>'/>
    <asp:RequiredFieldValidator
        ID="RequiredFieldValidator2"
        runat="server" Display="Dynamic"
        ControlToValidate="txtName"
        ErrorMessage="Required." /><br />
    <asp:Label ID="Label4" runat="server"
        BorderStyle="None" Width="80px"
        Height="45px"
        Text="Short Text:" />
    <asp:TextBox ID="txtShortText"               →27
        runat="server"
        ReadOnly="False"
TextMode="MultiLine"
        Height="40px" Width="200px"
        BackColor="LightBlue"
        Text='<%# Bind("shorttext") %>'/>
    <asp:RequiredFieldValidator
        ID="RequiredFieldValidator3"
        runat="server" Display="Dynamic"
        ControlToValidate="txtShortText"
        ErrorMessage="Required." /><br />
    <asp:Label ID="Label5" runat="server"
        BorderStyle="None" Width="80px"
        Height="65px"
        Text="Long Text:" />
    <asp:TextBox ID="txtLongText"                →28
        runat="server"
        ReadOnly="False"
TextMode="MultiLine"
        Height="60px" Width="200px"
        BackColor="LightBlue"
        Text='<%# Bind("longtext") %>'/>
    <asp:RequiredFieldValidator
        ID="RequiredFieldValidator4"
        runat="server" Display="Dynamic"
        ControlToValidate="txtLongText"
        ErrorMessage="Required." /><br />
    <asp:Label ID="Label6" runat="server"
        BorderStyle="None" Width="80px"
        Text="Price:" />
```

(continued)

Listing 7-7 *(continued)*

```
        <asp:TextBox ID="txtPrice"              →29
            runat="server"
            ReadOnly="False" Width="100px"
            BackColor="LightBlue"
            Text='<%# Bind("price") %>'/>
        <asp:RequiredFieldValidator
            ID="RequiredFieldValidator5"
            runat="server" Display="Dynamic"
            ControlToValidate="txtPrice"
            ErrorMessage="Required." />
        <asp:CompareValidator
            ID="CompareValidator1"
    runat="server"
            Display="Dynamic"
            ControlToValidate="txtPrice"
            ErrorMessage="Must be numeric."
            Operator="DataTypeCheck"
            Type="Double" /><br />
        <asp:Label ID="Label7" runat="server"
            BorderStyle="None" Width="80px"
            Text="Thumb URL:" />
        <asp:TextBox ID="txtThumbnail"          →30
            runat="server"
            ReadOnly="False" Width="200px"
            BackColor="LightBlue"
            Text='<%# Bind("thumbnail") %>'/>
        <asp:RequiredFieldValidator
            ID="RequiredFieldValidator7"
            runat="server" Display="Dynamic"
            ControlToValidate="txtThumbnail"
            ErrorMessage="Required." /><br />
        <asp:Label ID="Label8" runat="server"
            BorderStyle="None" Width="80px"
            Text="Image URL:" />
        <asp:TextBox ID="txtImage"              →31
            runat="server"
            ReadOnly="False" Width="200px"
            BackColor="LightBlue"
            Text='<%# Bind("image") %>'/>
        <asp:RequiredFieldValidator
            ID="RequiredFieldValidator8"
            runat="server" Display="Dynamic"
            ControlToValidate="txtImage"
            ErrorMessage="Required." />
        <br /><br />
        <asp:LinkButton ID="LinkButton1"        →32
            runat="server"
            CommandName="Update" Text="Update"
    />
```

```
             
            <asp:LinkButton ID="LinkButton3"          →33
                runat="server"
                CommandName="Cancel" Text="Cancel"
                CausesValidation="False" />
    </EditItemTemplate>
    <InsertItemTemplate>                              →34
            <asp:Label ID="Label1" runat="server"
                BorderStyle="None" Width="80px"
                Text="Product ID:" />
            <asp:TextBox ID="txtProductID"
                runat="server"
                ReadOnly="False" Width="100px"
                BackColor="LightBlue"
                Text='<%# Bind("productid") %>'/>
            <br />
            <asp:Label ID="Label2" runat="server"
                BorderStyle="None" Width="80px"
                Text="Category ID:" />
                <asp:DropDownList ID="DropDownList2"
                    runat="server"
                    BackColor="LightBlue"
                    DataSourceID="SqlDataSource3"
                    DataTextField="catid"
                    DataValueField="catid"
                    SelectedValue=
                        '<%# Bind("catid") %>'>
                </asp:DropDownList>
            <br />
            <asp:Label ID="Label3" runat="server"
                BorderStyle="None" Width="80px"
                Text="Name:" />
            <asp:TextBox ID="txtName" runat="server"
                ReadOnly="False" Width="200px"
                BackColor="LightBlue"
                Text='<%# Bind("name") %>'/>
            <asp:RequiredFieldValidator
                ID="RequiredFieldValidator2"
                runat="server" Display="Dynamic"
                ControlToValidate="txtName"
                ErrorMessage="Required." /><br />
            <asp:Label ID="Label4" runat="server"
                BorderStyle="None" Width="80px"
                Height="45px"
                Text="Short Text:" />
            <asp:TextBox ID="txtShortText"
                runat="server"
                ReadOnly="False"
TextMode="MultiLine"
                Height="40px" Width="200px"
                BackColor="LightBlue"
                Text='<%# Bind("shorttext") %>'/>
```

(continued)

Listing 7-7 *(continued)*

```
                    <asp:RequiredFieldValidator
                        ID="RequiredFieldValidator3"
                        runat="server" Display="Dynamic"
                        ControlToValidate="txtShortText"
                        ErrorMessage="Required." /><br />
                    <asp:Label ID="Label5" runat="server"
                        BorderStyle="None" Width="80px"
                        Height="65px"
                        Text="Long Text:" />
                    <asp:TextBox ID="txtLongText"
                        runat="server"
                        ReadOnly="False"
        TextMode="MultiLine"
                        Height="60px" Width="200px"
                        BackColor="LightBlue"
                        Text='<%# Bind("longtext") %>'/>
                    <asp:RequiredFieldValidator
                        ID="RequiredFieldValidator4"
                        runat="server" Display="Dynamic"
                        ControlToValidate="txtLongText"
                        ErrorMessage="Required." /><br />
                    <asp:Label ID="Label6" runat="server"
                        BorderStyle="None" Width="80px"
                        Text="Price:" />
                    <asp:TextBox ID="txtPrice"
        runat="server"
                        ReadOnly="False" Width="100px"
                        BackColor="LightBlue"
                        Text='<%# Bind("price") %>'/>
                    <asp:RequiredFieldValidator
                        ID="RequiredFieldValidator5"
                        runat="server" Display="Dynamic"
                        ControlToValidate="txtPrice"
                        ErrorMessage="Required." />
                    <asp:CompareValidator
                        ID="CompareValidator1"
        runat="server"
                        Display="Dynamic"
                        ControlToValidate="txtPrice"
                        ErrorMessage="Must be numeric."
                        Operator="DataTypeCheck"
                        Type="Double" /><br />
                    <asp:Label ID="Label7" runat="server"
                        BorderStyle="None" Width="80px"
                        Text="Thumb URL:" />
                    <asp:TextBox
                        ID="txtThumbnail" runat="server"
                        ReadOnly="False" Width="200px"
                        BackColor="LightBlue"
                        Text='<%# Bind("thumbnail") %>'/>
```

```
                <asp:RequiredFieldValidator
                    ID="RequiredFieldValidator7"
                    runat="server" Display="Dynamic"
                    ControlToValidate="txtThumbnail"
                    ErrorMessage="Required." /><br />
                <asp:Label ID="Label8" runat="server"
                    BorderStyle="None" Width="80px"
                    Text="Image URL:" />
                <asp:TextBox
                    ID="txtImage" runat="server"
                    ReadOnly="False" Width="200px"
                    BackColor="LightBlue"
                    Text='<%# Bind("image") %>'/>
                <asp:RequiredFieldValidator
                    ID="RequiredFieldValidator8"
                    runat="server" Display="Dynamic"
                    ControlToValidate="txtImage"
                    ErrorMessage="Required." />
                <br /><br />
                <asp:LinkButton ID="LinkButton1"
                    runat="server"
                    CommandName="Insert" Text="Insert"
  />
                 
                <asp:LinkButton ID="LinkButton2"
                    runat="server"
                    CommandName="Cancel" Text="Cancel"
                    CausesValidation="False"/>
        </InsertItemTemplate>
</asp:FormView>
<asp:SqlDataSource ID="SqlDataSource2"              →35
    runat="server"
    ConnectionString=
      "<%$ ConnectionStrings:ConnectionString
%>"
    ConflictDetection="CompareAllValues"

OldValuesParameterFormatString="original_{0}"
    OnDeleted="SqlDataSource2_Deleted"
    OnUpdated="SqlDataSource2_Updated"
    OnInserted="SqlDataSource2_Inserted"
    SelectCommand=                                  →36
      "SELECT [productid], [catid],
            [name], [shorttext], [longtext],
            [price], [thumbnail], [image]
        FROM [Products]
        WHERE ([productid] = @productid)"
    InsertCommand="INSERT                           →37
        INTO [Products]
            ([productid], [catid], [name],
            [shorttext], [longtext], [price],
            [thumbnail], [image])
```

(continued)

Listing 7-7 *(continued)*

```
              VALUES (@productid, @catid, @name,
                     @shorttext, @longtext, @price,
                     @thumbnail, @image)"
UpdateCommand="UPDATE [Products]              →38
    SET [catid] = @catid, [name] = @name,
        [shorttext] = @shorttext,
        [longtext] = @longtext,
        [price] = @price,
        [thumbnail] = @thumbnail,
        [image] = @image
    WHERE [productid] = @original_productid"
DeleteCommand="DELETE                         →39
  FROM [Products]
  WHERE [productid] = @original_productid" >
<SelectParameters>                            →40
    <asp:ControlParameter
        ControlID="GridView1"
        Name="productid"
        PropertyName="SelectedValue"
        Type="String" />
</SelectParameters>
<InsertParameters>                            →41
    <asp:Parameter Name="productid"
        Type="String" />
    <asp:Parameter Name="catid"
        Type="String" />
    <asp:Parameter Name="name"
        Type="String" />
    <asp:Parameter Name="shorttext"
        Type="String" />
    <asp:Parameter Name="longtext"
        Type="String" />
    <asp:Parameter Name="price"
        Type="Decimal" />
    <asp:Parameter Name="thumbnail"
        Type="String" />
    <asp:Parameter Name="image"
        Type="String" />
</InsertParameters>
<UpdateParameters>                            →42
    <asp:Parameter Name="catid"
        Type="String" />
    <asp:Parameter Name="name"
        Type="String" />
    <asp:Parameter Name="shorttext"
        Type="String" />
    <asp:Parameter Name="longtext"
        Type="String" />
```

```
                    <asp:Parameter Name="price"
                        Type="Decimal" />
                    <asp:Parameter Name="thumbnail"
                        Type="String" />
                    <asp:Parameter Name="image"
                        Type="String" />
                    <asp:Parameter Name="original_productid"
                        Type="String" />
                </UpdateParameters>
                <DeleteParameters>                        →43
                    <asp:Parameter Name="original_productid"
                        Type="String" />
                </DeleteParameters>
            </asp:SqlDataSource>
            <asp:SqlDataSource ID="SqlDataSource3"      →44
                runat="server"
                ConnectionString=
                  "<%$ ConnectionStrings:ConnectionString
              %>"
                SelectCommand="SELECT [catid]
                    FROM [Categories]
                    ORDER BY [catid]">
            </asp:SqlDataSource>
            <asp:Label ID="lblMessage"                  →45
                runat="server"
                EnableViewState="False" ForeColor="Red" />
        </td>
      </tr>
    </table>
    <asp:LinkButton ID="LinkButton1"                    →46
        runat="server"
        PostBackUrl="~/Default.aspx"
        CausesValidation="false" >
        Return to Home Page
    </asp:LinkButton>
</asp:Content>
```

Whew! That was a long listing. Any listing that long deserves a correspond-
ingly long list of explanations (might as well kick back for a read):

→ **1** The `Page` directive specifies the Master Page and other information for the page. Note that to use the Visual Basic version of the
code-behind file (shown in Listing 7-9), you must change the
`AutoEventWireup` attribute to `false`.

→ **2** The `<Content>` element provides the content that's displayed in
the `<ContentPlaceHolder>` element of the Master Page.

→ **3**   An HTML table displays the `GridView` and `FormView` controls side by side. The table consists of a single row with two columns, one for the `GridView`, the other for the `FormView`.

→ **4**   The `GridView` control displays the products from the Products table so the user can select a product to update or delete. The data source is `SqlDataSource1`, and paging is enabled. As a result, only ten product rows are displayed at a time.

→ **5**   The first column defined for the `GridView` control displays the `productid` field from the data source.

→ **6**   The second column displays the `name` field.

→ **7**   The third column is a command field that displays a <u>Select</u> link. When the user clicks this link, the indicated product is selected — which (in turn) displays the detail data for the selected product in the `FormView` control.

→ **8**   The first data source, named `SqlDataSource1`, provides the data displayed by the `GridView` control. Its `Select` statement simply selects all rows from the `Products` table.

→ **9**   The `FormView` control displays the detail data for the product selected by the `GridView1` control. Note that the connection to the `GridView1` control isn't specified in the `FormView` control itself. Instead, the data source that the `FormView` control is bound to (`SqlDataSource2`) handles this relationship.

→ **10**   The `FormView` control uses templates to specify how its data is to be displayed. The first of these is the `EmptyDataTemplate` — used when the data source has no data — in which case, the `FormView` control displays this instruction: `Please select a product`. In addition, a link lets the user place the `FormView` control in Insert mode by specifying `New` for the `CommandName` attribute.

→ **11**   The `ItemTemplate` displays the data for the row selected by the data source. This template consists of several labels and text fields that display product data; the text boxes are all marked read-only so the user can't change their contents. (Note that I could have used labels instead of text boxes to display the data in the item template. Then I wouldn't have to use the `ReadOnly` attribute. I chose to use read-only text fields instead because I wanted the bordered look provided by the `TextBox` control.)

→ **12** The first text box in the item template displays the product ID. Note how an ASP.NET 2.0 binding expression is used to bind the Text property of the text box to the productid field of the data source. The new Eval method provides a simple way to provide one-way binding for display-only fields.

→ **13** The next TextBox control displays the category ID. Here, the Bind method is used instead of the Eval method to provide two-way (input and output) data binding.

→ **14** This text box displays the product name.

→ **15** This text box displays the shorttext field of the data source. Note that the MultiLine attribute is specified for the text box so the user can enter more than one line of text.

→ **16** This text box displays the longtext field — again, using the MultiLine attribute so the user can enter more than one line of text.

→ **17** This text box binds to the price field of the data source. In this case, a format string is used along with the Bind method to apply currency formatting to the price.

→ **18** This text box displays the thumbnail field.

→ **19** This text box displays the image field.

→ **20** This link button, which appears at the bottom of the item template, allows the user to edit the product data. Note that the CommandName attribute specifies Edit as the command name. The FormView control displays the EditItemTemplate, defined in line 23, when the user clicks this button.

→ **21** This link button lets the user delete the product. Its CommandName attribute specifies Delete as the command name. As a result, the product row is automatically deleted when the user clicks this button.

→ **22** The New link button displays the InsertItem template, defined starting at line 34. Then the user can enter the data for a new product.

→ **23** The EditItemTemplate defines the data that's displayed when the user clicks the Edit link, placing the FormView control in Edit mode. As you can see, the contents of this template are very similar to the contents of the item template.

→ **24**   The text box for the product ID is read-only to prevent the user from modifying the `product ID` column of the `Products` table.

→ **25**   Instead of typing into a text box, the user chooses a product category from a drop-down list bound to `SqlDataSource3` (which is defined in line 44).

→ **26**   The next text box is bound to the `name` field. Note that it is followed by a `RequiredFieldValidator` control so the user must enter a name for the product.

→ **27**   This text box is bound to the `shorttext` field. A `RequiredFieldValidator` control requires the user to enter a value for this field.

→ **28**   The text box for the `longtext` field is also followed by a `RequiredFieldValidator`.

→ **29**   The text box for the `price` field does *not* use a format string to apply the currency format to the price. That's to avoid the dollar sign (or other currency symbol), which can complicate the parsing required to convert the string value of the `Text` property to a decimal value when the data is entered. Notice also that in addition to a `RequiredFieldValidator`, this field also uses a `CompareValidator` to ensure that the user enters a valid number.

→ **30**   The text box for the `thumbnail` field uses a `RequiredFieldValidator` to ensure the user enters a value.

→ **31**   The text box for the `image` field is also associated with a `RequiredFieldValidator`.

→ **32**   This link button's `CommandName` attribute is set to `Update`. As a result, the database is updated with new information when the user clicks this link.

→ **33**   The `CommandName` attribute of this link button is set to `Cancel`. As a result, whatever data the user enters is discarded when this link is clicked, and the database is not updated. `CausesValidation = "False"` is specified so the page's validators are ignored when the user clicks this link.

→ **34**   The `InsertItemTemplate` template is displayed when the `FormView` control is placed in Insert mode. The controls defined for this template are the same ones defined for the `EditItemTemplate` template.

→ **35**   This `SqlDataSource` control, named `SqlDataSource2`, provides the data for the `FormView` control. The `OnDeleted`, `OnUpdated`, and `OnInserted` attributes specify the methods called to handle the `Deleted`, `Updated`, and `Inserted` events for the data source.

If you're using the Visual Basic version of the code-behind file for this page, you should omit these attributes.

→ **36**   The `SelectCommand` attribute provides the `SELECT` statement that retrieves a specific product from the `Products` table. Notice that the `WHERE` clause uses the `@productid` parameter. As you can see in line 40, this parameter comes from the `SelectedValue` property of the `GridView` control. As a result, this data source retrieves the `Product` row selected by the user via the `GridView` control.

→ **37**   The `InsertCommand` attribute specifies the `INSERT` statement that inserts a new row into the `Products` table.

→ **38**   The `UpdateCommand` attribute specifies the `UPDATE` statement that updates product rows.

→ **39**   The `DeleteCommand` attribute specifies the `DELETE` statement that deletes products.

→ **40**   The `<SelectParameters>` element defines the parameters used by the `SELECT` statement. In this case, only one parameter is used: a `Control` parameter that's bound to the `SelectedValue` property of the `GridView1` control. Thus the value of this parameter is automatically set to the product ID selected by the user (via the `GridView` control).

→ **41**   The `<InsertParameters>` element provides the parameters used by the `INSERT` statement.

→ **42**   The `<UpdateParameters>` element provides the parameters used by the `UPDATE` statement.

→ **43**   The `<DeleteParameters>` element provides the parameters used by the `DELETE` statement.

→ **44**   The third data source used by this page, `SqlDataSource3`, retrieves all rows from the `Categories` table and uses them to populate the Categories drop-down list in the `EditItemTemplate` and `InsertItemTemplate` templates of the `FormView1` control.

→ **45**   A label control named `lblMessage` appears beneath the `FormView` control. This label displays messages about the success or failure of database updates.

→ **46**   Finally, a link button provides a convenient way for the user to get back to the menu page.

The FormView Control

The new `FormView` control is similar to the `DetailsView` control used in the Product Catalog application (shown in Chapter 5). The main difference is that the `DetailsView` control renders its data using an HTML table — with one row for each field in the data source. In contrast, the `FormView` control is based on templates that you supply. Then it's up to you to specify exactly how you want to render the data.

The `FormView` control lets you create one or more of the following templates:

✔ `EmptyItemTemplate`: This template is rendered if the data source is empty.

✔ `ItemTemplate`: Used to display data in Read-Only mode.

✔ `EditItemTemplate`: Used to render data when the `FormView` control is in Edit mode.

✔ `InsertItemTemplate`: Used to render data when the `FormView` control is in Insert mode.

✔ `HeaderTemplate`: Displayed at the top of the control.

✔ `FooterTemplate`: Displayed at the bottom of the control.

✔ `PagerTemplate`: Displayed when paging is enabled.

You can use the `Eval` or `Bind` methods in binding expressions to display data from the data source in a template. For example, here's a label that's bound to a data-source field named `lastname`:

```
<asp:Label ID="lblLastName"
    runat="server"
        Text='<%#
    Eval("lastname") %>'/>
```

And here's a text box bound to the same field:

```
<asp:TextBox ID="txtProductID"
    runat="server"
    Width="100px"
    Text='<%# Bind("lastname")
    %>'/>
```

Notice that you have to use `Bind` instead of `Eval` when you want the binding to be two-way — that is, for input as well as for output.

A template can include a link that specifies a command name via the `CommandName` attribute. Then when the user clicks the link, the specified command will be sent to the `FormView` control. The following commands are allowed:

✔ `Edit`: Places the `FormView` control in Edit mode and displays the `EditItemTemplate` template.

✔ `New`: Places the `FormView` control in Insert mode and uses the `InsertItemTemplate`.

✔ `Update`: Accepts changes made while in Edit mode and updates the data source.

✔ `Insert`: Inserts a row using data entered while in Insert mode.

✔ `Cancel`: Cancels Edit or Insert mode and ignores any changes.

✔ `Delete`: Deletes a row.

✔ `Page`: Used to support paging operations.

The code-behind file for the Product Maintenance page

Like the `CatMaint.aspx` page, the `ProdMaint.aspx` page requires a code-behind file. The C# version of this code-behind file is shown in Listing 7-8, and Listing 7-9 shows the Visual Basic version.

Listing 7-8:   The code-behind file for the Product Maintenance page (C#)

```csharp
using System;
using System.Data;
using System.Configuration;
using System.Collections;
using System.Web;
using System.Web.Security;
using System.Web.UI;
using System.Web.UI.WebControls;
using System.Web.UI.WebControls.WebParts;
using System.Web.UI.HtmlControls;

public partial class ProdMaint : System.Web.UI.Page
{
    protected void SqlDataSource2_Deleted(              →1
        object sender,
        SqlDataSourceStatusEventArgs e)
    {
        if (e.AffectedRows == 0 | e.Exception != null)
        {
            lblMessage.Text = "<br />Product could not "
                + "be deleted. Please try again.";
            e.ExceptionHandled = true;
        }
        else
        {
            lblMessage.Text = "<br />Product deleted.";
            GridView1.SelectedIndex = -1;
            this.DataBind();
        }

    }
```

(continued)

Listing 7-8 *(continued)*

```
protected void SqlDataSource2_Updated(                →2
    object sender,
    SqlDataSourceStatusEventArgs e)
{
    if (e.AffectedRows == 0 | e.Exception != null)
    {
        lblMessage.Text = "Product could not "
            + "be updated. Please try again.";
        e.ExceptionHandled = true;
    }
    else
        lblMessage.Text = "Product updated.";

}

protected void SqlDataSource2_Inserted(               →3
    object sender,
    SqlDataSourceStatusEventArgs e)
{
    if (e.AffectedRows == 0 | e.Exception != null)
    {
        lblMessage.Text = "Product could not "
            + "be inserted. Please try again.";
        e.ExceptionHandled = true;
    }
    else
    {
        lblMessage.Text = "Product inserted.";
        this.DataBind();
    }
}
}
```

As you can see, the code-behind file consists of just three methods:

→ **1**   SqlDataSource2_Deleted: This method is called when a row
has been deleted from the Products table — whether or not the
row was *successfully* deleted. As a result, both the AffectedRows
and the Exception properties are checked to see whether an
error occurred. If so, an appropriate error message is displayed in
the lblMessage label. If the deletion was successful, what shows
up is a message indicating that the product was deleted. Then the
SelectedIndex property of the GridView control is set to -1
automatically to deselect the row, and the DataBind method is
called to re-bind the controls.

→ **2**   `SqlDataSource2_Updated`: This method is similar to the `SqlDataSource2_Deleted` method. It's called when a row has been updated. Again, both the `AffectedRows` and the `Exception` properties are checked to see whether an error occurred.

→ **3**   `SqlDataSource2_Inserted`: This method is called when a row has been inserted. If the `AffectedRows` or `Exception` properties indicate that an error has occurred, an appropriate error message is displayed. Otherwise what shows up is a message indicating that the product has been inserted; then the page is re-bound.

Listing 7-9:   The code-behind file for the Catalog Maintenance page (VB)

```
Partial Class ProdMaint
    Inherits System.Web.UI.Page

    Protected Sub SqlDataSource2_Deleted( _                    →1
            ByVal sender As Object, _
            ByVal e As System.Web.UI.WebControls. _
                SqlDataSourceStatusEventArgs) _
            Handles SqlDataSource2.Deleted
        If e.AffectedRows = 0 _
                Or Not e.Exception Is Nothing Then
                lblMessage.Text = "<br />Product could not " _
                + "be deleted. Please try again."
                e.ExceptionHandled = True
        Else
                lblMessage.Text = "<br />Product deleted."
                GridView1.SelectedIndex = -1
                Me.DataBind()
        End If
    End Sub

    Protected Sub SqlDataSource2_Updated( _                    →2
            ByVal sender As Object, _
            ByVal e As System.Web.UI. _
            WebControls.SqlDataSourceStatusEventArgs) _
            Handles SqlDataSource2.Updated
        If e.AffectedRows = 0 _
                Or Not e.Exception Is Nothing Then
                lblMessage.Text = "Product could not " _
                + "be updated. Please try again."
                e.ExceptionHandled = True
        Else
                lblMessage.Text = "<br />Product updated."
                GridView1.SelectedIndex = -1
                Me.DataBind()
        End If
    End Sub
```

(continued)

Listing 7-9 *(continued)*

```
Protected Sub SqlDataSource2_Inserted( _                    →3
        ByVal sender As Object, _
        ByVal e As System.Web.UI.WebControls. _
        SqlDataSourceStatusEventArgs) _
        Handles SqlDataSource2.Inserted
    If e.AffectedRows = 0 _
            Or Not e.Exception Is Nothing Then
        lblMessage.Text = "<br />Product could not " _
        + "be inserted. Please try again."
        e.ExceptionHandled = True
    Else
        lblMessage.Text = "<br />Product inserted."
        GridView1.SelectedIndex = -1
        Me.DataBind()
    End If
End Sub

End Class
```

Chapter 8

Building a Report Application

*R*eport applications are an important part of almost all but the most trivial Web applications. Report applications extract data from a database and present it in a meaningful form for the users. In some cases, the Report page includes a link to a printable version of the page that doesn't have banner graphics or other distractions.

This chapter presents a simple report application — called the Order Listing application — that lists orders entered by users. The Order Listing application works in a way that's consistent with the other applications in this book:

✔ It uses the same database as the Shopping Cart application in Chapter 6.

✔ It lets the user select an order in the Orders table, and then displays an invoice for the order.

✔ It includes a link to a printable version of the invoice.

The Application's User Interface

This application has a simple user interface that consists of just two pages: the main page and the Master Page. The main page (`Default.aspx`), shown in Figure 8-1, is the equivalent of a home page for the application. After the banner image that's displayed by the Master Page, a drop-down list lets the user choose the order to be displayed. Then the details for the selected order are displayed in nicely formatted tables.

Notice the <u>Print this page</u> link near the top of the page. If the user clicks this link, the `PrintOrder.aspx` page shown in Figure 8-2 is displayed. This page is almost identical to the page shown in Figure 8-1, with two differences: (1) the banner image isn't displayed and (2) the <u>Print this page</u> link is omitted. Then the user can use the browser's File⇨Print command to print a copy of the page.

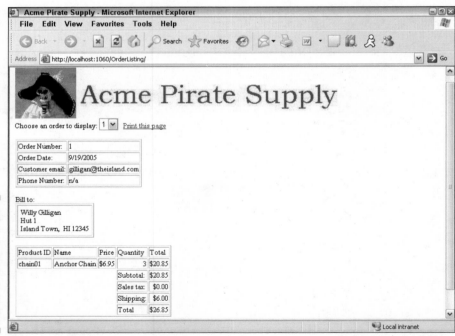

Figure 8-1: The Orders application displays information for the selected order.

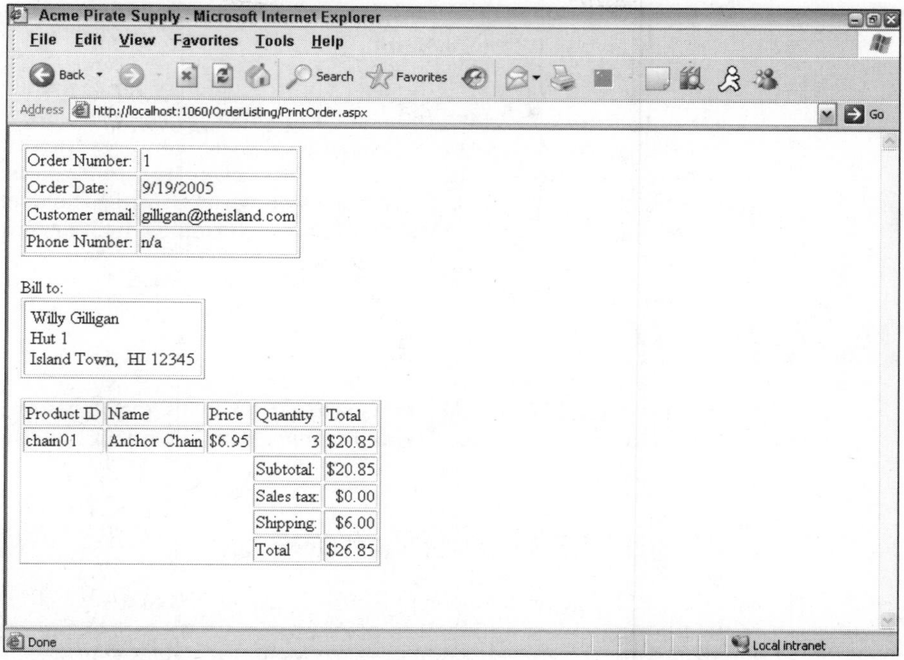

Figure 8-2:
The Print
Order page.

Designing the Application

Even though this application is simple, there are several important design decisions that should be made before you begin writing the application's code. These decisions are described in the following paragraphs:

- ✔ You'll need to decide the details of how the database will store the data to be shown in the report. Because this application uses the same database as the Shopping Cart application presented in Chapter 6, the database design decisions have already been made. For more information, refer to Chapter 6.

- ✔ There are several ways to create reports in ASP.NET. If you have a professional edition of Visual Studio, you can use Crystal Reports to create the reports. Visual Web Developer Express Edition doesn't include Crystal Reports, however, so the application that's the subject of this chapter uses standard ASP.NET controls to build its report.

- ✔ The invoice report shown in the main application page and the Print Order page should be identical. You could simply duplicate the code used to create the report in both pages, but that would be inefficient. A better way is to create a user control that displays the printable data for an order. Then you simply include the user control in both the

`Default.aspx` page and the `PrintOrder.aspx` page. That's the technique used in this application.

✔ You'll need a way to tell the user control which order to display. There are, of course, several ways you can do that. For this application, a session variable named `ordernum` is used. When the user uses the drop-down list to select an order in the `Default.aspx` page, the application saves the order number in the `ordernum` session variable. Then the user control retrieves this session state variable to determine which order to display.

Building the Database

First things first: Before you can use the Order Listing application, you must create the database it uses. The following sections explain how to do that.

Designing the database

The Order Listing application uses the same database design that was used in the Shopping Cart application presented in Chapter 6. I won't review all the details of this database design here. (If necessary, refer to Chapter 6 to catch up on those details.)

To save you some page-flipping, though, Tables 8-1 through 8-3 list the columns defined for the three database tables used by the Order Listing application: `Customers`, `Orders`, and `OrderItems`.

Although the design of the database is the same, this application doesn't use the same *physical* database as the one presented in Chapter 6. That database was named `Cart`. This application uses a database named `Orders`.

Table 8-1		The Customers Table
Column name	*Type*	*Description*
email	VARCHAR(50)	The customer's e-mail address. This column also serves as the table's primary key.
lastname	VARCHAR(50)	The customer's last name.
firstname	VARCHAR(50)	The customer's first name.
address	VARCHAR(50)	The customer's street address.
city	VARCHAR(50)	The customer's city.

Column name	Type	Description
state	VARCHAR(2)	The customer's two-character state code.
zipcode	VARCHAR(9)	The customer's Zip code, up to nine characters.
phone	VARCHAR(20)	The customer's phone number.

Table 8-2	The Orders Table	
Column name	**Type**	**Description**
ordernum	INT	This column uniquely identifies each order and serves as the the table's primary key.
orderdate	SMALLDATETIME	The date the order was placed.
custemail	VARCHAR(50)	The customer's e-mail address. This serves as a foreign key that relates the order to a particular row in the Customers table.
subtotal	MONEY	The sum of the totals for each item associated with the order.
salestax	MONEY	The sales tax for the order.
shipping	MONEY	The shipping charges for the order.
total	n/a	The order total. This field is calculated by adding the subtotal, salestax, and shipping fields.

Table 8-3	The OrderItems Table	
Column name	**Type**	**Description**
ordernum	INT	The order number for the order this item is associated with.
productid	VARCHAR(10)	The ID for the product represented by this item. Note that this column along with the ordernum columns comprise the primary key for this table.

Table 8-3 *(continued)*

Column name	Type	Description
name	VARCHAR(50)	The product's name.
price	MONEY	The product's price.
quantity	SMALLINT	The quantity ordered.
total	n/a	The total for the item, calculated by multiplying the price by the quantity.

Creating the database

The CD that comes with this book includes a script named CreateOrdersDB. sql that you can use to create this database. To run this script, open a command-prompt window and change to the directory that contains the script. Then enter this command:

```
sqlcmd -S localhost\SQLExpress -i CreateOrdersDB.sql
```

Note that this command assumes you're running SQL Server Express on your own computer. If you're using SQL Server on a different server, you'll need to change localhost\SQLExpress to the correct name.

If you're curious about the contents of this script, refer to Listing 6-1 in Chapter 6. The only difference between that script and the CreateOrdersDB.sql script is the name of the database that's created. Otherwise the scripts are identical.

Adding test data

You can add some useful test data to the Orders database by running the InsertOrdersData.sql script that's included on this book's companion CD. In addition to adding category and product data to the database, it also creates two customers (Willy Gilligan and Jonas Grumby), each with an order in the Orders table. The test data is simple, but enough to test the application.

To run the InsertData.sql script, open a command window, change to the directory that contains the script, and run this command:

```
sqlcmd -S localhost\SQLExpress -i InsertData.sql
```

Again, you'll need to change the server instance name if it is other than SQLExpress.

SQL statements to retrieve the order data

The Order Listing application uses three SQL SELECT statements to retrieve data from the Customers, Orders, and OrderItems tables. These SQL statements are described in the following paragraphs:

✔ The following SELECT statement fills the drop-down list with order numbers:

```
SELECT [ordernum]
FROM [orders] ORDER BY [ordernum]
```

✔ The SELECT statement used to retrieve a specific order requires a join to retrieve data from both the Orders table and the Customers table:

```
SELECT Orders.ordernum,
       Orders.orderdate,
       Orders.custemail,
       Orders.subtotal,
       Orders.salestax,
       Orders.shipping,
       Orders.total,
       Customers.lastname,
       Customers.firstname,
       Customers.address,
       Customers.city,
       Customers.state,
       Customers.zipcode,
       Customers.phone
FROM Orders
INNER JOIN Customers
    ON Orders.custemail = Customers.email
WHERE Orders.ordernum = @ordernum
ORDER BY Orders.ordernum"
```

✔ The following statement retrieves the items for a given order:

```
SELECT [productid],
       [name],
       [price],
       [quantity],
       [total],
       [ordernum]
FROM [OrderItems]
WHERE ([ordernum] = @ordernum)
ORDER BY [productid]"
```

Connecting to the database

The connection string for the Order Listing application is stored in the `web.config` file, like this:

```
<connectionStrings>
    <add name="ConnectionString"
          connectionString="Data
             Source=localhost\SQLExpress;
Initial Catalog=Orders;Integrated Security=True"/>
</connectionStrings>
```

You'll need to change this connection string if your server isn't named `localhost\SQLExpress` or if you want to run the application against a different database.

Building the Master Page

Listing 8-1 shows the Master Page (`MasterPage.master`), which displays a banner at the top of each page.

Listing 8-1:   The Master Page (MasterPage.master)

```
<%@ Master Language="C#"                                      →1
    AutoEventWireup="true"
    CodeFile="MasterPage.master.cs"
    Inherits="MasterPage" %>

<!DOCTYPE html PUBLIC "-//W3C//DTD XHTML 1.1//EN"
    "http://www.w3.org/TR/xhtml11/DTD/xhtml11.dtd">

<html xmlns="http://www.w3.org/1999/xhtml" >
<head runat="server">
    <title>Acme Pirate Store</title>
</head>
<body>
    <form id="form1" runat="server">
    <div>
        <img src="Images/Banner.jpg" /><br />       →2
        <asp:contentplaceholder                       →3
            id="ContentPlaceHolder1"
            runat="server">
        </asp:contentplaceholder>
        <br /><br />
    </div>
    </form>
</body>
</html>
```

Three key points stand out in this listing:

→ **1**   The `Master` directive indicates that the file is a Master Page. Note that if you want to use Visual Basic rather than C# for the application's code-behind files, you should change the `AutoEventWireup` attribute to `false`.

→ **2**   The `Image` control displays the banner image that appears at the top of each page.

→ **3**   The `ContentPlaceHolder` control indicates where the content for each page will appear.

Building the Order User Control

The `Order` user control (`Orders.aspx`) displays the details for a particular order. The order to be displayed is specified via a session variable named `ordernum`. Then the order details are formatted using simple HTML tables.

Remarkably, the code-behind file for this user control is empty. The order number — a corresponding SQL parameter created for this purpose by the `<SessionParameter>` element — is automatically retrieved from the session state.

Listing 8-2 shows the code for the `Order` user control.

Listing 8-2:   The Order user control (Order.aspx)

```
<%@ Control Language="C#"                              →1
    AutoEventWireup="true"
    CodeFile="Order.ascx.cs"
    Inherits="Order" %>

<asp:FormView ID="FormView1" runat="server"           →2
    DataSourceID="SqlDataSource1"
    DataKeyNames="ordernum" >
  <ItemTemplate>                                       →3
      <table border="1">                               →4
      <tr><td>
      Order Number:
      </td><td>
      <asp:Label ID="ordernumLabel" runat="server"     →5
          Text='<%# Eval("ordernum") %>' />
      </td></tr>
      <tr><td>
      Order Date:
      </td><td>
      <asp:Label ID="orderdateLabel" runat="server"    →6
          Text='<%# Eval("orderdate", "{0:d}") %>' />
```

(continued)

Listing 8-2 *(continued)*

```
</td></tr>
<tr><td>
Customer email:
</td><td>
<asp:Label ID="custemailLabel" runat="server"            →7
    Text='<%# Eval("custemail") %>' />
</td></tr>
<tr><td>
Phone Number:
</td><td>
<asp:Label ID="Label10" runat="server"                   →8
    Text='<%# Eval("phone") %>' />
</td></tr>
</table>                                                  →9
<br />
Bill to:<br />
<table border="1" cellpadding="5" >                       →10
  <tr><td>
  <asp:Label ID="lblFirstName" runat="server"             →11
      Text='<%# Eval("firstname") %>' />
  <asp:Label ID="lblLastName" runat="server"              →12
      Text='<%# Eval("lastname") %>' /><br />
  <asp:Label ID="lblAddress" runat="server"               →13
      Text='<%# Eval("address") %>' /><br />
  <asp:Label ID="lblCity" runat="server"                  →14
      Text='<%# Eval("city") %>' />, 
  <asp:Label ID="lblState" runat="server"                 →15
      Text='<%# Eval("state") %>' />
  <asp:Label ID="lblZipCode" runat="server"               →16
      Text='<%# Eval("zipcode") %>' /><br />
</td></tr>
</table>                                                  →17
<br />
<table border="1">                                        →18
  <asp:Repeater ID="Repeater1" runat="server"             →19
      DataSourceID="SqlDataSource2">
    <HeaderTemplate>                                      →20
      <tr>
        <td>Product ID</td>
          <td>Name</td>
          <td>Price</td>
          <td>Quantity</td>
          <td>Total</td>
      </tr>
    </HeaderTemplate>
    <ItemTemplate>                                        →21
      <tr>
        <td>
          <asp:Label ID="Label1" runat="server"           →22
              Text='<%# Eval("productid") %>' />
        </td>
        <td>
```

```
                <asp:Label ID="Label2" runat="server"        →23
                    Text='<%# Eval("name") %>' />
            </td>
            <td>
              <asp:Label ID="Label3" runat="server"          →24
                  Text='<%# Eval("price", "{0:c}") %>' />
            </td>
            <td align="right">
              <asp:Label ID="Label4" runat="server"          →25
                  Text='<%# Eval("quantity") %>' />
            </td>
            <td align="right">
              <asp:Label ID="Label5" runat="server"          →26
                  Text='<%# Eval("total", "{0:c}") %>' />
            </td>
          </tr>
        </ItemTemplate>                                       →27
      </asp:Repeater>                                         →28
      <tr>
        <td></td><td></td><td></td>
        <td>Subtotal:</td>
        <td align="right">
          <asp:Label ID="Label5" runat="server"              →29
              Text='<%# Eval("subtotal", "{0:c}") %>' />
        </td>
      </tr>
      <tr>
        <td></td><td></td><td></td>
        <td>Sales tax:</td>
        <td align="right">
          <asp:Label ID="Label6" runat="server"              →30
              Text='<%# Eval("salestax", "{0:c}") %>' />
        </td>
      </tr>
      <tr>
        <td></td><td></td><td></td>
        <td>Shipping:</td>
        <td align="right">
          <asp:Label ID="Label7" runat="server"              →31
              Text='<%# Eval("shipping", "{0:c}") %>' />
        </td>
      </tr>
      <tr>
        <td></td><td></td><td></td>
        <td>Total</td>
        <td align="right">
          <asp:Label ID="Label8" runat="server"              →32
              Text='<%# Eval("total", "{0:c}") %>' />
        </td>
      </tr>
    </table>                                                  →33
</ItemTemplate>                                               →34
```

(continued)

Listing 8-2 *(continued)*

```
</asp:FormView>                                              →35
<asp:SqlDataSource ID="SqlDataSource1"                       >36
     runat="server"
     ConnectionString=
     "<%$ ConnectionStrings:CartConnectionString %>"
     SelectCommand="SELECT Orders.ordernum,
             Orders.orderdate,
             Orders.custemail,
             Orders.subtotal,
             Orders.salestax,
             Orders.shipping,
             Orders.total,
             Customers.lastname,
             Customers.firstname,
             Customers.address,
             Customers.city,
             Customers.state,
             Customers.zipcode,
             Customers.phone
         FROM Orders
         INNER JOIN Customers
             ON Orders.custemail = Customers.email
         WHERE Orders.ordernum = @ordernum
         ORDER BY Orders.ordernum" >
     <SelectParameters>
         <asp:SessionParameter                               →37
             Name="ordernum"
             SessionField="ordernum"
             Type="Int32" />
     </SelectParameters>
</asp:SqlDataSource>
<asp:SqlDataSource ID="SqlDataSource2"                       →38
     runat="server"
     ConnectionString=
     "<%$ ConnectionStrings:ConnectionString %>"
     SelectCommand="SELECT [productid],
             [name],
             [price],
             [quantity],
             [total],
             [ordernum]
         FROM [OrderItems]
         WHERE ([ordernum] = @ordernum)
         ORDER BY [productid]" >
     <SelectParameters>
         <asp:ControlParameter                               →39
             Name="ordernum"
             ControlID="FormView1"
             PropertyName="SelectedValue"
             Type="Int32" />
     </SelectParameters>
</asp:SqlDataSource>
```

Lots going on here — so here are explanations of key lines in this user control:

→ **1** The Control directive marks the start of the user control. Note that although the Control directive specifies the AutoEvent Wireup, CodeFile, and Inherits attributes, the code-behind file is empty. (You could delete it, but then you'd have to remove the CodeFile and Inherits attributes.)

→ **2** This line marks the start of the code for the FormView control that displays the order data. This FormView control is bound to the data source named SqlDataSource1, which retrieves data from the Orders table. The end tag completes this FormView control in line 35.

→ **3** The <ItemTemplate> element defines the content that's displayed for the order. The end tag for this element is found in line 34.

→ **4** The<ItemTemplate> uses three separate HTML tables to display the order data. This line marks the start of the first of these tables, which displays the order number and date as well as the customer's e-mail address and phone number.

→ **5** This label displays the order number. It uses the Eval method to bind to the data source's ordernum field.

→ **6** This label displays the order date. The Eval method binds this label to the orderdate field and formats it using the short date format.

→ **7** This label displays the customer's e-mail address.

→ **8** This label displays the customer's phone number.

→ **9** The </table> tag marks the end of the first table.

→ **10** The second table will display the customer's bill-to information.

→ **11** This label displays the customer's first name.

→ **12** This label displays the customer's last name.

→ **13** This label displays the customer's street address.

→ **14** This label displays the customer's city.

→ **15** This label displays the customer's state.

→ **16** This label displays the customer's Zip code.

→ **17** This line marks the end of the second table.

→ **18** The third table displays the line items and totals for the order.

→ **19** A Repeater control is used to display the table rows that show the order's line items. This Repeater control is bound to the

SqlDataSource2 data source, which retrieves data from the Orders table. The <Repeater> element ends at line 28.

→ **20** The header template provides the column headers for the table. It consists of a single row with cells for the Name, Price, Quantity, and Total columns.

→ **21** The <ItemTemplate> defines the table row that's rendered for each of the order's line items. This <ItemTemplate> for the Repeater control (not to be confused with the <ItemTemplate> for the FormView control) ends in line 27.

→ **22** This label displays the product ID.

→ **23** This label displays the product name.

→ **24** This label displays the price, formatted as currency.

→ **25** This label displays the quantity.

→ **26** This label displays the line item total, formatted as currency.

→ **27** This line marks the end of the Repeater control's <ItemTemplate>.

→ **28** This line marks the end of the Repeater control.

→ **29** This label displays the order subtotal, formatted as currency.

→ **30** This label displays the sales tax for the order, formatted as currency.

→ **31** This label displays the shipping charges for the order, formatted as currency.

→ **32** This label displays the order total, formatted as currency.

→ **33** This line marks the end of the third table, which was started in line 18.

→ **34** This line marks the end of the FormView control's <ItemTemplate>.

→ **35** This line marks the end of the FormView control.

→ **36** The first SQL data source retrieves data for an order from the Customers and Orders tables.

→ **37** The <asp:SessionParameter> element defines a parameter whose value is automatically retrieved from session state. In this case, the @ordernum parameter's value is retrieved from the session state variable named ordernum.

→ **38** The second SQL data source retrieves the line items from the OrderItems table. It uses a parameter named @ordernum to indicate the order whose items are to be retrieved.

→ **39** The @ordernum parameter is defined using an <asp:ControlParameter> element. Here the ControlID attribute is set to FormView1 and the PropertyName attribute specifies `SelectedValue`. By default, the `SelectedValue` attribute of a `FormView` control returns the primary key of the item currently displayed by the `FormView` control. As a result, this parameter's value will be the order number of the order currently displayed by the `FormView` control.

Building the Default Page

The `Default.aspx` displays a link to the `OrderPrint.aspx` page, a drop-down list that lets the user pick an order, and the `Order` user control that displays the order. This page requires a small code-behind file, whose only function is to create the `ordernum` session variable required by the `Order` user control. The value for this variable is taken from the drop-down list.

The Default.aspx file

Listing 8-3 shows the `.aspx` code for the default page. Refer to Figure 8-1 to see how this page looks on-screen.

Listing 8-3:   The Default page (Default.aspx)

```
<%@ Page Language="C#"                               →1
    MasterPageFile="~/MasterPage.master"
    AutoEventWireup="true"
    CodeFile="Default.aspx.cs"
    Inherits="_Default"
    Title="Acme Pirate Supply" %>
<%@ Register Src="Order.ascx"                        →2
    TagName="Order"
    TagPrefix="uc1" %>
<asp:Content ID="Content1"                           →3
    ContentPlaceHolderID="ContentPlaceHolder1"
    Runat="Server">
    Choose an order to display:
    <asp:DropDownList ID="ddlOrder" runat="server"   →4
        DataSourceID="SqlDataSource1"
        DataTextField="ordernum"
        DataValueField="ordernum"
        AutoPostBack="True" />
     
    <asp:LinkButton ID="LinkButton1"                 →5
        runat="server"
        PostBackUrl="~/PrintOrder.aspx">
    Print this page</asp:LinkButton>
    <asp:SqlDataSource ID="SqlDataSource1"           →6
```

(continued)

Listing 8-3 *(continued)*

```
        runat="server"
        ConnectionString=
        "<%$ ConnectionStrings:CartConnectionString %>"
        SelectCommand="SELECT ordernum
            FROM Orders ORDER BY ordernum" >
    </asp:SqlDataSource>
    <br /><br />
    <uc1:Order ID="Order1" runat="server" />                →7
</asp:Content>
```

The following list explains the numbered lines in this listing:

→ **1**   The `Page` directive specifies the Master Page and other information for the page.

       To use the Visual Basic version of the code-behind file (shown in Listing 8-5), you'll have to change the `AutoEventWireup` attribute to `false` and the `CodeFile` attribute to `Default.aspx.vb`.

→ **2**   The `Register` directive is required to register the `Order` user control. It specifies that the source file for the user control is `Order.ascx`. Then the `TagName` and `TagPrefix` attributes indicate that you can include the user control on the page by using the tag `uc1:Order`.

→ **3**   The `<Content>` element provides the content that's displayed in the `<ContentPlaceHolder>` element of the Master Page.

→ **4**   The drop-down list control displays a list of all order numbers currently in the `Orders` table. This drop-down list is bound to the data source named `SqlDataSource1`; auto post-back is enabled so the page is posted back to the server when the user selects an order.

→ **5**   The link button posts back to the `PrintOrder.aspx` page.

→ **6**   The SQL data source retrieves the order numbers from the `Orders` table, using them to populate the drop-down list.

→ **7**   The `uc1:Order` tag places the `Order` user control on the page. This user control is responsible for displaying the data for the selected order.

The code-behind file for the default page

The `Default.aspx` page requires a simple code-behind file to create the session state variable that stores the selected order number. Listing 8-4 shows the C# version of this code-behind file, and Listing 8-5 shows the Visual Basic version.

Listing 8-4: The code-behind file for the default page (C#)

```csharp
using System;
using System.Data;
using System.Configuration;
using System.Collections;
using System.Web;
using System.Web.Security;
using System.Web.UI;
using System.Web.UI.WebControls;
using System.Web.UI.WebControls.WebParts;
using System.Web.UI.HtmlControls;

public partial class _Default : System.Web.UI.Page
{
    protected void Page_Load(object sender, EventArgs e)
    {
        if (!IsPostBack)
            ddlOrder.DataBind();
        Session["ordernum"] = ddlOrder.SelectedValue;
    }
}
```

The `Page_Load` method is called when the `Default.aspx` page is loaded. It starts by calling the `DataBind` method for the drop-down list if the page is being posted for the first time. This statement is required — without it, no data binding occurs for the drop-down list, so the order number for the first order in the `Orders` file won't be set. On subsequent posts of the page (that is, when `IsPostBack` is `True`), the drop-down list will retain its values because of the view state. Then, the `DataBind` method doesn't need to be called.

The second statement in this method creates the `ordernum` session variable if it doesn't already exist and assigns the order number selected by the user to it.

Listing 8-5: The code-behind file for the default page (VB)

```vb
Partial Class _Default
    Inherits System.Web.UI.Page

    Protected Sub Page_Load( _
            ByVal sender As Object, _
            ByVal e As System.EventArgs) _
            Handles Me.Load

        If Not IsPostBack Then
            ddlOrder.DataBind()
        End If
        Session("ordernum") = ddlOrder.SelectedValue

    End Sub

End Class
```

Building the Print Order page

The Print Order page is about as simple as it could be: It simply includes the `Order` user control, with no other extraneous information to clutter up the page. The Print Order page is shown in Listing 8-6. The code-behind file for this page is empty.

Listing 8-6: The Print Order page (PrintOrder.aspx)

```
<%@ Page Language="C#"                                          →1
    AutoEventWireup="true"
    CodeFile="PrintOrder.aspx.cs"
    Inherits="PrintOrder" %>

<%@ Register Src="Order.ascx"                                   →2
        TagName="Order"
        TagPrefix="uc1" %>

<!DOCTYPE html PUBLIC "-//W3C//DTD XHTML 1.1//EN"
    "http://www.w3.org/TR/xhtml11/DTD/xhtml11.dtd">

<html xmlns="http://www.w3.org/1999/xhtml" >
<head runat="server">
    <title>Acme Pirate Supply</title>
</head>
<body>
    <form id="form1" runat="server">
    <div>
        <uc1:Order ID="Order1" runat="server" />        →3
    </div>
    </form>
</body>
</html>
```

Here's a short-but-sweet list of important elements in the code for this page:

→ **1**   Unlike nearly all the other pages I describe in this book, this `Page` directive does *not* specify a Master Page. That way the banner image doesn't appear at the top of the page.

→ **2**   The `Register` directive is required to register the `Order` user control.

→ **3**   The `uc1:Order` tag places the `Order` user control on the page. Then the user control handles the details of formatting the order data.

Part V

Building Community Applications

In this part . . .

Among the most popular types of Web applications today are those used to build online communities. This part presents three such applications. Chapter 9 presents a basic content-management system that makes it easy to create a Web site whose content changes on a regular basis. Then Chapter 10 presents a discussion-forum application, which gives users a way to post messages and reply to messages from other users. And finally, Chapter 11 presents a simple blog application that lets users create their own online journal (weblog) pages.

Chapter 9

Building a Content Management System

A *Content Management System* is a Web site that lets users manage the content displayed by the site without requiring a detailed knowledge of HTML. In short, the Content Management System provides an administrative interface that lets the user add, delete, or edit content items that are displayed on the Web site. Of course, you can limit access to the administrative pages so only those users who are authorized to administer the Web site can add, edit, or delete content items.

In this chapter, I present a simple Content Management System written in ASP.NET. The content displayed by this system is stored in a SQL database, and the system provides an easy way for authorized users to add, edit, and delete content.

Making Some Basic Decisions

Before we get into the specifics of how the Content Management System in this chapter works, consider some basic decisions that you should make early on when you create a Content Management System:

> ✔ **Will the content itself be stored in a database or as separate HTML files?** There are two basic options for how you can store the actual content that's managed by the Content Management System. One approach is to build a database that contains the text content that's managed by the system. Then, the Content Management System's main job is extracting information from this database to display. Building this type of

Content Management System is the easiest, but it also limits the type of content that can be managed by the system to text with simple formatting.

The alternative is to let users create the actual HTML files that provide the content for the system. Then, the Content Management System's job is to manage these files. You'll usually use a database to track the files, and you'll need to provide a way for users to upload files to the server.

The Content Management System presented in this chapter stores all of the content data in a database. To keep things simple, the content is limited to simple text.

✔ **How will the content be organized?** The Content Management System in this chapter provides two levels of organization for its content items: by department and by type. Both the departments and the types are stored in SQL tables, so users can easily add or remove departments or types. Depending on your organization's needs, you may need to provide a different way to organize or categorize content items.

✔ **Will users be required to log in?** You'll almost certainly require that users log in before you let them modify the Web site's content. That way, you can grant administration privileges to just certain users. However, you may also want to allow all users to log in. Then, you can restrict access to some or all of the content based on the user's identity.

In addition, you'll need to decide how you'll handle the registration of new users. For tight control over the user list, you'll want to allow only certain users to create new user accounts. For a more open Web site, you can let users register themselves.

For more information about adding login capabilities to a Web site, see Chapter 4. The Content Management System presented in this chapter requires the user to log in. To do that, it borrows the `login.aspx` page from the User Authentication application that was presented in Chapter 4.

The application shown in this chapter doesn't provide for user registration, password changes, or password recovery — but those features should be easy enough to add if you use the application presented in Chapter 4 as a guide.

The Content Management System uses the ASP.NET roles feature to assign each registered user to one or more departments. Any user can view content from any department, but only users assigned to a department can add, update, or delete content for the department.

✔ **How will you handle expired content?** For simplicity, the application in this chapter displays all of the content in the database. Users can add, modify, or delete content items any time they wish, but the system doesn't provide an automatic way to limit how long an item should be displayed or to automatically remove items that are expired. (You shouldn't have much trouble adding such a feature on your own, though.)

The Content Management System's User Interface

The Content Management System is designed to create an intranet Web site for a company so that each department within the company can provide its own content items. For example, the Human Resources department might want to provide information about company policies, while the Information Technology department may be interested in providing information about the computer network. The department names are stored in a database table so the company can create any department it wishes for the Content Management System.

Besides organizing its content by department, the Content Management System also categorizes content by type. As with departments, the Content Management System stores the type names in a database table. That way you can create as many different content types as you want.

One of the interesting things about the Content Management System is that it lets you create the illusion of a Web site with many different pages, while in reality getting by with only five distinct pages. Figure 9-1 shows how these pages work together to create the Content Management System, and the following sections describe each page in greater detail.

Figure 9-1:
The Content Management System requires these five pages.

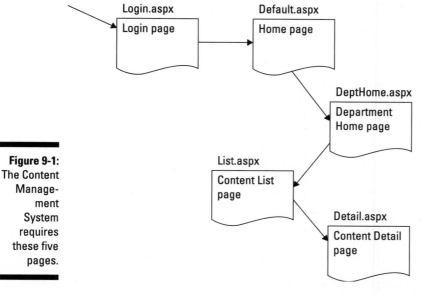

The Login page

The Login page (shown in Figure 9-2) appears whenever the user tries to access any page of the Content Management System without first logging in. As you can see, this page simply prompts the user to enter his or her user name and password. A checkbox lets the user store the name and password in a cookie — which then allows the user to automatically log in whenever he or she returns to the site.

The Home page

The Home page is shown in Figure 9-3. Note that the user must get through the Login page to reach this or any other page in the Content Management System. The Home page displays a brief text introduction, followed by a list of links to the various departments of the company.

Notice that the departments also appear in a list at the left side of the page. This sidebar list is actually a part of the Master Page used throughout the application. As a result, the user can quickly jump to the Home page for any department by clicking the department in the sidebar list.

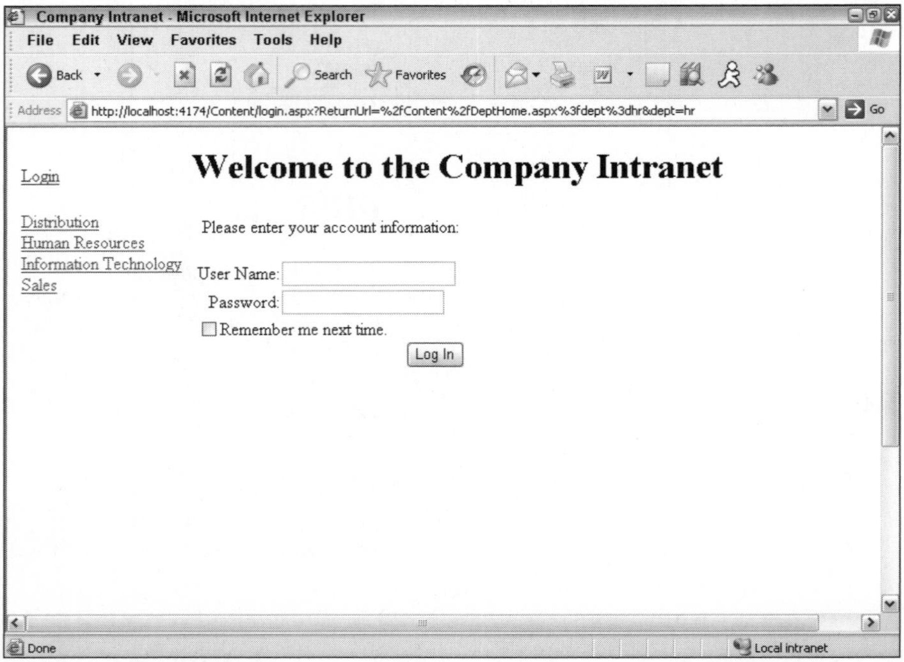

Figure 9-2:
The Login page.

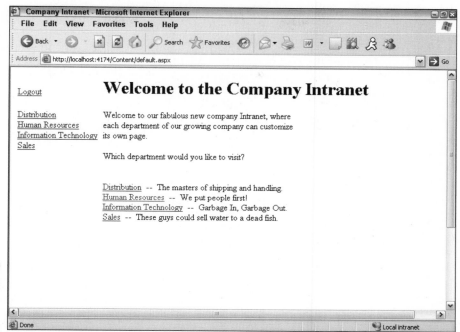

Figure 9-3:
The Home
page.

An enhancement you may want to make to the Content Management System is to store the text displayed on the Home page in a database table. (I'll leave you to your own devices to figure out how to do that. It shouldn't be too hard.)

The Department Home page

When the user clicks one of the department names in the Home page (or in the sidebar menu that appears at the left side of each page), the Home page for that department appears, as shown in Figure 9-4. As you can see, this page displays the name of the department, followed by a catchy description that's retrieved from the database. Then it displays links for each type of content managed by the system. (For example, the user can click the FAQ link to display a list of all the FAQ items for the selected department.)

Note that there is only one Department Home page for the entire Web site; each department doesn't have its own home page. Instead, the content for the selected department is retrieved from the database and displayed on the Department Home page.

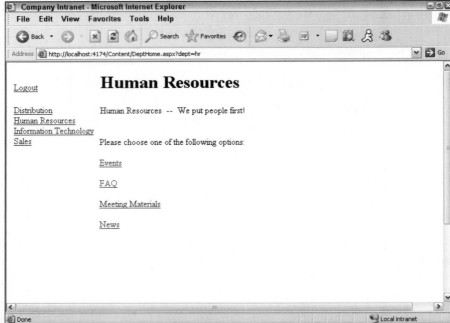

Figure 9-4:
The
Department
Home page.

The Content List page

The Content List page is shown in Figure 9-5. This page lists all content items for the department and type selected by the user. For example, if the user clicks Human Resources on the Home page, and then clicks FAQ on the Department Home Page, what shows up on-screen is a list of all FAQ items for the Human Resources department.

Notice the Add link beneath the list of content items. This link allows the user to add a new content item to the database. The Add link appears only if the user is assigned to the administrative role for the department. The Content List page includes code that checks whether the user is a member of the department's administrative role. If not, the Add link is hidden.

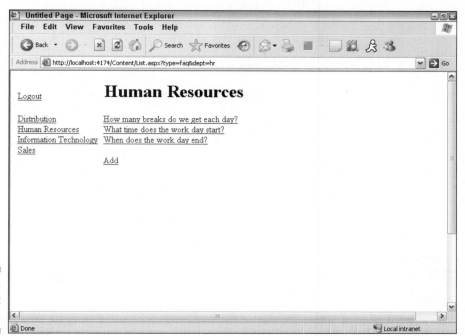

Figure 9-5:
The Content
List page.

The Content Detail page

Figure 9-6 shows the Content Detail page, which is displayed when the user selects one of the content items from the Content List page. As you can see, each content item has just two elements: a title and text. The Content Detail page simply displays the title and text for the item selected by the user.

Beneath the text are Edit and Delete links that let the user edit or delete the content item. Like the Add link on the Content List page, these links are displayed only if the user has been assigned to the administrative role for the department. The code-behind file for this page includes code that checks the user's role(s) — and hides these links if the user is in a role that shouldn't see them.

If the user clicks the Delete link, the content item is summarily deleted and the Content List page is redisplayed. But if the user clicks the Edit link, the page goes into Edit mode, as shown in Figure 9-7. Then the user can change the title or text to match the content item.

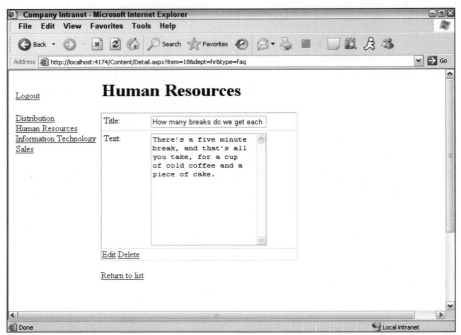

Figure 9-6:
The Content
Detail page.

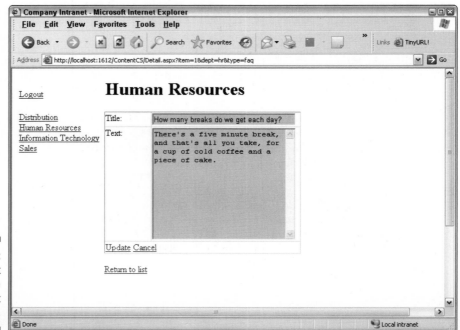

Figure 9-7:
The Content
Detail page
in Edit
mode.

Designing the Database

The Content Management System stores its content in a database named, appropriately enough, Content. The Content database consists of just three tables:

- ✔ Departments
- ✔ ContentTypes
- ✔ ContentItems

Figure 9-8 shows a diagram of this database, and the following sections describe each table individually.

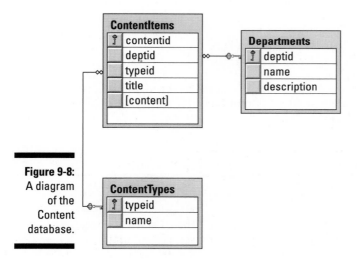

Figure 9-8: A diagram of the Content database.

The Departments table

The Departments table stores the information about the departments represented in the Content Management System. Table 9-1 lists the columns defined for this table.

Table 9-1	The Departments Table	
Column name	*Type*	*Description*
deptid	VARCHAR(10)	An alphanumeric code (up to 10 characters) that uniquely identifies each department. This is the primary key for the Departments table.
name	VARCHAR(255)	The department name.
description	VARCHAR(255)	A short description of the department. This text is displayed next to the department name on the Home page.

The ContentTypes table

The ContentTypes table stores information about the different types of content that can be managed by the Content Management System. Table 9-2 lists the columns defined for this table.

Table 9-2	The ContentTypes Table	
Column name	*Type*	*Description*
typeid	VARCHAR(10)	An alphanumeric code (up to 10 characters) that uniquely identifies each content type. This is the primary key for the ContentTypes table.
name	VARCHAR(255)	The name of the content type.

The ContentItems table

The ContentItems table stores the actual content that's managed by the Content Management System. Its columns are listed in Table 9-3.

Table 9-3		The ContentItems Table
Column name	*Type*	*Description*
contentid	INT IDENTITY	A column that uniquely identifies each content item. This identity column is the primary key for the ContentItems table.
deptid	VARCHAR(10)	An alphanumeric code (up to 10 characters) that indicates which department this content item belongs to. This is a foreign key.
typeid	VARCHAR(10)	An alphanumeric code (up to 10 characters) that indicates the content type. This is a foreign key.
title	VARCHAR(255)	The title for this content item.
content	TEXT	The text displayed for the content.

Creating the Database

On the CD that comes with this book, you'll find the script shown in Listing 9-1, which creates the Content database. To run this script, open a command-prompt window and change to the directory that contains the script. Then enter this command:

```
sqlcmd -S localhost\SQLExpress -i CreateContentDB.sql
```

(I assume you're running SQL Server Express on your own computer. If not, you'll need to change localhost\SQLExpress to the correct name.)

Listing 9-1: The CreateContentsDB.sql script

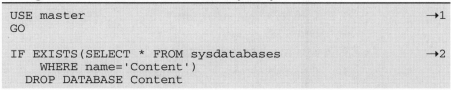

```
USE master                                              →1
GO

IF EXISTS(SELECT * FROM sysdatabases                    →2
    WHERE name='Content')
  DROP DATABASE Content
```

(continued)

Listing 9-1 *(continued)*

```
GO

CREATE DATABASE Content                                    →3
ON (NAME=Product,
     FILENAME = 'C:\APPS\Content.mdf',
     SIZE=10 )
GO

USE Content                                                →4

CREATE TABLE Departments (                                 →5
   deptid        VARCHAR(10)     NOT NULL,
   name          VARCHAR(255)    NOT NULL,
   description   VARCHAR(255)    NOT NULL,
   PRIMARY KEY(deptid)
   )
GO

CREATE TABLE ContentTypes (                                →6
   typeid VARCHAR(10)    NOT NULL,
   name    VARCHAR(255)   NOT NULL,
   PRIMARY KEY(typeid)
   )
GO

CREATE TABLE ContentItems (                                →7
   contentid      INT IDENTITY,
   deptid         VARCHAR(10)     NOT NULL,
   typeid         VARCHAR(10)     NOT NULL,
   title          VARCHAR(255)    NOT NULL,
   content        TEXT            NOT NULL,
   PRIMARY KEY(contentid),
   FOREIGN KEY(deptid) REFERENCES Departments(deptid),
   FOREIGN KEY(typeid) REFERENCES ContentTypes(typeid)
   )
GO
```

The following comments draw out the pertinent details of this listing:

→ **1**   Sets the database context to master.

→ **2**   Deletes the existing Content database if it exists.

→ **3**   Creates a database named Content, placing the database file C:\Apps.

→ **4**   Sets the database context to Content.

→ **5**   Creates the Departments table.

→ **6**   Creates the ContentTypes table.

→ **7**   Creates the ContentItems table.

Adding Test Data

The `InsertData.sql` script, also found on the companion CD, has a series of `INSERT` statements that insert some test data for you to work with. First it creates the following four departments:

deptid	name	description
hr	Human Resources	We put people first!
sales	Sales	These guys could sell water to a dead fish.
distr	Distribution	The masters of shipping and handling.
it	Information Technology	Garbage In, Garbage Out.

Then it creates some content types:

typeid	name
news	News
events	Events
faq	FAQ
meeting	Meeting Materials

Finally, it adds three FAQ items for the Human Resources department:

Title: How many breaks do we get each day?

Text: There's a five-minute break, and that's all you take, for a cup of cold coffee and a piece of cake.

Title: What time does the workday start?

Text: Up at eight, you can't be late, for Matthew and Son, he won't wait.

Title: When does the workday end?

Text: The files in your head, you take them to bed, you're never ever through.

To run the `InsertData.sql` script, open a command window, change to the directory that contains the script, and run this command:

```
sqlcmd -S localhost\SQLExpress -i InsertData.sql
```

Note that you'll need to change the server name if it is other than `localhost\SQLExpress`.

SQL statements for working with the database

The Content Management system uses a variety of SQL statements to retrieve and update data in the Content database. Here's a closer look at what these SQL statements do:

- The query that lists the departments on the Home page is simple:

```
SELECT [deptid],
       [name],
       [description]
  FROM [Departments]
  ORDER BY [name]
```

- The Department Home page uses the following query to retrieve name and description for the selected department:

```
SELECT [deptid],
       [name]
  FROM [Departments]
  WHERE [deptid] = @deptid
  ORDER BY [name]
```

- A similar query retrieves the description, as well as the department ID and name:

```
SELECT [deptid],
       [name]
  FROM [Departments]
  WHERE [deptid] = @deptid
  ORDER BY [name]
```

- The following query is used to list the content types on the Department Home page:

```
SELECT [typeid], [name]
  FROM [ContentTypes]
  ORDER BY [name]
```

- This next query is for use on the Content List page to get content items for a given department and content type:

```
SELECT [contentid], [title]
  FROM [ContentItems]
 WHERE [deptid] = @deptid
   AND [typeid] = @typeid
```

✔ Finally, the Content Detail page uses the following SQL statements to
select, update, delete, and insert content items:

```
SELECT [contentid],
       [title],
       [content]
  FROM [ContentItems]
  WHERE ([contentid] = @contentid)

UPDATE [ContentItems]
   SET [title] = @title,
       [content] = @content
   WHERE [contentid] = @original_contentid

DELETE FROM [ContentItems]
   WHERE [contentid] = @original_contentid

INSERT INTO [ContentItems]
          ([title], [content], [typeid], [deptid])
   VALUES (@title, @content, @typeid, @deptid)
```

Connecting to the database

The connection string for the Content Management System is stored in the
<connectionStrings> section of the web.config file, like this:

```
<connectionStrings>
    <add name="ConnectionString"
         connectionString="Data
           Source=localhost\SQLExpress;
Initial Catalog=Content;Integrated Security=True"/>
</connectionStrings>
```

You may have to modify the connection strings to match your server and
database names.

Creating the User Accounts

The Content Management System relies on ASP.NET 2.0's built-in authentication database to store information about users and roles. First, you must
modify the web.config file to configure the application to use forms-based
security, to deny access to users who haven't logged on, and to enable roles.
To do that, add the following lines to the <system.web> section of the
web.config file:

```
<authorization>
  <deny users="?" />
</authorization>
<roleManager enabled="true" />
<authentication mode="Forms" />
```

When you've configured the application to use forms-based security, you can create roles and user accounts by using the Web Site Administration Tool. If you want to get right into that, choose Web Site⇨ASP.NET Configuration from within Visual Studio, and then follow these steps:

1. **From the main page of the Web Site Administration Tool, click** Security.

   This brings up a page with security-configuration options.

2. **Click the** Create or Manage Roles **link.**

   This brings up the page that lets you manage roles.

3. **Create a role for each department.**

   If you're using the sample data provided on the CD, you should create roles named hr, sales, distr, and it.

4. **Click the Back button to return to the main Security page, and then choose** Create User.

   This brings up a page that lets you create user accounts.

5. **Create one or more user accounts using any names and passwords you wish.**

   Note that the password must include at least one non-alphanumeric character, such as a dollar sign ($) or ampersand (&). Otherwise the Create User page won't accept your password.

   Note also that you can using the check boxes in the Roles list to select which department(s) the user is a member of.

6. **Close the browser window to close the Web Site Administration Tool.**

Building the Master Page

Listing 9-2 shows the .aspx code for Master Page, MasterPage.master. This Master Page provides two content areas, one for a heading and one for content information, as well as a sidebar navigation area that contains a link for each department. An HTML table is used to control the basic layout of the page.

Listing 9-2: The Master Page (MasterPage.master)

```
<%@ Master Language="C#"                                        →1
    AutoEventWireup="true"
    CodeFile="MasterPage.master.cs"
    Inherits="MasterPage" %>

<!DOCTYPE html PUBLIC "-//W3C//DTD XHTML 1.1//EN"
"http://www.w3.org/TR/xhtml11/DTD/xhtml11.dtd">

<html xmlns="http://www.w3.org/1999/xhtml" >
<head runat="server">
    <title>Company Intranet</title>
</head>
<body>
    <form id="form1" runat="server">
    <div>
        <table width="800" border=0>
          <tr height="50px">
            <td width="150px" valign="Bottom">
                <asp:LoginStatus ID="LoginStatus1"          →2
                    runat="server" /><br /><br />
            </td>
            <td width="650px">
              <asp:contentplaceholder                       →3
                  id="ContentPlaceHolder1"
                  runat="server" />
            </td>
          </tr>
          <tr height="550px">
            <td width="150px" valign="top">
                <asp:Repeater ID="Repeater1"                →4
                  runat="Server"
                  DataSourceID="SqlDataSource1" >
                <ItemTemplate>
                    <asp:LinkButton                         →5
                        ID="LinkButton1"
                        runat="server"
                        Text='<% #Eval("name") %>'
                        PostBackUrl='<% #Eval("deptid",
            "DeptHome.aspx?dept={0}") %>' />
                    <br />
                </ItemTemplate>
                </asp:Repeater>
                <asp:SqlDataSource                          →6
                  ID="SqlDataSource1"
                  runat="server"
                  ConnectionString="<%$ ConnectionStrings:
                      ConnectionString %>"
                  SelectCommand="SELECT [deptid], [name]
```

(continued)

Listing 9-2 *(continued)*

```
                        FROM [Departments] ORDER BY [name]">
            </asp:SqlDataSource>
        </td>
        <td width="650px" valign="top">
            <asp:contentplaceholder                    →7
                id="ContentPlaceHolder2"
                runat="server" />
        </td>
    </tr>
    </table>
    </div>
    </form>
</body>
</html>
```

Okay, heads up for the key points of this listing:

→ **1**   The `Master` directive indicates that the file is a Master Page. Note that if you want to use Visual Basic rather than C# for the application's code-behind files, you should change the `AutoEventWireup` attribute to `false`. That won't matter for this application, though, since the Master Page doesn't require a code-behind file.

→ **2**   A `LoginStatus` control is used to let the user log out of the application. When the user clicks the <u>Logout</u> link, the user will be redirected to the Login page and will have to log in again (perhaps with a different account) to continue using the application.

→ **3**   The first `ContentPlaceHolder` control provides a heading area that displays the department name or some other heading information.

→ **4**   This `Repeater` control provides the sidebar menu that lists the departments. It's bound to the data source named `SqlDataSource1`.

→ **5**   The `LinkButton` control is a bit tricky because it uses the `Eval` method two times. The first call binds the `Text` property of the link to the `name` field in the data source. As a result, the link displays the department name. The second call to `Eval` uses a format string to create a `PostBack` URL that includes the `deptid` field from the data source in a query string. For example, if the department ID is `sales`, the `PostBack` URL for the link will be `DeptHome.aspx?dept=sales`.

Note that in the actual source file for the Master Page, the expression in the `PostBackUrl` attribute is contained on one line, not broken into two lines as shown here. I kept it on one line in the source file so the expression will be acceptable for both C# and Visual Basic, which requires continuation characters when you use line breaks within an expression.

→ **6**   This SQL data source is bound to the `Repeater` control. Its
          `SELECT` statement retrieves the `deptid` and `name` columns from
          the `Departments` table.

→ **7**   The second `ContentPlaceHolder` control provides the main dis-
          play area for the content of each page.

Building the Login Page

The Login page, shown back in Figure 9-2, is automatically displayed when
the user tries to access any other page of the Content Management System
without first logging in. Thus, the user must log in before accessing the application. The `.aspx` code for the Login page is shown in Listing 9-3.

Listing 9-3:   The Login page (Login.aspx)

```
<%@ Page Language="C#"                                          →1
    MasterPageFile="~/MasterPage.master"
    AutoEventWireup="true"
    CodeFile="Login.aspx.cs"
    Inherits="Login"
    Title="Company Intranet" %>
<asp:Content ID="Content1"                                      →2
    ContentPlaceHolderID="ContentPlaceHolder1"
    Runat="Server">
    <h1>
    Welcome to the Company Intranet
    </h1>
</asp:Content>
<asp:Content ID="Content2" Runat="Server"                       →3
    ContentPlaceHolderID="ContentPlaceHolder2" >
    <asp:Login ID="Login1" runat="Server"                       →4
        DestinationPageUrl="~/Default.aspx"
        TitleText="Please enter your account information:
<br /><br />" />
</asp:Content>
```

Here's a more detailed rundown on the numbered parts of this listing:

→ **1**   The `Page` directive indicates that `MasterPage.master` is used
          as the master file. If you're using Visual Basic instead of C#, this
          directive will indicate VB instead of C# as the language and
          `AutoEventWireup` will be set to `false`.

→ **2**   The first `<Content>` element defines the content displayed at the
          top of the page. In this case, the simple heading "Welcome to the
          Company Intranet" is displayed.

→ **3**   The second <Content> element provides the content displayed in the main portion of the page. For the Login page, the only item here is the Login control, described in the next paragraph.

→ **4**   The Login control displays the labels, text boxes, and buttons necessary to let the user log in. For more information about using the Login control, refer to Chapter 4.

Building the Home Page

The Home page (Default.aspx) displays a greeting and a list of the departments. The department list is a little redundant, since the sidebar in the Master Page also displays a list of the departments. However, the list displayed in the main area of the Home page includes the department descriptions in addition to the names. Listing 9-4 shows the .aspx code for this page. A code-behind file isn't required. Refer to Figure 9-3 for a refresher of what this page looks like.

Listing 9-4:   The Home page (Default.aspx)

```
<%@ Page Language="C#"                                    →1
    MasterPageFile="~/MasterPage.master"
    AutoEventWireup="true"
    CodeFile="Default.aspx.cs"
    Inherits="_Default"
    Title="Company Intranet" %>
<asp:Content ID="Content1"                                →2
    ContentPlaceHolderID="ContentPlaceHolder1"
    Runat="Server">
  <h1>
  Welcome to the Company Intranet
  </h1>
</asp:Content>
<asp:Content ID="Content2"                                →3
    ContentPlaceHolderID="ContentPlaceHolder2"
    Runat="Server">
Welcome to our fabulous new company Intranet, where<br />
each department of our growing company can customize<br />
its own page.<br /><br />

Which department would you like to visit?<br /><br /><br
        />
  <asp:Repeater ID="Repeater1" runat="Server"             →4
      DataSourceID="SqlDataSource1" >
      <ItemTemplate>
          <asp:LinkButton ID="LinkButton1"                →5
              runat="server"
              Text='<% #Eval("name") %>'
              PostBackUrl='<% #Eval("deptid",
```

```
            "DeptHome.aspx?dept={0}") %>' />
         --                                     →6
        <asp:Label ID="Label1" runat="server"            →7
            Text='<% #Eval("description") %>' />
        <br />
    </ItemTemplate>
  </asp:Repeater>
  <asp:SqlDataSource ID="SqlDataSource1"                  →8
      runat="server"
      ConnectionString="<%$ ConnectionStrings:
          ConnectionString %>"
      SelectCommand="SELECT [deptid], [name],
          [description]
        FROM [Departments] ORDER BY [name]">
  </asp:SqlDataSource>
</asp:Content>
```

Here are the secrets to understanding this listing:

→ **1**   As usual, the `Page` directive has to be changed if you're working in VB. Specifically, you should change the `Language`, `AutoEventWireup`, and `CodeFile` attributes.

→ **2**   The first `<Content>` element provides the heading `Welcome to the Company Intranet` at the top of the page.

→ **3**   The second `<Content>` element begins with several lines of text.

→ **4**   The `Repeater` control displays the list of departments. It's bound to the data source named `SqlDataSource1`.

→ **5**   The `LinkButton` control displays the `name` field and uses the `deptid` field as the value of the `dept` query string in the `PostBack` URL. For example, if the user clicks the link for the Human Resources department, the `PostBack` URL will be `DeptHome.aspx?dept=hr`.

→ **6**   This odd-looking construction displays a space, two hyphens, and another space to separate the department name from the description.

→ **7**   This `Label` control displays the `description` field from the data source.

→ **8**   The data source uses a simple `SELECT` statement to retrieve the `deptid`, `name`, and `description` columns for each row in the `Departments` table.

Building the Department Home Page

The Department Home page (`DeptHome.aspx`) is the home page for the department, as chosen by the user. It displays the department's description and a list of the content types. This page was illustrated back in Figure 9-4, and Listing 9-5 shows the `.aspx` code. No code-behind file is required for this page — but the page does contain an expression that must be coded differently depending on the language you're using.

This page is displayed when the user clicks one of the department links that appear in the Master Page or on the Home page (`Default.aspx`). Either way, the `PostBack` URL for the <u>Department</u> link passes the ID of the selected department as a query string with the name `dept`.

Listing 9-5:   The Department Home page (DeptHome.aspx)

```
<%@ Page Language="C#"                                       →1
    MasterPageFile="~/MasterPage.master"
    AutoEventWireup="true"
    CodeFile="DeptHome.aspx.cs"
    Inherits="DeptHome"
    Title="Company Intranet" %>

<asp:Content ID="Content1" Runat="Server"                    →2
    ContentPlaceHolderID="ContentPlaceHolder1" >

    <asp:FormView ID="FormView1" runat="server"              →3
        DataKeyNames="deptid"
        DataSourceID="SqlDataSource1">
        <ItemTemplate>
            <h1>
            <asp:Label ID="nameLabel" runat="server"         →4
                Text='<%# Eval("name") %>'></asp:Label>
            </h1>
        </ItemTemplate>
    </asp:FormView>

    <asp:SqlDataSource ID="SqlDataSource1"                    →5
        runat="server"
        ConnectionString="<%$ ConnectionStrings:
            ConnectionString %>"
        SelectCommand="SELECT [deptid], [name]
            FROM [Departments]
            WHERE [deptid] = @deptid
            ORDER BY [name]">
        <SelectParameters>
            <asp:QueryStringParameter                         →6
                Name="deptid"
                QueryStringField="dept"
                Type="String" />
        </SelectParameters>
    </asp:SqlDataSource>

</asp:Content>

<asp:Content ID="Content2" Runat="Server"                    →7
```

```
ContentPlaceHolderID="ContentPlaceHolder2" >

<asp:FormView ID="FormView2" runat="server"            →8
    DataSourceID="SqlDataSource2">
    <ItemTemplate>
        <asp:Label ID="nameLabel" runat="server"        →9
            Text='<%# Eval("name") %>' />
         -- 
        <asp:Label ID="Label1" runat="server"          →10
            Text='<%# Eval("description") %>' />
    </ItemTemplate>
</asp:FormView>

<br /><br />
Please choose one of the following options:
<br /><br />

<asp:Repeater ID="Repeater1" runat="server"           →11
    DataSourceID="SqlDataSource3" >
  <ItemTemplate>
    <asp:LinkButton ID="linkContent"                   →12
        runat="server"
        Text='<% #Eval("name") %>'
        PostBackUrl='<% #Eval("typeid",
            "List.aspx?type={0}")
        + "&dept="
        + Request.QueryString["dept"] %>' />
    <br /><br />
  </ItemTemplate>
</asp:Repeater>

<asp:SqlDataSource ID="SqlDataSource2"                 →13
    runat="server"
    ConnectionString="<%$ ConnectionStrings:
        ConnectionString %>"
    SelectCommand="SELECT [deptid],
            [name],
            [description]
        FROM [Departments]
        WHERE [deptid] = @deptid
        ORDER BY [name]" >
    <SelectParameters>
        <asp:QueryStringParameter
            Name="deptid"
            QueryStringField="dept"
            Type="String" />
    </SelectParameters>
</asp:SqlDataSource>

<asp:SqlDataSource ID="SqlDataSource3"                 →14
    runat="server"
    ConnectionString="<%$ ConnectionStrings:
        ConnectionString %>"
```

(continued)

Listing 9-5 *(continued)*

```
        SelectCommand="SELECT [typeid], [name]
            FROM [ContentTypes]
            ORDER BY [name]">
    </asp:SqlDataSource>

</asp:Content>
```

And now, here comes the play-by-play commentary for this listing:

→ **1**   The Page directive does its normal job of identifying the Master Page and other details. Some of these details are dependent on the language being used, so you'll need to change them if you're working with VB instead of C#.

→ **2**   The first <Content> element defines the information that will be displayed at the top of the page. This <Content> element includes a FormView control and a DataView control so it can retrieve the department name from the database and display it in the heading area.

→ **3**   This FormView control is bound to a specific SQL data source named SqlDataSource1. It might seem a little strange to use a FormView control to display just one field, but the FormView control is needed to provide a binding context for the Eval method described in Line 4.

→ **4**   This Label control displays the name field retrieved by the data source. Notice that this label is sandwiched between <h1> and </h1> tags, so the department name is formatted as a level-1 heading.

→ **5**   The first SQL data source for this form retrieves the department information from the Departments table. The WHERE clause in the SELECT statement uses a parameter named deptid to indicate which department to retrieve.

→ **6**   The deptid parameter is defined by this <QueryParameter> element, which specifies that the parameter's value is taken from the query string field named dept. As a result, this data source retrieves the department row indicated by the dept query string field.

→ **7**   The second <Content> element provides the main content for the page: the department description and a list of links to the available content types.

→ **8**   A FormView control (similar to the one defined in Line 3) displays the name and description fields retrieved by the SqlDataSource2 data source.

→ **9**   This label displays the name field from the data source.

→ **10**   Then, another label displays the description field.

→ **11**   A `Repeater` control displays a list of links for the content types. The `Repeater` control is bound to a third data source, `SqlDataSource3`.

→ **12**   The `LinkButton` control includes a complicated expression that builds the `PostBack` URL with two query string fields, one named `type`, the other named `dept`. For example, if the user has chosen the `faq` type for the `hr` department, the `PostBack` URL will be `List.aspx?type=faq&dept=hr`. Notice that `Request.QueryString` is used to retrieve the value for the `dept` query string field.

If you're working in Visual Basic, you'll need to make two changes to this expression. First, Visual Basic requires continuation characters to break the expression across lines. And second, you'll need to replace the brackets on the `QueryString` parameter with parentheses. Thus, the Visual Basic version of this `<LinkButton>` element should look like this:

```
<asp:LinkButton ID="linkContent"
    runat="server"
    Text="<% #Eval("name") %>'
    PostBackUrl='<% #Eval("typeid", _
        "List.aspx?type={0}") _
        + "&dept=" _
        + Request.QueryString("dept") %>' />
```

→ **13**   This data source retrieves the `name` and `description` fields displayed by the `FormView` control that was defined in Line 8.

→ **14**   This data source retrieves all rows from the `Types` table so they can be displayed by the `Repeater` control defined in Line 11.

Building the Content List Page

The Content List page, which was pictured back in Figure 9-5, displays a list of the content items for the selected department. Two query string fields are passed to this page — one for the department ID and the other for the type ID. For example, a typical request string for this page would look like this:

```
List.aspx?type=faq&dept=hr
```

Here, the FAQ items for the Human Resources department are being requested.

Unlike the other pages of this application presented so far, this page requires a code-behind file. The following sections present the `List.aspx` file and both the C# and Visual Basic versions of the code-behind file.

The List.aspx file

Listing 9-6 shows the .aspx code that defines the Content List page. For a refresher on how this page looks when the application is run, please refer to Figure 9-5.

Listing 9-6:   The Content List page (List.aspx)

```
<%@ Page Language="C#"                                          →1
    MasterPageFile="~/MasterPage.master"
    AutoEventWireup="true"
    CodeFile="List.aspx.cs"
    Inherits="List"
    Title="Company Intranet" %>
<asp:Content ID="Content1"                                      →2
    ContentPlaceHolderID="ContentPlaceHolder1"
    Runat="Server">
    <asp:FormView ID="FormView1" runat="server"                 →3
        DataKeyNames="deptid"
        DataSourceID="SqlDataSource1">
        <ItemTemplate>
            <h1>
            <asp:Label ID="nameLabel"                            →4
                runat="server"
                Text='<%# Eval("name") %>' />
            </h1>
        </ItemTemplate>
    </asp:FormView>
    <asp:SqlDataSource ID="SqlDataSource1"                       →5
        runat="server"
        ConnectionString="<%$ ConnectionStrings:
            ConnectionString %>"
        SelectCommand="SELECT [deptid], [name]
            FROM [Departments]
            WHERE ([deptid] = @deptid)
            ORDER BY [name]">
        <SelectParameters>
            <asp:QueryStringParameter                            →6
                Name="deptid"
                QueryStringField="dept"
                Type="String" />
        </SelectParameters>
    </asp:SqlDataSource>
</asp:Content>
<asp:Content ID="Content2"                                      →7
    ContentPlaceHolderID="ContentPlaceHolder2"
    Runat="Server">
    <asp:Repeater ID="Repeater1" runat="server"                 →8
        DataSourceID="SqlDataSource2">
      <ItemTemplate>
        <asp:LinkButton ID="Link1" runat="server"               →9
            Text='<%# Eval("title") %>'
```

```
                    PostBackUrl='<%# Eval("contentid",
                    "Detail.aspx?item={0}") +
                    "&dept=" + Request.QueryString["dept"] +
                    "&type=" + Request.QueryString["type"] %>'
                />
                    <br />
            </ItemTemplate>
        </asp:Repeater>
        <asp:SqlDataSource ID="SqlDataSource2"                    →10
            runat="server"
            ConnectionString="<%$ ConnectionStrings:
                ConnectionString %>"
            SelectCommand="SELECT [contentid], [title]
                FROM [ContentItems]
                WHERE [deptid] = @deptid
                AND [typeid] = @typeid">
            <SelectParameters>
                <asp:QueryStringParameter                          →11
                    Name="deptid"
                    QueryStringField="dept"
                    Type="String" />
                <asp:QueryStringParameter                          →12
                    Name="typeid"
                    QueryStringField="type"
                    Type="String" />
            </SelectParameters>
        </asp:SqlDataSource>
        <br />
        <asp:LinkButton ID="btnAdd" runat="server"                 →13
            Text="Add"
            OnClick="btnAdd_Click" />
</asp:Content>
```

For your reading pleasure, the following paragraphs summarize the key points that are necessary to understand this page:

→ **1**   As usual, you'll need to modify the Page directive if you want to use the VB version of the code-behind file. In particular, you'll need to change the Language attribute to VB, the AutoEventWireup attribute to false, and the CodeFile attribute to List.aspx.vb.

→ **2**   The first `<Content>` element displays the department name at the top of the page.

→ **3**   This FormView control displays the department name. It's bound to a SQL data source named SqlDataSource1.

→ **4**   This is the Label control that displays the name field, formatted by the `<h1>` and `</h1>` tags.

→ **5**   The SqlDataSource1 data source retrieves the department name. The deptid parameter indicates which department should be retrieved.

→ **6**   The `<QueryParameter>` element defines the `deptid` parameter. Its value is taken from the `dept` query string.

→ **7**   The second `<Content>` element provides the main content for the page.

→ **8**   A `Repeater` control is used to display the content types. This control is bound to `SqlDataSource2`, which is defined in Line 10.

→ **9**   The `LinkButton` control in the `Repeater`'s item template displays the links to the content types. As you can see, it uses a simple `Eval` expression to bind the `Text` attribute to the title field. However, a more complicated expression specifies the `PostBack` URL. This URL includes three query strings, named `item`, `dept`, and `type`. The `item` query string's value comes from the contented field of the data source; the other two query strings are simply carried forward from the `request` query string. If (for example) the user selects the content item whose ID is 2 while viewing the FAQ items for the Human Resources department, then the `PostBack` URL is `Detail.aspx?item=2&dept=hr&type=faq`.

If you're working in Visual Basic, you'll need to modify this expression so it uses VB continuation characters and parentheses instead of brackets. In that case, the entire `<LinkButton>` element looks like this:

```
<asp:LinkButton ID="Link1" runat="server" →9
    Text='<%# Eval("title") %>'
    PostBackUrl='<%# Eval("contentid", _
        "Detail.aspx?item={0}") + _
        "&dept=" + Request.QueryString("dept") + _
        "&type=" + Request.QueryString("type") %>' />
```

→ **10** The `SqlDataSource2` data source retrieves the list of content items for the selected department and type. As you can see, the `SELECT` statement requires two parameters, `deptid` and `typeid`.

→ **11** The `deptid` parameter is defined with a `<QueryString>` element, taking its value from the `dept` query string.

→ **12** The `deptid` parameter is defined with a `<QueryString>` element. It takes its value from the `dept` query string.

→ **13** This `LinkButton` control displays the <u>Add</u> link, which lets the user add a new content item. Note that the code-behind file hides this link if the user is not an administrator for the department.

If you're working in Visual Basic, you should remove the `<OnClick>` element.

The code-behind file for the Content List page

The List.aspx page requires a code-behind file to show or hide the Add
link — depending on the user's departmental role(s) — and to handle the
Click event for the Add link. The C# version of this code-behind file is
shown in Listing 9-7, and Listing 9-8 shows the Visual Basic version.

Listing 9-7:   The code-behind file for the Content List page (C#)

```csharp
using System;
using System.Data;
using System.Configuration;
using System.Collections;
using System.Web;
using System.Web.Security;
using System.Web.UI;
using System.Web.UI.WebControls;
using System.Web.UI.WebControls.WebParts;
using System.Web.UI.HtmlControls;

public partial class List : System.Web.UI.Page
{
    protected void Page_Load(                              →1
        object sender, EventArgs e)
    {
        string deptid =
            (String)Request.QueryString["dept"];
        if (User.IsInRole(deptid))
            btnAdd.Visible = true;
        else
            btnAdd.Visible = false;
    }

    protected void btnAdd_Click(                           →2
        object sender, EventArgs e)
    {
        Response.Redirect("Detail.aspx?item=-1&type="
            + Request.QueryString["type"]
            + "&dept=" + Request.QueryString["dept"]);
    }
}
```

Here's how the two methods work in this code-behind file:

→ **1**   `Page_Load`: This method begins by retrieving the department ID from the `dept` query string. Then, it calls `User.IsInRole` to find out if the user is an administrator for the department. If so, the Add link is made visible; if not, it's hidden.

→ **2**   `btnAdd_Click`: This method is called when the user clicks the Add link. It redirects to the `Detail.aspx` page, setting the `item` query string to `-1` to indicate that a new row should be inserted. The redirect URL also includes query strings that pass the content-type ID and the department ID.

Listing 9-8:   The code-behind file for the Content List page (VB)

```
Partial Class List
    Inherits System.Web.UI.Page

    Protected Sub Page_Load( _                              →1
        ByVal sender As Object, _
        ByVal e As System.EventArgs) _
        Handles Me.Load
      Dim deptid As String
      deptid = Request.QueryString("dept")
      If User.IsInRole(deptid) Then
          btnAdd.Visible = True
      Else
          btnAdd.Visible = False
      End If
    End Sub

    Protected Sub btnAdd_Click( _                          →2
        ByVal sender As Object, _
        ByVal e As System.EventArgs) _
        Handles btnAdd.Click
      Response.Redirect("Detail.aspx?item=-1&type=" _
          + Request.QueryString("type") _
          + "&dept=" + Request.QueryString("dept"))
    End Sub
End Class
```

Building the Content Detail Page

The last page for this application is the Content Detail page, pictured way back in Figure 9-6. This page displays the content item selected by the user; if the user is an administrator for the current department, the page lets the user edit or delete the item — or insert a new content item.

This page uses three query string fields. A typical request looks like this:

```
Detail.aspx?item=3&type=faq&dept=hr
```

Here, content item 3 is requested. The Content Detail page itself doesn't need the `type` and `dept` values, but passing them as query string fields makes it easier for the detail page to display the department name in the heading area — and these values are required to insert a content item.

Speaking of inserting rows, the special value `-1` is used in the `item` query string field to indicate that a new content item should be inserted. For example, to create a new FAQ for the Human Resources department, the request string looks like this:

```
Detail.aspx?item=-1&type=faq&dept=hr
```

The following sections present the `.aspx` code for the Content Details page, as well as both the C# and VB versions of the required code-behind file.

The Detail.aspx file

Listing 9-9 shows the `.aspx` code for the Content Details page.

Listing 9-9: The Content Details page (Detail.aspx)

```
<%@ Page Language="C#"                                          →1
    MasterPageFile="~/MasterPage.master"
    AutoEventWireup="true"
    CodeFile="Detail.aspx.cs"
    Inherits="Detail"
    Title="Company Intranet" %>
<asp:Content ID="Content1" Runat="Server"                       →2
    ContentPlaceHolderID="ContentPlaceHolder1" >
    <asp:FormView ID="FormView2" runat="server"                 →3
        DataSourceID="SqlDataSource1">
        <ItemTemplate>
          <h1>
            <asp:Label ID="nameLabel"                            →4
                runat="server"
                Text='<%# Eval("name") %>' /><br />
          </h1>
        </ItemTemplate>
    </asp:FormView>
    <asp:SqlDataSource ID="SqlDataSource1"                       →5
        runat="server"
        ConnectionString="<%$ ConnectionStrings:
            ConnectionString %>"
        SelectCommand="SELECT [name] FROM Departments
            WHERE deptid = @deptid" >
```

(continued)

Listing 9-9 *(continued)*

```
            <SelectParameters>
                <asp:QueryStringParameter                        →6
                    Name="deptid"
                    QueryStringField="dept" />
            </SelectParameters>
        </asp:SqlDataSource>
</asp:Content>
<asp:Content ID="Content2" Runat="Server"                        →7
    ContentPlaceHolderID="ContentPlaceHolder2" >
    <asp:DetailsView ID="DetailsView1"                           →8
        runat="server"
        AutoGenerateRows="False"
        DataSourceID="SqlDataSource2"
        DataKeyNames="contentid"
        BorderStyle="None"
        Height="50px" Width="350px"
        OnItemDeleted="DetailsView1_ItemDeleted"
        OnItemInserted="DetailsView1_ItemInserted"
        OnItemCommand="DetailsView1_ItemCommand" >
    <Fields>
        <asp:TemplateField ShowHeader="True"                     →9
            HeaderText="Title:"
            HeaderStyle-Width="80px"
            HeaderStyle-VerticalAlign="Top" >
        <ItemTemplate>                                           →10
            <asp:TextBox ID="txtItemTitle"
                runat="server"
                Text='<%# Eval("title") %>'
                ReadOnly="True"
                Width="250px" />
        </ItemTemplate>
        <EditItemTemplate>                                       →11
            <asp:TextBox ID="txtEditTitle"
                runat="server"
                Text='<%# Bind("title") %>'
                Width="250px"
                BackColor="LightBlue" />
            <asp:RequiredFieldValidator
                ID="RequiredFieldValidator1"
                runat="server"
                ControlToValidate="txtEditTitle"
                ErrorMessage="Title is required."
                Display="Dynamic" />
        </EditItemTemplate>
        <InsertItemTemplate>                                     →12
            <asp:TextBox ID="txtInsertTitle"
                runat="server"
                Text='<%# Bind("title") %>'
                Width="250px"
                BackColor="LightBlue" />
            <asp:RequiredFieldValidator
                ID="RequiredFieldValidator2"
                runat="server"
```

```
                         ControlToValidate="txtInsertTitle"
                         ErrorMessage="Title is required."
                         Display="Dynamic" />
           </InsertItemTemplate>
        </asp:TemplateField>
        <asp:TemplateField ShowHeader="True"                    →13
           HeaderText="Text:"
           HeaderStyle-Width="80px"
           HeaderStyle-VerticalAlign="Top" >
           <ItemTemplate>                                       →14
              <asp:TextBox ID="txtItemContent"
                  runat="server"
                  Text='<%# Eval("content") %>'
                  ReadOnly="True"
                  TextMode="MultiLine"
                  Width="250px" Height="200px" /><br />
           </ItemTemplate>
           <EditItemTemplate>                                   →15
              <asp:TextBox ID="txtEditContent"
                  runat="server"
                  Text='<%# Bind("content") %>'
                  TextMode="MultiLine"
                  Width="250px" Height="200px"
                  BackColor="LightBlue" /><br />
              <asp:RequiredFieldValidator
                  ID="RequiredFieldValidator3"
                  runat="server"
                  ControlToValidate="txtEditContent"
                  ErrorMessage="Text is required."
                  Display="Dynamic" />
           </EditItemTemplate>
           <InsertItemTemplate>                                 →16
              <asp:TextBox ID="txtInsertContent"
                  runat="server"
                  Text='<%# Bind("content") %>'
                  TextMode="MultiLine"
                  Width="250px" Height="200px"
                  BackColor="LightBlue" /><br />
              <asp:RequiredFieldValidator
                  ID="RequiredFieldValidator4"
                  runat="server"
                  ControlToValidate="txtInsertContent"
                  ErrorMessage="Text is required."
                  Display="Dynamic" />
           </InsertItemTemplate>
        </asp:TemplateField>
     </Fields>
  </asp:DetailsView>
<asp:SqlDataSource ID="SqlDataSource2"                          →17
     runat="server"
     ConnectionString="<%$ ConnectionStrings:
        ConnectionString %>"
     OldValuesParameterFormatString="original_{0}"
```

(continued)

Listing 9-9 *(continued)*

```
        SelectCommand="SELECT                          →18
            [contentid],
            [title],
            [content]
        FROM [ContentItems]
        WHERE ([contentid] = @contentid)"
        UpdateCommand="UPDATE [ContentItems]            →19
            SET [title] = @title,
            [content] = @content
        WHERE [contentid] = @original_contentid"
        DeleteCommand="DELETE                           →20
            FROM [ContentItems]
            WHERE [contentid] = @original_contentid"
        InsertCommand="INSERT                           →21
            INTO [ContentItems]
            ([title], [content], [typeid], [deptid])
            VALUES (@title, @content, @typeid, @deptid)" >
        <SelectParameters>                              →22
            <asp:QueryStringParameter
                Name="contentid"
                QueryStringField="item"
                Type="Int32" />
        </SelectParameters>
        <UpdateParameters>                              →23
            <asp:Parameter Name="title"
                Type="String" />
            <asp:Parameter Name="content"
                Type="String" />
            <asp:Parameter Name="original_contentid"
                Type="Int32" />
        </UpdateParameters>
        <DeleteParameters>                              →24
            <asp:Parameter Name="original_contentid"
                Type="Int32" />
        </DeleteParameters>
        <InsertParameters>                              →25
            <asp:Parameter Name="title"
                Type="String" />
            <asp:Parameter Name="content"
                Type="String" />
            <asp:QueryStringParameter Name="deptid"
                QueryStringField="dept" Type="String" />
            <asp:QueryStringParameter Name="typeid"
                QueryStringField="type" Type="String" />
        </InsertParameters>
    </asp:SqlDataSource>
    <br />
    <asp:LinkButton ID="btnReturn"                      →26
        runat="server"
        Text="Return to list"
        OnClick="btnReturn_Click" />
</asp:Content>
```

Brace yourself — the following paragraphs describe the 26 essential tenets of this listing:

→ **1**   You will need to change this `Page` directive if you use the VB version of the code-behind file. Specifically, you'll need to change the `Language`, `AutoEventWireup`, and `CodeFile` attributes to `VB`, `False`, and `Detail.aspx.vb`.

→ **2**   The first `<Content>` element displays the department name at the top of the page.

→ **3**   This `FormView` is bound to the `SqlDataSource1` data source and displays the department name.

→ **4**   This `Label` control displays the `name` field.

→ **5**   The first SQL data source (`SqlDataSource1`) retrieves the department name, using a parameter named `deptid` to specify the department to retrieve.

→ **6**   The `deptid` parameter is a query parameter, taking its value from the `dept` query string.

→ **7**   The second `<Content>` element provides the main content for the page.

→ **8**   The `DetailsView` control displays the title and text for the selected content item, which is retrieved by the `SqlDataSource2` data source.

      If you're working in Visual Basic, you should drop the `OnItemDeleted`, `OnItemInserted`, or `OnItemCommand` attributes.

→ **9**   This `<TemplateField>` element is the first of two fields contained in the `<Fields>` element for the `DetailsView` control.

→ **10**   The `Item` template is used to display the content item's title when the `DetailsView` control is displayed in Read-Only mode. It consists of a single read-only text box that uses the `Eval` method to bind to the `title` field of the data source.

→ **11**   The `EditItem` template is displayed when the user clicks the <u>Edit</u> link to edit a content item. It includes two controls: a text box that uses the `Bind` method to bind to the `title` field, and a `RequiredFieldValidator` that ensures that the user enters a value for the title. (Notice that the background color for the text box is set to `blue` to provide a visual clue that the page is in Edit mode.)

→ **12**   The InsertItem template is displayed when the `DetailsView` control enters Insert mode. That happens when the `Details.aspx` page is called with `-1` as the value of the `item` query string. This template contains the same text box and `RequiredField Validator` controls as the `EditItem` template.

→ **13**   This `<TemplateField>` field is the second field contained in the `<Fields>` element for the `DetailsView` control. It displays the content item's text.

→ **14**   The item template displays the text in Read-Only mode. It uses a read-only text box that (in turn) uses the `Eval` method to bind to the `text` field. Notice that the text box allows multiple lines and is 200 pixels high.

→ **15**   The `EditItem` template provides a text box that binds to the text field and to a `RequiredFieldValidator`.

→ **16**   The `InsertItem` template contains the same text box and `RequiredFieldValidator` controls as the `EditItem` template.

→ **17**   The `SqlDataSource2` data source provides the SQL statements necessary to retrieve, update, delete, and insert rows in the ContentItems table.

→ **18**   The `SELECT` statement retrieves the `contentid`, `title`, and `content` fields for the content item specified by the `contentid` parameter.

→ **19**   The `UPDATE` statement updates the `title` and `content` fields with values provided by the `title` and `content` parameters.

→ **20**   The `DELETE` statement deletes the content item indicated by the `contentid` parameter.

→ **21**   The `INSERT` statement inserts a new item into the `ContentItems` table.

→ **22**   The `<SelectParameters>` element specifies that the `contentid` parameter gets its value from the `item` query string.

→ **23**   The `<UpdateParameters>` element provides the parameters necessary to execute the `UPDATE` statement.

→ **24**   The `<DeleteParameters>` element provides the parameters necessary to execute the `DELETE` statement.

→ **25**   The `<InsertParameters>` element provides the parameters necessary to execute the `INSERT` statement.

→ **26**   The `LinkButton` control returns the user to the Content List page.

If you're working in Visual Basic, you'll want to remove the `OnClick` attribute.

The code-behind file for the Content Detail page

Like the `List.aspx` page, the `Detail.aspx` page requires a code-behind file. The C# version of this code-behind file is shown in Listing 9-10, and Listing 9-11 shows the Visual Basic version.

Listing 9-10:   The code-behind file for the Content Detail page (C#)

```csharp
using System;
using System.Data;
using System.Configuration;
using System.Collections;
using System.Web;
using System.Web.Security;
using System.Web.UI;
using System.Web.UI.WebControls;
using System.Web.UI.WebControls.WebParts;
using System.Web.UI.HtmlControls;

public partial class Detail : System.Web.UI.Page
{
    string deptid;
    string typeid;

    protected void Page_Load(                              →1
        object sender, EventArgs e)
    {
        deptid = (String)Request.QueryString["dept"];
        typeid = (string)Request.QueryString["type"];
        if (User.IsInRole(deptid))
        {
            DetailsView1.AutoGenerateDeleteButton = true;
            DetailsView1.AutoGenerateEditButton = true;
            if (Request.QueryString["item"] == "-1")
            {
              DetailsView1.DefaultMode
                  = DetailsViewMode.Insert;
                DetailsView1.AutoGenerateInsertButton =
            true;
            }
        }
        else
        {
            DetailsView1.AutoGenerateDeleteButton = false;
            DetailsView1.AutoGenerateEditButton = false;
```

(continued)

Listing 9-10 *(continued)*

```
        }
    }

    protected void DetailsView1_ItemDeleted(          →2
        object sender, DetailsViewDeletedEventArgs e)
    {
        Response.Redirect("List.aspx?type=" + typeid
            + "&dept=" + deptid);
    }

    protected void DetailsView1_ItemInserted(         →3
        object sender, DetailsViewInsertedEventArgs e)
    {
        Response.Redirect("List.aspx?type=" + typeid
            + "&dept=" + deptid);
    }

    protected void DetailsView1_ItemCommand(          →4
        object sender, DetailsViewCommandEventArgs e)
    {
        if (e.CommandName=="Cancel")
            if (DetailsView1.DefaultMode
                    == DetailsViewMode.Insert)
                Response.Redirect(
                    "List.aspx?type=" + typeid
                    + "&dept=" + deptid);
    }

    protected void btnReturn_Click(                   →5
        object sender, EventArgs e)
    {
        Response.Redirect("List.aspx?type=" + typeid
            + "&dept=" + deptid);
    }
}
```

To end the suspense, the following paragraphs explain the purpose of each method in this code-behind file:

→ **1**   Page_Load: This method is called each time the page is loaded. It starts by extracting the values of the dept and type query string fields and saving them in class instance variables named deptid and typeid.

Next, it calls User.IsInRole to determine if the user is an administrator for the current department. If so, the DetailsView control is configured to automatically generate Update and Delete links. Otherwise the DetailsView control is configured to suppress the Update and Delete links.

Finally, the value of the `item` query string is tested. If it is -1, the `DetailsView` control is placed in Insert mode to allow the user to create a new content item.

→ **2**   `DetailsView1_ItemDeleted`: This method is called when an item has been successfully deleted from the `DetailsView` control. It simply redirects the user back to the List page, passing on the `dept` query string that it received.

→ **3**   `DetailsView1_ItemInserted`: This method is called when an item has been successfully inserted into the `DetailsView` control. It redirects the user back to the List page, passing on the `dept` query string that it received.

→ **4**   `DetailsView1_ItemCommand`: This method is called whenever the `DetailsView` control receives a command, such as `Update`, `Edit`, `Insert`, and `Cancel`. You can determine which command caused the method to be invoked by checking the `CommandName` property of the e argument.

The purpose of this method is to return to the List page if the user clicks <u>Cancel</u> while inserting a new content item. As a result, it calls `Response.Redirect` if e.`Command` is `Cancel` and if the `DetailsView` control is in Insert mode. Otherwise, this method doesn't do anything.

→ **5**   `LinkButton_Click`: This method returns to the List page when the user clicks the <u>Return</u> link.

Listing 9-11:   The code-behind file for the Content Detail page (VB)

```
Partial Class Detail
    Inherits System.Web.UI.Page

    Private deptid As String
    Private typeid As String

    Protected Sub Page_Load( _                               →1
            ByVal sender As Object, _
            ByVal e As System.EventArgs) _
            Handles Me.Load
        deptid = Request.QueryString("dept")
        typeid = Request.QueryString("type")
        If User.IsInRole(deptid) Then
            DetailsView1.AutoGenerateDeleteButton = True
            DetailsView1.AutoGenerateEditButton = True
            If Request.QueryString("item") = "-1" Then
                DetailsView1.DefaultMode _
                    = DetailsViewMode.Insert
```

(continued)

Listing 9-11 *(continued)*

```
            DetailsView1.AutoGenerateInsertButton = True
        End If
        Else
            DetailsView1.AutoGenerateDeleteButton = False
            DetailsView1.AutoGenerateEditButton = False
        End If
    End Sub

    Protected Sub DetailsView1_ItemDeleted( _            →2
            ByVal sender As Object, _
            ByVal e As System.Web.UI.WebControls _
                .DetailsViewDeletedEventArgs) _
            Handles DetailsView1.ItemDeleted
        Response.Redirect("List.aspx?type=" + typeid _
            + "&dept=" + deptid)
    End Sub

    Protected Sub DetailsView1_ItemInserted( _           →3
            ByVal sender As Object, _
            ByVal e As System.Web.UI.WebControls _
                .DetailsViewInsertedEventArgs) _
            Handles DetailsView1.ItemInserted
        Response.Redirect("List.aspx?type=" + typeid _
            + "&dept=" + deptid)
    End Sub

    Protected Sub DetailsView1_ItemCommand( _            →4
            ByVal sender As Object, _
            ByVal e As System.Web.UI.WebControls _
                .DetailsViewCommandEventArgs) _
            Handles DetailsView1.ItemCommand
        Response.Redirect("List.aspx?type=" + typeid _
            + "&dept=" + deptid)
    End Sub

    Protected Sub btnReturn_Click( _                     5
            ByVal sender As Object, _
            ByVal e As System.EventArgs) _
            Handles btnReturn.Click
        Response.Redirect("List.aspx?type=" + typeid _
            + "&dept=" + deptid)
    End Sub
End Class
```

Chapter 10

Building a Web Forum

A *Web forum* is, essentially, a form of online communication — a Web application that lets users post messages as well as reply to messages left by other users. Forums are sort of like the back fences of the Internet, where people gather to talk about the important topics of the day.

Most forums are devoted to a particular subject so people with similar interests can gather to discuss topics that are important to them. For example, a forum might be devoted to music, politics, religion, or even (yes, it's true) computer programming. And because these subjects tend to be broad, most forums are further organized into more focused discussion topics. For example, a forum on computer programming might have topics on programming languages, database programming, Web programming, and Windows programming.

Because forums are so popular as Web applications, many prebuilt forum applications are available to save you the trouble of creating your own — though you may still want to do so for a variety of reasons. If so, this chapter is for you. Here you'll find a simple forum application written in ASP.NET.

Designing the Forum Application

The basic function of the Forum application is to let users post messages, which others can then display later and reply to. But within this basic requirement, there are many design decisions to be made along the way. Here's a quick review of some of these basic decisions:

✔ **How will your forum messages be organized?** A popular forum can receive hundreds, thousands, or even tens of thousands of posts per day. Clearly, you'll need a way to keep all that information reasonably organized. The most common way to organize forum messages is to divide them into related *topics*. Then, when a user posts a message, he or she can specify the appropriate topic for the message. The Forum application presented in this chapter lets you organize your forum into any number of topics.

To provide an additional layer of organization, the Forum application lets you group the topics together into *forums*. For example, if you're hosting discussions about holiday decorating, you might have a forum for each holiday. Then you might create topics for more specific subjects such as decorating, party tips, costumes, and so on.

Besides breaking down the site into forums and topics, each topic consists of one or more *threads*. A thread consists of an initial message posted by a user and additional messages posted in response to the initial message. Typically, the first message in a thread will be a question, and the follow-up messages will be answers to the initial question. There are two ways to organize replies within a thread:

- **Associate each reply with a specific message in the thread.** Then threads take on a tree-like structure.

- **Associate each reply with the thread itself.** Then the threads have a simple list structure.

For simplicity, the Forum application presented in this chapter associates replies with threads, not with other messages.

✔ **Will users be required to log in?** If you want your forum's membership to be limited, you should require that your users log in before they can post messages. To keep the code for this chapter's application simple, it doesn't require users to log in. Instead, each user must supply an e-mail address whenever he or she posts a message.

For more information about requiring users to log in, see Chapter 4.

✔ **Will the discussions be moderated?** In an *unmoderated forum*, any user can post messages, and those messages are immediately viewable by other users. Unmoderated threads tend to be lively and free-flowing, but can also become unfocused and sometimes offensive.

The alternative to such potential chaos is to offer a *moderated forum*, in which a moderator must approve all messages posted to the forum. Moderated forums tend to stay closer to the topic at hand. Plus, the moderator can ban offensive posts. However, moderated forums require ongoing work from the moderator, and the time required for the moderator to approve new posts can stifle discussion.

For the sake of simplicity, the Forum application presented in this chapter is not moderated.

The User Interface for the Forum Application

The Forum application uses the five pages shown in Figure 10-1. These pages are described in detail in the following sections.

The Forum Home page

The home page for the Forum application, `Default.aspx`, is shown in Figure 10-2. As you can see, this page lists the forums and topics that are available at the forum site. In this case, there are two forums and a total of five topics. To view the threads in one of the topics, the user clicks the link for the topic.

In case you're wondering how the forums and topics are displayed, nested `Repeater` controls do the trick. The outer `Repeater` control displays the forums; then, for each forum, the inner `Repeater` control displays the available topics. (More about how to pull off this bit of programming trickery later in this chapter.)

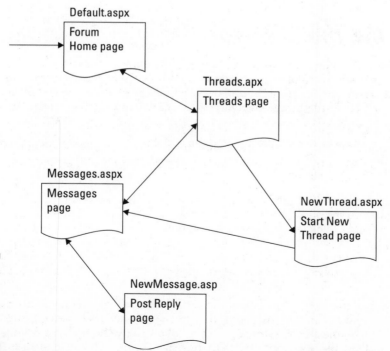

Figure 10-1:
The page flow for the Forum application.

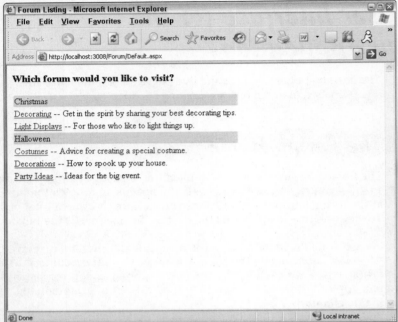

Figure 10-2:
The Forum
Home page.

The Threads page

The Threads page, shown in Figure 10-3, displays the threads in a given topic. For each thread, the page lists the thread's subject, the e-mail address of the person who initiated the thread, the number of replies to the thread, and the date the thread was last replied to. A `GridView` control is used to display this list.

Note that the thread subjects are links. If the user clicks one of these links, the Forum application displays the messages for that thread, as described in the next section.

Notice also that beneath the list of threads are two links. The first takes the user to the New Thread page to create a new thread. The second link takes the user back to the forum's Home page.

The Messages page

When the user clicks one of the threads in the Threads page, the messages for that thread are displayed, as shown in Figure 10-4. This page displays the topic name and the thread subject, followed by the thread's original message and any replies. Note that each message is preceded by a header that identifies who posted the message and when.

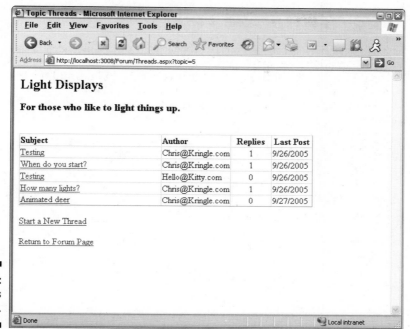

Figure 10-3:
The Threads
page.

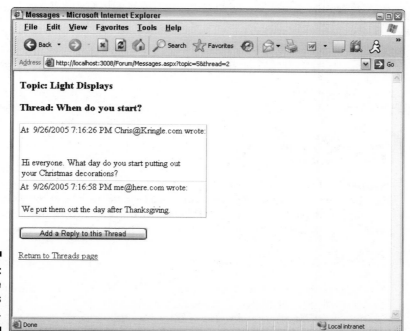

Figure 10-4:
The
Messages
page.

The New Thread page

If the user clicks the Start a New Thread link from the Threads page, the New Thread page is displayed, as shown in Figure 10-5. This page simply lets the user enter his or her e-mail address, a subject line, and the text for the thread's initial message. Then, when the user clicks the Post Message button, the new thread is written to the Forum application's database.

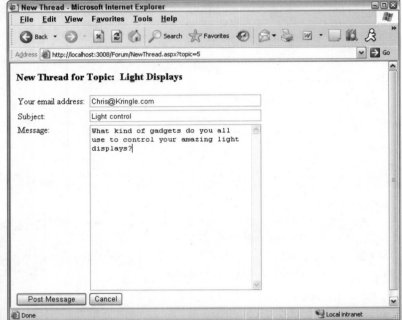

Figure 10-5:
The New
Thread
page.

The Post Reply page

Figure 10-6 shows the Post Reply page, where you can add a message to an existing thread. To post a reply, you must enter your e-mail address and the text of your reply, then click the Post Reply button. This updates the database, then returns the user to the Messages page.

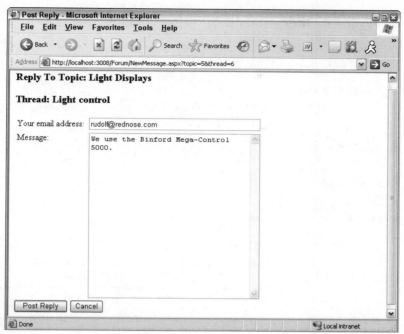

Designing the Database

The database for the Forum application requires the following four tables:

- Forums
- Topics
- Threads
- Messages

Figure 10-7 presents a diagram that shows how these tables are related, and the following sections describe each table individually.

The Forums table

The Forums table stores information about each forum supported by the Web site. Table 10-1 lists the columns defined for this table.

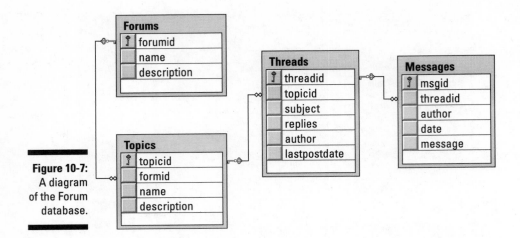

Figure 10-7:
A diagram
of the Forum
database.

Table 10-1		The Forums Table
Column name	*Type*	*Description*
forumid	INT IDENTITY	An identity column that provides a unique ID number for each forum supported by the site. This is the primary key for the Forums table.
name	VARCHAR(255)	The forum's name.
description	VARCHAR(255)	A short description of the forum.

The Topics table

The Topics table stores information for each of the topic areas available to users. Table 10-2 lists the columns defined for this table.

Table 10-2		The Topics Table
Column name	*Type*	*Description*
topicid	INT IDENTITY	An identity column that provides a unique ID number for each topic area supported by the site. This is the primary key for the Topics table.

Column name	Type	Description
forumid	INT	Indicates the Forum that this topic is associated with. This column is a foreign key to the forumid column in the Forums table.
name	VARCHAR(255)	The topic name.
description	VARCHAR(255)	A short description of the topic.

The Threads table

The Threads table stores information about the discussion threads that are active on the system. Its columns are listed in Table 10-3.

Table 10-3		The Threads Table
Column name	**Type**	**Description**
threadid	INT IDENTITY	An identity column that uniquely identifies each thread. This is the primary key for the Threads table.
topicid	INT	The topic ID of the topic the thread belongs to. This is a foreign key to the topicid column of the Topics table.
subject	VARCHAR(100)	The subject line for the thread.
replies	INT	A count of the number of replies that have been made to the thread. This number will be one less than the total number of rows in the Messages table for the thread.
author	VARCHAR(100)	The e-mail address of the user who created the thread.
lastpostdate	DATETIME	The date of the last message posted to the thread.

The Messages table

The Messages table stores the actual messages that have been posted to the Forum Web site. Its columns are listed in Table 10-4.

Table 10-4		The Messages Table
Column name	**Type**	**Description**
msgid	INT IDENTITY	An identity column that uniquely identifies each message. This is the primary key for the Messages table.
threadid	INT	The ID of the thread this message belongs to. This is a foreign key to the threadid column of the Threads table.
author	VARCHAR(100)	The e-mail address of the user who created the message.
date	DATETIME	The date the message was posted.
message	VARCHAR(MAX)	The text of the message.

Creating the Database

Listing 10-1 shows a SQL script named CreateForumDB.sql which creates the Forum database. To run this script, open a command prompt window and change to the directory that contains the script. Then enter this command:

```
sqlcmd -S localhost\SQLExpress -i CreateForumsDB.sql
```

Change the host name if you're not using SQL Server Express on your own computer.

Listing 10-1: The CreateForumDB.sql script

```
USE master                                                →1
GO

IF EXISTS(SELECT * FROM sysdatabases                      →2
    WHERE name='Forum')
DROP DATABASE Forum
```

```
GO

CREATE DATABASE Forum                                          →3
ON (NAME=Product,
    FILENAME = 'C:\APPS\Forum.mdf',
    SIZE=10 )
GO

USE Forum                                                      →4

CREATE TABLE Forums (                                          →5
    forumid      INT IDENTITY,
    name         VARCHAR(255)   NOT NULL,
    description VARCHAR(255)    NOT NULL,
    PRIMARY KEY(forumid)
    )
GO

CREATE TABLE Topics (                                          →6
    topicid      INT IDENTITY,
    forumid      INT,
    name         VARCHAR(255)   NOT NULL,
    description VARCHAR(255),
    PRIMARY KEY(topicid),
    FOREIGN KEY(forumid) REFERENCES Forums(forumid)
    )
GO

CREATE TABLE Threads (                                         →7
    threadid     INT IDENTITY,
    topicid      INT            NOT NULL,
    subject      VARCHAR(100)   NOT NULL,
    replies      INT            NOT NULL,
    author       VARCHAR(100)   NOT NULL,
    lastpostdate DATETIME,
    PRIMARY KEY(threadid),
    FOREIGN KEY(topicid) REFERENCES Topics(topicid)
    )
GO

CREATE TABLE Messages (                                        →8
    msgid        INT IDENTITY,
    threadid     INT            NOT NULL,
    author       VARCHAR(100)   NOT NULL,
    date         DATETIME,
    message      VARCHAR(MAX)   NOT NULL,
    PRIMARY KEY(msgid),
    FOREIGN KEY(threadid) REFERENCES Threads(threadid)
    )
GO
```

Eight quick comments draw out the pertinent details of this listing:

→ **1**   Sets the database context to master.

→ **2**   Deletes the existing Forum database if it exists.

→ **3**   Creates a database named Forum, placing the database in the folder C:\Apps.

→ **4**   Sets the database context to Forum.

→ **5**   Creates the Forums table.

→ **6**   Creates the Topics table.

→ **7**   Creates the Threads table.

→ **8**   Creates the Messages table.

Adding Test Data

The companion CD also includes a script named InsertData.sql script, which creates test data for the database. It creates the forums and topics — for example, these:

forum	*topic*
Christmas	Decorating
	Light Displays
Halloween	Costumes
	Decorations
	Party Ideas

After the forums and topics are set up, you can create threads and messages yourself by running the Forum application.

To run the InsertData.sql script, open a command window, change to the directory that contains the script, and run this command:

```
sqlcmd -S localhost\SQLExpress -i InsertData.sql
```

Note that you'll need to change the server name if it is other than local-host\SQLExpress.

SQL statements for working with the database

The Forum application uses several SQL statements to retrieve and update data in the Forum. Here's a rundown on what the various SQL statements do:

✔ These SELECT statements list the forums and topics on the home page:

```
SELECT [forumid], [name]
    FROM Forums
    ORDER BY [name]
SELECT [forumid], [topicid], [name], [description]
    FROM Topics
    ORDER BY [name]
```

✔ Several pages use the following SELECT statements to retrieve names for the topic and thread being displayed:

```
SELECT [name], [description]
    FROM [Topics]
    WHERE ([topicid] = @topicid)
SELECT [subject]
    FROM [Threads]
    WHERE ([threadid] = @threadid)
```

✔ The following query retrieves all threads for a given topic:

```
SELECT [threadid], [topicid], [subject],
       [replies], [author], [lastpostdate]
    FROM [Threads]
    WHERE ([topicid] = @topicid)
    ORDER BY [lastpostdate]
```

✔ The following query retrieves all messages for a given thread:

```
SELECT [author], [date], [message]
    FROM [Messages]
    WHERE ([threadid] = @threadid)
    ORDER BY [date]
```

✔ The following statements insert rows into the Threads and Messages tables when the user creates a new thread:

```
INSERT Threads
        (topicid, subject, replies,
        author, lastpostdate)"
    VALUES(@topicid, @subject, @replies,
        →uthor, @lastpostdate)

INSERT Messages
        (threadid, author, date, message)
    VALUES(@threadid, →uthor, @date, @message)
```

↙ Finally, the following statements post a reply to a thread:

```
INSERT Messages
          (threadid, author, date, message)
    VALUES(@threadid, →uthor, @date, @message)

UPDATE Threads
    SET replies = replies + 1
    WHERE threadid = @threadid
```

Here, the UPDATE statement is required to update the replies column in the Threads table.

Connecting to the database

The connection string for the Forum Application is stored in the <connectionStrings> section of the web.config file, like this:

```
<connectionStrings>
    <add name="ForumConnectionString"
         connectionString="Data
            Source=localhost\SQLExpress;
Initial Catalog=Forum;Integrated Security=True"/>
</connectionStrings>
```

You may have to modify the connection string to match your server and database name.

Building the Master Page

The Forum application uses the simple Master Page that's shown in Listing 10-2. As you can see, this Master Page includes a content placeholder — and nothing else. (When you develop your own Forum application, you'll probably want to put additional information in the Master Page.)

Listing 10-2:   The Master Page (MasterPage.master)

```
<%@ Master Language="C#"                              →1
    AutoEventWireup="true"
    CodeFile="MasterPage.master.cs"
    Inherits="MasterPage" %>

<!DOCTYPE html PUBLIC "-//W3C//DTD XHTML 1.1//EN"
    "http://www.w3.org/TR/xhtml11/DTD/xhtml11.dtd">

<html xmlns="http://www.w3.org/1999/xhtml" >
<head runat="server">
```

```
        <title>Untitled Page</title>
    </head>
    <body>
        <form id="form1" runat="server">
        <div>
            <asp:contentplaceholder                    →2
                id="ContentPlaceHolder1"
                runat="server">
            </asp:contentplaceholder>
        </div>
        </form>
    </body>
</html>
```

Just two key points for this listing:

→ **1**   The `Master` directive indicates that the file is a Master Page.

Note that if you want to use Visual Basic rather than C# for the application's code-behind files, you should change the `AutoEventWireup` attribute to `false`. (That won't matter for this application; the Master Page doesn't require a code-behind file.)

→ **2**   The `ContentPlaceHolder` control marks where to display the content for each page of the application.

Building the Forum Home Page

The Forum Home page (`Default.aspx`) displays a list of the forums and topics that are available on the Forum Web site. You can refer back to Figure 10-2 to see how this page appears when the application is run.

You might think a page that displays a list like this would be relatively simple — in fact, the forum and topics list are pretty tricky to create. To create this list, I used a pair of nested `Repeater` controls. The outer `Repeater` control displays the forums. For each forum, a second `Repeater` control lists the topics associated with that forum.

The following sections present the `.aspx` and code-behind files for this page.

The Default.aspx page

Listing 10-3 presents the .aspx code for the Forum Home page, which uses nested Repeater controls to display the topics for each forum provided by the application.

Listing 10-3: The Forum Home page (Default.aspx)

```
<%@ Page Language="C#"                                            →1
    MasterPageFile="~/MasterPage.master"
    AutoEventWireup="true"
    CodeFile="Default.aspx.cs"
    Inherits="_Default"
    Title="Forum Listing" %>
<asp:Content ID="Content1" Runat="Server"                         →2
    ContentPlaceHolderID="ContentPlaceHolder1" >
<h3>Which forum would you like to visit?</h3>
<table border=0>                                                  →3
<asp:Repeater ID="ForumRepeater" runat="Server"                  →4
    OnItemDataBound="ForumRepeater_ItemDataBound" >
    <ItemTemplate>                                                →5
      <tr bgcolor="Gainsboro">
        <td>
          <asp:Label ID="lblForumName"
            runat="Server"
            Text='<% #Eval("name") %>' />
        </td>
      </tr>
      <asp:Repeater ID="TopicRepeater"                            →6
        runat="Server" >
        <ItemTemplate>                                            →7
          <tr><td>
            <asp:LinkButton ID="linkTopicName"                    →8
                runat="Server"
                Text='<% #Eval("name")%>'
                PostBackUrl='<% #Eval("topicid",
                  "Threads.aspx?topic={0}")%>'/>
                --
            <asp:Label ID="lblTopicDescr"                         →9
                runat="Server"
                Text='<% #Eval("description")%>' />
          </td></tr>
        </ItemTemplate>                                           →10
      </asp:Repeater>                                             →11
    </ItemTemplate>                                               →12
</asp:Repeater>                                                   →13
</table>                                                          →14
</asp:Content>
```

And here's another set of 14 key points for this listing:

→ **1**   You'll need to change the Language, AutoEventWireup, and CodeFile attributes in the Page directive if you're working with Visual Basic rather than C#.

→ **2**   The <Content> element provides the content displayed for the page.

→ **3**   This <table> element marks the start of the HTML table used to display the list of forums and topics.

→ **4**   This is the first of the two Repeater controls on this page. Note that although this application uses data binding to provide the data for the Repeater controls, the data binding is done procedurally in code provided by the code-behind file. As a result, the .aspx file provides no data source and the Repeater control does not specify the DataSourceID attribute.

The OnItemDataBound attribute specifies that the ForumRepeater_DataBound method should be called for each item in the Repeater control's data source. If you're working in Visual Basic, omit this attribute; the Handles clause is used instead to specify the method called when the ItemDataBound event occurs.

→ **5**   The <ItemTemplate> element for the first Repeater control begins with an HTML table row (<tr>) that includes a Label control. The Text attribute for the label uses the Eval method to display the name field from the data source.

The code-behind file specifies the data source at run time.

→ **6**   Next, the item template includes a Repeater control that displays the topics for the current forum. Like the first Repeater control, the data binding for this Repeater control is handled in the code-behind file.

→ **7**   The item template for the second Repeater control displays an HTML table row for each topic associated with the current forum.

→ **8**   A LinkButton control is used to display the topic name. The PostBackUrl address for the link button uses the Eval method to pass the ID for the selected topic to the Threads.aspx page as a query string. For example, if the user clicks the link button for a topic whose topicid is 4, the PostBackUrl will be Threads.aspx?topic=4.

→ **9**   This label displays the topic description.

→ **10** This `</ItemTemplate>` tag marks the end of the item template for the inner `Repeater` control, which was started in Line 7.

→ **11** This `</asp:Repeater>` tag marks the end of the inner `Repeater` control. It pairs with the `<Repeater>` tag in Line 6.

→ **12** This `</ItemTemplate>` tag marks the end of the item template for the outer `Repeater` control, started in Line 5.

→ **13** This `</asp:Repeater>` tag marks the end of the outer `Repeater` control. It matches up with the `<Repeater>` tag in Line 4.

→ **14** This line marks the end of the HTML table started in Line 3.

The code-behind file for the Forum Home page

The code-behind file for the Forum Home page handles the details of retrieving the forum and topic information from the database. Then it binds the outer `Repeater` control to the list of forums. Finally, each time an item is bound for the outer `Repeater` control, this process binds the inner `Repeater` control and displays topics for the current forum.

Listings 10-4 and 10-5 show the C# and Visual Basic versions of this code-behind file.

Listing 10-4: The code-behind file for the home page (C# version)

```
using System;
using System.Data;
using System.Configuration;
using System.Collections;
using System.Web;
using System.Web.Security;
using System.Web.UI;
using System.Web.UI.WebControls;
using System.Web.UI.WebControls.WebParts;
using System.Web.UI.HtmlControls;
using System.Web.Configuration;                              →1
using System.Data.SqlClient;                                 →2

public partial class _Default : System.Web.UI.Page
{
    DataSet ds;                                              →3

    protected void Page_Load(object sender,                  →4
```

```
        EventArgs e)
    {
        string con = WebConfigurationManager          →5
            .ConnectionStrings["ForumConnectionString"]
            .ConnectionString;

        ds = new DataSet();                            →6

        // fill the Forums table                       →7
        string sel = "SELECT [forumid], [name] "
            + "FROM Forums "
            + "ORDER BY [name]";
        SqlDataAdapter da = new SqlDataAdapter(sel, con);
        da.Fill(ds, "Forums");

        // fill the Topics table                       →8
        sel = "SELECT [forumid], [topicid], "
            + "[name], [description] "
            + "FROM Topics "
            + "ORDER BY [name]";
        da = new SqlDataAdapter(sel, con);
        da.Fill(ds, "Topics");

        // bind the Forum repeater                      →9
        ForumRepeater.DataSource = ds.Tables["Forums"]
            .DefaultView;
        ForumRepeater.DataBind();
    }

    public void ForumRepeater_ItemDataBound(           →10
        Object sender, RepeaterItemEventArgs e)
    {
        Repeater r = ((Repeater)e.Item                 →11
            .FindControl("TopicRepeater"));

        DataRowView drv                                →12
            = (DataRowView)e.Item.DataItem;
        string forumid = drv["forumid"].ToString();

        DataView dv                                    →13
            = ds.Tables["Topics"].DefaultView;
        dv.RowFilter = "forumid=" + forumid;

        r.DataSource = dv;                             →14
        r.DataBind();
    }
}
```

Here's a set of 14 explanations, matched to the 14 key lines of this listing:

→ **1** The code-behind file needs access to the `System.Web.Configuration` namespace because it uses the `WebConfigurationManager` class to retrieve the database connection string from the `web.config` file.

→ **2** The `System.Data.SqlClient` namespace is required to use ADO.NET classes such as `DataSet`, `SqlConnection`, and `SqlCommand`.

→ **3** This line defines a class instance variable of type `DataSet`. That way, the dataset will be available to both of the methods in the code-behind file.

→ **4** The `Page_Load` method executes when the page loads. It fills the dataset with data retrieved from the `Forums` and `Topics` tables; it also sets up data binding for the `ForumRepeater` control and calls that control's `DataBind` method, which completes the binding.

→ **5** This line retrieves the connection string from the `web.config` file.

→ **6** This statement creates an empty dataset object and assigns it to the `ds` variable.

→ **7** These lines create a table in the `ds` dataset named `Forums` by a) creating a data adapter that retrieves rows from the Forums table and b) calling the data adapter's `Fill` method.

→ **8** These lines create a second table in the dataset (named `Topics`) by creating a data adapter (which retrieves data from this new `Topics` table) and calling the data adapter's `Fill` method.

→ **9** These lines set the data source for the `ForumRepeater` control to the `Forums` table in the dataset, and then call the `DataBind` method to bind the `Repeater` control to its data.

→ **10** This method is called each time an item is bound to the outer `Repeater`. It binds the inner `Repeater` control to the topics that are associated with the forum represented by the item.

→ **11** The e argument includes a property named `Item` that represents the item being bound. This statement calls that item's `FindControl` method to find the `Repeater` control named `TopicRepeater`. That particular `Repeater` is then assigned to the variable named r so it can be used later.

→ **12** These lines retrieve the id of the forum represented by the current `Repeater` item. First, `e.Item.DataItem` is used to retrieve a `DataRowView` object that lets you access the individual data fields for the `Repeater` item. Then the `forumid` field is retrieved and saved in a local variable named `forumid`.

→ **13**   These lines retrieve a `DataView` object for the `Topics` table of the data set and set its row filter so it views only those rows whose `forumid` field matches the value of the `forumid` variable.

→ **14**   These lines bind the `Repeater` control to the data view. This causes the `Repeater` control to create a line for each topic that's associated with the forum.

Listing 10-5:   The code-behind file for the home page (VB version)

```
Imports System.Web.Configuration                           →1
Imports System.Data.SqlClient                              →2
Imports System.Data

Partial Class _Default
    Inherits System.Web.UI.Page

    Private ds As DataSet                                  →3

    Protected Sub Page_Load( _                             →4
            ByVal sender As Object, _
            ByVal e As System.EventArgs) _
            Handles Me.Load
        Dim con As String _                                →5
            = WebConfigurationManager _
            .ConnectionStrings("ForumConnectionString") _
            .ConnectionString

        ds = New DataSet()                                 →6

        'fill the Forums table                             →7
        Dim sel As String _
            = "SELECT [forumid], [name] " _
            + "FROM Forums " _
            + "ORDER BY [name]"
        Dim da As SqlDataAdapter _
            = New SqlDataAdapter(sel, con)
        da.Fill(ds, "Forums")

        'fill the Topics table                             →8
        sel = "SELECT [forumid], [topicid], " _
            + "[name], [description] " _
            + "FROM Topics " _
            + "ORDER BY [name]"
        da = New SqlDataAdapter(sel, con)
        da.Fill(ds, "Topics")

        'bind the Forum repeater                           →9
        ForumRepeater.DataSource = ds.Tables("Forums") _
            .DefaultView
        ForumRepeater.DataBind()
    End Sub
```

(continued)

Listing 10-5 *(continued)*

```
    Protected Sub ForumRepeater_ItemDataBound( _         →10
        ByVal sender As Object, _
        ByVal e As RepeaterItemEventArgs) _
        Handles ForumRepeater.ItemDataBound

        Dim r As Repeater                                →11
        r = e.Item.FindControl("TopicRepeater")

        Dim drv As DataRowView                           →12
        drv = e.Item.DataItem
        Dim forumid As String = drv("forumid")

        Dim dv As DataView                               →13
        dv = ds.Tables("Topics").DefaultView
        dv.RowFilter = "forumid=" + forumid

        r.DataSource = dv                                →14
        r.DataBind()
    End Sub
End Class
```

Building the Threads Page

The Threads page displays all threads for the topic selected by the user. The Threads page knows which topic to display because the topic is passed as a query string field from the Default.aspx page. Then the Threads page uses a simple GridView control bound to a SqlDataSource to retrieve and display the threads.

A code-behind file is required to handle the Click event raised by the Start a New Thread link or the SelectedItemChanged event raised by the GridView control.

The Threads.aspx page

Listing 10-6 presents the .aspx code for the Threads page. There's nothing unusual about the code for this page, so you shouldn't have much trouble following it.

Listing 10-6:   The Threads.aspx page

```
<%@ Page Language="C#"                                   →1
    MasterPageFile="~/MasterPage.master"
    AutoEventWireup="true"
    CodeFile="Threads.aspx.cs"
    Inherits="Threads"
```

```
        Title="Topic Threads" %>
<asp:Content ID="Content1" Runat="Server"                    →2
    ContentPlaceHolderID="ContentPlaceHolder1" >
    <asp:FormView ID="FormView1" runat="server"              →3
        DataSourceID="SqlDataSource1">
        <ItemTemplate>
            <h2>
                <asp:Label ID="nameLabel" runat="server"
                    Text='<%# Bind("name") %>' />
            </h2>
            <h3>
                <asp:Label ID="descriptionLabel"
                    runat="server"
                    Text='<%# Bind("description") %>' />
            </h3>
        </ItemTemplate>
    </asp:FormView>
    <asp:SqlDataSource ID="SqlDataSource1"                   →4
        runat="server"
        ConnectionString="<%$ ConnectionStrings
:ForumConnectionString %>"
        SelectCommand="SELECT [name], [description]
            FROM [Topics] WHERE ([topicid] = @topicid)">
        <SelectParameters>
            <asp:QueryStringParameter                        →5
                Name="topicid"
                QueryStringField="topic"
                Type="Int32" />
        </SelectParameters>
    </asp:SqlDataSource>
    <br />
    <asp:GridView ID="GridView1" runat="server"              →6
        AutoGenerateColumns="False"
        DataSourceID="SqlDataSource2"
        DataKeyNames="threadid"
        AllowPaging="True"
        PageSize="15"
        PagerSettings-Mode="NumericFirstLast"
        OnSelectedIndexChanged
            ="GridView1_SelectedIndexChanged">
        <Columns>
            <asp:ButtonField                                 →7
                CommandName="Select"
                DataTextField="subject"
                HeaderText="Subject"
                Text="Button">
                <ItemStyle HorizontalAlign="Left"
                    Width="250px" />
                <HeaderStyle HorizontalAlign="Left" />
            </asp:ButtonField>
            <asp:BoundField                                  →8
                DataField="author"
                HeaderText="Author" >
```

(continued)

Listing 10-6 *(continued)*

```
                <HeaderStyle HorizontalAlign="Left" />
                <ItemStyle Width="100px" />
            </asp:BoundField>
            <asp:BoundField                                      →9
                DataField="replies"
                HeaderText="Replies" >
                <HeaderStyle HorizontalAlign="Center" />
                <ItemStyle HorizontalAlign="Center"
                    Width="70px" />
            </asp:BoundField>
            <asp:BoundField                                      →10
                DataField="lastpostdate"
                HeaderText="Last Post"
                DataFormatString="{0:d}" >
                <HeaderStyle HorizontalAlign="Center" />
                <ItemStyle Width="70px" />
            </asp:BoundField>
        </Columns>
    </asp:GridView>
    <asp:SqlDataSource ID="SqlDataSource2"                       →11
        runat="server"
        ConnectionString="<%$ ConnectionStrings
:ForumConnectionString %>"
        SelectCommand="SELECT [threadid], [topicid],
            [subject], [replies], [author], [lastpostdate]
            FROM [Threads]
            WHERE ([topicid] = @topicid)
            ORDER BY [lastpostdate]">
        <SelectParameters>
            <asp:QueryStringParameter                            →12
            Name="topicid"
            QueryStringField="topic"
            Type="Int32" />
        </SelectParameters>
    </asp:SqlDataSource>
    <br />
    <asp:LinkButton ID="LinkButton1"                             →13
        runat="server"
        Text="Start a New Thread"
        OnClick="LinkButton1_Click" />
    <br /><br />
    <asp:LinkButton ID="btnReturn"                               →14
        runat="server"
        PostBackUrl="~/Default.aspx"
        Text="Return to Forum Page" />
</asp:Content>
```

This listing has 14 key points to explain:

→ **1** If you use the Visual Basic version of the code-behind file, be sure to change the Language, AutoEventWireup, and CodeFile attributes in the Page directive.

→ **2**   The `<Content>` element provides the content that's displayed for the page.

→ **3**   This `FormView` control displays the topic name and description. It's bound to the data source named `SqlDataSource1`.

→ **4**   The `SqlDataSource1` data source retrieves the topic information from the `Topics` row, using the `topicid` parameter to specify the topic to be retrieved.

→ **5**   The value of the `topicid` parameter is bound to the query string named `topic`.

→ **6**   The `GridView` control displays the threads for the selected topic. It's bound to the `SqlDataSource2` data source, and paging is enabled. Note that the `GridView1_SelectedIndexChanged` method is called if the user selects a thread.

If you're working with Visual Basic, remove the `OnSelectedIndexChanged` attribute.

→ **7**   The first column for the `GridView` control is a button field that displays the thread subject. The `CommandName` attribute specifies `Select`, so the row is selected when the user clicks this link.

→ **8**   The next column displays the e-mail address of the user that initially started the thread.

→ **9**   This column displays the number of replies to the thread.

→ **10**   This column displays the date of the last message posted to the thread.

→ **11**   The `SqlDataSource2` data source provides the data for the `GridView` control. Its `SelectCommand` attribute specifies a `SELECT` statement that retrieves threads for the topic specified by the `topicid` parameter.

→ **12**   The `topicid` parameter is bound to the `topic` query string field.

→ **13**   This `LinkButton` control lets the user start a new thread.

If you're using Visual Basic, you should omit the `OnClick` attribute.

→ **14**   This `LinkButton` sends the user back to the Forum Home page.

The code-behind file for the Threads page

The code-behind file for the Threads page handles the `Click` event for the Start a New Thread link and the `SelectedIndexChanged` event for the `GridView` control. Listings 10-7 and 10-8 show the C# and Visual Basic versions of this code-behind file.

Listing 10-7: The code-behind file for the Threads page (C# version)

```csharp
using System;
using System.Data;
using System.Configuration;
using System.Collections;
using System.Web;
using System.Web.Security;
using System.Web.UI;
using System.Web.UI.WebControls;
using System.Web.UI.WebControls.WebParts;
using System.Web.UI.HtmlControls;

public partial class Threads : System.Web.UI.Page
{
    protected void LinkButton1_Click(object sender,        →1
        EventArgs e)
    {
        Response.Redirect("NewThread.aspx?topic="
            + Request.QueryString["topic"]);
    }

    protected void GridView1_SelectedIndexChanged(         →2
        object sender, EventArgs e)
    {
        string threadid
            = GridView1.SelectedValue.ToString();
        string topicid = Request.QueryString["topic"];
        Response.Redirect("Messages.aspx?topic=" + topicid
            + "&thread=" + threadid);
    }
}
```

The two methods in this code-behind file are the heart of how it works:

→ 1   The `LinkButton1_Click` method is called when the user clicks the Start a New Thread link. It simply redirects to the `NewThread.aspx` page, passing the `topic` query string so the New Thread page knows which topic to create the thread in.

→ 2   The `GridView1_SelectedIndexChanged` method is called when the user selects a thread in the `GridView` control. It retrieves the thread ID from the `GridView` control's `SelectedValue` property and the topic ID from the `topic` query string field, then redirects to the `Messages.aspx` page, passing the thread and topic IDs as query string fields.

Listing 10-8:   The code-behind file for the Threads page (VB version)

```
Partial Class Threads
    Inherits System.Web.UI.Page


    Protected Sub LinkButton1_Click( _                    →1
        ByVal sender As Object, _
        ByVal e As System.EventArgs) _
        Handles LinkButton1.Click
      Response.Redirect("NewThread.aspx?topic=" _
        + Request.QueryString("topic"))
    End Sub


    Protected Sub GridView1_SelectedIndexChanged( _       →2
        ByVal sender As Object, _
        ByVal e As System.EventArgs) _
        Handles GridView1.SelectedIndexChanged
      Dim threadid As String
      Dim topicid As String
      threadid = GridView1.SelectedValue.ToString()
      topicid = Request.QueryString("topic")
      Response.Redirect("Messages.aspx?topic=" _
        + topicid _
        + "&thread=" + threadid)
    End Sub
End Class
```

Building the Messages Page

The Messages page displays all messages for the thread selected by the user. The thread to be displayed is passed to the Messages page as a query string named `thread`. In response, the Messages page uses a `GridView` control to display the messages.

The Messages.aspx page

Listing 10-9 presents the `Messages.apsx` file. As you can see, this page uses three SQL data sources, two `FormView` controls, and a `GridView` control to display the messages for the selected topic.

Listing 10-9: The Messages.aspx page

```
<%@ Page Language="C#"                                              →1
    MasterPageFile="~/MasterPage.master"
    AutoEventWireup="true"
    CodeFile="Messages.aspx.cs"
    Inherits="Messages"
    Title="Messages" %>
<asp:Content ID="Content1" Runat="Server"                           →2
    ContentPlaceHolderID="ContentPlaceHolder1" >

    <asp:FormView ID="FormView1" runat="server"                     →3
        DataSourceID="SqlDataSource1">
        <ItemTemplate>
            <h3>
                Topic:
                <asp:Label ID="topicNameLabel"
                    runat="server"
                    Text='<%# Bind("name") %>' />
            </h3>
        </ItemTemplate>
    </asp:FormView>

    <asp:SqlDataSource ID="SqlDataSource1"                           →4
        runat="server"
        ConnectionString
          ="<%$ ConnectionStrings:ForumConnectionString
          %>"
        SelectCommand="SELECT [name], [description]
            FROM [Topics]
            WHERE ([topicid] = @topicid)">
        <SelectParameters>                                          →5
            <asp:QueryStringParameter
            Name="topicid"
            QueryStringField="topic"
            Type="Int32" />
        </SelectParameters>
    </asp:SqlDataSource>

    <asp:FormView ID="FormView2" runat="server"                     →6
        DataSourceID="SqlDataSource2">
        <ItemTemplate>
            <h3>
                Thread:
                <asp:Label ID="threadNameLabel"
                    runat="server"
                    Text='<%# Bind("subject") %>' />
            </h3>
        </ItemTemplate>
    </asp:FormView>

    <asp:SqlDataSource ID="SqlDataSource2"                           →7
        runat="server"
        ConnectionString
```

```
          ="<%$ ConnectionStrings:ForumConnectionString
          %>"
      SelectCommand="SELECT [subject]
          FROM [Threads]
          WHERE ([threadid] = @threadid)">
      <SelectParameters>
          <asp:QueryStringParameter                    →8
          Name="threadid"
          QueryStringField="thread"
          Type="Int32" />
      </SelectParameters>
  </asp:SqlDataSource>

  <asp:GridView ID="GridView1" runat="server"          →9
      AutoGenerateColumns="False"
      DataSourceID="SqlDataSource3"
      ShowHeader="False"
      AllowPaging="True" >
    <Columns>
      <asp:TemplateField>                               →10
        <ItemTemplate>
        At
          <asp:Label ID="Label1" runat="server"
          Text='<% #Eval("date") %>' />
          <asp:Label ID="Label2" runat="server"
          Text='<% #Eval("author") %>' />
          wrote:
          <br /><br />
          <table border=0>
          <tr><td width=300>
          <asp:Label ID="Label3" runat="server"
          Text='<% #Eval("message") %>' />
          </td></tr></table>
        </ItemTemplate>
      </asp:TemplateField>
    </Columns>
  </asp:GridView>

  <asp:SqlDataSource ID="SqlDataSource3"                →11
      runat="server"
      ConnectionString
        ="<%$ ConnectionStrings:ForumConnectionString
        %>"
      SelectCommand="SELECT [author], [date], [message]
          FROM [Messages]
          WHERE ([threadid] = @threadid)
          ORDER BY [date]">
      <SelectParameters>
          <asp:QueryStringParameter                     →12
              Name="threadid"
              QueryStringField="thread" Type="Int32" />
      </SelectParameters>
```

(continued)

Listing 10-9 *(continued)*

```
        </asp:SqlDataSource><br />

        <asp:Button ID="btnAdd" runat="server"           →13
            Text="Add a Reply to this Thread"
            OnClick="btnAdd_Click" />
        <br /><br />

        <asp:LinkButton ID="btnReturn"                    →14
            runat="server"
            Text="Return to Threads page"
            OnClick="btnReturn_Click" />
</asp:Content>
```

This page has 14 key points:

→ 1   You'll need to change the Language, AutoEventWireup, and
       CodeFile attributes in the Page directive if you use Visual Basic
       instead of C#.

→ 2   The <Content> element provides the content that's displayed for
       the page.

→ 3   This FormView control displays the topic name and description.
       It's bound to the data source named SqlDataSource1.

→ 4   The SqlDataSource1 data source retrieves the topic information
       from the Topics table, using the topicid parameter to specify
       the topic to be retrieved.

→ 5   The value of the topicid parameter is bound to the query string
       named topic.

→ 6   This FormView control displays the thread subject. It's bound to
       the data source named SqlDataSource2.

→ 7   The SqlDataSource2 data source retrieves the thread subject
       from the Threads table.

→ 8   The value of the threadid parameter is bound to the query
       string named thread.

→ 9   The GridView control displays the messages for the selected
       thread. Paging is enabled, and the data source is
       SqlDataSource3.

→ 10   The <Columns> element consists of a single template field that
       displays the date of the post, the e-mail address of the poster, and
       the text of the message.

→ 11   The SqlDataSource3 data source retrieves all messages for the
       selected thread.

→ **12**　The value of the `threadid` parameter is taken from the `thread` query string.

→ **13**　The `btnAdd` button lets the user add a reply to the thread. (If you're working with Visual Basic, you should omit the `OnClick` attribute.)

→ **14**　The `btnReturn` button returns the user to the Threads page.

The code-behind file for the Messages page

Listings 10-10 and 10-11 show the C# and Visual Basic versions of the code-behind file for the Messages page, which handles the `Click` events for the two buttons on this page.

Listing 10-10:　The code-behind file for the Messages page (C# version)

```
using System;
using System.Data;
using System.Configuration;
using System.Collections;
using System.Web;
using System.Web.Security;
using System.Web.UI;
using System.Web.UI.WebControls;
using System.Web.UI.WebControls.WebParts;
using System.Web.UI.HtmlControls;

public partial class Messages : System.Web.UI.Page
{
    protected void btnAdd_Click(object sender,          →1
        EventArgs e)
    {
        string topicid = Request.QueryString["topic"];
        string threadid = Request.QueryString["thread"];
        Response.Redirect("NewMessage.aspx?topic="
            + topicid + "&thread=" + threadid);
    }

    protected void btnReturn_Click(object sender,       →2
        EventArgs e)
    {
        Response.Redirect("Threads.aspx?topic="
            + Request.QueryString["topic"]);
    }
}
```

The two methods in this code-behind file merit a closer look:

→ **1**   The `btnAdd_Click` method is called when the user clicks the Add a Reply to this Thread button. It simply redirects the user to the `NewMessage.aspx` page, passing the `topic` and `thread` query strings so the New Thread page knows which topic and thread to create the message for.

→ **2**   The `btnReturn_Click` method is called when the user clicks the Return link. It redirects to the `Threads.aspx` page, passing the topic-query string so the Threads page will know which topic to display.

Listing 10-11:   The code-behind file for the Messages page (VB version)

```
Partial Class Messages
    Inherits System.Web.UI.Page

    Protected Sub btnAdd_Click( _                              →1
            ByVal sender As Object, _
            ByVal e As System.EventArgs) _
            Handles btnAdd.Click
        Dim topicid As String
        Dim threadid As String
        topicid = Request.QueryString("topic")
        threadid = Request.QueryString("thread")
        Response.Redirect("NewMessage.aspx?topic=" _
            + topicid + "&thread=" + threadid)
    End Sub

    Protected Sub btnReturn_Click( _                           →2
            ByVal sender As Object, _
            ByVal e As System.EventArgs) _
            Handles btnReturn.Click
        Response.Redirect("Threads.aspx?topic=" _
            + Request.QueryString("topic"))
    End Sub
End Class
```

Building the New Thread Page

The New Thread page lets the user start a new thread. The topic in which the thread should be created is passed to the page via a query string named `topic`.

The NewThread.aspx page

The `.aspx` file for the New Thread page is shown in Listing 10-12. This page displays the topic name in a `FormView` control at the top of the page. Text boxes are displayed to get the user's e-mail address, the thread subject, and the text for the first message in the thread.

Listing 10-12:   The NewThread.aspx page

```
<%@ Page Language="C#"                                           →1
    MasterPageFile="~/MasterPage.master"
    AutoEventWireup="true"
    CodeFile="NewThread.aspx.cs"
    Inherits="NewThread"
    Title="New Thread" %>
<asp:Content ID="Content1" Runat="Server"                        →2
    ContentPlaceHolderID="ContentPlaceHolder1" >
    <asp:FormView ID="FormView1" runat="server"                  →3
        DataSourceID="SqlDataSource1">
        <ItemTemplate>
            <h3>
                New Thread for Topic: 
                <asp:Label ID="nameLabel" runat="server"
                    Text='<%# Bind("name") %>' />
            </h3>
        </ItemTemplate>
    </asp:FormView>
    <asp:SqlDataSource ID="SqlDataSource1"                        →4
        runat="server"
        ConnectionString
          ="<%$ ConnectionStrings:ForumConnectionString
          %>"
        SelectCommand="SELECT [name], [description]
          FROM [Topics]
          WHERE ([topicid] = @topicid)">
        <SelectParameters>
            <asp:QueryStringParameter                             →5
                Name="topicid"
                QueryStringField="topic"
                Type="Int32" />
        </SelectParameters>
    </asp:SqlDataSource>
    <table border=0>
      <tr><td Width="125">
         Your email address:
        </td><td width="300" valign="top">
          <asp:TextBox ID="txtEmail" runat="server"              →6
            Width="300px" />
          <asp:RequiredFieldValidator
            ID="RequiredFieldValidator1"
            runat="server"
```

(continued)

Listing 10-12 *(continued)*

```
                    ControlToValidate="txtEmail"
                    ErrorMessage="Required." />
          </td></tr>
          <tr><td Width="125">
              Subject:
            </td><td width="300" valign="top">
              <asp:TextBox ID="txtSubject" runat="server"        →7
                  Width="300px" />
              <asp:RequiredFieldValidator
                  ID="RequiredFieldValidator2"
                  runat="server"
                  ControlToValidate="txtMessage"
                  ErrorMessage="Required." />
          </td></tr>
          <tr><td width="125" valign="top">
              Message:
            </td><td width="300">
              <asp:TextBox ID="txtMessage" runat="server"        →8
                  TextMode="MultiLine"
                  Width="300px" Height="300px"/>
              <asp:RequiredFieldValidator
                  ID="RequiredFieldValidator3"
                  runat="server"
                  ControlToValidate="txtSubject"
                  ErrorMessage="Required." />
          </td></tr>
        </table>
        <asp:Button ID="btnPost" runat="server"                  →9
            OnClick="btnPost_Click"
            Text="Post Message" /> 
        <asp:Button ID="btnCancel" runat="server"                →10
            OnClick="btnCancel_Click" Text="Cancel" />
</asp:Content>
```

Here are details of the ten most important lines of this file:

→ **1** You'll need to change the `Language`, `AutoEventWireup`, and `CodeFile` attributes in the `Page` directive if you use Visual Basic instead of C#.

→ **2** The `<Content>` element provides the content that's displayed for the page.

→ **3** This `FormView` control displays the topic name and description. It's bound to the data source named `SqlDataSource1`.

→ **4** The `SqlDataSource1` data source retrieves the topic information from the `Topics` row, using the `topicid` parameter to specify the topic to be retrieved.

→ **5** The value of the `topicid` parameter is bound to the query string named `topic`.

→ **6**   This text box accepts the user's e-mail address. A
`RequiredFieldValidator` is used to make sure the user enters
an address.

→ **7**   This text box accepts the thread subject. Again, a
`RequiredFieldValidator` makes sure the user enters a
subject.

→ **8**   This multi-line text box accepts the message. A
`RequiredFieldValidator` is used to make sure the user enters
a message.

→ **9**   The `btnPost` button creates the new thread.

If you're working in Visual Basic, omit the `OnClick` attribute.

→ **10**   The `btnCancel` button cancels the new thread.

Omit the `OnClick` attribute if you're working in Visual Basic.

The code-behind file for the New Thread page

The C# and Visual Basic versions of the code-behind file for the New Thread
page are shown in Listings 10-13 and 10-14, respectively. As you can see,
these code-behind files contain just two methods, which handle the `Click`
event for the buttons that appear at the bottom of the New Thread page.

Listing 10-13:   The code-behind file for the New Thread page (C# version)

```
using System;
using System.Data;
using System.Configuration;
using System.Collections;
using System.Web;
using System.Web.Security;
using System.Web.UI;
using System.Web.UI.WebControls;
using System.Web.UI.WebControls.WebParts;
using System.Web.UI.HtmlControls;
using System.Web.Configuration;                                →1
using System.Data.SqlClient;                                   →2

public partial class NewThread : System.Web.UI.Page
{
    protected void btnPost_Click(                              →3
            object sender, EventArgs e)
    {
        // set up the data objects                             →4
```

(continued)

Listing 10-13 *(continued)*

```
string cs = WebConfigurationManager
    .ConnectionStrings["ForumConnectionString"]
    .ConnectionString;
string insertThread = "INSERT Threads "
    + "(topicid, subject, replies, "
    + "author, lastpostdate)"
    + "VALUES(@topicid, @subject, @replies, "
    + "→uthor, @lastpostdate)";
string getThreadID = "SELECT @@IDENTITY";
string insertMessage = "INSERT Messages "
    + "(threadid, author, date, message) "
    + "VALUES(@threadid, →uthor, @date, @message)";
SqlConnection con = new SqlConnection(cs);
SqlCommand cmd = new SqlCommand(insertThread,
    con);

// insert the thread                               →5
cmd.Parameters.AddWithValue("topicid",
    Request.QueryString["topic"]);
cmd.Parameters.AddWithValue("subject",
    txtSubject.Text);
cmd.Parameters.AddWithValue("replies", 0);
cmd.Parameters.AddWithValue("author",
    txtEmail.Text);
cmd.Parameters.AddWithValue("lastpostdate",
    DateTime.Now);
con.Open();
cmd.ExecuteNonQuery();

// get the thread ID                               →6
cmd.CommandText = getThreadID;
string threadid = cmd.ExecuteScalar().ToString();

// insert the message                              →7
cmd.CommandText = insertMessage;
cmd.Parameters.Clear();
cmd.Parameters.AddWithValue("threadid",
    threadid);
cmd.Parameters.AddWithValue("author",
    txtEmail.Text);
cmd.Parameters.AddWithValue("date",
    DateTime.Now);
cmd.Parameters.AddWithValue("message",
    txtMessage.Text);
cmd.ExecuteNonQuery();
con.Close();

Response.Redirect("Messages.aspx?topic="        →8
    + Request.QueryString["topic"]
    + "&thread=" + threadid);
```

```
    }

    protected void btnCancel_Click(                          →9
            object sender, EventArgs e)
    {
        Response.Redirect("Threads.aspx?topic="
            + Request.QueryString["topic"]);
    }
}
```

Here are the highlights of this code-behind file:

→ **1**   Because the code-behind file uses the `WebConfigurationManager` class to retrieve the database connection string from the `web.config` file, the code-behind file requires the `System.Web.Configuration` namespace.

→ **2**   Similarly, the `System.Data.SqlClient` namespace is required because the code-behind file uses ADO.NET classes.

→ **3**   The `btnPost_Click` method executes when the user clicks the Post Message button, writing a row to both the `Threads` table and the `Messages` table.

→ **4**   These lines create the ADO.NET database objects used by the `btnPost_Click` method, in a specific sequence:

    1.   The connection string is retrieved from `web.config`.

    2.   Three string variables are created and initialized to the `INSERT` statements needed to insert data into the `Threads` and `Messages` tables.

    3.   The `SELECT` statement used to determine the `threadid` created for the new thread.

    4.   `SqlConnection` and `SqlCommand` objects are created.

→ **5**   These lines insert the thread data into the Threads table. First the parameters used by the `INSERT` statement for the `Threads` table are created. Then the connection opens and the `INSERT` statement executes.

→ **6**   These lines use the SQL statement `SELECT @@IDENTITY` to retrieve the `threadid` value that was assigned to the newly created thread. The `threadid` value is saved in a local variable named `threadid`.

→ **7**   These lines insert the message for the thread into the `Messages` table. First, the parameters used by the `INSERT` statement are created. Then, the `INSERT` statement executes and the connection is closed.

→ **8**   This line redirects the user to the `Messages.aspx` page, which shows the newly created thread.

→ **9**   This method executes when the user clicks the Cancel button. It simply redirects the user back to the `Threads.aspx` page.

Listing 10-14:   **The code-behind file for the New Thread page (VB version)**

```
Imports System.Web.Configuration                            →1
Imports System.Data.SqlClient                               →2

Partial Class NewThread
    Inherits System.Web.UI.Page

    Protected Sub btnPost_Click( _                          →3
            ByVal sender As Object, _
            ByVal e As System.EventArgs) _
            Handles btnPost.Click

        'set up the data objects                            →4
        Dim cs As String
        cs = WebConfigurationManager _
            .ConnectionStrings("ForumConnectionString") _
            .ConnectionString
        Dim insertThread As String
        insertThread = "INSERT Threads " _
            + "(topicid, subject, replies, " _
            + "author, lastpostdate)" _
            + "VALUES(@topicid, @subject, @replies, " _
            + "→uthor, @lastpostdate)"
        Dim getThreadID As String
        getThreadID = "SELECT @@IDENTITY"
        Dim insertMessage As String
        insertMessage = "INSERT Messages " _
            + "(threadid, author, date, message) " _
            + "VALUES(@threadid, →uthor, @date,
          @message)"
        Dim con As SqlConnection
        con = New SqlConnection(cs)
        Dim cmd As SqlCommand
        cmd = New SqlCommand(insertThread, con)

        'insert the thread                                  →5
        cmd.Parameters.AddWithValue("topicid", _
            Request.QueryString("topic"))
        cmd.Parameters.AddWithValue("subject", _
            txtSubject.Text)
        cmd.Parameters.AddWithValue("replies", 0)
```

```
        cmd.Parameters.AddWithValue("author", _
            txtEmail.Text)
        cmd.Parameters.AddWithValue("lastpostdate", _
            DateTime.Now)
        con.Open()
        cmd.ExecuteNonQuery()

        'get the thread ID                                      →6
        cmd.CommandText = getThreadID
        Dim threadid As String
        threadid = cmd.ExecuteScalar().ToString()

        'insert the message                                     →7
        cmd.CommandText = insertMessage
        cmd.Parameters.Clear()
        cmd.Parameters.AddWithValue("threadid", _
            threadid)
        cmd.Parameters.AddWithValue("author", _
            txtEmail.Text)
        cmd.Parameters.AddWithValue("date", _
            DateTime.Now)
        cmd.Parameters.AddWithValue("message", _
            txtMessage.Text)
        cmd.ExecuteNonQuery()
        con.Close()

        Response.Redirect("Messages.aspx?topic=" _          →8
            + Request.QueryString("topic") _
            + "&thread=" + threadid)
    End Sub

    Protected Sub btnCancel_Click( _                        →9
            ByVal sender As Object, _
            ByVal e As System.EventArgs) _
            Handles btnCancel.Click
        Response.Redirect("Threads.aspx?topic=" _
            + Request.QueryString("topic"))
    End Sub
End Class
```

Building the New Message Page

The last page of the Forum application is the New Message page, which lets the user post a reply to an existing thread. The following sections lay out the details of the .aspx and code-behind files for this page.

The NewMessage.aspx page

The `.aspx` file for the New Message page is shown in Listing 10-15. This page displays the topic name in a `FormView` control at the top of the page. Then text boxes are used to get the user's e-mail address and the message text. Note that there is no text box for the subject. That's because the thread — not the individual messages that make it up — provides the subject.

Listing 10-15:   The NewMessage.aspx page

```
<%@ Page Language="C#"                                              →1
    MasterPageFile="~/MasterPage.master"
    AutoEventWireup="true"
    CodeFile="NewMessage.aspx.cs"
    Inherits="NewMessage"
    Title="Post Reply" %>
<asp:Content ID="Content1" Runat="Server"                           →2
    ContentPlaceHolderID="ContentPlaceHolder1" >

    <asp:FormView ID="FormView1" runat="server"                     →3
        DataSourceID="SqlDataSource1">
        <ItemTemplate>
            <h3>
                Reply To Topic:
                <asp:Label ID="nameLabel"
                    runat="server"
                    Text='<%# Bind("name") %>' />
            </h3>
        </ItemTemplate>
    </asp:FormView>

    <asp:SqlDataSource ID="SqlDataSource1"                          →4
        runat="server"
        ConnectionString
          ="<%$ ConnectionStrings:ForumConnectionString
          %>"
        SelectCommand="SELECT [name], [description]
          FROM [Topics]
          WHERE ([topicid] = @topicid)">
        <SelectParameters>                                          →5
            <asp:QueryStringParameter
            Name="topicid"
            QueryStringField="topic"
            Type="Int32" />
        </SelectParameters>
    </asp:SqlDataSource>

    <asp:FormView ID="FormView2" runat="server"                     →6
        DataSourceID="SqlDataSource2">
        <ItemTemplate>
            <h3>
                Thread:
```

```
                    <asp:Label ID="subjectLabel"
                        runat="server"
                        Text='<%# Bind("subject") %>' />
            </h3>
        </ItemTemplate>
</asp:FormView>

<asp:SqlDataSource ID="SqlDataSource2"                        →7
    runat="server"
    ConnectionString
      ="<%$ ConnectionStrings:ForumConnectionString
      %>"
    SelectCommand="SELECT [subject]
        FROM [Threads]
        WHERE ([threadid] = @threadid)">
    <SelectParameters>                                        →8
        <asp:QueryStringParameter
            Name="threadid"
            QueryStringField="thread"
            Type="Int32" />
    </SelectParameters>
</asp:SqlDataSource>

<table border=0>

  <tr><td Width="125" valign="top">
     Your email address:
     </td><td width="300">
        <asp:TextBox ID="txtEmail" runat="server"           →9
           Width="300px" />
        <asp:RequiredFieldValidator
           ID="RequiredFieldValidator1"
           runat="Server"
           ControlToValidate="txtEmail"
           ErrorMessage="Required." />
  </td></tr>

  <tr><td width="125" valign="top">
     Message:
     </td><td width="300">
        <asp:TextBox ID="txtMessage"                         →10
           runat="server"
           TextMode="MultiLine"
           Width="300px" Height="300px"/>
        <asp:RequiredFieldValidator
           ID="RequiredFieldValidator2"
           runat="Server"
           ControlToValidate="txtMessage"
           ErrorMessage="Required." />
  </td></tr>
```

(continued)

Listing 10-15 *(continued)*

```
    </table>

    <asp:Button ID="btnPost" runat="server"          →11
        OnClick="btnPost_Click"
        Text="Post Reply" /> 

    <asp:Button ID="btnCancel" runat="server"         →12
        OnClick="btnCancel_Click"
        Text="Cancel" />

</asp:Content>
```

Here's a closer look at 12 key elements of this file:

→ **1**   If you use Visual Basic instead of C#, you'll need to change the `Language`, `AutoEventWireup`, and `CodeFile` attributes.

→ **2**   The `<Content>` element provides the content that's displayed for the page.

→ **3**   This `FormView` control, which is bound to the `SqlDataSource1` data source, displays the topic name and description.

→ **4**   The `SqlDataSource1` data source retrieves the topic information from the `Topics` table.

→ **5**   The value of the `topicid` parameter is bound to the query string named `topic`.

→ **6**   This `FormView` control displays the thread subject, which is bound to `SqlDataSource2`.

→ **7**   The `SqlDataSource2` data source retrieves the thread subject from the `Threads` table.

→ **8**   The `threadid` parameter is bound to the thread query string.

→ **9**   This text box accepts the user's e-mail address. A `RequiredFieldValidator` is used to make sure the user enters an address.

→ **10**   This multi-line text box accepts the message. A `RequiredFieldValidator` is used to make sure the user enters a message.

→ **11**   The `btnPost` button creates the new thread. If you're working in Visual Basic, you'll need to omit the `OnClick` attribute.

→ **12**   The `btnCancel` button cancels the new thread. Again, you'll need to omit the `OnClick` attribute if you're working in Visual Basic.

The code-behind file for the New Message page

Listings 10-16 and 10-17 show the C# and Visual Basic versions of the code-behind file required by the New Message page. These code-behind files contain methods that handle the `Click` event for the Post Message and Cancel buttons.

Listing 10-16:   The code-behind file for the New Message page (C#)

```
using System;
using System.Data;
using System.Configuration;
using System.Collections;
using System.Web;
using System.Web.Security;
using System.Web.UI;
using System.Web.UI.WebControls;
using System.Web.UI.WebControls.WebParts;
using System.Web.UI.HtmlControls;
using System.Web.Configuration;                                →1
using System.Data.SqlClient;                                   →2
public partial class NewMessage : System.Web.UI.Page
{
    protected void btnPost_Click(                              →3
        object sender, EventArgs e)
    {
        // set up the data objects                             →4
        string cs = WebConfigurationManager
            .ConnectionStrings["ForumConnectionString"]
            .ConnectionString;
        string insertMessage = "INSERT Messages "
          + "(threadid, author, date, message) "
          + "VALUES(@threadid, →uthor, @date, @message);"
          + "UPDATE Threads "
          + "SET replies = replies + 1"
          + "WHERE threadid = @threadid";
        SqlConnection con = new SqlConnection(cs);
        SqlCommand cmd
            = new SqlCommand(insertMessage, con);

        // get the query strings                               →5
        string threadid = Request.QueryString["thread"];
        string topicid = Request.QueryString["topic"];

        // insert the message                                  →6
        cmd.CommandText = insertMessage;
```

(continued)

Listing 10-16 *(continued)*

```
        cmd.Parameters.Clear();
        cmd.Parameters.AddWithValue("threadid",
            threadid);
        cmd.Parameters.AddWithValue("author",
            txtEmail.Text);
        cmd.Parameters.AddWithValue("date",
            DateTime.Now);
        cmd.Parameters.AddWithValue("message",
            txtMessage.Text);
        con.Open();
        cmd.ExecuteNonQuery();
        con.Close();

        Response.Redirect("Messages.aspx?topic="          →7
            + topicid + "&thread=" + threadid);
    }

    protected void btnCancel_Click(                       →8
        object sender, EventArgs e)
    {
        Response.Redirect("Messages.aspx?topic="
            + Request.QueryString["topic"]
            + "&thread="
            + Request.QueryString["thread"]);
    }
}
```

The following paragraphs guide you through the most important lines of these listings:

→ **1**   This line is required because the code-behind file uses the WebConfigurationManager class to retrieve the database-connection string from the web.config file.

→ **2**   This line is required so the code-behind file can use ADO.NET classes to access SQL databases.

→ **3**   The btnPost_Click method executes when the user clicks the Post Message button. This method writes a row to the Messages table and updates the reply count in the Threads table.

→ **4**   These lines set up the ADO.NET database objects used by the btnPost_Click method, one at a time, in a specific sequence:

   1.   The connection string is retrieved.

   2.   A string variable is created and initialized with the INSERT and UPDATE statement that writes the new message row and updates the thread reply count.

   3.   A database connection object is created.

   4.   A new SqlCommand object is created.

→ **5**   These lines retrieve the `thread` and `topic` query strings and assign them to local variables named (respectively) `threadid` and `topicid`.

→ **6**   These lines set up the parameters required by the `INSERT` and `UPDATE` statement, open the connection, execute the `INSERT` and `UPDATE` commands, and close the connection.

→ **7**   This line redirects the user to the `Messages.aspx` page, which shows the new message added to the end of the thread.

→ **8**   This method executes when the user clicks the Cancel button. It simply redirects the user back to the `Messages.aspx` page.

Listing 10-17:   The code-behind file for the New Message page (VB)

```
Imports System.Web.Configuration                            →1
Imports System.Data.SqlClient                               →2

Partial Class NewMessage
    Inherits System.Web.UI.Page

    Protected Sub btnPost_Click( _                          →3
            ByVal sender As Object, _
            ByVal e As System.EventArgs) _
            Handles btnPost.Click

        'set up the data objects                            →4
        Dim cs As String
        cs = WebConfigurationManager _
            .ConnectionStrings("ForumConnectionString") _
            .ConnectionString
        Dim insertMessage As String
        insertMessage = "INSERT Messages " _
            + "(threadid, author, date, message) " _
            + "VALUES(@threadid, →uthor, @date, @message);"
            _
            + "UPDATE Threads " _
            + "SET replies = replies + 1" _
            + "WHERE threadid = @threadid"
        Dim con As SqlConnection
        con = New SqlConnection(cs)
        Dim cmd As SqlCommand
        cmd = New SqlCommand(insertMessage, con)

        'get the query strings                              →5
        Dim threadid As String
        Dim topicid As String
        threadid = Request.QueryString("thread")
        topicid = Request.QueryString("topic")

        'insert the message                                 →6
        cmd.CommandText = insertMessage
```

(continued)

Listing 10-17 *(continued)*

```
        cmd.Parameters.Clear()
        cmd.Parameters.AddWithValue("threadid", _
            threadid)
        cmd.Parameters.AddWithValue("author", _
            txtEmail.Text)
        cmd.Parameters.AddWithValue("date", _
            DateTime.Now)
        cmd.Parameters.AddWithValue("message", _
            txtMessage.Text)
        con.Open()
        cmd.ExecuteNonQuery()
        con.Close()

        Response.Redirect("Messages.aspx?topic="            →7
            + topicid + "&thread=" + threadid)
    End Sub

    Protected Sub btnCancel_Click( _                        →8
        ByVal sender As Object, _
        ByVal e As System.EventArgs) _
        Handles btnCancel.Click
        Response.Redirect("Messages.aspx?topic=" _
            + Request.QueryString("topic") _
            + "&thread=" _
            + Request.QueryString("thread"))
    End Sub

End Class
```

Chapter 11

Building a Blog Application

In This Chapter

▶ Designing the Blog application

▶ Creating the database for the Blog application

▶ Building the Blog application's pages

A blog (short for *weblog*) is a Web application that lets users create their own Web pages where they can post their thoughts. Other users can visit the blog, read the blog owner's posts, and leave comments of their own. These days, blogging is one of the most popular activities — and applications — on the Internet.

There are many Web sites that let you create blogs, and free or inexpensive applications are available to host your own blogs. Still, you may want to create your own blogging application. If so, this chapter is for you. It presents a simple blog application written in ASP.NET 2.0.

The Blog application presented in this chapter requires that users register and log in to create a blog. Each registered user can create as many different blogs as he or she wants. Any visitor can read a blog and post comments without having to register or log in. The application relies on the built-in user registration features of ASP.NET 2.0. (You may want to refer to the User Authentication application presented in Chapter 3 for further details of how the user-registration and login pages work.)

Designing the Blog Application

Because blogs are so popular on the Web, you can find plenty of examples of blog applications to provide inspiration for your design. The blog application in this chapter is relatively simple. It provides the following features:

✔ Any visitor to the Web site can register to create an account. Once registered, a user can create one or more blogs.

✔ When a registered user logs in, a My Blogs page is displayed to list the blogs that user has created. This page includes a link that lets the user create a new post for any of his or her blogs.

✔ Blog posts consist of simple text with no embedded HTML or images.

✔ Unregistered visitors can view blogs and leave comments but can't create blogs. Comments consist of simple text with no HTML or images.

✔ To keep things simple, this Blog application doesn't provide for editing the blog title, description, posts, or comments once they've been created. In the real blogosphere, those features are desirable to include.

✔ The Home page for the Blog application lists all blogs that have been created on the site. The title displayed for each blog is a link that takes the user to that blog.

✔ When the visitor first displays a blog, the most recently created post is displayed, along with a list of previous posts. The visitor can use this list to display previous posts.

✔ The Blog page also includes links that display comments for the current post and lets the visitor leave a comment.

Designing the User Interface

The Blog application uses a total of seven pages, as shown in Figure 11-1. Two of them are for logging in and registering; two of them are accessible only to registered users who have logged in. The other three are for viewing blogs and leaving comments.

The Blog Home page

The Home page for the Blog application (`Default.aspx`) is shown in Figure 11-2. As you can see, this page lists the blogs that are available on the site. In this example, two users have created blogs. (In a popular blog site, of course, there would be many more than two blogs to choose from.)

The "Blog-O-Rama" title and the links beneath it are provided by the Master Page, so they're available throughout the site. They let the user return to the Home page, log in (or log out if the user is already logged in), register a new user account, and go to the My Blogs page. (The My Blogs page, as you'll soon see, lists the blogs created by the currently logged-in user, lets the user add a new post to one of his or her blogs, and lets the user create a new blog.)

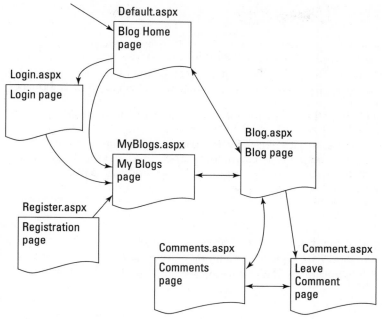

Figure 11-1:
The page
flow for
the Blog
application.

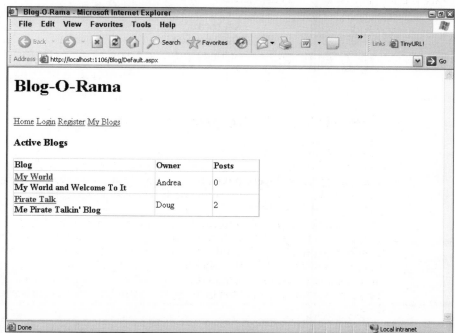

Figure 11-2:
The Blog
Home page.

The Blog page

When the user selects a blog from the application's Home page (or from the My Blogs page, as you'll see in a moment), the Blog page is displayed, as shown in Figure 11-3. This page displays the most recent post for the blog as well as a list of older posts; the user can click and view the posts in this list as well. Beneath the post, a count of comments made for the post is displayed, along with a link to view the comments and a link to leave a new comment.

This page uses a `FormView` control to display the post itself and a `GridView` control to display the list of posts. The `SELECT` statement for the `FormView` control's data source is tied to the `SelectedValue` property of the `GridView` control. As a result, the `FormView` control displays the post selected by the user. When the page is first displayed, the most recent post is automatically selected.

Notice that the URL in the address bar includes a query string named `blog`. This query string is set to the ID of the blog selected by the user in the Blog Home page. The Blog page uses this query string to determine which blog to display.

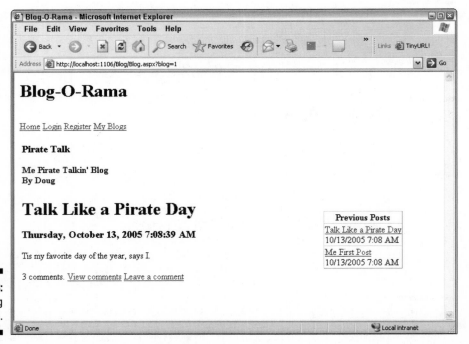

Figure 11-3:
The Blog
page.

The Comments page

When the user clicks the <u>View Comments</u> link in the Blog page, the Comments page is displayed, as shown in Figure 11-4. This page displays any comments left by other users. The comments are listed in descending date sequence, so the most recent comment is displayed first. A query string field named `postid` is used to determine the post whose comments are to be displayed. (The other query string fields shown in the URL for this page, `post` and `blogid`, are used so to remember which blog and post to display when the user returns to the Blog page. (There's more to know about these query string fields; you can see it in the source code for the `Blog.aspx` page.)

This page also includes a <u>Return</u> link that returns to the Blog page and a <u>Leave Comment</u> link that lets the user add a new comment.

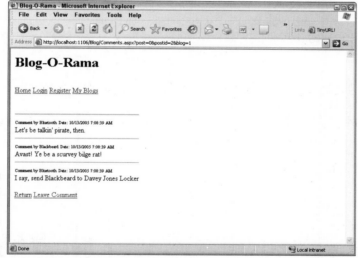

Figure 11-4:
The
Comments
page.

The Leave Comment page

If the user clicks the <u>Leave a Comment</u> link on the Blog page or the Comments page, the Leave Comment page is displayed (as shown in Figure 11-5). Here the user can leave a comment that's associated with a particular post. The Leave Comment page has text boxes for the user to enter his or her name and comment. Note that the user doesn't have to register or log in to leave a comment. As a result, the user can enter any name he or she pleases in the `Name` text box.

This page also includes two buttons. To post a comment, the user clicks the Post button. To return to the previous page without posting a comment, the user clicks the Cancel button.

The Login page

If the user clicks the <u>Log In</u> link that appears in the Master page (and thus on each page in the site) or attempts to access the My Blogs page without first logging in, the Login page shown in Figure 11-6 is displayed. This page simply uses a standard ASP.NET Login control to prompt the user for a username and password.

In Chapter 4, you can find information about enhancing this login page by providing links that let the user change his or her password or retrieve a forgotten password.

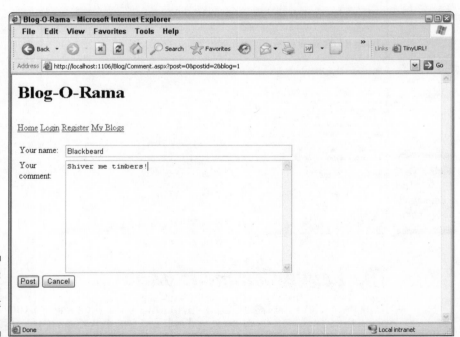

Figure 11-5:
The Leave
Comment
page.

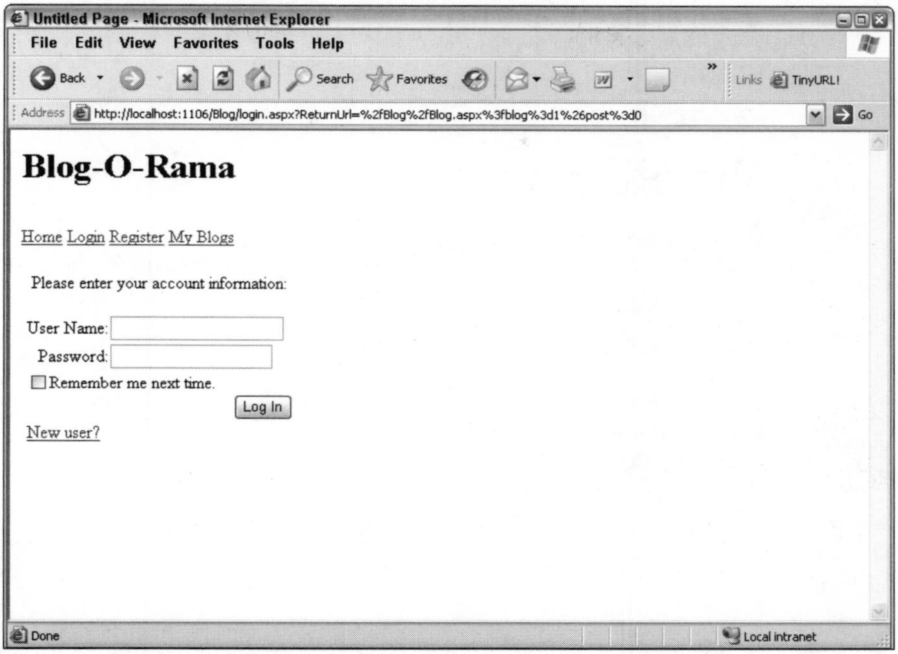

Figure 11-6:
The Login
page.

The Register page

To create a new user account, the user can click the <u>Register</u> link that appears in the Master Page. Then the Register page appears, as shown in Figure 11-7. This page uses an ASP.NET CreateUserWizard control to create a new user account. (For more information about this control, refer to Chapter 4.)

The My Blogs page

Figure 11-8 shows the My Blogs page, which is displayed when the user clicks the <u>My Blogs</u> link that appears in the Master Page and has logged in. This page displays the blogs the user has created, lets the user post a new article to one of his or her blogs, and lets the user create a new blog. To post a new article to a blog, the user simply clicks the <u>New Post</u> link for the blog. To create a new blog, the user enters the blog's name and description and clicks the Create Blog button.

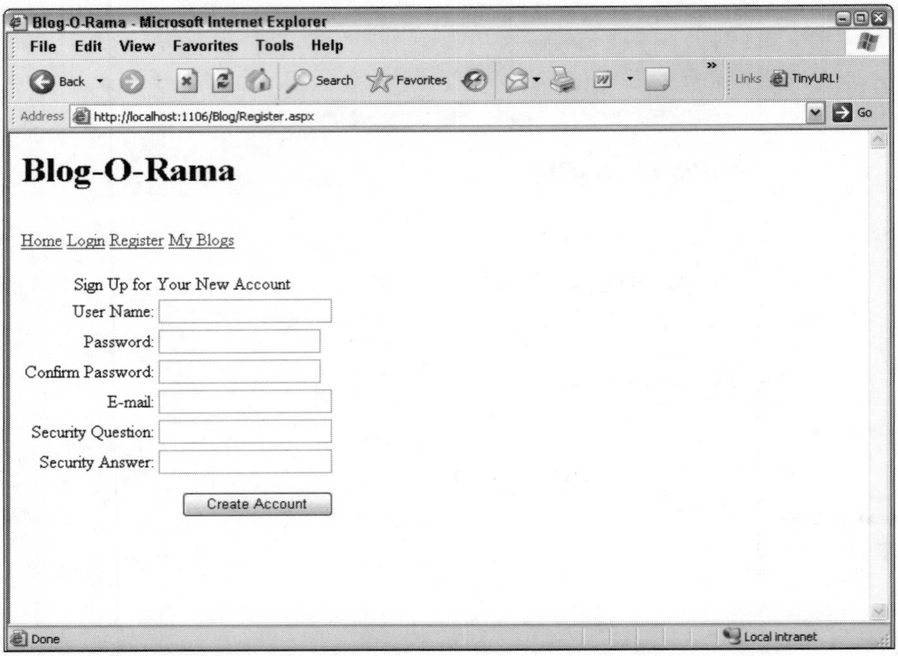

Figure 11-7:
The Register
page.

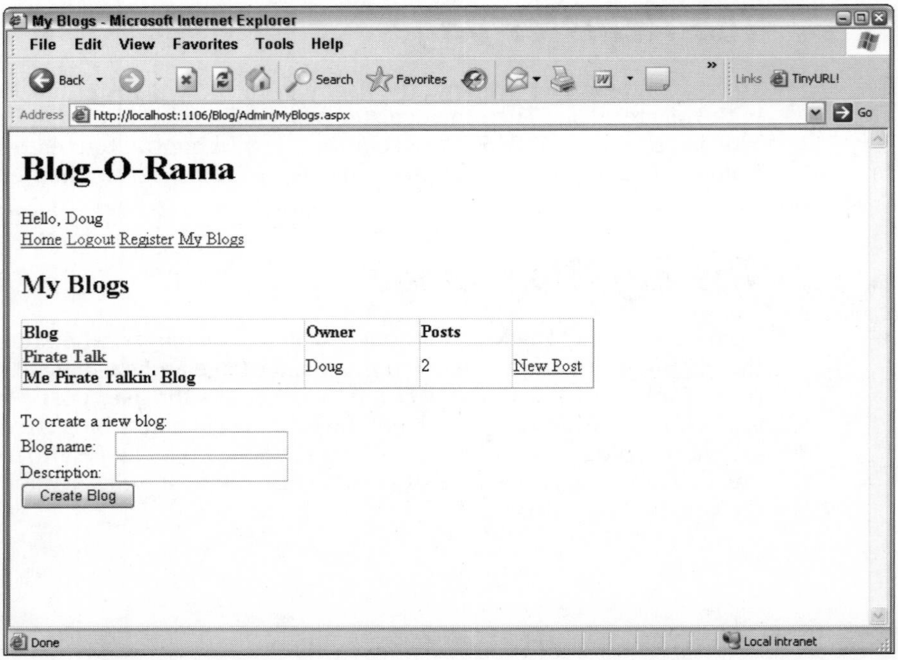

Figure 11-8:
The My
Blogs page.

The New Post page

The New Post page is shown in Figure 11-9. This page is displayed when the user clicks the <u>New Post</u> link on the My Blogs page. It lets the user enter the subject and text for a new article to be posted to the user's blog. Note that the blog the article should be posted to is passed to the New Post page as a query string field.

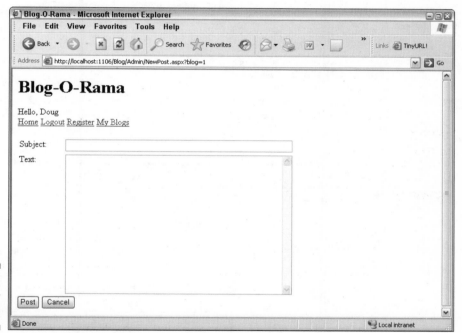

Figure 11-9: The New Post page.

Designing the Database

The database for the Blog application uses just three tables:

- ✔ Blogs
- ✔ Posts
- ✔ Comments

Figure 11-10 shows a diagram for the database, and the following sections describe each table individually.

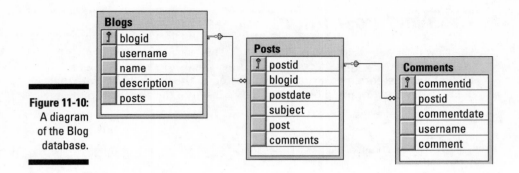

Figure 11-10:
A diagram
of the Blog
database.

The Blogs table

The Blogs table records vital information about the blogs that have been created by users of the Web site. The columns for the Blogs table are listed in Table 11-1.

Table 11-1		The Blogs Table
Column name	**Type**	**Description**
blogid	INT IDENTITY	This column provides a unique ID number for each blog created by the site's users, and serves as the primary key for the Blogs table.
username	VARCHAR(100)	The name of the user that created the blog.
name	VARCHAR(255)	The blog's name.
description	VARCHAR(255)	A short description of the blog.
posts	INT	The number of posts that have been made to this blog. A trigger updates this field automatically whenever a row is inserted into the Posts table.

The Posts table

The Posts table stores the posts that users have made to their blogs. Table 11-2 lists the columns defined for this table.

Table 11-2		The Posts Table
Column name	*Type*	*Description*
postid	INT IDENTITY	This column provides a unique ID number for each post, and serves as the primary key for the Posts table.
blogid	INT	This column specifies the blog that the post is associated with, and serves as a foreign key to the blogid column in the Blogs table.
postdate	DATETIME	The date and time the post was made. The default value for this column is the current date and time.
subject	VARCHAR(255)	The subject title for the post.
post	VARCHAR(MAX)	The text of the post.
comments	INT	The number of comments that have been made to this blog. A trigger updates this field automatically whenever a row is inserted into the Comments table.

The Comments table

The Comments table records comments made by visitors to the blog site. The columns of the Comments table are listed in Table 11-3.

Table 11-3		The Comments Table
Column name	*Type*	*Description*
commentid	INT IDENTITY	This column uniquely identifies each comment and serves as the primary key for the Comments table.
postid	INT	The ID of the post the comment belongs to. This is a foreign key to the postid column of the Posts table.

(continued)

Table 11-3 *(continued)*

Column name	Type	Description
commentdate	DATETIME	The date and time the comment was recorded. The default value for this column is the current date and time.
username	VARCHAR(100)	The name of the person who left the comment.
comment	VARCHAR(MAX)	The text of the comment.

Creating the Database

You can create the Blog database by running the script that's shown in Listing 11-1. To run this script, open a command prompt window and change to the directory that contains the script. Then enter this command:

```
sqlcmd -S localhost\SQLExpress -i CreateBlogDB.sql
```

As usual, you'll need to change the host name from localhost if you're not using SQL Server Express on your own computer.

Listing 11-1: The CreateBlogDB.sql script

```
USE master                                              →1
GO

IF EXISTS(SELECT * FROM sysdatabases                    →2
     WHERE name='Forum')
DROP DATABASE Blog
GO

CREATE DATABASE Blog                                    →3
ON (NAME=Product,
     FILENAME = 'C:\APPS\Blog.mdf',
     SIZE=10 )
GO

USE Blog                                                →4
GO

CREATE TABLE Blogs (                                    →5
   blogid        INT IDENTITY,
   username      VARCHAR(100)   NOT NULL,
   name          VARCHAR(255)   NOT NULL,
```

```
      description VARCHAR(255)   NOT NULL,
      posts          INT         NOT NULL
                                 DEFAULT 0,
      PRIMARY KEY(blogid)
      )
GO

CREATE TABLE Posts (                                          →6
      postid       INT IDENTITY,
      blogid       INT           NOT NULL,
      postdate     DATETIME      NOT NULL
                                 DEFAULT CURRENT_TIMESTAMP,
      subject      VARCHAR(255)  NOT NULL,
      post         VARCHAR(MAX)  NOT NULL,
      comments     INT           NOT NULL
                                 DEFAULT 0,
      PRIMARY KEY(postid),
      FOREIGN KEY(blogid) REFERENCES Blogs(blogid)
      )
GO

CREATE TABLE Comments (                                       →7
      commentid    INT IDENTITY,
      postid       INT           NOT NULL,
      commentdate  DATETIME      NOT NULL
                                 DEFAULT CURRENT_TIMESTAMP,
      username     VARCHAR(100)  NOT NULL,
      comment      VARCHAR(MAX)  NOT NULL,
      PRIMARY KEY(commentid),
      FOREIGN KEY(postid) REFERENCES Posts(postid)
      )
GO

CREATE TRIGGER tr_PostCount                                   →8
      ON Posts
      AFTER INSERT
AS
      DECLARE @blogid INT

      SELECT @blogid = blogid
          FROM inserted

      UPDATE blogs
          SET posts = posts + 1
          WHERE blogid = @blogid

      RETURN
GO

CREATE TRIGGER tr_CommentCount                                →9
      ON Comments
      AFTER INSERT
```

(continued)

Listing 11-1 *(continued)*

```
AS
    DECLARE @postid INT

    SELECT @postid = postid
        FROM inserted

    UPDATE posts
        SET comments = comments + 1
        WHERE postid = @postid

    RETURN
GO
```

Nine rapid-fire paragraphs draw out the pertinent details of this listing:

→ **1**   Sets the database context to `master`.

→ **2**   Deletes the existing `Blog` database if it exists.

→ **3**   Creates a database named `Blog`. The data file is stored in `C:\Apps`.

→ **4**   Sets the database context to `Blog`.

→ **5**   Creates the `Blogs` table.

→ **6**   Creates the `Posts` table.

→ **7**   Creates the `Comments` table.

→ **8**   Creates a trigger named `tr_PostCount`. This trigger executes whenever a row is inserted in the `Posts` table. It defines a variable named `@blogid` which is set to the value of the `blogid` column in the inserted row. Then it executes an `UPDATE` statement that increments the `posts` column for the Blogs row that the new post was added to.

→ **9**   Creates a trigger named `tr_CommentCount`. This trigger executes whenever a row is inserted in the `Comments` table. It defines a variable named `@postid` which is set to the value of the `postid` column in the inserted row. Then it executes an `UPDATE` statement that increments the `comments` column of the appropriate row in the `Posts` table.

Adding test data

On the companion CD, you'll find a script named `InsertData.sql`, which creates test data for the database. It creates two blogs, along with several posts and comments.

To run the `InsertData.sql` script, open a command window, change to the directory that contains the script, and run this command:

```
sqlcmd -S localhost\SQLExpress -i InsertData.sql
```

You'll need to change the server name if it is other than `localhost\ SQLExpress`.

SQL statements for working with the database

The Blog application uses several SQL statements to retrieve and update data in the Blog database, as described in the following paragraphs:

✔ To list the Blogs on the `default.aspx`, this `SELECT` statement is used:

```
SELECT [blogid], [name],
       [description], [username], [posts]
  FROM [Blogs]
  ORDER BY [name]
```

✔ The `MyBlogs.aspx` page uses a similar `SELECT` statement to retrieve the blogs for the current user:

```
SELECT [blogid], [name],
       [description],  [username], [posts]
  FROM [Blogs]
  WHERE [username]=@username
  ORDER BY [name]
```

✔ The `Blog.aspx` page uses the following `SELECT` statement to list the posts in a particular blog:

```
SELECT [postid], [blogid],
       [postdate], [subject]
  FROM [Posts]
  WHERE ([blogid] = @blogid)
  ORDER BY [postdate] DESC
```

The posts are sorted in descending date sequence, so the newest post is listed first.

✔ The `Blog.aspx` page also uses this `SELECT` statement to retrieve the details for the selected post:

```
SELECT [postid], [blogid],
       [postdate], [subject],
       [post], [comments]
  FROM [Posts]
  WHERE ([postid] = @postid)
```

✔ The `Comments.aspx` page uses this `SELECT` statement to retrieve all of the comments for a given post:

```
SELECT [commentdate], [username], [comment]
        FROM [Comments]
        WHERE ([postid] = @postid)
        ORDER BY [commentdate]
```

✔ The `MyBlogs.aspx` page uses this statement to create a new blog:

```
INSERT INTO [Blogs]
        ([username], [name],
        [description], [posts])
    VALUES (@username, @name,
        @description, @posts)
```

✔ To create a new post, the `NewPost.aspx` page uses this statement:

```
INSERT INTO [Posts]
        ([blogid], [subject], [post])
    VALUES (@blogid, @subject, @post)
```

✔ Finally, the `Comment.aspx` page uses the following `INSERT` statement to create a new comment:

```
INSERT INTO [Comments]
        ([postid], [username], [comment])
    VALUES (@postid, @username, @comment)
```

Connecting to the database

As with the other applications in this book, the connection string for the Blog application is stored in the `<connectionStrings>` section of the `web.config` file:

```
<connectionStrings>
    <add name="BlogConnectionString"
        connectionString="Data
          Source=localhost\SQLExpress;
Initial Catalog=Blog;Integrated Security=True"/>
</connectionStrings>
```

Note that if you're not using SQL Server Express on your local computer, you'll have to modify the connection string to provide the correct server name.

Building the Master Page

The Master page for the Blog application is shown in Listing 11-2. The code-behind file for this Master Page has no methods, so it isn't shown here.

Listing 11-2:   The master page (MasterPage.master)

```
<%@ Master Language="C#"                                        →1
    AutoEventWireup="true"
    CodeFile="MasterPage.master.cs"
    Inherits="MasterPage" %>

<!DOCTYPE html PUBLIC "-//W3C//DTD XHTML 1.1//EN"
    "http://www.w3.org/TR/xhtml11/DTD/xhtml11.dtd">

<html xmlns="http://www.w3.org/1999/xhtml" >
<head runat="server">
    <title>Blog-O-Rama</title>
</head>
<body>
    <form id="form1" runat="server">
    <div>
        <h1>Blog-O-Rama</h1>
        <asp:LoginName ID="LoginName1"                          →2
            runat="server"
            FormatString="Hello, {0}" />
        <br />

        <asp:LinkButton ID="btnHome" runat="server"             →3
            Text="Home"
            PostBackUrl="~/Default.aspx" />

        <asp:LoginStatus ID="LoginStatus1"                      →4
            runat="server"
            LogoutAction="Refresh" />

        <asp:LinkButton ID="btnRegister"                        →5
            runat="server"
            Text="Register"
            CausesValidation="False"
            PostBackUrl="~/Register.aspx" />

        <asp:LinkButton ID="btnMyBlogs"                         →6
            runat="server"
            Text="My Blogs"
            CausesValidation="False"
            PostBackUrl="~/Admin/MyBlogs.aspx" />
        <br /><br />

        <asp:contentplaceholder                                 →7
            id="ContentPlaceHolder1"
            runat="server">
        </asp:contentplaceholder>
    </div>
    </form>
</body>
</html>
```

Here's a rundown on the key points of this listing:

→ **1**   If you're using Visual Basic rather than C# for the application's code-behind files, you should change the `Language` attribute to `C#` and the `AutoEventWireup` attribute to `false`.

→ **2**   The `LoginName` control displays the name of the user if the user has logged in. The `FormatString` attribute adds the word `Hello` before the user name.

→ **3**   This link button returns the user to the home page (`Default.aspx`).

→ **4**   The `LoginStatus` control displays a link button that lets the user log in or out.

→ **5**   This link button posts back to the `Register.aspx` page so new users can register.

→ **6**   This link button posts to the `MyBlogs.aspx` page. This page is in the `Admin` folder, which contains a `web.config` file that prohibits anonymous access. As a result, the user must log in to access this page. If the user is not already logged in, ASP.NET will automatically redirect the user to the `Login.aspx` page. To accomplish this, the `web.config` file in the `Admin` folder contains the following lines:

```
<system.web>
    <authorization>
        <deny users="?" />
    </authorization>
</system.web>
```

→ **7**   The `ContentPlaceHolder` control marks the location where the content for each page of the application will be displayed.

Building the Blog Home Page

The Blog Home page (`Default.aspx`) displays a list of the blogs that are available on the Blog Web site. You can refer back to Figure 11-2 to see how this page appears when the application runs.

The Blog Home page consists mostly of a `GridView` control that displays a list of the blogs in the Blogs table. The `GridView` control displays three columns. The first displays the name and description of the blog, with the name presented as a link button that posts to the `Blog.aspx` page and passes the ID of the selected blog as a query string field. The second column displays the name of the user that created the blog, and the third displays the number of posts that have been made to the blog.

Listing 11-3 presents the `.aspx` code for this page. A code-behind file isn't required.

Listing 11-3:   The Blog Home page (Default.aspx)

```
<%@ Page Language="C#"                                            →1
    MasterPageFile="~/MasterPage.master"
    AutoEventWireup="true"
    CodeFile="Default.aspx.cs"
    Inherits="_Default"
    Title="Blog-O-Rama" %>
<asp:Content ID="Content1" Runat="Server"                         →2
    ContentPlaceHolderID="ContentPlaceHolder1" >
    <h3>Active Blogs</h3>

    <asp:GridView ID="GridView1" runat="server"                   →3
        AllowPaging="True"
        AutoGenerateColumns="False"
        DataSourceID="SqlDataSource1">
        <Columns>
        <asp:TemplateField>                                       →4
            <HeaderTemplate>
                Blog
            </HeaderTemplate>
            <ItemTemplate>
            <b>
              <asp:LinkButton ID="LinkButton1"
                runat="server"
                Text='<% #Bind("name") %>'
                PostBackUrl
                  ='<% #Bind("blogid",
        "Blog.aspx?blog={0}") %>' />
              <br />
              <asp:Label ID="Label2" runat="server"
                  Text='<% #Bind("description") %>' />
            </ItemTemplate>
            <HeaderStyle HorizontalAlign="Left" />
            <ItemStyle Width="250px" />
        </asp:TemplateField>
        <asp:BoundField                                           →5
            DataField="username"
            HeaderText="Owner" >
            <HeaderStyle HorizontalAlign="Left" />
            <ItemStyle HorizontalAlign="Left"
                Width="100px" />
        </asp:BoundField>
        <asp:BoundField                                           →6
            DataField="posts"
            HeaderText="Posts" >
            <HeaderStyle HorizontalAlign="Left" />
            <ItemStyle HorizontalAlign="Left"
                Width="80px" />
        </asp:BoundField>
        </Columns>
    </asp:GridView>
```

(continued)

Listing 11-3 *(continued)*

```
<asp:SqlDataSource ID="SqlDataSource1"                        →7
        runat="server"
        ConnectionString
          ="<%$ ConnectionStrings:BlogConnectionString %>"
        SelectCommand="SELECT [blogid], [name],
            [description], [username], [posts]
            FROM [Blogs]
            ORDER BY [name]">
    </asp:SqlDataSource>
</asp:Content>
```

Seven important lines in this listing merit a little closer look:

→ **1** You should change the `Language`, `AutoEventWireup`, and `CodeFile` attributes in the `Page` directive if you're working with Visual Basic rather than C#. (It doesn't really matter for this page, since no code-behind file is needed, but you should change it nonetheless.)

→ **2** The `<Content>` element provides the content that's displayed for the page.

→ **3** The `GridView` control lists the blogs retrieved from the Blogs table by the SQL data source named `SqlDataSource1`. Note that paging is enabled for this `GridView` control. As a result, ten blogs will be listed at a time.

→ **4** The first column defined for the `GridView` control is a template column. This column specifies two templates:

The header template displays the word "Blog" as the column heading.

The item template displays the blog name and title. The blog name is shown as a link button that uses binding expressions for the `Text` and `PostBackUrl` attributes. The binding expression for the `Text` attribute simply retrieves the `name` field from the data source. The binding expression for the `PostBackUrl` attribute is a little more complicated. It retrieves the `blogid` field from the data source and uses a format string to create a URL that specifies the `blogid` as a query string field. For example, if the `blogid` value is 3, the `PostBackUrl` attribute's value will be `Blog.aspx?blog=3`.

→ **5** The second column in the `GridView` control is bound to the `username` field in the data source.

→ **6** The third column in the `GridView` control is bound to the `posts` field in the data source.

→ **7** The data source uses a `SELECT` statement to retrieve the `blogid`, `name`, `description`, `username`, and `posts` columns from the `Blogs` table.

Building the Blog Page

The Blog page displays one post from a selected blog (by default, the most recent) as well as a list of all the posts that have been made to the blog. The Blog page is passed a query string field to indicate which blog to display. In addition, a query string field is used to indicate which post should be displayed. If this query string is not present, the most recent post for the blog is displayed by default.

A code-behind file is used here to determine which post to display based on the post query string and to handle the `Click` events for the buttons that display comments for the post or enable a visitor to leave a comment. The following sections present the `Blog.aspx` file and both the C# and Visual Basic versions of the code-behind file.

The Blog.aspx page

Listing 11-4 presents the `.aspx` code for the Blog page. Most of the code for this page is straightforward, so you shouldn't have any trouble following it.

Listing 11-4:   The Blog.aspx page

```
<%@ Page Language="C#"                                          →1
    MasterPageFile="~/MasterPage.master"
    AutoEventWireup="true"
    CodeFile="Blog.aspx.cs"
    Inherits="Blog"
    Title="Blog-O-Rama" %>
<asp:Content ID="Content1" Runat="Server"                       →2
    ContentPlaceHolderID="ContentPlaceHolder1" >
<table border="0">                                              →3
  <tr>
    <td width="700">
      <asp:FormView ID="FormView1" runat="server"               →4
        DataSourceID="SqlDataSource1">
        <ItemTemplate>
          <asp:Label ID="lblName" runat="server"                →5
            Text='<%# Bind("name",
"<h3>{0}</h3>") %>' />
          <asp:Label ID="lblDesc" runat="server"                →6
            Text='<%# Bind("description",
"<h4>{0}") %>' />
          <asp:Label ID="lblUser" runat="server"                →7
            Text='<%# Bind("username",
```

(continued)

Listing 11-4 *(continued)*

```
"<br/>By {0}</h4>") %>' />
      </ItemTemplate>
   </asp:FormView>
   <asp:SqlDataSource ID="SqlDataSource1"                     →8
      runat="server"
      ConnectionString=
        "<%$ ConnectionStrings:BlogConnectionString
        %>"
      SelectCommand="SELECT [name], [description],
           [username], [posts]
           FROM [Blogs]
           WHERE ([blogid] = @blogid)">
   <SelectParameters>
      <asp:QueryStringParameter Name="blogid"               →9
         QueryStringField="blog" Type="Int32" />
   </SelectParameters>
   </asp:SqlDataSource>
  </td>
 </tr>
 <tr>
   <td width="350" valign="Top">
      <asp:FormView ID="FormView2" runat="server"           →10
          DataKeyNames="postid"
          DataSourceID="SqlDataSource2" >
      <ItemTemplate>
          <asp:Label ID="lblSubject"                        →11
             runat="server"
             Text='<%# Bind("subject",
"<h1>{0}</h1>") %>' />
          <asp:Label ID="lblDate"                           →12
             runat="server"
             Text='<%# Bind("postdate",
"<h3>{0:F}</h3>") %>' />
          <asp:Label ID="lblPost"                           →13
             runat="server"
             Text='<%# Bind("post", "<p>{0}</p>") %>' />
          <asp:Label ID="lblComments"                       →14
             runat="server"
             Text='<%# Bind("comments",
"{0} comments.") %>'/>
          <asp:LinkButton ID="btnViewComments"              →15
             runat="server"
             OnClick="btnViewComments_Click"
             Text="View comments" />
          <asp:LinkButton ID="btnLeaveComment"              →16
             runat="server"
             OnClick="btnLeaveComment_Click"
             Text="Leave a comment" />
      </ItemTemplate>
   </asp:FormView>
```

```
          <asp:SqlDataSource ID="SqlDataSource2"              →17
            runat="server"
            ConnectionString=
             "<%$ ConnectionStrings:BlogConnectionString
            %>"
            SelectCommand="SELECT [postid], [blogid],
                [postdate], [subject],
                [post], [comments]
                FROM [Posts]
                WHERE ([postid] = @postid)">
            <SelectParameters>
              <asp:ControlParameter                          →18
                ControlID="GridView1"
                Name="postid"
                PropertyName="SelectedValue"
                Type="Int32" />
          </SelectParameters>
        </asp:SqlDataSource>
    </td>
    <td width="250">
      <asp:GridView ID="GridView1" runat="server"            →19
          AutoGenerateColumns="False"
          DataSourceID="SqlDataSource3"
          DataKeyNames="postid"
          AllowPaging="True" >
        <Columns>
          <asp:TemplateField                                 →20
            HeaderText="Previous Posts" >
            <ItemTemplate>
              <asp:LinkButton ID="btnPost"
                runat="server"
                Text='<%# Bind("subject") %>'
                CommandName="Select" />
              <br />
              <asp:Label ID="lblDate"
                runat="server"
                Text='<%# Bind("postdate", "{0:g}") %>' />
            </ItemTemplate>
          </asp:TemplateField>
        </Columns>
      </asp:GridView>
      <asp:SqlDataSource ID="SqlDataSource3"                 →21
          runat="server"
          ConnectionString=
           "<%$ ConnectionStrings:BlogConnectionString %>"
          SelectCommand="SELECT [postid], [blogid],
              [postdate], [subject]
              FROM [Posts]
              WHERE ([blogid] = @blogid)
              ORDER BY [postdate] DESC">
```

(continued)

Listing 11-4 *(continued)*

```
            <SelectParameters>
              <asp:QueryStringParameter                →22
                Name="blogid"
                QueryStringField="blog"
                Type="Int32" />
            </SelectParameters>
          </asp:SqlDataSource>
        </td>
      </tr>
    </table>
  </asp:Content>
```

The following paragraphs draw your attention irresistibly to the highlights of this listing:

→ **1**   If you use the Visual Basic version of the code-behind file, be sure to change the `Language`, `AutoEventWireup`, and `CodeFile` attributes in the `Page` directive.

→ **2**   The `<asp:Content>` element provides the content displayed by this page.

→ **3**   A table is used to format the controls on the page. The table consists of two rows. The first has a single cell and contains a `FormView` control that displays the blog name, description, and owner. The second row has two cells. The first displays the selected post with a `FormView` control, and the second displays the list of posts for the blog using a `GridView` control.

→ **4**   This `FormView` control displays the blog name and description as well as the name of the user that created the blog. It's bound to the data source named `SqlDataSource1`.

→ **5**   The first control in the item template is a label that displays the blog name. Its `Text` attribute uses a binding expression that retrieves the `name` field from the data source and formats it using `<h3>` and `</h3>` tags.

→ **6**   The second control in the item template is a label that displays the blog description. Its `Text` attribute uses a binding expression that retrieves the `description` field from the data source and formats it using an `<h4>`. Note that this label doesn't include the closing `</h4>` tag. Instead, the closing tag is provided by the label in line 7.

→ **7**   The third control in the item template is a label that displays the name of the user who created the blog. Its `Text` attribute uses a binding expression that retrieves the `username` field from the data source and formats it with a closing `</h4>` tag.

→ **8**   The `SqlDataSource1` data source retrieves the information from the Blogs table, using the `blogid` parameter to specify the blog to be retrieved.

→ **9**   The value of the `blogid` parameter is bound to the query string field named `blog`.

→ **10**   This `FormView` control displays the selected post for the current blog. It is bound to `SqlDataSource2`.

→ **11**   The first control in the item template displays the post subject. The subject is formatted using `<h1>` and `</h1>` tags.

→ **12**   The second control in the item template displays the date of the post, which is formatted using `<h3>` and `</h3>` tags.

→ **13**   The third control in the item template displays the text of the post, which is formatted between a matched set of `<p>` and `</p>` tags.

→ **14**   The fourth control in the item template displays the number of comments associated with the post.

→ **15**   The fifth control in the item template is a link button that takes the user to the Comments page.

→ **16**   The final control in the item template is a link button that lets the user leave a comment.

→ **17**   The `SqlDataSource2` data source retrieves the information for the current post from the `Posts` table, using the `postid` parameter to specify the post to be retrieved.

→ **18**   The value of the `postid` parameter is bound to the `SelectedValue` property of the `GridView1` control.

→ **19**   The `GridView` control displays a list of the posts for the current blog. It is bound to `SqlDataSource3`. Paging is enabled to display ten posts at a time.

→ **20**   The first (and only) column for this `GridView` control is a template field column whose item template contains two controls: a link button that displays the post subject (bound to the `subject` field) and a label that displays the date (bound to the `postdate` field). Note that the link button includes a `CommandName` attribute that specifies `Select` as the command name. Thus the `GridView` row is selected when the user clicks this button.

→ **21**   The `SqlDataSource3` data source retrieves the posts for the current blog, as indicated by the `blogid` parameter.

→ **22**   The `blogid` parameter is bound to the `blog` query string.

The code-behind file for the Blog page

The code-behind file for the Blog page must handle the `PageLoad` event to determine which post should be displayed. In addition, it must handle the `click` events for the <u>View Comments</u> and <u>Leave a Comment</u> links so it can set up the query strings passed to the `Comments.aspx` and `Comment.aspx` page. Listings 11-5 and 11-6 show the C# and Visual Basic versions of this code-behind file.

Listing 11-5: The code-behind file for the Blog page (C# version)

```
using System;
using System.Data;
using System.Configuration;
using System.Collections;
using System.Web;
using System.Web.Security;
using System.Web.UI;
using System.Web.UI.WebControls;
using System.Web.UI.WebControls.WebParts;
using System.Web.UI.HtmlControls;

public partial class Blog : System.Web.UI.Page
{
    protected void Page_Load(                               →1
        object sender, EventArgs e)
    {
        if (!IsPostBack)
        {
            if (Request.QueryString["post"] == null)
                GridView1.SelectedIndex = 0;
            else
            {
                GridView1.SelectedIndex
                    = Int16.Parse(
                        Request.QueryString["post"]);
            }
            this.DataBind();
        }
    }

    protected void btnViewComments_Click(                   →2
        object sender, EventArgs e)
    {
        Response.Redirect("Comments.aspx?post="
            + GridView1.SelectedIndex.ToString()
            + "&postid="
            + GridView1.SelectedValue.ToString()
            + "&blog="
            + Request.QueryString["blog"]);
    }

    protected void btnLeaveComment_Click(                   →3
        object sender, EventArgs e)
    {
        Response.Redirect("Comment.aspx?post="
            + GridView1.SelectedIndex.ToString()
            + "&postid="
```

```
                        + GridView1.SelectedValue.ToString()
                        + "&blog="
                        + Request.QueryString["blog"]);
        }
}
```

The following paragraphs describe the three methods in this code-behind file:

→ **1** The `Page_Load` method sets the `SelectedIndex` property of the `GridView` control to the value indicated by the `post` query string field, if the `post` query string is present. If the `post` query string is missing, the `SelectedIndex` property is set to `zero`. Then the `DataBind` method is called to bind the controls on the page.

→ **2** The `btnViewComments_Click` method is called when the user clicks the <u>View Comments</u> link. It simply redirects the user to the `Comments.aspx` page, passing query string fields that contain the ID of the selected post (`postid`), the index of the selected post (`post`), and the ID of the current blog (`blog`).

→ **3** The `btnLeaveComment_Click` method is called when the user clicks the <u>Leave a Comment</u> link. It redirects the user to the `Comment.aspx` page, passing the same query string fields as the `btnViewComments_Click` method.

Listing 11-6:   The code-behind file for the Blog page (VB version)

```
Partial Class Blog
    Inherits System.Web.UI.Page

    Protected Sub Page_Load( _                                    →1
            ByVal sender As Object, _
            ByVal e As System.EventArgs) _
            Handles Me.Load
        If Not IsPostBack Then
            If Request.QueryString("post") Is Nothing Then
                GridView1.SelectedIndex = 0
            Else
                GridView1.SelectedIndex _
                    = Int16.Parse( _
                        Request.QueryString("post"))
            End If
            Me.DataBind()
        End If
    End Sub

    Protected Sub btnViewComments_Click( _                       →2
            ByVal sender As Object, _
            ByVal e As System.EventArgs)
        Response.Redirect("Comments.aspx?post=" _
```

(continued)

Listing 11-6 *(continued)*

```
            + GridView1.SelectedIndex.ToString() _
            + "&postid=" _
            + GridView1.SelectedValue.ToString() _
            + "&blog=" _
            + Request.QueryString("blog"))
    End Sub

    Protected Sub btnLeaveComment_Click( _       →3
            ByVal sender As Object, _
            ByVal e As System.EventArgs) _
    End Sub

End Class
```

Building the Comments Page

The Comments page uses a `GridView` control to display all comments left for a particular post. The ID of the post whose comments are to be displayed is passed to the page via a query string field. You can refer back to Figure 11-4 for a glimpse of what this page looks like.

The Comments.aspx page

Listing 11-7 shows the `Comments.aspx` page. As you can see, this page uses three SQL data sources, two `FormView` controls, and a `GridView` control to display the comments that have been created for the post.

Listing 11-7:   The Comments.aspx page

```
<%@ Page Language="C#"                                →1
    MasterPageFile="~/MasterPage.master"
    AutoEventWireup="true"
    CodeFile="Comments.aspx.cs"
    Inherits="Comments"
    Title="Blog-O-Rama" %>
<asp:Content ID="Content1" Runat="Server"             →2
    ContentPlaceHolderID="ContentPlaceHolder1" >
    <asp:FormView ID="FormView2" runat="server"       →3
        DataSourceID="SqlDataSource1"
        DataKeyNames="postid" >
        <ItemTemplate>
            <asp:Label ID="lblSubject"                →4
                runat="server"
                Text='<%# Bind("subject",
                    "<h1>{0}</h1>") %>'>
            </asp:Label>
```

```
            <asp:Label ID="lblDate" runat="server"          →5
                Text='<%# Bind("postdate",
                   "<h3>{0:F}</h3>") %>'>
            </asp:Label>
        </ItemTemplate>
</asp:FormView>
<asp:SqlDataSource ID="SqlDataSource1"                       →6
    runat="server"
    ConnectionString
      ="<%$ ConnectionStrings:BlogConnectionString %>"
    SelectCommand="SELECT [postid], [blogid],
        [postdate], [subject]
        FROM [Posts]
        WHERE ([postid] = @postid)">
    <SelectParameters>
        <asp:QueryStringParameter                            →7
            Name="postid"
            QueryStringField="post"
            Type=Int32 />
    </SelectParameters>
</asp:SqlDataSource>
<br />
<asp:DataList ID="DataList1" runat="server"                  →8
    DataSourceID="SqlDataSource2">
    <ItemTemplate>
        <hr>
        <asp:Label ID="lblUserName"                          →9
            runat="server"
            Text='<%# Bind("username",
                "Comment by {0}") %>'
            Font-Size="X-Small" />
        <asp:Label ID="lblDate" runat="server"               →10
            Text='<%# Bind("commentdate",
                " Date: {0:G}") %>'
            Font-Size="X-Small" />
        <br />
        <asp:Label ID="lblComment"                           →11
            runat="server"
            Text='<%# Bind("comment") %>'
            Width="300px"/>
    </ItemTemplate>
</asp:DataList>
<asp:SqlDataSource ID="SqlDataSource2"                        →12
    runat="server"
    ConnectionString
      ="<%$ ConnectionStrings:BlogConnectionString %>"
    SelectCommand="SELECT [commentdate],
        [username], [comment]
        FROM [Comments]
        WHERE ([postid] = @postid)
        ORDER BY [commentdate]">
    <SelectParameters>
```

(continued)

Listing 11-7 *(continued)*

```
            <asp:QueryStringParameter                    →13
                Name="postid"
                QueryStringField="postid"
                Type="Int32" />
        </SelectParameters>
    </asp:SqlDataSource>
    <br />
    <asp:LinkButton ID="btnReturn" runat="server"        →14
        Text="Return"
        OnClick="btnReturn_Click" />
    <asp:LinkButton ID="btnComment" runat="server"       →15
        Text="Leave Comment"
        OnClick="btnComment_Click" />
</asp:Content>
```

To help you follow along, the following paragraphs describe the key points of this listing:

→ 1   You'll need to change the `Language`, `AutoEventWireup`, and `CodeFile` attributes in the `Page` directive if you use Visual Basic instead of C#.

→ 2   The `<Content>` element provides the content that's displayed for the page.

→ 3   This `FormView` control displays the subject and date of the post that the comments apply to. The `FormView` control is bound to the `SqlDataSource1` data source.

→ 4   The first control in the `FormView` control's item template is a label that displays the subject.

→ 5   The second control in the item template is another label that displays the date.

→ 6   The `SqlDataSource1` data source retrieves data for the post specified by the `postid` parameter.

→ 7   The value of the `postid` parameter is bound to the query string field named `post`.

→ 8   The `DataList` control displays the comments for the post. It's bound to the data source named `SqlDataSource2`.

→ 9   The first control in the data list's item template is a label that displays the user name.

→ 10   The second control in the item template is a label that displays the date the comment was created.

→ 11   The third control in the item template is a label that displays the comment text.

→ 12   The `SqlDataSource2` data source retrieves the comments for the post specified by the `postid` parameter.

→ **13**   The value of the `postid` parameter is bound to the query string field named `postid`.

→ **14**   The `btnReturn` button returns the user to the Blog page. The `btnReturn_Click` method in the code-behind file executes when the user clicks this button.

For this line and the next, note that if you're working with Visual Basic, you should omit the `OnClick` attribute.

→ **15**   The `btnComment` button lets the user add a new comment to the post. (Again, if you're working with Visual Basic, omit the `OnClick` attribute.)

The code-behind file for the Comments page

Listings 11-8 and 11-9 show the C# and Visual Basic versions of the code-behind file for the Comments page, which handles the `click` events for the two links on this page.

Listing 11-8:   The code-behind file for the Comments page (C# version)

```
using System;
using System.Data;
using System.Configuration;
using System.Collections;
using System.Web;
using System.Web.Security;
using System.Web.UI;
using System.Web.UI.WebControls;
using System.Web.UI.WebControls.WebParts;
using System.Web.UI.HtmlControls;

public partial class Comments : System.Web.UI.Page
{
    protected void btnReturn_Click(                  →1
        object sender, EventArgs e)
    {
        Response.Redirect("Blog.aspx?post="
            + Request.QueryString["post"]
            + "&postid="
            + Request.QueryString["postid"]
            + "&blog="
            + Request.QueryString["blog"]);
    }

    protected void btnComment_Click(                 →2
        object sender, EventArgs e)
```

(continued)

Listing 11-8 *(continued)*

```
    {
        Response.Redirect("Comment.aspx?post="
            + Request.QueryString["post"]
            + "&postid="
            + Request.QueryString["postid"]
            + "&blog="
            + Request.QueryString["blog"]);
    }
}
```

The two methods in this code-behind file have some details worth noting:

→ **1**   The `btnReturn_Click` method is called when the user clicks the <u>Return</u> link. It simply redirects to the `Blog.aspx` page, passing back the three query strings that were in the request (via the redirect URL).

→ **2**   The `btnComment_Click` method is called when the user clicks the <u>Leave a Comment</u> link. It redirects to the `Comment.aspx` page, again passing the three query strings via the redirect URL.

Listing 11-9:   **The code-behind file for the Comments page (VB version)**

```
Partial Class Comments
    Inherits System.Web.UI.Page

    Protected Sub btnReturn_Click( _                              →1
            ByVal sender As Object, _
            ByVal e As System.EventArgs) _
            Handles btnReturn.Click
        Response.Redirect("Blog.aspx?post=" _
            + Request.QueryString("post") _
            + "&postid=" _
            + Request.QueryString("postid") _
            + "&blog=" _
            + Request.QueryString("blog"))
    End Sub

    Protected Sub btnComment_Click( _                             →2
            ByVal sender As Object, _
            ByVal e As System.EventArgs) _
            Handles btnComment.Click
        Response.Redirect("Comment.aspx?post=" _
            + Request.QueryString("post") _
            + "&postid=" _
            + Request.QueryString("postid") _
            + "&blog=" _
            + Request.QueryString("blog"))
    End Sub
End Class
```

Building the Leave Comment Page

The Leave Comment page lets a Web site visitor add a comment to a post. To see what this page looks like, flip back to Figure 11-5. The following sections present the `.aspx` file and the code-behind files for this page.

The Comment.aspx page

The `.aspx` file for the Leave Comment page is shown in Listing 11-10. This page displays the topic name in a `FormView` control at the top of the page. Then text boxes are used to get the user's name and comment.

Listing 11-10:   The Comment.aspx page

```
<%@ Page Language="C#"                                              →1
    MasterPageFile="~/MasterPage.master"
    AutoEventWireup="true"
    CodeFile="Comment.aspx.cs"
    Inherits="Comment"
    Title="Blog-O-Rama" %>
<asp:Content ID="Content1" Runat="Server"                          →2
    ContentPlaceHolderID="ContentPlaceHolder1" >
<table border="0" width="700" >                                    →3
  <tr>
    <td width="80" valign="top">
      Your name:
    </td>
    <td width="620" valign="top">
      <asp:TextBox ID="txtName" runat="server"                     →4
          Width="400px"/>
    </td>
  </tr>
  <tr>
    <td width="80" valign="top">
      Your comment:
    </td>
    <td width="620" valign="top">
      <asp:TextBox ID="txtComment" runat="server"                  →5
          TextMode="MultiLine"
          Height="200px"
          Width="400px" />
    </td>
  </tr>
</table>
<asp:Button ID="btnPost" runat="server"                            →6
    Text="Post"
    OnClick="btnPost_Click" />
```

(continued)

Listing 11-10 *(continued)*

```
<asp:Button ID="btnCancel" runat="server"                    →7
    Text="Cancel"
    OnClick="btnCancel_Click"/>
<asp:SqlDataSource ID="SqlDataSource1"                       →8
    runat="server"
    ConnectionString
      ="<%$ ConnectionStrings:BlogConnectionString %>"
    InsertCommand="INSERT INTO [Comments]
        ([postid], [username], [comment])
        VALUES (@postid, @username, @comment)" >
    <InsertParameters>
        <asp:QueryStringParameter Name="postid"              →9
            Type="String"
            QueryStringField="postid" />
        <asp:ControlParameter Name="username"                →10
            Type="String"
            ControlID="txtName"
            PropertyName="Text" />
        <asp:ControlParameter Name="comment"                 →11
            Type="String"
            ControlID="txtComment"
            PropertyName="Text" />
    </InsertParameters>
</asp:SqlDataSource>
</asp:Content>
```

The critical lines of this listing are described in the following paragraphs:

→ **1** Don't forget to change the `Language`, `AutoEventWireup`, and `CodeFile` attributes in the `Page` directive if you use Visual Basic instead of C#.

→ **2** The `<Content>` element provides the content that's displayed for the page.

→ **3** This page uses an HTML table to manage the layout of its controls.

→ **4** This text box lets the Web site visitor enter his or her name.

→ **5** This multi-line text box lets the Web site visitor enter the text of his or her comment.

→ **6** The Web site visitor clicks this button to record the comment.

For this line and the next, you should remove the `OnClick` attribute if you're using Visual Basic instead of C#.

→ **7** This button cancels the comment and returns to the Blog page. (Again, remove the `OnClick` attribute if you're using VB instead of C#.)

→ **8** Even though this page doesn't contain any bound controls, it still uses `SqlDataSource1` to insert the comment into the `Comments` table. The `InsertCommand` attribute specifies an `INSERT` statement that requires three parameters: `postid`, `username`, and `comment`.

→ **9**   The value of the `postid` parameter is obtained from the query string field named `postid`.

→ **10**   The `username` parameter is bound to the `txtName` text box.

→ **11**   The `comment` parameter is bound to the `txtComment` text box.

The code-behind file for the Leave Comment page

Listings 11-11 and 11-12 show the C# and Visual Basic versions of the code-behind file for the Leave Comment page. As you can see, these code-behind files contain just two methods, which handle the `click` event for the Post and Cancel buttons.

Listing 11-11:   The code-behind file for the Leave Comment page (C#)

```
using System;
using System.Data;
using System.Configuration;
using System.Collections;
using System.Web;
using System.Web.Security;
using System.Web.UI;
using System.Web.UI.WebControls;
using System.Web.UI.WebControls.WebParts;
using System.Web.UI.HtmlControls;

public partial class Comment : System.Web.UI.Page
{
    protected void btnPost_Click(                        →1
        object sender, EventArgs e)
    {
        SqlDataSource1.Insert();
        Response.Redirect("Blog.aspx?blog="
            + Request.QueryString["blog"]
            + "&post="
            + Request.QueryString["post"]);
    }

    protected void btnCancel_Click(                      →2
        object sender, EventArgs e)
    {
        Response.Redirect("Blog.aspx?blog="
            + Request.QueryString["blog"]
            + "&post="
            + Request.QueryString["post"]);
    }

}
```

You'll sleep better tonight if you read the following paragraphs, which describe the most important two lines of this code-behind file:

→ **1**   The `btnPost_Click` method executes when the user clicks the Post button. This method calls the `Insert` method of the data source to insert the comment into the `Comments` table. Then it redirects to the `Blog.aspx` page.

→ **2**   The `btnCancel_Click` method is similar to the `btnPost_Click` method, with one important exception: it doesn't call the `INSERT` method of the data source. As a result, any comment entered by the user is ignored.

Listing 11-12:   The code-behind file for the Leave Comment page (VB)

```
Partial Class Comment
    Inherits System.Web.UI.Page

    Protected Sub btnPost_Click( _                          →1
            ByVal sender As Object, _
            ByVal e As System.EventArgs) _
            Handles btnPost.Click
        SqlDataSource1.Insert()
        Response.Redirect("Blog.aspx?blog=" _
            + Request.QueryString("blog") _
            + "&post=" _
            + Request.QueryString("post"))
    End Sub

    Protected Sub btnCancel_Click( _                        →2
            ByVal sender As Object, _
            ByVal e As System.EventArgs) _
            Handles btnCancel.Click
        Response.Redirect("Blog.aspx?blog=" _
            + Request.QueryString("blog") _
            + "&post=" _
            + Request.QueryString("post"))
    End Sub
End Class
```

Building the Login Page

The Login page is displayed if the user clicks the Login button provided by the Master Page or tries to access the My Blogs page without first logging in. The `.aspx` code for this page (pictured back in Figure 11-6) is shown in Listing 11-13.

Listing 11-13:   The Login.aspx page

```
<%@ Page Language="C#"                                          →1
    MasterPageFile="~/MasterPage.master"
    AutoEventWireup="true"
    CodeFile="Login.aspx.cs"
    Inherits="Login"
    Title="Blog-O-Rama" %>
<asp:Content ID="Content1" Runat="Server"                       →2
    ContentPlaceHolderID="ContentPlaceHolder1" >
<asp:Login ID="Login1" runat="Server"                           →3
  DestinationPageUrl="~/Default.aspx"
  TitleText="Please enter your account information:
<br /><br />"
  CreateUserText="New user?"
  CreateUserUrl="~/Register.aspx" />
</asp:Content>
```

A quick list explains the details of three key lines in this listing:

→ **1**   Remember to change the `Language`, `AutoEventWireup`, and
`CodeFile` attributes in the `Page` directive if you use Visual Basic.

→ **2**   The `<Content>` element provides the content that's displayed for
the page.

→ **3**   This page displays just one control, a `Login` control that lets the
user enter a name and password to log in. For more information
about how this control works, refer to Chapter 4.

Building the Register Page

The Register page is displayed if the user clicks the <u>New User?</u> link on the
Login page or the <u>Register</u> link displayed by the Master Page. (To see what
the Register page looks like, flip back to Figure 11-7.) The `.aspx` file for this
page, which doesn't require a code-behind file, is shown in Listing 11-14.

Listing 11-14:   The Register.aspx page

```
<%@ Page Language="C#"                                          →1
    AutoEventWireup="true"
    MasterPageFile="~/MasterPage.master"
    CodeFile="Register.aspx.cs"
    Inherits="Register"
    title="Blog-O-Rama" %>
<asp:Content ID="Content1" Runat="Server"                       →2
```

(continued)

Listing 11-14 *(continued)*

```
    ContentPlaceHolderID="ContentPlaceHolder1" >
   <asp:CreateUserWizard ID="CreateUserWizard1"              →3
       runat="server"
       CreateUserButtonText="Create Account"
       ContinueDestinationPageUrl="~\Admin\MyBlogs.aspx" >
   </asp:CreateUserWizard>
 </asp:Content>
```

Here are the details of three key lines in this listing:

→ **1**   Remember to change the Language, AutoEventWireup, and CodeFile attributes in the Page directive if you use Visual Basic.

→ **2**   The <Content> element provides the content that's displayed for the page.

→ **3**   This page displays just one control, a CreateUserWizard control that walks the user through the steps required to register a new user account. The ContinueDestinationPageUrl attribute provides the URL of the page to be displayed when the user completes the Wizard. In this case, the My Blogs page will be displayed. (For more information about how the CreateUserWizard control works, refer to Chapter 4.)

Building the My Blogs Page

The My Blogs page was originally shown back in Figure 11-8. It is similar to the Blog Home page (Default.aspx), with four key differences:

1. It's stored in the \Admin folder, which is protected from anonymous access. That means that only users who have registered and logged in can view it.

2. Rather than display all of the blogs in the Blogs table, it displays only the blogs that were created by the current user.

3. It includes a link that takes the user to the Post page to add a new post to one of his or her blogs.

4. It includes controls that let the user create a new blog.

The following sections present the .aspx code and code-behind files for this page.

The MyBlogs.aspx page

The `.aspx` file for the My Blogs page is shown in Listing 11-15. It includes a `GridView` control to display the user's blogs and a set of text boxes, field validators, and buttons that enable the user to create a new blog. In addition, two `SqlDataSource` controls are used.

Listing 11-15:   The My Blogs page (MyBlogs.aspx)

```
<%@ Page Language="C#"                                        →1
    MasterPageFile="~/MasterPage.master"
    AutoEventWireup="true"
    CodeFile="MyBlogs.aspx.cs"
    Inherits="MyBlogs"
    Title="My Blogs" %>
<asp:Content ID="Content1" Runat="Server"                     →2
    ContentPlaceHolderID="ContentPlaceHolder1" >
    <h2>My Blogs</h2>

        <asp:GridView ID="GridView1" runat="server"           →3
        AllowPaging="True"
        AutoGenerateColumns="False"
        DataSourceID="SqlDataSource1">
        <Columns>

        <asp:TemplateField>                                   →4
            <HeaderTemplate>
                Blog
            </HeaderTemplate>
            <ItemTemplate>
            <b>
            <asp:LinkButton ID="LinkButton1"
                runat="server"
                Text='<% #Bind("name") %>'
                PostBackUrl='<% #Bind("blogid",
                    "~\Blog.aspx?blog={0}") %>'
                CausesValidation="False" />
            <br />
            <asp:Label ID="Label2" runat="server"
                Text='<% #Bind("description") %>' />
            </ItemTemplate>
            <HeaderStyle HorizontalAlign="Left" />
            <ItemStyle HorizontalAlign="Left"
                Width="250px" />
        </asp:TemplateField>

        <asp:BoundField                                       →5
            DataField="username"
```

(continued)

Listing 11-15 *(continued)*

```
            HeaderText="Owner" >
            <HeaderStyle HorizontalAlign="Left" />
            <ItemStyle Width="100px" />
        </asp:BoundField>

        <asp:BoundField                                    →6
            DataField="posts"
            HeaderText="Posts" >
            <HeaderStyle HorizontalAlign="Left" />
            <ItemStyle Width="80px" />
        </asp:BoundField>

        <asp:HyperLinkField                                →7
            DataNavigateUrlFields="blogid"
            DataNavigateUrlFormatString
                ="NewPost.aspx?blog={0}"
            Text="New Post">
            <ItemStyle Width="70px" />
        </asp:HyperLinkField>

    </Columns>
</asp:GridView>
<asp:SqlDataSource ID="SqlDataSource1"                     →8
    runat="server"
    ConnectionString
      ="<%$ ConnectionStrings:BlogConnectionString %>"
    SelectCommand="SELECT [blogid], [name],
        [description], [username], [posts]
        FROM [Blogs]
        WHERE [username]=@username
        ORDER BY [name]">
    <SelectParameters>
        <asp:Parameter Name="username"                     →9
            Type="String" />
    </SelectParameters>
</asp:SqlDataSource>

<br />To create a new blog:<br />

<asp:Label ID="Label3" runat="server"                      →10
    BorderStyle="None" Text="Blog name:"
    Width="80px" />
<asp:TextBox ID="txtBlogName" runat="server" />
<asp:RequiredFieldValidator
    ID="RequiredFieldValidator1" runat="server"
    ControlToValidate="txtBlogName"
    Display="Dynamic"
    ErrorMessage="Required." /><br />

<asp:Label ID="Label4" runat="server"                      →11
    BorderStyle="None" Text="Description:"
    Width="80px" />
```

```
    <asp:TextBox ID="txtDescription" runat="server" />
    <asp:RequiredFieldValidator
        ID="RequiredFieldValidator2" runat="server"
        ControlToValidate="txtDescription"
        Display="Dynamic"
        ErrorMessage="Required." /><br />

    <asp:Button ID="btnCreate" runat="server"              →12
        OnClick="btnCreate_Click"
        Text="Create Blog" />

    <asp:SqlDataSource ID="SqlDataSource2"                 →13
        runat="server"
        ConnectionString
          ="<%$ ConnectionStrings:BlogConnectionString %>"
        InsertCommand="INSERT INTO [Blogs]
            ([username], [name], [description])
            VALUES (@username, @name, @description)" >
        <InsertParameters>                                 →14
            <asp:Parameter
                Name="username" Type="String" />
            <asp:Parameter
                Name="name" Type="String" />
            <asp:Parameter
                Name="description" Type="String" />
        </InsertParameters>
    </asp:SqlDataSource>
</asp:Content>
```

The following paragraphs describe the important lines of this listing:

→ 1   You must change the `Language`, `AutoEventWireup`, and `CodeFile` attributes in the `Page` directive if you use Visual Basic instead of C#.

→ 2   The `<Content>` element provides the content that's displayed for the page.

→ 3   The `GridView` control lists the blogs retrieved from the Blogs table by the SQL data source named `SqlDataSource1`. Although it's unlikely that any user will have more than a few blogs (most will have only one), paging is enabled for this `GridView` control.

→ 4   The first column of the `GridView` control is a template column that specifies two templates:

- A header template displays the word `Blog` as the column heading.

- An item template displays the blog name and title; a link button displays the blog name. Binding expressions are used for the `Text` and `PostBackUrl` attributes.

→ 5   The second column is a bound column that displays the user-name field.

→ 6   The third column control is a bound column that displays the number of posts for the blog, as indicated by the posts field.

→ 7   The fourth column is a hyperlink field that provides a link to the NewPost.aspx page so the user can create a new post. A format string provides a value for the blog query string.

→ 8   The SqlDataSource1 data source uses a SELECT statement to retrieve five columns — blogid, name, description, username, and posts — for the user indicated by the username parameter.

→ 9   The username parameter is defined as a standard parameter. Its value will be supplied in the Page_Load method of the code-behind file.

→ 10   This label, text box, and RequiredFieldValidator let the user enter the name for a new blog.

→ 11   This label, text box, and RequiredFieldValidator let the user enter the description for a new blog.

→ 12   The Create button lets the user create a new blog using the name and description entered in the text boxes.

       If you're using Visual Basic, you should remove the OnClick attribute.

→ 13   The second data source (SqlDataSource2) provides the INSERT statement used to create a new blog.

→ 14   The INSERT statement uses three parameters — username, name, and description — whose values will be set in the code-behind file.

The code-behind file for the My Blogs page

Listings 11-16 and 11-17 show the C# and Visual Basic versions of the code-behind file for the My Blogs page. As you can see, it consists of just two methods: Page_Load (executed when the page loads) and btnCreate_Click, executed when the user creates a new blog.

Listing 11-16:   The code-behind file for the My Blogs page (C# version)

```
using System;
using System.Data;
using System.Configuration;
using System.Collections;
```

```
using System.Web;
using System.Web.Security;
using System.Web.UI;
using System.Web.UI.WebControls;
using System.Web.UI.WebControls.WebParts;
using System.Web.UI.HtmlControls;
using System.Web.Configuration;

public partial class MyBlogs : System.Web.UI.Page
{
    protected void Page_Load(                              →1
        object sender, EventArgs e)
    {
        SqlDataSource1.SelectParameters["username"]
            .DefaultValue = User.Identity.Name;

    }
    protected void btnCreate_Click(                        →2
        object sender, EventArgs e)
    {
        SqlDataSource2.InsertParameters["username"]
            .DefaultValue = User.Identity.Name;
        SqlDataSource2.InsertParameters["name"]
            .DefaultValue = txtBlogName.Text;
        SqlDataSource2.InsertParameters["description"]
            .DefaultValue = txtDescription.Text;
        SqlDataSource2.Insert();
        GridView1.DataBind();
    }
}
```

Two methods in this file merit closer inspection:

→ **1**   The `Page_Load` method executes when the page loads. It simply sets the value of the `username` parameter for the `SqlDataSource1` data source to the name of the logged-in user. That way the data source retrieves only the current user's blogs.

→ **2**   The `btnCreate_Click` method executes when the user clicks the Create Blog button. It sets the values of the three `Insert` parameters, calls the `Insert` method of the `SqlDataSource2` data source, then calls the `GridView` control's `DataBind` method so the `GridView` control will show the new blog.

Listing 11-17:   The code-behind file for the My Blogs page (VB version)

```
Partial Class MyBlogs
    Inherits System.Web.UI.Page

    Protected Sub Page_Load( _                             →1
            ByVal sender As Object, _
            ByVal e As System.EventArgs) _
```

(continued)

Listing 11-17 *(continued)*

```
            Handles Me.Load
        SqlDataSource1.SelectParameters("username") _
            .DefaultValue = User.Identity.Name
    End Sub

    Protected Sub btnCreate_Click( _                          →2
            ByVal sender As Object, _
            ByVal e As System.EventArgs) _
            Handles btnCreate.Click
        SqlDataSource2.InsertParameters("username") _
            .DefaultValue = User.Identity.Name
        SqlDataSource2.InsertParameters("name") _
            .DefaultValue = txtBlogName.Text
        SqlDataSource2.InsertParameters("description") _
            .DefaultValue = txtDescription.Text
        SqlDataSource2.Insert()
        GridView1.DataBind()
    End Sub

End Class
```

Building the New Post Page

The New Post page lets a registered and logged-in user add a new post to one of his or her blogs. To see this page in action, refer to Figure 11-9. The following sections present the .aspx file and the code-behind files for this page.

The NewPost.aspx page

The .aspx file for the New Post page is shown in Listing 11-18. This page uses text boxes to let the user enter the subject and text for the new post and a SqlDataSource control to provide the INSERT statement used to record the post.

Listing 11-18:   The NewPost.aspx page

```
<%@ Page Language="C#"                                       →1
    MasterPageFile="~/MasterPage.master"
    AutoEventWireup="true"
    CodeFile="NewPost.aspx.cs"
    Inherits="NewPost"
    Title="Blog-O-Rama" %>
<asp:Content ID="Content1" Runat="Server"                    →2
```

```
      ContentPlaceHolderID="ContentPlaceHolder1" >
<table border="0" width="700" >                              →3
  <tr>
    <td width="80" valign="top">
      Subject:
    </td>
    <td width="620" valign="top">
      <asp:TextBox ID="txtSubject" runat="server"         →4
          Width="400px"/>
      <asp:RequiredFieldValidator runat="server"
        ID="RequiredFieldValidator1"
        ControlToValidate="txtSubject"
        ErrorMessage="Subject is required"
        Display="Dynamic" />
    </td>
  </tr>
  <tr>
    <td width="80" valign="top">
      Text:
    </td>
    <td width="620" valign="top">
      <asp:TextBox ID="txtPostText" runat="server"        →5
          TextMode="MultiLine"
          Height="250px"
          Width="400px" />
      <asp:RequiredFieldValidator runat="server"
        ID="RequiredFieldValidator2"
        ControlToValidate="txtPostText"
        ErrorMessage="Text is required"
        Display="Dynamic" />
    </td>
  </tr>
</table>

<asp:Button ID="btnPost" runat="server"                    →6
    Text="Post" OnClick="btnPost_Click" />

<asp:Button ID="btnCancel" runat="server"                  →7
    PostBackUrl="~/Admin/MyBlogs.aspx"
    Text="Cancel" />

<asp:SqlDataSource ID="SqlDataSource1"                      →8
    runat="server"
    ConnectionString
      ="<%$ ConnectionStrings:BlogConnectionString %>"
    InsertCommand="INSERT INTO [Posts]
        ([blogid], [subject], [post])
        VALUES (@blogid, @subject, @post)" >
    <InsertParameters>
```

(continued)

Listing 11-18 *(continued)*

```
            <asp:QueryStringParameter Name="blogid"              →9
                QueryStringField="blog"
                Type="String" />
            <asp:ControlParameter Name="subject"                 →10
                ControlID="txtSubject"
                PropertyName="Text"
                Type="String" />
            <asp:ControlParameter Name="post"                    →11
                ControlID="txtPostText"
                PropertyName="Text"
                Type="String" />
    </InsertParameters>
    </asp:SqlDataSource>

</asp:Content>
```

The most important lines of this file are described in the following paragraphs:

→ **1**   You will have to change the `Language`, `AutoEventWireup`, and `CodeFile` attributes in the `Page` directive if you use Visual Basic instead of C#.

→ **2**   The `<Content>` element provides the content that's displayed for the page.

→ **3**   This page uses an HTML table to manage the layout of its controls.

→ **4**   A text box lets the user enter the subject for the new post. Note that a RequiredFieldValidator is used to ensure that the user doesn't leave the subject blank.

→ **5**   A multi-line text box lets the user enter the text of the new post. Again, a RequiredFieldValidator is used to make sure the post isn't left blank.

→ **6**   The Post button causes the new post to be added to the database. You should remove the `OnClick` attribute if you're using Visual Basic instead of C#.

→ **7**   The Cancel button cancels the post and returns to the My Blogs page.

→ **8**   Although this page doesn't use bound controls, a SQL Data Source is still used to insert the post into the database. The `INSERT` statement requires three parameters: `blogid`, `subject`, and `post`.

→ **9**   The value of the `blogid` parameter is obtained from the query string named `blog`.

→ **10**   The subject parameter is bound to the Text property of the txtSubject text box.

→ **11**   The post parameter is bound to the Text property of the txtPostText text box.

The code-behind file for the New Post page

Listings 11-19 and 11-20 present the C# and Visual Basic versions of the code-behind file for the New Post page. As you can see, these code-behind files contain just one method, which handles the click event for the Post button.

Listing 11-19:   The code-behind file for the New Post page (C#)

```
using System;
using System.Data;
using System.Configuration;
using System.Collections;
using System.Web;
using System.Web.Security;
using System.Web.UI;
using System.Web.UI.WebControls;
using System.Web.UI.WebControls.WebParts;
using System.Web.UI.HtmlControls;

public partial class NewPost : System.Web.UI.Page
{
    protected void btnPost_Click(                        →1
        object sender, EventArgs e)
    {
        SqlDataSource1.Insert();
        Response.Redirect("MyBlogs.aspx");
    }
}
```

There's only one numbered line to consider for this listing:

→ **1**   The btnPost_Click method executes when the user clicks the Post button. This method calls the Insert method of the data source to insert the new post into the Posts table. Then it redirects the user back to the MyBlogs.aspx page. Pretty simple, eh?

Listing 11-20: **The code-behind file for the New Post page (VB)**

```
Partial Class NewPost
    Inherits System.Web.UI.Page

    Protected Sub btnPost_Click( _                          →1
            ByVal sender As Object, _
            ByVal e As System.EventArgs) _
            Handles btnPost.Click
        SqlDataSource1.Insert()
        Response.Redirect("MyBlogs.aspx")
    End Sub
End Class
```

Part VI
The Part of Tens

The 5th Wave   By Rich Tennant

"So far our Web presence has been pretty good.
We've gotten some orders, a few inquiries, and
nine guys who want to date our logo."

In this part . . .

If you keep this book in the bathroom, the chapters in this section are the ones that you'll read most. Each chapter consists of ten (more or less) entertaining (okay, *useful*) things that are worth knowing about various aspects of ASP.NET programming. Without further ado, here they are, direct from the home office in sunny Fresno, California.

Chapter 12

Ten New Features of ASP.NET 2.0

*T*his book assumes that you already know a bit of ASP.NET programming. Okay, you don't have to be an expert, but this book is not a beginner's tutorial; it assumes you know the basics — concepts such as how to code ASP tags to create server controls, and how to write Visual Basic or C# code to handle events such as button clicks.

If you have never written a line of ASP.NET code, I suggest you put this book down momentarily and spend some quality time in a copy of my book, *ASP.NET 2.0 All-In-One Desk Reference For Dummies*, published (of course) by the good people at Wiley.

With that important disclaimer out of the way, I realize that although you may have worked with ASP.NET 1.0 or 1.1, this may well be your first exposure to ASP.NET 2.0, the new release issued in November 2005. ASP.NET 2.0 introduces a bevy of new and important features to the ASP.NET programmer's tool chest.

And so, without further ado, this chapter introduces you to ten of the best new features of ASP.NET 2.0. You'll find that all applications presented in this book use one or more of these new features. And each of these new features is used at least once in this book.

Note that this isn't a comprehensive list of what's new in ASP.NET 2.0. Instead, I've focused on the new programming features that I've utilized to create the applications in this book. I didn't include features that I didn't use in these applications, such as Web Parts or Themes.

The New Code-Behind Model

ASP.NET has always supported a programming technique called *code-behind*, but ASP.NET 2.0 introduces some important changes to the way code-behind works.

Code-behind lets you separate the code that *defines the appearance* of a Web page from the code that *executes in response to events* such as loading the page or clicking a button. The code that defines a page's appearance is stored in a file called an *aspx* file, which includes both HTML and ASP tags and has the extension `.aspx`. (For example, the `aspx` file for a page named `default` is `default.aspx`.) The file that contains the code that's run in response to page events — called the *code-behind file* — has the extension .vb or .cs, depending on the programming language being used. For example, if the language is Visual Basic, the code-behind file for the `default.aspx` page is `default.aspx.vb`. If the language is C#, this code-behind file is named `default.aspx.cs`.

In other words, there are two files for each page of an ASP.NET application: an `.aspx` file that defines the appearance of the page and a code-behind file that provides the executable code for the page.

From a simple programming perspective, the code-behind file in ASP.NET 2.0 works pretty much the same as it does in ASP.NET 1.*x*. For example, if you double-click a button in Visual Studio's Design view, the code editor opens and Visual Studio generates a method that handles the click event for the button. Then this method executes whenever a user clicks the button.

Looks familiar enough, but what's actually happening behind the scenes is very different in ASP.NET 2.0 from what it was in ASP.NET 1.*x*. The details (which are pretty intricate) depend on a new feature of ASP.NET 2.0 called *partial classes* — a capability of splitting the code that defines a class into two or more source files.

Aside from the behind-the-scenes differences, the new code-behind model has one very practical and important difference: the code-behind file in ASP.NET 2.0 does not have any code that's generated by Visual Studio. In ASP.NET 1.*x*, the code-behind file had a hidden region of code (labeled "Web Form Designer Generated Code") that was required to keep the code-behind file synchronized with the `.aspx` file. As a result, it was possible — and all too common — for the `.aspx` file and the code-behind file to fall out of sync with each other.

If (for example) you deleted or changed the name of a control in the `.aspx` file, the corresponding definition for the control in the code-behind file might not be deleted or changed. Then, when you tried to run the page, a compiling error would occur. This type of problem happens much less frequently in Visual Studio 2005 than it used to in previous versions — and that's because the code-behind file doesn't include any generated code.

ASP.NET 2.0 also provides a *code-beside model*, in which the C# or VB code is embedded within the `.aspx` file rather than stored as a partial class in a separate file. To use the code-beside model, you simply uncheck the Place Code in Separate File option in the dialog box that appears when you create a new page. As a general rule, I prefer code-behind to code-beside because code-behind provides better separation of the application's presentation and logic code. However, some programmers prefer code-beside because of its simplicity, especially for smaller projects. All of the examples in this book use code-behind.

App_ Folders

In addition to the difference in the way code-behind works, ASP.NET 2.0 also introduces a set of special application folders you can use in your applications.

These folders have reserved names, so you shouldn't create your own application folders using these names. Here's a list of the application folders you can use:

- ✔ `App_Data`: Contains any Access databases used by the application. Other types of databases can be stored here, too, but SQL server databases are typically stored in a separate folder that's not part of the application's folder structure.

- ✔ `App_Code`: Contains class files used by the application. If you create utility or helper classes, database-access classes, or classes that define business objects, this is where you should place them.

- ✔ `App_GlobalResources`: Contains resources you place in this folder to be accessed by any page in the application.

- ✔ `App_LocalResources`: Contains resources that are available only to pages in the same folder as the `App_LocalResources` folder.

- ✔ `App_WebReferences`: Contains references to Web services.

- ✔ `App_Browsers`: Contains browser-definition files. ASP.NET uses these files to identify the capabilities of individual browsers.

Note that some of these folders are created automatically by Visual Studio when they're needed and others can be added by right-clicking the Web site in Solution Explorer and choosing the Add ASP.NET Folder command.

Master Pages

One of the most common requirements for any Web application is to create a unified look for all the pages that make up the application. In ASP.NET 1.*x*, the only easy way to do that was to specify a user control to create every element common to all the application's Web pages. For example, you might create one user control apiece for the banner that appears at the top of each page and a navigation menu that appears on the left side of each page. Then you'd have to make sure that each page included these user controls, as well as layout elements (such as tables or CSS positioning elements) to provide a consistent layout for the page. (Hassles, anyone?)

ASP.NET 2.0 introduces a major new feature called *Master Pages* — an easy way to provide a consistent layout for all the pages in a Web site. A Master Page is a page that provides a layout within which the content from one or more *Content pages* is displayed. When a user requests a Content page, the elements from the Master Page specified by the Content page are added to the elements from the Content page to create the final page that's rendered to the browser. Figure 12-1 shows how this works.

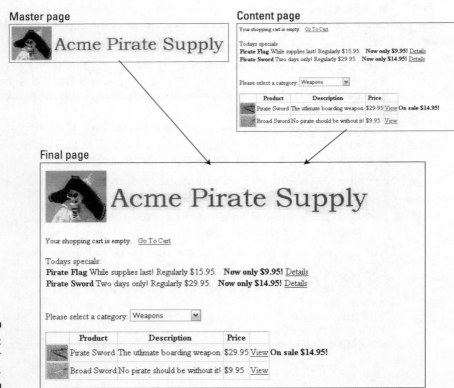

Figure 12-1:
How Master
Pages work.

The Master Page itself includes the content displayed on each page that uses the master. In addition, it contains one or more *content placeholder* controls (`contentplaceholder`) that specify where to display content from the Content page. For example, the Master Page shown in Figure 12-1 includes a banner and a sidebar displayed for each Content page that uses this master — plus a content placeholder that displays information from the Content page.

Creating a Master Page

To create a Master Page in Visual Studio 2005, follow these steps:

1. **Choose the Web Site⇨Add New Item command.**

   This brings up the Add New Item dialog box (shown in Figure 12-2), which lists the various templates available for adding new items to a project.

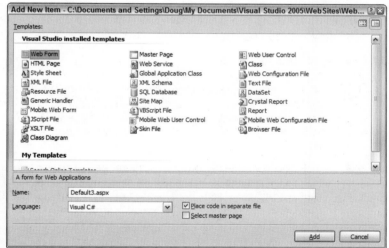

Figure 12-2: The Add New Item dialog box.

2. **Select Master Page from the list of templates.**

3. **Enter the name you want to use for the new Master Page.**

4. **Select the programming language you want to use.**

   Make sure the Place Code in Separate File option is selected.

5. **Click OK.**

   The Master Page is created.

Listing 12-1 shows the `.aspx` code that's generated for a new Master Page.

Listing 12-1:   The default code for a Master Page

```
<%@ Master Language="C#" AutoEventWireup="true"          →1
    CodeFile="MasterPage.master.cs" Inherits="MasterPage"
        %>

<!DOCTYPE html PUBLIC "-//W3C//DTD XHTML 1.1//EN"
        "http://www.w3.org/TR/xhtml11/DTD/xhtml11.dtd">

<html xmlns="http://www.w3.org/1999/xhtml" >
<head runat="server">
    <title>Untitled Page</title>
</head>
<body>
    <form id="form1" runat="server">
    <div>
        <asp:contentplaceholder id="ContentPlaceHolder1"→2
            runat="server">
        </asp:contentplaceholder>
    </div>
    </form>
</body>
</html>
```

Just two key points in this listing:

→ **1**   Instead of a `Page` directive, Master Pages begin with a `Master` directive. This directive indicates that the page is a Master Page and specifies the language used (in this case, C#), whether automatic event wiring is used, the name of the code-behind file, and the name of the class defined by the code-behind file.

→ **2**   The `<ContentPlaceHolder>` element (`<asp:ContentPlace Holder>`)is used to mark the location on the page where the content from the content file should appear. In the default Master Page, the `<ContentPlaceHolder>` simply fills the entire page; in an actual Master Page, you add elements outside the `<ContentPlaceHolder>`.

Completing a Master Page

Okay, the default Master Page shown in Listing 12-1 isn't very useful as is; it doesn't provide any elements that appear automatically on each page. You can fix this sad state of affairs by adding (well, yeah) elements that appear on each page: Simply edit the Master Page in Design or Source view. For example, Listing 12-2 shows the code for the Master Page that's illustrated in Figure 12-1.

Listing 12-2:   A Master Page with a banner image

```
<%@ Master Language="C#" %>

<!DOCTYPE html PUBLIC "-//W3C//DTD XHTML 1.1//EN"
            "http://www.w3.org/TR/xhtml11/DTD/xhtml11.dtd">

<html xmlns="http://www.w3.org/1999/xhtml" >
<head runat="server">
    <title>The Acme Pirate Shop</title>
</head>
<body>
    <form id="form1" runat="server">
    <div>
        <img src="Images/Banner.jpg" />
        <asp:contentplaceholder id="ContentPlaceHolder1"
            runat="server">
        </asp:contentplaceholder>
    </div>
    </form>
</body>
</html>
```

As you can see, the only difference between this code and the code in Listing
12-1 is that I added an .img tag immediately before the <ContentPlace
Holder> element. This image tag displays the banner that appears at the top
of each page that uses this Master Page.

Any content you add between the start and end tags of the <ContentPlace
Holder> element will be treated as *default content* — stuff that's rendered
only when the Master Page is used by a Content page that *doesn't* specifically
provide a <Content> element for the <ContentPlaceHolder>.

Creating a Content page

Listing 12-3 shows the code for an empty Content page. Of course, for this
page to be useful, you must add (what a concept) some actual content.

Listing 12-3:   The default code for a Content page

```
<%@ Page Language="C#"                                    →1
    MasterPageFile="~/MasterPage.master"
    AutoEventWireup="true" CodeFile="Default2.aspx.cs"
    Inherits="Default2" Title="Untitled Page" %>
<asp:Content ID="Content1"                                →2
    ContentPlaceHolderID="ContentPlaceHolder1"
    Runat="Server">
</asp:Content>
```

A few short, sweet paragraphs describe the key points of this listing:

→ 1   The `Page` directive uses the `MasterPageFile` attribute to indicate the name of the Master Page file to use for the page. In this example, the Master Page is `~/MasterPage.master`, which happens to be the name of the file that was shown in Listing 12-3.

In ASP.NET 2.0, the tilde (~) represents the application's root folder. Thus the line is saying that the `MasterPage.master` file is in the application's root folder.

→ 2   This is the `<Content>` element that defines the content that will appear on the page. The `ContentPlaceHolderID` attribute provides the name of the Master Page's `contentplaceholder` in which the content should appear. (In this case, the content will appear in the `ContentPlaceHolder1` placeholder.)

Note that the actual content for the page should appear between the opening tag (`<asp:Content>`) and the closing tag (`</asp:Content>`) for the placeholder.

New Data Controls

For ASP.NET 2.0, Microsoft has completely revamped data access. The old ADO.NET classes (such as `SqlConnection`, `SqlCommand`, `SqlDataAdapter`, and `DataSet`) are still there, as are the old data-bound controls (such as `Repeater`, `DataList`, and `DataGrid`). However, ASP.NET 2.0 introduces a new set of controls that are designed to replace the old way of controlling data. The new data controls include *data sources* such as `SqlDataSource` (which simplify the task of connecting to databases and retrieving and updating data) as well as new data controls such as `GridView`, `FormView`, and `DetailsView` that are designed to work with the new data sources.

The goal of the new data features is to dramatically reduce the amount of code you have to write for most database applications. And, for the most part, Microsoft has succeeded in this goal. In most of the applications in this book, you'll find at least one page that retrieves data from a database and doesn't require a code-behind file. That's because the database access is handled declaratively — and often the declarative code is generated entirely by Visual Studio, using wizards.

For most real-world applications, however, some code is still required — and you should be aware that some programmers take a dim view of providing database access through declarative code in the `.aspx` file. That's because this practice violates one of the basic principles of application design — keeping the presentation and data-management aspects of an application separate. For example, the Shopping Cart application presented in Chapter 6 keeps presentation apart from data access by providing separate classes that handle the application's data access. As a result, this application avoids using the declarative data-access features of ASP.NET 2.0.

The following sections describe the new data access controls you'll use most: `SqlDataSource`, `GridView`, `FormView`, and `DetailsView`.

The SqlDataSource control

The new `SqlDataSource` connects to a SQL database and binds controls such as `DataList`, `GridView`, and `DetailsView` to SQL data retrieved from SQL databases such as Microsoft's own SQL Server and Access. This control isn't rendered on the page, so it isn't visible to the user when the application runs. However, it is visible in the Web Designer in Visual Studio, so you can work with it in Design view.

The following paragraphs describe some of the more important features of the `SqlDataSource` control:

✔ It uses the ADO.NET data provider classes to connect to relational databases. As a result, you can use it to access several different types of databases, including Microsoft SQL Server, Access, and Oracle.

✔ The connection string can be automatically retrieved from the application's `web.config` file, so you don't have to code the connection string on the page.

✔ Each `SqlDataSource` control has a `Select` command associated with it via the `SelectCommand` property. The data source executes this command whenever it needs to retrieve data from the database. You can also manually execute this `Select` command by calling the data source's `Select` method.

✔ The `SqlDataSource` control can also have an `Insert`, `Update`, and `Delete` command associated with it via `InsertCommand`, `Update Command`, and `DeleteCommand` properties. When you bind a `SqlDataSource` control to a data control such as `GridView` or `FormView`, the data control executes these commands when the user inserts, updates, or deletes data. In addition, you can manually execute these commands by calling the data source's `Insert`, `Update`, or `Delete` methods.

✔ The `SqlDataSource` has three collections of parameters that provide values for the `Select`, `Insert`, `Update`, and `Delete` commands. These parameter collections are accessed via the `SelectParameters`, `InsertParameters`, `UpdateParameters`, and `DeleteParameters` collections. The parameters can be bound to a property of another control (for example, the `Text` property of a text box or the `SelectedValue` property of a drop-down list), a query string, a value retrieved from session state, a cookie, or a form field.

✔ You can configure a `SqlDataSource` so the `SELECT` statement returns an ADO.NET dataset or a data reader. The data reader is more efficient if you simply want to display read-only data on a page. If you want to update the data — or if you want to filter, sort, or page the data — you should use a dataset. (The default mode is `dataset`.)

✔ The `SqlDataSource` control can be configured to automatically cache data. As a result, you no longer have to write code to cache data.

The following example shows a basic `SqlDataSource` control from the Product Catalog application presented in Chapter 5:

```
<asp:SqlDataSource ID="SqlDataSource2"
    runat="server"
    ConnectionString=
        "<%$ ConnectionStrings:ConnectionString %>"
    SelectCommand="SELECT catid, name, [desc]
        FROM Categories ORDER BY name">
</asp:SqlDataSource>
```

This data source simply retrieves the `catid`, `name`, and `desc` columns from the `Categories` table in the database, sorting the rows by name.

Here's a more complicated `SqlDataSource` control, from the Maintenance application presented in Chapter 7:

```
<asp:SqlDataSource ID="SqlDataSource1"
    runat="server"
    ConflictDetection="CompareAllValues"
    ConnectionString=
    "<%$ ConnectionStrings:MaintConnectionString %>"
    SelectCommand="SELECT [catid],
                [name], [desc]
            FROM [Categories] ORDER BY [catid]"
    InsertCommand="INSERT INTO [Categories]
                ([catid], [name], [desc])
            VALUES (@catid, @name, @desc)"
    UpdateCommand="UPDATE [Categories]
            SET [name] = @name, [desc] = @desc
            WHERE [catid] = @original_catid
            AND [name] = @original_name
            AND [desc] = @original_desc"
    DeleteCommand="DELETE FROM [Categories]
            WHERE [catid] = @original_catid
            AND [name] = @original_name
            AND [desc] = @original_desc" >
    <InsertParameters>
        <asp:Parameter Name="catid"
            Type="String" />
        <asp:Parameter Name="name"
            Type="String" />
```

```
            <asp:Parameter Name="desc"
                Type="String" />
        </InsertParameters>
        <UpdateParameters>
            <asp:Parameter Name="name"
                Type="String" />
            <asp:Parameter Name="desc"
                Type="String" />
            <asp:Parameter Name="original_catid"
                Type="String" />
            <asp:Parameter Name="original_name"
                Type="String" />
            <asp:Parameter Name="original_desc"
                Type="String" />
        </UpdateParameters>
        <DeleteParameters>
            <asp:Parameter Name="original_catid"
                Type="String" />
            <asp:Parameter Name="original_name"
                Type="String" />
            <asp:Parameter Name="original_desc"
                Type="String" />
        </DeleteParameters>
    </asp:SqlDataSource>
```

This `SqlDataSource` specifies all four command types (`Select`, `Insert`, `Update`, and `Delete`) as well as parameters for the `INSERT`, `UPDATE`, and `DELETE` statements.

In some cases, you may want to access data from a `SqlDataSource` in code. For example, the Shopping Cart application presented in Chapter 6 needs to retrieve data from the current record so it can use the data to update the `ShoppingCart` item in session state. To do this, it calls the data source's `Select` method, which returns an object defined by the `DataView` class. It then uses the `DataView` object to get the `DataRowView` object for the first row returned by the `SELECT` statement. Then it can access the individual fields for the row. Here's the code (in C#):

```csharp
DataView dv = (DataView)SqlDataSource1.Select(
    DataSourceSelectArguments.Empty);
DataRowView dr = dv[0];
string ID = (String)dr["ProductID"];
string Name = (string)dr["Name"];
decimal Price;
if (dr["SalePrice"] is DBNull)
    Price = (decimal)dr["Price"];
else
    Price = (decimal)dr["SalePrice"];
```

Other Data Sources

Besides the `SqlDataSource` control, ASP.NET 2.0 includes several other data-source controls that let you work with different types of data. The other data-source controls include:

- `AccessDataSource`: A data source that connects directly to a Microsoft Access database.

- `ObjectDataSource`: A data source that connects to a custom business class. This data source lets you write custom classes to access your databases, while still taking advantage of the data-binding features

available in controls such as `GridView` and `DetailsView`. (Note, however, that programming with the `ObjectData Source` is more difficult and limited than programming with the `SqlDataSource`.)

- `XmlDataSource`: Lets you bind to XML data.

- `SiteMapDataSource`: A special data source that's used with ASP.NET 2.0 site-navigation controls, which let you create menus to navigate your Web site.

Notice that one of the fields (`SalePrice`) allows nulls, so its value must be tested for `DBNull`. Here's the equivalent code in Visual Basic:

```
Dim dv As DataView
dv = SqlDataSource1.Select( _
    DataSourceSelectArguments.Empty)
Dim dr As DataRowView = dv(0)
Dim ID As String = dr("ProductID")
Dim name As String = dr("Name")
Dim Price As Decimal
If TypeOf (dr("SalePrice")) Is DBNull Then
    Price = dr("Price")
Else
    Price = dr("SalePrice")
End If
```

The GridView control

The `GridView` control replaces the old `DataGrid` control as the way to display data in a tabular format. The `GridView` control has several features that weren't available in the `DataGrid` control. In particular:

- Binding to the new data source controls, including `SqlDataSource`.

- Automatic paging, which makes it easy to display just a subset of rows at a time. You can specify the number of rows to display on each page and can specify the appearance of the paging controls.

✔ Automatic sorting, which lets the user click a column heading to sort the data.

✔ Updating and deleting. However, you can't insert a new row using the `GridView` control.

Each column in a `GridView` control is represented by a column that can be bound to a data field. There are actually seven different types of columns you can create:

✔ `BoundField`: A column bound to a data source field.

✔ `ButtonField`: A column that contains a button.

✔ `CheckBoxField`: A column that displays a check box.

✔ `CommandField`: A column that displays one or more command buttons (command buttons include Select, Edit, and Delete).

✔ `HyperLinkField`: A column that displays a data source field as a hyperlink.

✔ `ImageField`: A column that displays an image. The URL for the image is provided by a data source field.

✔ `TemplateField`: A column that uses a template to specify its contents.

Here's a `GridView` control that has five columns. Three of the columns are bound to fields in the data source (`catid`, `name`, and `desc`). The other two columns display command buttons that let the user edit or delete a row, like this:

```
<asp:GridView ID="GridView1" runat="server"
    AutoGenerateColumns="False"
    DataKeyNames="catid"
    DataSourceID="SqlDataSource1"
    OnRowDeleted="GridView1_RowDeleted"
    OnRowUpdated="GridView1_RowUpdated">
    <Columns>
        <asp:BoundField DataField="catid"
            HeaderText="ID" ReadOnly="True">
            <HeaderStyle HorizontalAlign="Left" />
            <ItemStyle Width="80px" />
        </asp:BoundField>
        <asp:BoundField DataField="name"
            HeaderText="Name">
            <HeaderStyle HorizontalAlign="Left" />
            <ItemStyle Width="100px" />
        </asp:BoundField>
        <asp:BoundField DataField="desc"
            HeaderText="Description">
            <HeaderStyle HorizontalAlign="Left" />
```

```
            <ItemStyle Width="400px" />
    </asp:BoundField>
    <asp:CommandField
        CausesValidation="False"
        ShowEditButton="True" />
    <asp:CommandField
        CausesValidation="False"
        ShowDeleteButton="True" />
    </Columns>
</asp:GridView>
```

The DetailsView control

The DetailsView control displays one row from a data source at a time by rendering an HTML table. The HTML table contains one row for each field in the data source.

The DetailsView control supports paging, so you can use it to display one row of a data source that returns multiple rows. Then the DetailsView control displays paging controls that let the user navigate through the data.

But a more common way to use the DetailsView control is in combination with a GridView control or other list control that enables the user to select a row. Then the data source for the DetailsView control uses a Select parameter that's bound to the SelectedValue property of the GridView or other list control. When the user selects a row, the DetailsView control's data source retrieves the row and the DetailsView control displays the details for that row.

Here's a typical DetailsView control, adapted from the Product Catalog application that was presented in Chapter 5:

```
<asp:DetailsView ID="DetailsView1"
    runat="server"
    AutoGenerateRows="False"
    DataKeyNames="productid"
    DataSourceID="SqlDataSource1" >
    <Fields>
        <asp:BoundField DataField="name" />
        <asp:BoundField DataField="shorttext" />
        <asp:BoundField DataField="longtext" />
        <asp:BoundField DataField="price"
            DataFormatString="<br />{0:c}" />
    </Fields>
</asp:DetailsView>
```

This DetailsView control displays four fields from the data source: name, shorttext, longtext, and price. The price field uses a format string to apply a format to the data.

The FormView Control

The FormView control is similar to the DetailsView control. However, instead of rendering data as an HTML table, the FormView control uses templates that let you specify exactly how you want it to render the data. It gives you these template choices:

- ✔ EmptyItemTemplate: Rendered if the data source is empty.
- ✔ ItemTemplate: Displays data in read-only mode.
- ✔ EditItemTemplate: Displayed when the FormView control is in Edit mode.
- ✔ InsertItemTemplate: Displayed when the FormView control is in Insert mode.
- ✔ HeaderTemplate: Displayed at the top of the control.
- ✔ FooterTemplate: Displayed at the bottom of the control.
- ✔ PagerTemplate: Displayed when paging is enabled.

To display data from the data source, you can use the Eval or Bind methods. For example:

```
<asp:Label ID="lblLastName" runat="server"
    Text='<%# Eval("lastname") %>'/>
```

Here, a label is bound to a data-source field named lastname. Here's an example that shows how to bind a text box to the lastname field:

```
<asp:TextBox ID="txtProductID" runat="server"
    Width="100px"
    Text='<%# Bind("lastname") %>'/>
```

Notice that Bind is used instead of Eval when you want the binding to be two-way — that is, for input as well as output.

You can also include a command button in a template; when the user clicks the button, the specified command is sent to the FormView control. The following commands are allowed:

- ✔ Edit: Places the FormView control in Edit mode and displays the EditItemTemplate template.
- ✔ New: Places the FormView control in Insert mode and uses the InsertItemTemplate.
- ✔ Update: Accepts changes made while in Edit mode and updates the data source.

✔ `Insert`: Inserts a row using data entered while in Insert mode.

✔ `Cancel`: Cancels Edit or Insert mode and ignores any changes.

For a complete example of a `FormView` control, refer to the Product Details page presented in Chapter 5.

Login Controls

ASP.NET 2.0 provides an entire set of controls that make it easy to create applications for which users must register and log in. These controls include:

✔ `Login`: Lets the user log in by entering a user name and password.

✔ `CreateUserWizard`: Lets the user create a new user account.

✔ `PasswordRecovery`: Lets the user retrieve a forgotten password.

✔ `ChangePassword`: Lets the user change his or her password.

✔ `LoginView`: Displays the contents of a template as appropriate to the user's login status.

✔ `LoginStatus`: If the user is logged in, displays a link that logs the user off. If the user isn't logged in, displays a link that leads to the application's login page.

✔ `LoginName`: Displays the user's login name if the user is logged in.

You'll find more information about using these controls in Chapters 3 and 4.

The Wizard Control

The `Wizard` control lets you create wizards that walk the user through a series of steps. Each step can include any content and controls you want it to include. Only one step at a time is displayed, along with navigation buttons that let the user move from step to step.

To define the steps of a Wizard, you use the `<WizardSteps>` element. This element, in turn, can contain one or more `<WizardStep>` child elements. There are five different types of steps you can create:

✔ **Start:** The first step, which includes a Next button but not a Previous button.

✔ **Step:** An intermediate step, with both a Next and a Previous button.

✔ **Finish:** The next-to-last step. Instead of a Next button, this step includes a Finish button.

✔ **Complete:** The final step, displayed after the user clicks the Finish button. No navigation buttons are included on this step.

✔ **Auto:** The Wizard control determines the step type according to its position in the `<WizardSteps>` element. For example, the first step declared is the start step.

Here's a basic skeleton of a simple `Wizard` control with three steps:

```
<asp:Wizard id="Wizard1" runat="server">
    <WizardSteps>
        <asp:WizardStep steptype="Start" title="Step One">
            Content for step one goes here.
        </asp:WizardStep>
        <asp:WizardStep steptype="Step" title="Step Two">
            Content for step two goes here.
        </asp:WizardStep>
        <asp:WizardStep steptype="Finish"
            title="Step Three">
            Content for step three goes here.
        </asp:WizardStep>
    </WizardSteps>
</asp:Wizard>
```

For more information about using the Wizard control, refer to Chapter 6.

The Generics Feature

Generics is a new language feature introduced with ASP.NET 2.0. It applies to both C# and Visual Basic. The basic idea of the Generics feature is to let you create type-specific classes — particularly, to create strongly typed collection classes that have specified uses.

One of the problems most common to working with collections is that the collections store objects of type `Object` — that is, a collection can store *any* type of object. So, if you want to store a collection of `Product` objects, you might declare an `ArrayList` and add `Product` objects to it. Note, however, that nothing prevents you from adding a `Customer` object to the array list; the `Add` method of the `ArrayList` class accepts any object. Result (all too often): mishmash.

With the Generics feature, you can designate the type of object a collection can hold when you declare the collection. For example, you can create an `ArrayList` that can hold only `Product` objects. Then the compiler won't let you add a `Customer` object to the list.

Other New Features of ASP.NET 2.0

This chapter describes the new ASP.NET 2.0 features that I used in the applications presented in this book. But ASP.NET 2.0 has many other new features as well. Here are a few of the more important ones:

✔ **Navigation controls:** A set of controls that let you build site-navigation features into your Web applications. These controls include a Menu control for creating menus, a SiteMapPath control that displays a path to the current page, and a TreeView control that displays the site's navigation structure as a tree.

✔ **WebParts:** A set of controls that let you create pages that the user can customize by selecting components called *Web parts*. The WebParts feature is designed to build portal sites similar to the Microsoft portal, MSN.com.

✔ **Themes:** A feature that lets you apply formatting to controls and other page elements throughout the application.

The generics features introduces a new namespace (System.Collections.Generic) that provides typed collection classes, including these:

✔ List: A generic array list.

✔ SortedList: A generic list that's kept in sorted order.

✔ LinkedList: A generic linked list.

✔ Stack: A generic last-in, first-out stack.

✔ Queue: A generic first-in, first-out queue.

✔ Dictionary: A generic collection of key/value pairs.

✔ SortedDictionary: A generic collection of key/value pairs kept in sorted order.

Here's an example in C# that creates a list of Product objects:

```
List<Product> plist;
plist = new List<Product>();
```

Note that you specify the type of object you want contained in a collection by using greater-than (>) and less-than (<) symbols, both when you declare the list and when you instantiate it.

Here it is in Visual Basic, which uses the Of keyword rather than angle brackets:

```
Dim custlist As List(Of Customer)
custlist = New List(Of Customer)()
```

The Web Site Administration Tool

ASP.NET 2.0 includes a new feature called the *Web Site Administration Tool* that lets you configure web.config settings from a browser-based interface. You can also create the user accounts used by the new Login controls. To use this tool, choose the Web Site⇨ASP.NET Configuration command from within Visual Studio. Note that this tool works only for file system Web sites, which means you probably won't be able to use it for applications that have been deployed to an IIS server and are in production. Figure 12-3 shows the opening page of the Web Site Administration Tool.

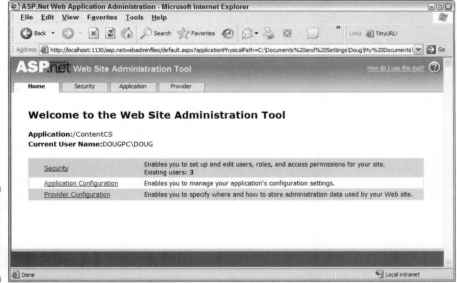

Figure 12-3:
The Web
Site
Administrati
on Tool.

Chapter 13

Ten Rookie Mistakes

*I*f you're relatively new to programming in general or ASP.NET Web programming in particular, this chapter is for you. It forewarns you about some of the most common mistakes made by inexperienced developers. Human nature being what it is, experienced developers make these mistakes too; most of them are caused by our desire to get on with the nitty-gritty of programming rather than getting stuck in the more tedious — but vital — aspects of development, such as planning, testing, and documenting our code.

Coding Too Soon

Probably the most common application development mistake is to start coding too soon. This is a natural mistake to make, since *programming* is what programmers do. But you should resist the temptation to begin writing code for your application until you've thoroughly designed the application and thought through how you will handle the more challenging aspects of the code. In particular, you should make sure your application design addresses the following issues:

✔ **How will database access be handled?** Will you use ASP.NET data source controls such as `SqlDataSource` to handle data access declaratively, or will you write custom data access classes? Will you include SQL statements in your code, or will you use stored procedures to store the SQL statements in the database?

✔ **How will you pass state information from page to page?** Will you rely on ASP.NET's session-state feature, or will you pass query strings around among the application's pages?

✔ **How will you protect the application from security breaches?** In what ways will the application be vulnerable to attacks such as SQL injections, and how can you design the application to protect itself from such attacks?

✔ **How will the application handle error situations?** For example, how do you want it to respond to database-connection problems?

Don't start coding your application until you've resolved these issues.

For more complicated applications, it's sometimes a good idea to do a simple version of the application before you write the complete application, just to make sure the application can be done. This proof-of-concept version should focus on the most troublesome parts of the application, such as linkages to other existing applications or tricky database design issues. Once you've established that the application is doable, you'll have the knowledge and confidence you need to prepare a detailed application design.

Skimping On Documentation

Most developers love good documentation in other people's programs, but they hate *doing* it because it's tedious work. And it involves writing. (I happen to like to write, but I realize that I'm a bit weird. Most people don't like to write.)

Another reason most developers hate documentation is that it doesn't seem productive. Why waste the day writing about what you did yesterday, when you could be writing more code?

The answer is that today you probably *remember* what you did yesterday and why you did it. But six months from now, you won't. So even if you hate doing the documentation, suffer through it; your future self will be glad you did.

Remember that there are two basic kinds of documentation you should prepare. First, you should liberally sprinkle your code with inline comments that explain what's going on. And second, you should prepare separate documents that explain what the application does, how it is designed, and how to use the application.

Inadequate Testing

The most common mistake when testing a computer program is to assume that the purpose of testing is to make sure your program works. That's exactly the opposite of the approach you should take. Instead of trying to prove your program right, you should *try to prove it wrong*. Do everything you can think of to make your program fail.

Always keep in mind the many ways your users will use and abuse your program. Here are just a few crazy things to try when you're testing your applications:

✔ Try leaving all the input fields blank.

✔ Try entering data that includes angle brackets < >.

✔ After you type data into a data-entry page, hit the browser's Back button to return to the data-entry page — and enter the same data again.

✔ After you delete or update a record, hit the browser's Back button, then try to delete or update the same record again.

✔ Have someone who has never seen the application before test the application. We developers tend to get into a rut when we test our applications, testing the same things over and over again. You'll be surprised at the errors discovered by someone who has never before seen the application.

Also, remember the principle of *regression testing*: Whenever you make any change to the application, you need to retest the entire application, not just the part you change. You never know what unintended consequences the change may have.

Abusing State Features

ASP.NET provides several convenient ways to save state information, including session state and view state. However, it's easy to overuse these features. Here are some ways you can improve the way your application works with state features:

✔ Disable view state for controls that don't need it. By default, most ASP.NET controls enable view state. This needlessly sends state information to the browser for each page. The application will run more efficiently if you use view state only when necessary.

- ✔ Try not to save excessive amounts of data in session state. Session state is usually stored in server RAM, which is a precious resource shared by all users of the application.

- ✔ Remove data from session state as soon as you know you won't need it any more.

Not Validating Input Data

All data allowed into an application should be validated. ASP.NET includes a rich set of validation controls, and you should rarely code a text box or other input control without at least one validation control to go along with it. At minimum, a text box should include a `RequiredFieldValidator` if it gathers required data; text boxes that gather numeric data should use validators to ensure that the data is of the correct type (and, if appropriate, within the correct range).

One common omission is to forget to check for negative numbers for values that must be positive. For example, a quantity field in a shopping cart application shouldn't allow negative values.

Another common mistake is to forget to treat query strings as input data. ASP.NET lets you use validation controls to automatically validate input data received from text boxes and other input controls. However, query strings are a form of input data too, but ASP.NET doesn't provide an automatic way to validate them. So you have to write code that manually validates query string fields before your program uses those values. If you don't, malicious users can alter or fake query string values in an attempt to hack your application. A word to the wise: Never assume that a query string contains valid or legitimate data.

Reinventing the Wheel

I recently needed to write a routine that would sort the letters of a word into alphabetical order. I was working in C, not C# or Visual Basic, so I had no sort function or method available. Rather than work out the details of how to write a sort routine from scratch, I just grabbed a book off my shelf, looked up *sort* in the index, found a good routine, and shamelessly copied it into my program.

Before you spend hours, days, or weeks writing code, find out if the code you're developing is already available. Odds are it is.

In fact, you should apply this principal to the entire application. You may find that you can purchase a ready-made application that does exactly — or almost exactly — what your application will do. Depending on the purchase price, of course, it may be considerably less expensive to buy the ready-made solution.

Not Asking for Help

There are plenty of places on the Internet where you can ask for help and get good (and sometimes useful) answers. One of the best-known (and best) is the forums section of `www.asp.net`. There you can post a question and get answers, usually within a few hours or a day. It always amazes me that other ASP.NET programmers are so often willing to help others with programming problems.

Of course, you shouldn't abuse the willingness of others to help. Don't post questions before you've spent a reasonable amount of time researching the answer yourself and trying several different solutions. In particular, be sure to read whatever the online help has to say about the controls and classes you're having trouble with.

Before you post, search the forum for similar questions. You may well find that someone has already asked your question and the answer to your problem is there, waiting for you to read it.

Chapter 14

Ten Database Design Tips

*O*ne of the most important aspects of any application-development project is the database design. And so, without further ado, here are ten-or-so tips for designing good databases, straight from the Home Office in sunny Fresno, California.

Use the Right Number of Tables

In *Amadeus* (one of my all-time favorite flicks from the '80s), the Emperor of Germany criticizes one of Mozart's works as having "too many notes." Mozart replies indignantly that he uses neither too many nor too few notes, but the exact number of notes that the composition requires.

So it should be with database design. Your database should have as many tables as the application requires — not more, not fewer. There is no single "right" number of tables for all databases.

Inexperienced database designers have a tendency to use too few tables — sometimes trying to cram an entire database-worth of information into a single table. At the other extreme are databases with dozens of tables, each consisting of just a few fields.

Avoid Repeating Data

One of the core principles of relational database design is to handle repeating data by breaking it out into a separate table. For example, in the old days of flat-file processing, it was common to create invoice records that had room for a certain number of line items. Thus the invoice record would have fields with names like Item1, Item2, Item3, and so on.

Bad!

Whenever you find yourself numbering field names like that, you should create a separate table. In the case of the invoice record, you should create a separate table to store the line item data.

Avoid Redundant Data

When designing the tables that make up your database, try to avoid creating redundant data. Whenever redundant data creeps into a database, it introduces the likelihood that the data will become corrupt. For example, suppose you store a customer's name in two different tables. Then, if you update the name in one of the tables but not the other, the database has become inconsistent.

The most obvious type of redundant-data mistake is to create a field that exists in two or more tables. But there are more subtle types of redundant data. For example, consider an Invoice table that contains a LineItemTotal field that represents the sum of the Total fields in each of the invoice's line items. Technically, this field represents redundant data; the data is also stored in the Total fields of each line item.

Whether you should allow this type of redundancy depends on the application. In many cases, it's better to put up with the redundancy for the convenience and efficiency of not having to recalculate the total each time the data is accessed. But it's always worth considering whether the added convenience is worth the risk of corrupting the data.

Use a Naming Convention

To avoid confusion, pick a naming convention for your database objects and stick to it. That way your database tables, columns, constraints, and other objects will be named in a consistent and predictable way. (Just think of the savings on aspirin.)

You can argue from now until St. Swithen's day about what the naming conventions *should* be. That doesn't matter so much. What does matter is that you make a convention — and follow it.

Avoid nulls

Allowing nulls in your database tables significantly complicates the application programming required to access the tables. As a result, I suggest you avoid nulls by specifying NOT NULL whenever you can. Use nulls rarely, and only when you truly need them.

Nulls are often misused anyway. The correct use of null is for a value that is unknown; *not* for a blank or empty value. For example, consider a typical address record that allows two address lines, named `Address1` and `Address2`. Most addresses have only one address, so the second address line is blank. The value of this second address line is, in fact, known — it's blank. That's not the same thing as null. Null would imply that the address may have a second address line; we just don't know what it is.

Even for columns that might seem appropriate for nulls, it's usually more convenient to just leave the column value blank for values that aren't known. For example, consider a `phone number` column in a `Customer` table. It's safe to assume that all your customers have phone numbers, so it would be correct to use null for phone numbers that you don't know. However, from a practical point of view, it's just as easy to disallow nulls for the phone number column, and leave the unknown phone numbers blank.

Avoid Secret Codes

Avoid fields with names like `CustomerType`, where the value of the field is one of several constants that aren't defined elsewhere in the database, such as R for `Retail` or W for `Wholesale`. You may have only these two types of customers today, but the needs of the application may change in the future, requiring a third customer type.

An alternative would be to create a separate table of customer-type codes (call it `CustomerTypes`), and then create a foreign-key constraint so the value of the `CustomerType` column must appear in the `CustomerTypes` table.

Use Constraints Wisely

Constraints let you prevent changes to the database that violate the internal consistency of your data. For example, a check constraint lets you validate only data that meets certain criteria. For example, you can use a check constraint to make sure the value of a field named `Price` is greater than zero.

A *foreign-key constraint* requires that the value of a column in one table must match the value that exists in some other table. For example, if you have a `LineItems` table with a column named `ProductID`, and a `Products` table with a column also named `ProductID`, you could use a foreign-key constraint to make sure that the `ProductID` value for each row in the `LineItems` table matches an existing row in the `Products` table.

Use Triggers When Appropriate

A *trigger* is a procedure that kicks in when certain database data is updated or accessed. Triggers are a great way to enforce those database rules that are more complicated than simple constraints. For example, suppose an `Invoice` table contains an `ItemCount` column whose value is the number of line items for the invoice. One way to maintain the value of this column automatically would be to create triggers that increment the `ItemCount` column whenever a line item is inserted, and decrement the `ItemCount` column whenever a line item is deleted. Sometimes automation is a beautiful thing.

Use Stored Procedures

Stored procedures are SQL procedures that are tucked away in the database and are part of it. There are several advantages to using stored procedures instead of coding SQL in your applications:

- Using stored procedures removes the burden of SQL programming from your application programmers. Instead, it makes the SQL used to access the database a part of the database itself — no fuss, no muss. All the application programs have to do is call the appropriate stored procedures to select, insert, update, or delete database data.

- Stored procedures are more efficient as a way of handling transactions, because the database server handles the entire transaction.

- Stored procedures are also more efficient because they reduce the amount of network traffic between the database server and the Web server.

- Finally, stored procedures are more secure because they reduce the risk of SQL injection attacks.

Appendix

About the CD

I included a CD to provide you with all the source code for the applications presented in this book. That way you won't have to type everything in from scratch. In this appendix, I explain the requirements for using the CD — and show you how to install and use the applications.

System Requirements

Basically, any modern PC will be sufficient to run the applications on this CD, provided the computer is powerful enough to run Visual Studio 2005 or Visual Web Developer 2005 Express Edition. Here's what you need at minimum:

- A PC with a Pentium processor, running at 600MHz or faster. (The faster the better, of course.)
- 128MB of RAM.
- Windows XP with Service Pack 2. Or, Windows 2003 Server or Windows 2000 Service Pack 4.
- At least 1.3 GB of space available on your hard drive. (That's to install Visual Web Developer 2005 Express Edition. The applications on the CD don't require nearly that much disk space.)
- A monitor that can display at least 800x600 pixels in 256 colors.
- A mouse or other pointing device.
- A CD-ROM drive.

Any way your system can exceed these requirements is, by and large, all to the good — and the more it exceeds them, the better.

Using the CD

To install the applications on the CD, follow these steps:

1. **Insert the CD into your CD-ROM drive.**

   The license agreement should automatically appear. Note that if you have disabled the AutoRun feature in Windows, you'll have to start the installation program manually. To do so, choose Start⇨Run, and then enter d:\start.exe. (Replace d: with the proper drive letter if your CD drive isn't drive d.)

2. **Read the license agreement, and then click the Accept button to access the CD.**

   The CD interface appears, which allows you to install the applications.

Using the Source Files

The CD contains the source files for all applications presented in this book. Both the C# and Visual Basic versions are included. You can copy any or all of these applications to your hard drive, and then access them from Visual Studio 2005 or Visual Web Developer 2005 Express Edition as file-system applications. Note that the installation program will let you chose to copy just the C# or VB versions of the applications if you want.

Here is the folder structure for the applications:

```
Apps\LoginCS
Apps\LoginVB

Apps\CatalogCS
Apps\CatalogVB

Apps\CartCS
Apps\CartVB

Apps\MaintCS
Apps\MaintVB

Apps\OrderListingCS
Apps\OrderListingVB

Apps\ContentCS
Apps\ContentVB
```

```
Apps\ForumCS
Apps\ForumVB

Apps\BlogCS
Apps\BlogVB
```

Troubleshooting

If you encounter any problems with the applications on the CD, please check my Web site (www.lowewriter.com/apps) for more information. I'll be sure to post any updates or corrections based on feedback from readers like you. You may also find updated versions of the applications.

Customer care: If you have trouble with the CD-ROM, please call the Wiley Product Technical Support phone number at (800) 762-2974. Outside the United States, call (317) 572-3994. You can also contact Wiley Product Technical Support at www.wiley.com/techsupport. Wiley Publishing provides technical support only for installation and other general quality-control items.

To place additional orders or to request information about other Wiley products, please call (877) 762-2974.

Index

• *I* •

• *K* •

• T •

• *X* •

USINESS, CAREERS & PERSONAL FINANCE

Grant Writing FOR DUMMIES

A Reference for the Rest of Us!

0-7645-5307-0

Home Buying FOR DUMMIES

A Reference for the Rest of Us!

0-7645-5331-3 *†

Also available:

- Accounting For Dummies †
  0-7645-5314-3
- Business Plans Kit For Dummies †
  0-7645-5365-8
- Cover Letters For Dummies
  0-7645-5224-4
- Frugal Living For Dummies
  0-7645-5403-4
- Leadership For Dummies
  0-7645-5176-0
- Managing For Dummies
  0-7645-1771-6

- Marketing For Dummies
  0-7645-5600-2
- Personal Finance For Dummies *
  0-7645-2590-5
- Project Management For Dummies
  0-7645-5283-X
- Resumes For Dummies †
  0-7645-5471-9
- Selling For Dummies
  0-7645-5363-1
- Small Business Kit For Dummies *†
  0-7645-5093-4

OME & BUSINESS COMPUTER BASICS

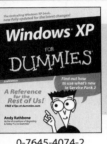

Windows XP FOR DUMMIES

A Reference for the Rest of Us!

0-7645-4074-2

Microsoft Office Excel 2003 ALL-IN-ONE DESK REFERENCE FOR DUMMIES

9 BOOKS IN 1

0-7645-3758-X

Also available:

- ACT! 6 For Dummies
  0-7645-2645-6
- iLife '04 All-in-One Desk Reference
  For Dummies
  0-7645-7347-0
- iPAQ For Dummies
  0-7645-6769-1
- Mac OS X Panther Timesaving
  Techniques For Dummies
  0-7645-5812-9
- Macs For Dummies
  0-7645-5656-8

- Microsoft Money 2004 For Dummies
  0-7645-4195-1
- Office 2003 All-in-One Desk Reference
  For Dummies
  0-7645-3883-7
- Outlook 2003 For Dummies
  0-7645-3759-8
- PCs For Dummies
  0-7645-4074-2
- TiVo For Dummies
  0-7645-6923-6
- Upgrading and Fixing PCs For Dummies
  0-7645-1665-5
- Windows XP Timesaving Techniques
  For Dummies
  0-7645-3748-2

OOD, HOME, GARDEN, HOBBIES, MUSIC & PETS

Feng Shui FOR DUMMIES

A Reference for the Rest of Us!

0-7645-5295-3

Poker FOR DUMMIES

A Reference for the Rest of Us!

0-7645-5232-5

Also available:

- Bass Guitar For Dummies
  0-7645-2487-9
- Diabetes Cookbook For Dummies
  0-7645-5230-9
- Gardening For Dummies *
  0-7645-5130-2
- Guitar For Dummies
  0-7645-5106-X
- Holiday Decorating For Dummies
  0-7645-2570-0
- Home Improvement All-in-One
  For Dummies
  0-7645-5680-0

- Knitting For Dummies
  0-7645-5395-X
- Piano For Dummies
  0-7645-5105-1
- Puppies For Dummies
  0-7645-5255-4
- Scrapbooking For Dummies
  0-7645-7208-3
- Senior Dogs For Dummies
  0-7645-5818-8
- Singing For Dummies
  0-7645-2475-5
- 30-Minute Meals For Dummies
  0-7645-2589-1

NTERNET & DIGITAL MEDIA

Digital Photography FOR DUMMIES

A Reference for the Rest of Us!

0-7645-1664-7

Starting an eBay Business FOR DUMMIES

A Reference for the Rest of Us!

0-7645-6924-4

Also available:

- 2005 Online Shopping Directory
  For Dummies
  0-7645-7495-7
- CD & DVD Recording For Dummies
  0-7645-5956-7
- eBay For Dummies
  0-7645-5654-1
- Fighting Spam For Dummies
  0-7645-5965-6
- Genealogy Online For Dummies
  0-7645-5964-8
- Google For Dummies
  0-7645-4420-9

- Home Recording For Musicians
  For Dummies
  0-7645-1634-5
- The Internet For Dummies
  0-7645-4173-0
- iPod & iTunes For Dummies
  0-7645-7772-7
- Preventing Identity Theft For Dummies
  0-7645-7336-5
- Pro Tools All-in-One Desk Reference
  For Dummies
  0-7645-5714-9
- Roxio Easy Media Creator For Dummies
  0-7645-7131-1

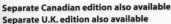

Separate Canadian edition also available
Separate U.K. edition also available

WILEY

SPORTS, FITNESS, PARENTING, RELIGION & SPIRITUALITY

0-7645-5146-9

0-7645-5418-2

Also available:
- Adoption For Dummies
  0-7645-5488-3
- Basketball For Dummies
  0-7645-5248-1
- The Bible For Dummies
  0-7645-5296-1
- Buddhism For Dummies
  0-7645-5359-3
- Catholicism For Dummies
  0-7645-5391-7
- Hockey For Dummies
  0-7645-5228-7

- Judaism For Dummies
  0-7645-5299-6
- Martial Arts For Dummies
  0-7645-5358-5
- Pilates For Dummies
  0-7645-5397-6
- Religion For Dummies
  0-7645-5264-3
- Teaching Kids to Read For Dummies
  0-7645-4043-2
- Weight Training For Dummies
  0-7645-5168-X
- Yoga For Dummies
  0-7645-5117-5

TRAVEL

0-7645-5438-7

0-7645-5453-0

Also available:
- Alaska For Dummies
  0-7645-1761-9
- Arizona For Dummies
  0-7645-6938-4
- Cancún and the Yucatán For Dummies
  0-7645-2437-2
- Cruise Vacations For Dummies
  0-7645-6941-4
- Europe For Dummies
  0-7645-5456-5
- Ireland For Dummies
  0-7645-5455-7

- Las Vegas For Dummies
  0-7645-5448-4
- London For Dummies
  0-7645-4277-X
- New York City For Dummies
  0-7645-6945-7
- Paris For Dummies
  0-7645-5494-8
- RV Vacations For Dummies
  0-7645-5443-3
- Walt Disney World & Orlando For Dummies
  0-7645-6943-0

GRAPHICS, DESIGN & WEB DEVELOPMENT

0-7645-4345-8

0-7645-5589-8

Also available:
- Adobe Acrobat 6 PDF For Dummies
  0-7645-3760-1
- Building a Web Site For Dummies
  0-7645-7144-3
- Dreamweaver MX 2004 For Dummies
  0-7645-4342-3
- FrontPage 2003 For Dummies
  0-7645-3882-9
- HTML 4 For Dummies
  0-7645-1995-6
- Illustrator CS For Dummies
  0-7645-4084-X

- Macromedia Flash MX 2004 For Dummies
  0-7645-4358-X
- Photoshop 7 All-in-One Desk
  Reference For Dummies
  0-7645-1667-1
- Photoshop CS Timesaving Techniques
  For Dummies
  0-7645-6782-9
- PHP 5 For Dummies
  0-7645-4166-8
- PowerPoint 2003 For Dummies
  0-7645-3908-6
- QuarkXPress 6 For Dummies
  0-7645-2593-X

NETWORKING, SECURITY, PROGRAMMING & DATABASES

0-7645-6852-3

0-7645-5784-X

Also available:
- A+ Certification For Dummies
  0-7645-4187-0
- Access 2003 All-in-One Desk
  Reference For Dummies
  0-7645-3988-4
- Beginning Programming For Dummies
  0-7645-4997-9
- C For Dummies
  0-7645-7068-4
- Firewalls For Dummies
  0-7645-4048-3
- Home Networking For Dummies
  0-7645-42796

- Network Security For Dummies
  0-7645-1679-5
- Networking For Dummies
  0-7645-1677-9
- TCP/IP For Dummies
  0-7645-1760-0
- VBA For Dummies
  0-7645-3989-2
- Wireless All In-One Desk Reference
  For Dummies
  0-7645-7496-5
- Wireless Home Networking For Dummies
  0-7645-3910-8